ENJOYING WHAT WE DON'T HAVE

SYMPLOKĒ STUDIES IN CONTEMPORARY THEORY

Series editor: *Jeffrey R. Di Leo*

Enjoying What We Don't Have

The POLITICAL PROJECT
of PSYCHOANALYSIS

TODD MCGOWAN

University of Nebraska Press / Lincoln and London

© 2013 by the Board of Regents of
the University of Nebraska

Acknowledgments for the use of copyrighted
material appear on page ix, which constitutes
an extension of the copyright page.

All rights reserved
Manufactured in the United
States of America

Set in Arno by Laura Wellington.
Designed by Nathan Putens.

Library of Congress
Cataloging-in-Publication Data
McGowan, Todd.
Enjoying what we don't have: the political
project of psychoanalysis / Todd McGowan.
pages cm. — (Symploke studies
in contemporary theory)
Includes bibliographical references and index.
ISBN 978-0-8032-4511-2 (pbk.: alk. paper)
1. Psychoanalysis—Political
aspects. 2. Loss (Psychology)
3. Psychoanalysis and culture. I. Title.
BF175.4.S65M25 2013
150.19'5—dc23   2012049860

*For Sheila Kunkle, who
manifests for me the paradox
of a psychoanalytic politics
and the generosity it requires*

Contents

Acknowledgments
ix

Introduction: Psychoanalytic Hostility to Politics
1

PART I: SUBJECTIVITY

1. The Formation of Subjectivity
25

2. The Economics of the Drive
52

3. Class Status and Enjoyment
79

4. Sustaining Anxiety
99

5. Changing the World
121

PART II: SOCIETY

6. The Appeal of Sacrifice
143

7. Against Knowledge
167

8. The Politics of Fantasy
196

9. Beyond Bare Life
223

10. The Necessity of Belief
243

11. The Case of the Missing Signifier
263

Conclusion:
A Society of the Death Drive
283

Notes
287

Index
339

Acknowledgments

This book developed over a number of years, and many people helped with the ideas and their presentation.

Chapters 10 and 11 contain work revised from earlier publications. Thanks to the *International Journal of Žižek Studies* for permission to publish material that appeared as "The Necessity of Belief, Or, the Trouble with Atheism," *International Journal of Žižek Studies* 4, no. 1 (2010), http://zizekstudies.org/index.php/ijzs/article/view/226/324. Thanks also to Palgrave Macmillan for permission to publish material that appeared as "The Case of the Missing Signifier," *Psychoanalysis, Culture & Society* 12, no. 1 (2008): 48–66.

I appreciate the support of Kristen Rowley at the University of Nebraska Press and Jeffrey Di Leo from Symplokē. Without their efforts, the book would not have come to light.

The film students at the University of Vermont played a decisive role in helping me to work through the political implications of psychoanalysis in various courses and seminars. Jason Clemence and Adam Cottrel especially helped, as did Kelly Samaris.

My film studies colleagues at the University of Vermont—Deb Ellis, Dave Jenemann, Hilary Neroni, Sarah Nilsen, and Hyon Joo Yoo—have all provided a stimulating intellectual field in which to work. Outside of film studies, Joseph Acquisto, John Waldron, Eric Lindstrom, Andrew Barnaby, Emily Bernard, and Ching Selao have helped to create a universe, if not a university, in which thought is valued above all else. And Bea Bookchin has constantly insisted, despite my resistance, that I place politics ahead of psychoanalysis in my attempt to bring them together.

I appreciate the thoughtful readings of the manuscript provided by Paul Taylor and Heiko Feldner. Both helped me to advance the argument in new directions and to correct its most embarrassing moments.

Anna Kornbluh read through chapters of the manuscript and offered invaluable suggestions along the way.

Thanks to Jonathan Mulrooney for his indefatigable intellectual energy, which has functioned as a reservoir for me.

Frances Restuccia has provided a way for me to think through ideas that did not yet merit any articulation.

I owe a great debt to Fabio Vighi, who has become a true comrade and philosophical ally.

Thanks to Rob Rushing, Hugh Manon, and Danny Cho, who have advanced my thinking about the philosophical implications of psychoanalysis and who have demanded an unceasing engagement with theory.

Jennifer Friedlander and Henry Krips were instrumental in helping me to see how a political position might emerge out of psychoanalysis.

Thanks to Quentin Martin for his skeptical reading of several chapters. He has consistently kept many of my mistakes from becoming more widely known.

Jean Wyatt also provided a conscientious reading that enabled a reexamination of many paths.

I owe a debt to Ken Reinhard, who invited me to present ideas that began new threads in the book. Ken has also been a crucial theoretical resource.

I would like to thank Jill Delaney-Shal for being a reminder of the possibility that inheres in impossibility and for her continued belief in me, despite my incessant failures to earn that belief.

Thanks also to Slavoj Žižek for his infinite support and his effort to bring the political dimension of psychoanalytic thought to the fore.

Sheila Kunkle has been my longtime collaborator in this project. She has read many of the chapters and provided too many points of revision to acknowledge.

Finally, this book would be unthinkable without the collaboration of Walter Davis, Paul Eisenstein, and Hilary Neroni. They have all sustained a confrontation with loss and have demonstrated that there is no enjoyment outside of this confrontation.

ENJOYING WHAT WE DON'T HAVE

Introduction

PSYCHOANALYTIC HOSTILITY TO POLITICS

The Politics of a Nonpolitical Theory

Psychoanalysis begins with individual subjects and their suffering. By allowing subjects to speak freely in the analytic session and by offering an interpretative intervention in this speech, psychoanalysis aims to reduce the impairment that their psychic disorder creates in their lives. In contrast to Marxism, which also attempts to ameliorate human suffering, psychoanalysis has no explicit political program designed to lessen the misery that Freud and his descendants find in their patients. There is no revolt of the patients that would correspond to the revolt of the proletariat. When Freud makes political pronouncements, they tend to be negative ones, expressing his skepticism about plans for social betterment. But it is my contention that a viable political project does inhere within psychoanalytic theory and that this project provides an avenue for emancipatory politics after the end of Marxism in the twentieth century. There are points at which this psychoanalytic politics remains proximate to Marxism, but it represents a genuine alternative that has the virtue of explaining the latter's failures. The task of this book will be to lay out the contours of this political project, one that has never been fully developed despite numerous attempts at bringing psychoanalytic thinking to bear on politics.

Unlike most previous formulations of a psychoanalytic politics, what follows will take as its point of departure not the early Freud of the sexual drive but the later Freud of the death drive (and its development in the thought of Jacques Lacan and his followers). I will conspicuously ignore all psychoanalytic thinking that deviates from Freud and from his specific rendering of the death drive. This means that psychoanalytic luminaries such as Alfred Adler, Carl Jung, Melanie Klein, Donald Winnicott, Wilfred Bion, and even Freud's own daughter Anna Freud will have no role to play in this account of the psychoanalytic political project.

The death drive has historically acted as a stumbling block for psychoanalytic politics because it involves our self-sabotage. It leads us to work unconsciously against social betterment. This is why, after its discovery in 1920, Freud becomes so much more pessimistic as a thinker. But just as the death drive leads to self-sabotage, it also acts as the source of our enjoyment, and by shifting the terrain of emancipatory politics to that of enjoyment, psychoanalysis offers what Marxism's political program could not. The politics of psychoanalysis after Marxism is an emancipatory project based on the self-sacrificing enjoyment located in the death drive. Marxism is able to theorize sacrifice as necessary for future pleasure, but it is unable to conceive sacrifice as an end in itself, as a source of enjoyment.[1] This represents its fundamental limitation.

The efforts to marry psychoanalysis and a political program since Freud's discovery of the unconscious have come from both sides of the aisle. Marxist thinkers such as Theodor Adorno and Louis Althusser have turned to psychoanalysis in order to supplement Marxism with a mode of thought that would address the complexities of subjectivity, while psychoanalytic thinkers such as Erich Fromm and Wilhelm Reich have turned to Marxism as a way of giving a sociohistorical importance to their understanding of the suffering that they discovered in psychoanalytic practice. Today this intersection animates the thought of many of the most compelling voices in contemporary political thought: Alain Badiou, Étienne Balibar, Ernesto Laclau, Chantal Mouffe, Jacques Rancière, and Slavoj Žižek, to name just a few.

But the relationship between psychoanalytic theory and politics has never freed itself of the fundamental divergence that animates it. Something about psychoanalytic thought inherently resists appropriation by a program aimed at the common good. Rather than helping with such a program, it almost inevitably testifies to the reasons for its failure. The attempt to give political relevance to the insights of psychoanalysis seems a hopeless one, and yet this is precisely the aim of this book. Without minimizing the psychoanalytic critique of progress and the common good, it lays out the contours of a political theory and practice derived from psychoanalytic thought. In doing so, it challenges the very history of psychoanalysis itself.

While Freud expresses sympathy with the Russian Revolution and contends that it seemed "like the message of a better future," he continually emphasizes the intractable barriers that any project of emancipatory politics would encounter.[2] About the Soviet Union in particular, he speculatively grasps the incipient horrors of Stalinism at a time when no one in the West had any direct knowledge of them (and the worst had yet to occur). In *Civilization and Its Discontents* he notes, "One only wonders, with concern, what the Soviets will do after they've wiped out their bourgeois."[3] This is a psychoanalytic insight into the nature of the emancipatory political project that pursues the good society. For Freud, the Soviet attempt to create a better future not only chases an impossible goal, but it also exacerbates existing human suffering. It is not simply Freud's personal judgment or prejudice that renders this verdict and installs an incompatibility between psychoanalytic thought and progressive political programs; this incompatibility inheres within the very psychoanalytic approach to the world.

On the face of it, this claim appears counterintuitive: one can imagine, for instance, a psychoanalytic understanding of the nature of desire aiding political theorists in their attempts to free desire from ideology, which is the recurring difficulty of leftist politics. There are even historical examples of this theoretical assistance at work. Louis Althusser develops his theory of ideological interpellation through his acquaintance with Jacques Lacan's conception of the subject's entrance into language, and Juliet Mitchell elaborates her critique of the structural effects of patriarchy through her experience with Freudian conceptions of masculinity and femininity. In each case, psychoanalysis allows the theorist to understand how a prevailing social structure operates, and this provides a foundation for imagining a way to challenge this structure. As Mitchell claims, "Psychoanalysis is not a recommendation *for* a patriarchal society, but an analysis *of* one. If we are interested in understanding and challenging the oppression of women, we cannot afford to neglect it."[4] Precisely because she sees psychoanalysis as a useful tool for political struggle, Mitchell here dismisses feminism's longstanding quarrel with psychoanalysis for its complicity with patriarchy.[5]

Underlying a position like Mitchell's (which almost all political theorists who turn to psychoanalysis embrace) is the idea that the political usefulness of psychoanalysis stems, ironically, from its lack of a political commitment. That is to say, psychoanalysis aims to discover the unconscious truth of the subject and the society in which the subject exists, not to change this truth. It is thus at the most basic level a descriptive rather than a prescriptive art. Even the psychoanalytic cure itself does not portend radical change for the subject who accomplishes it. This subject simply recognizes, in Jacques Lacan's words, "I am that." The cure is more a recognition of who one is rather than a transformation of one's subjectivity. Though psychoanalysis does view this recognition as the most radical kind of revolution, the revolution changes how the subject relates to its activity, not the activity itself. In this sense, psychoanalysis has no political axe to grind, which allows it to devote its energies to the project of interpretation and understanding. The understanding it produces can then form the basis for the different sorts of leftist political contestation that may appropriate it.

The problem with this appropriation is the point at which it arrests the descriptive process of psychoanalytic interpretation. Psychoanalysis does not merely describe the structure of one culture or socioeconomic formation (such as patriarchy or capitalism); it instead insists on a fundamental validity across cultural and socioeconomic boundaries. It also insists on this validity across different historical epochs. It is, in short, a universal theory concerning the relationship between the individual subject and society.[6] Of course, Freud discovered psychoanalysis in a particular historical situation that shaped how he presented his insights and even the ideas he could formulate. But one can separate the particular elements (like the Oedipus complex or the labeling of homosexuality as a perversion) from the universal ones (like the antagonistic nature of society or the fact of castration as the requirement for entrance into society). The challenge for the psychoanalytic theorist is discovering the universality in Freud's discoveries, but it is this universality that presents an obstacle for any political project. If the antagonism between the subject and the social order is irreducible, then the stumbling block is not just capitalism or patriarchy but human society itself.

The insights of psychoanalysis, if valid at all, apply not simply to the past and the present but also to whatever future society we might envision or even realize. Though Freud developed the insights of psychoanalysis in a particular historical situation, this situation enabled him to discover universal structures of subjectivity and of the social order, even if his way of conceptualizing these structures initially reflected the constraints of his historical situation. The insights apply not only to contemporary patriarchal society but also, pace Juliet Mitchell, to the future society that frees itself from patriarchy. This is not to say that we will always have the same forms of neurosis and psychosis that we have now but that we will not surmount the fundamental antagonism between the social order and the individual subject that produces these specific disorders. As a result, for psychoanalysis the good society becomes an unattainable fiction.

You're No Good

The great challenge that psychoanalysis poses for emancipatory politics — and for politics as such — is its absolute rejection of the good or the good society. In the opening of the *Politics*, Aristotle describes the good as the basic aim of political activity, and this aim has remained constant in the intervening 2,500 years.[7] Aristotle never attempts to prove this constitutive remark in his treatise but simply takes it as an unassailable postulate of political thinking. For subsequent political thinkers, the question does not concern Aristotle's claim about the good but in what the good consists. There is unanimity about the political pursuit of the good not just among political theorists but among almost everyone who thinks about politics at all.

From the perspective of psychoanalysis, however, there is no good at all. The good society is unattainable not just as a result of the competing desires of the individuals within the society. The theory that aligns social conflict with the coexistence of competing individual desires fails to go far enough in envisioning the antagonistic nature of the social order. No matter how divergent individual desires are, one could always imagine reconciling them with each other through some sort of compromise. A thinker such as John Rawls can imagine a just society despite positing a society divided by innumerable competing desires on the level of the individual. Justice here would consist in the idea of fairness — using one's imagination to envision society through what Rawls labels a "veil of ignorance" that allows one to make decisions about justice without taking into account one's individual interests or desires or social position.[8] This would facilitate a good society in which any inequality would be socially justified, and it would thus reconcile competing individual desires with each other.

But the barrier to the good society runs deeper than this. It derives from the very idea of the good, which Freud sees as fundamentally at odds with itself. The good itself, not our failures to achieve it, is the problem. This is the fundamental political insight that psychoanalysis brings to the table. It is at once the challenge that it poses to emancipatory politics and the basis for its implicit project for emancipation. As we get closer to the ideal of a good society, we simultaneously approach the emptiness concealed within the ideal. The notion of the good does not emerge simply from moral reasoning and speculation about the proper arrangement of society. We develop this notion only through the experience of its prohibition. That is to say, the prohibition of the good doesn't form an obstacle to a preexisting ideal but constitutes the ideal as such.

The good has no existence outside of the barriers that we erect around realizing it. As Jacques Lacan points out in one of his most important political statements, "The step taken by Freud at the level of the pleasure principle is to show us that there is no Sovereign Good — that the Sovereign Good, which is *das Ding*, which is the mother, is also the object of incest, is a forbidden good, and that there is no other good. Such is the foundation of the moral law as turned on its head by Freud."[9] The foundational link between the good and prohibition renders its pursuit completely contradictory. Every step toward the good occasions a corresponding step away from it. The closer we come, the more we undermine the social stability that we hoped to achieve. This occurs not just among the many utopian socialist projects that have failed but across all types of social structures.

For psychoanalysis, the good is not just an unrealizable ideal but a deception incapable of orienting a coherent and sustainable politics. This critique threatens to undermine the very idea of a political project because political theorists write in order to help bring about change, which means moving society in the direction of the good (even if they admit that the ideal itself is not realizable). Conservative theorists seem immune to this critique, but they envision a return to the good or the creation of a social stability that they associate implicitly with the good.[10] Political theorists of all stripes write to change the world and assist its progression (or its return to a better state), whereas psychoanalysis interprets the world and uncovers the repetition at work where it seems to be progressing.

For this reason, Julia Kristeva theorizes the political project inherent in psychoanalysis as one of permanent revolt. Rather than forming a positive program, psychoanalysis, like modernist literature, exists simply as a negation of identity and power. In *The Sense and Non-sense of Revolt*, she argues, "psychoanalysis, on the one hand, and a certain literature, on the other, perhaps constitute possible instances of revolt culture."[11] From Kristeva's point of view, psychoanalysis is completely political insofar as it demands revolt, but this revolt can never become revolution. Psychoanalytic revolt is destined to remain revolt against some existing power structure toward which it will continue to provide resistance. Kristeva views psychoanalytic thought as a hiccup in the hegemony of scientific rationality and progress. Any attempt to create a positive psychoanalytic politics would obviate its role as a key part of revolt culture.

Kristeva's dismissal of positive psychoanalytic politics fails to take cognizance of the implicit positive program in every revolt. When one revolts, one relies on and sustains the system against which one revolts. Nowhere is this truer than within the capitalist system, in which revolt forms the lifeblood. If psychoanalysis is nothing but revolt, it is politically vacuous. And yet, Kristeva does correctly recognize the seemingly inherent hostility of psychoanalysis to progressive change. Rather than aid in this process, psychoanalysis highlights the moments of its interruption and suspension.

This position puts psychoanalysis directly at odds with Marxism's emphasis on the centrality of praxis. Marx theorizes in order to facilitate social change, and every political project by its very nature shares this goal with Marxism. What distinguishes both Marx and Freud as thinkers is their understanding of social antagonism. Where Freud sees antagonism manifesting itself in the excessive suffering of the individual subject, Marx sees it playing out in class struggle. Despite this difference in focus, they share a belief in the fundamental status of antagonism, which separates them from political thinkers (such as John Stuart Mill and John Rawls) who view the social order as whole, as divided by conflicts but not by a fundamental antagonism. We can resolve conflicts through mediation and negotiation, but antagonism implies the impossibility of resolution.

An antagonism doesn't just involve two opposing positions — like that of the bourgeoisie and the proletariat — but conceives of opposition as internal to each position. This idea of each position being internally opposed to itself is what liberal political thinkers cannot grant (if they wish to remain liberal political thinkers). Just as they view society as whole, they also view each conflicting position within society as unified and identical with itself. Not so with Marx and Freud. For Marx, the conflict between the bourgeoisie and the proletariat is at the same time the indication of an internal conflict within the bourgeoisie itself. In fact, the bourgeoisie produces the proletariat out of itself through the contradictions of the capitalist mode of production. For Freud, the conflict between the individual and the social order is also an internal conflict within the individual and within the social order.

Even societies that lack the concept of an individual must nonetheless reckon with this universal antagonism. That is, they must attempt to reconcile the continued existence of the social order with the entrance of new subjects into that order. Though the individual may be a Western idea, the social antagonism resulting from the subject's entrance into the social order is not. The elaborate marriage rules that Claude Lévi-Strauss uncovered in various societies attest to the problem of this antagonism surfacing universally.[12] The individual emerges as a distinct being because the social order cannot reproduce itself without producing a remainder, even if this remainder doesn't take the form of the individual that is familiar to the Western world.

The idea of antagonism allows Marx and Freud to author their radical social critiques. It allows them to see how the proletariat or the individual invests itself in its own oppression, or how the bourgeoisie or the social order contributes to its own subversion. Antagonism is both the cause of social stasis and the possibility for revolutionary change. For Marx and Freud, interpretation must take antagonism as its point of departure, though Marx sees, in the last instance, the possibility of overcoming antagonism through the victory of the proletariat and the consequent elimination of class struggle.

Marx envisioned a society in which production would take place for the good of the society rather than for the sake of the accumulation of capital, a change that would allow production to develop without limit. Within the capitalist mode of production, according to Marx,

> the *true barrier* to capitalist production is *capital itself*. It is that capital and its self-valorization appear as the starting and finishing point as the motive and purpose of production; production is production only for

capital, and not the reverse, i.e. the means of production are not simply means for a steadily expanding pattern of life for the *society* of the producers. . . . The means — the unrestricted development of the social forces of production — comes into persistent conflict with the restricted end, the valorization of the existing capital. If the capitalist mode of production is therefore a historical means for developing the material powers of production and for creating a corresponding world market, it is at the same time the constant contradiction between this historical task and the social relations of production corresponding to it.[13]

Included in this critique of the capitalist mode of production is the idea of a society in which the means and the end would no longer be in conflict with each other. For Marx, "the unrestricted development of the social forces of production" — a society without antagonism — represents a genuine historical possibility. This is a possibility that Freud rejects because he conceives of antagonism as constitutive of the social structure itself.

Unprotected Sex

Before writing *Beyond the Pleasure Principle* in 1920, Freud did not yet see antagonism in this way. Though never a utopian believing that society might someday overcome the need for repression altogether, early in the development of psychoanalysis he does argue against the excesses of contemporary moral restrictions on sexual activity. While he prefaces his statement by admitting that "it is certainly not a physician's business to come forward with proposals for reform," he nonetheless claims that "it seemed to me that I might support the urgency of such proposals if I were to amplify [Christian] Von Ehrenfel's description of the injurious effects of our 'civilized' sexual morality by pointing to the important bearing of that morality upon the spread of modern nervous illness."[14] Freud made this claim in 1908, when his focus remained almost wholly on the sexual drives. At this time he saw a conflict between these drives and the interests of the ego because "the 'ego' feels threatened by the claims of the sexual instincts and fends them off by repressions."[15] Though no one can definitively overcome this conflict, Freud saw it as ameliorable, which allowed him to support a program for the reform of restrictions on sexual activity. We can lessen the bite that the ego takes out of the sexual drives on a societal level and thereby improve the relative satisfaction of subjects living within society.

When Freud discovered the death drive in 1920, this optimism became theoretically untenable and disappeared from Freud's writings. While Freud's discovery of the unconscious disrupted the thought of others, the discovery of the death drive disrupted his own and that of his followers — and this disruption makes itself felt in the halting and backtracking style of *Beyond the Pleasure Principle*. Though he continues to posit sexual drives and thus retains his psychic dualism (albeit in a completely modified form), Freud comes to see the death drive or the compulsion to repeat as the predominant force within the psyche and within society at large. He believes that it is more powerful than the sexual drives, just as before he saw the sexual drives as having more power than the drives associated with the ego. Despite this continued dualism, the discovery of the death drive radically alters Freud's ability to accept the possibility of reform or progressive political change of any sort.

When the sexual drives remained at the basis of Freudian thought, positive change existed as a possibility because dissatisfaction was not inherent within the sexual drives themselves. Psychic illness such as neurosis developed through a conflict between the sexual drives and other forces aligned with the ego (which also embodied the restrictive morality imposed on the subject by society). Even if we could not completely free the sexual drives from the repression associated with the ego, we could nonetheless lighten the burden and establish a degree of freedom. Seen in this way, we can imagine a Freudian politics of sexual liberation. This is the project of leftist psychoanalytic thinkers such as Otto Gross, Wilhelm Reich, and Erich Fromm, each of whom attacks repressive society and focuses on sexual liberation.

For these theorists, the early Freud before the discovery of the death drive is the more politically viable Freud. Gross, Reich, and Fromm develop disparate theoretical perspectives, but Reich and Fromm — Gross died in 1920, though he undoubtedly would have adopted their opposition as well had he lived — see the concept of the death drive as an unfortunate deviation on Freud's part. Each tries to marry psychoanalysis with some form of Marxist or socialist thought, and by doing so, they take up Marx's belief that society can overcome antagonism, that sexual liberation is possible within the social order. Repression, for these psychoanalytic thinkers, is not the necessary cost of social life but a fact of what Reich calls authoritarian rule.

Even before Freud comes up with the death drive, he insists that the sexual drive does not function smoothly but rather is constantly at odds with itself. His self-proclaimed dualistic conception of the drives — first the sex drive and the self-preservative drive, then the life drive and the death drive — is actually a dialectical conception in which a single drive produces an antagonistic struggle. The psychoanalytic leftists do not see things this way. From their perspective, the sexual drive doesn't run aground on its own but hits an opposing force — social restriction. As a result, the political project of psychoanalysis becomes perfectly clear: lift social restrictions and allow the free play of the sexual drive.

Wilhelm Reich gives this politics its most detailed early formulation. As both a committed Marxist and a psychoanalyst, he aligns the proletarian revolution with sexual liberation. Reich visited the Soviet Union in 1927 and found the realization of this theoretical alignment, though he would later attest to the Soviet retreat from sexual liberation and return to the conservative ideology of the family. By freeing subjects from repressive restrictions on sexuality, the social order can allow the subject's natural libido to flourish. The struggle, as Reich sees it, is entirely straightforward. An authoritarian rule imposes restrictions on natural sexuality, and these restrictions create the neurotic disorders that psychoanalysis treats. Reich contends that Freud fails to take up a critical position relative to social restrictions and thus blames the victims of society for the problems created by an oppressive authoritarian structure.[16]

Erich Fromm takes a position similar to that of Reich, though he never associates himself directly with the Communist revolution. Unlike Reich, Fromm does accept a version of the death drive. He believes that a death drive can form, but he doesn't grant it any independent status. The death drive, which is a drive to destroy oneself and others, emerges with the repression of the life drive. If life successfully expresses itself, the subject will not turn against itself and will instead develop loving relations with others and with the self. Despite this modification of Reich, the psychoanalytic political project is basically the same for both Reich and Fromm. Psychoanalysis takes the side of the natural libido or sexual drive and argues for its liberation. Rather than accepting the psychoanalytic critique of the good, they see a sexually liberated society as a good society that psychoanalytic thought and therapy can help to produce.

Though Gross, Reich, and Fromm develop the political dimension of psychoanalysis, they do so as practicing psychoanalysts. This investment in psychoanalytic treatment restricts the extent to which they are able to construct a political theory. They are psychoanalysts first and political thinkers second. They also collectively refuse to account for the later Freud's turn to the death drive, even if only to see it as a necessary obstacle with which political struggle must contend.[17] Herbert Marcuse suffers from neither of these limitations. He is a philosopher and cultural theorist who comes to psychoanalysis to assist in thinking through political difficulties, and he recognizes that any political project has to incorporate the death drive. Marcuse announces his own unique marriage of Marx and Freud in *Eros and Civilization*, one of the two great attempts to construct a politics grounded on psychoanalysis. It is a book that bears the subtitle *A Philosophical Inquiry into Freud*.[18]

Marcuse envisions a society that would eliminate scarcity to such an extent that it would no longer require the repression of our sexual drives, or eros. In this type of society, the need for labor would disappear, and the predominance of the reality principle (or the delaying of satisfaction) could give way to an unleashing of the pleasure principle (or the direct path to satisfaction). While Marcuse admits that up to this point in history progress has increased the amount of repression, he believes the end of labor—and the socialist revolution necessary to accomplish it—would occasion a dialectical reversal in which progress suddenly liberated eros rather than augmenting its repression. This vision allows us to imagine a world in which even death loses its traumatic dimension because individual subjects would be reconciled with the social whole that would survive them.

In constructing his vision of a better future, Marcuse does not lose sight of the principle that opposes eros—the death drive, or what he calls thanatos. He views thanatos as an aggressive instinct, an instinct toward destruction that, unlike eros, demands repression in order for society to function.[19] But there is a way to mitigate the power of this instinct for destruction: by eliminating the repression of eros, a society lessens the aggression that subjects experience because much of this aggression arises in response to a lack of erotic satisfaction, though this aggression would not disappear altogether.

Marcuse's ideal society appears to figure a way out of the antagonism that Freud sees animating the relation between the individual subject and the social order. He does so, despite borrowing terminology from the later Freud, by focusing on the liberation of the sexual drives in the way that the early Freud and the leftist Freudians advocate.

But such a program is constitutively incapable of admitting the idea of the death drive with all of its theoretical force. Marcuse acknowledges the death drive in order to show how an ideal society might minimize its power, but the existence of the death drive sabotages the political program as such. It leads Freud to say, toward the end of *Civilization and Its Discontents*, "I have not the courage to rise up before my fellow-men as a prophet, and I bow to their reproach that I can offer them no consolation."[20] The death drive eliminates the possibility of offering consolation in the form of a traditional political program because it erects a fundamental barrier to progress to an extent that Marcuse cannot fully recognize due to his Marxist political commitment.

Death at the Bottom of Everything

The death drive is neither (contra Marcuse) aggressiveness nor an impulse to return to an inorganic state (as Freud's metaphor in *Beyond the Pleasure Principle* might imply) but an impetus to return to an originary traumatic and constitutive loss. The death drive emerges with subjectivity itself as the subject enters into the social order and becomes a social and speaking being by sacrificing a part of itself. This sacrifice is an act of creation that produces an object that exists only insofar as it is lost. This loss of what the subject doesn't have institutes the death drive, which produces enjoyment through the repetition of the initial loss.

Subjects engage in acts of self-sacrifice and self-sabotage because the loss enacted reproduces the subject's lost object and enables the subject to enjoy this object. Once it is obtained, the object ceases to be *the* object. As a result, the subject must continually repeat the sacrificial acts that produce the object, despite the damage that such acts do to the subject's self-interest. From the perspective of the death drive, we turn to violence not in order to gain power but in order to produce loss, which is our only source of enjoyment. Without the lost object, life becomes bereft of any satisfaction. The repetition of sacrifice, however, creates a life worth living, a life in which one can enjoy oneself through the lost object.

The repetition involved with the death drive is not simply repetition of any particular experience. The repetition compulsion leads the subject to repeat specifically the experiences that have traumatized it and disturbed its stable functioning. The better things are going for the subject, the more likely that the death drive will derail the subject's activity. According to the theory implied by the death drive, any movement toward the good — any progress — will tend to produce a reaction that will undermine it. This occurs both on the level of the individual and on the level of society. In psychoanalytic treatment, it takes the form of a negative therapeutic reaction, an effort to sustain one's disorder in the face of the imminence of the cure. We can also think of individuals who continue to choose romantic relationships that fail according to a precise pattern. Politically, it means that progress triggers the very forms of oppression that it hopes to combat and thereby incessantly undermines itself. There is a backlash written into every progressive program from the outset.

The death drive creates an essentially masochistic structure within the psyche. It provides the organizing principle for the subject and orients the subject relative to its enjoyment, and this enjoyment remains always linked to trauma. This structure renders difficult all attempts to prompt subjects to act in their own self-interest or for their own good. The death drive leads subjects to act contrary to their own interests, to sabotage the projects that would lead to their good.

Common sense tells us that sadism is easier to understand than masochism, that the sadist's lust for power over the object makes sense in a way that the masochist's self-destruction does not. But for psychoanalysis, masochism functions as the paradigmatic form of subjectivity. Considering the structure of the death drive, masochism becomes easily explained, and sadism becomes a mystery. Masochism provides the subject the enjoyment of loss, while sadism seems to give this enjoyment to the other.

This is exactly the claim of Jacques Lacan's revolutionary interpretation of sadism in his famous article "Kant with Sade." Though most readers focus on the essay's philosophical coupling of Kantian morality with Sadean perversion, the more significant step that Lacan takes here occurs in his explanation of sadism's appeal. Traditionally, most people vilify sadists for transforming their victims into objects for their own satisfaction, but Lacan contends that they actually turn themselves into objects for the other's enjoyment. He notes: "The sadist discharges the pain of existence into the Other, but without seeing that he himself thereby turns into an 'eternal object.'"[21] Though the other suffers pain, the other also becomes the sole figure of enjoyment. What the sadist enjoys in the sadistic act is the enjoyment attributed to the other, and the sadistic act attempts to bring about this enjoyment. In this sense, sadism is nothing but an inverted form of masochism, which remains the fundamental structure of subjectivity.[22] Self-destruction plays such a prominent role in human activities because the death drive is the drive that animates us as subjects.

Unlike Herbert Marcuse, Norman O. Brown, another celebrated proponent of psychoanalytically informed political thought, attempts to construct a psychoanalytic political project that focuses on the death drive. He does not simply see it as the unfortunate result of the repression of eros but as a powerful category on its own. In *Life against Death* Brown conceives of the death drive as a self-annihilating impulse that emerges out of the human incapacity to accept death and loss. As he puts it, "The death instinct is the core of the human neurosis. It begins with the human infant's incapacity to accept separation from the mother, that separation which confers individual life on all living organisms and which in all living organisms at the same time leads to death."[23] For Brown, we pursue death and destruction, paradoxically, because we cannot accept death. If we possessed the ability to accept our own death, according to Brown's view, we would avoid falling into the death drive and would thereby rid ourselves of human violence and destructiveness.

Like Marcuse, Brown's societal ideal involves the unleashing of the sexual drives and the minimizing or elimination of the death drive. He even raises the stakes, contending that unless we manage to realize this ideal, the human species, under the sway of the death drive, will die out like the dinosaurs. Despite making more allowances for the death drive (and for death itself) than Marcuse, Brown nonetheless cannot avoid a similar error: the belief that the death drive is a force that subjects can overcome. For Freud, in contrast, it is the force that revenges itself on every overcoming, the repetition that no utopia can fully leave behind. An authentic recognition of the death drive and its primacy would demand that we rethink the idea of progress altogether.

INTRODUCTION

Progressing Backward

And yet some idea of progress seems essential to politics. Without progress as a possibility, it seems obvious that one would have no reason to involve oneself in political contestation. All political activity would become futile, which is why few dispense with it altogether. Even a thinker such as Jacques Derrida who struggles incessantly against the ideology of progress nonetheless implicitly retains some notion of authentic progress within his thought. Without it, he would have no position from which to criticize the idea while still endorsing political activity.

The problem with progress as an idea, according to someone like Derrida, lies in the way that it places a teleology on the movement of history and thereby prescribes a certain future that will serve to constrain our political activity. Rather than helping to increase our freedom, the idea of progress diminishes it by closing down the opening that the future represents. Despite his deconstruction of progress, Derrida aligns deconstruction with hope for a better future — with what he calls an "emancipatory promise." In *Specters of Marx* he elaborates: "Well, what remains irreducible to any deconstruction, what remains as undeconstructible as the possibility itself of deconstruction is, perhaps, a certain experience of the emancipatory promise; it is perhaps even the formality of a structural messianism, a messianism without religion, even a messianic without messianism."[24] Though deconstruction leaves its emancipatory promise always to be fulfilled and refuses to actualize it, Derrida tacitly conceives the movement toward it as progressive.

The political dimension of deconstruction is founded on the belief that a better world is possible: by deconstructing hierarchies, by insisting on a justice to come, and by struggling against illusions of presence, we can lessen human suffering and help to forge a more egalitarian world. There is a good, even if fully realizing this good would transform it into its opposite (which is Derrida's contention). One must ensure that the good society always remains to come, or *arrivant*, as Derrida puts it, but far from minimizing the status of the good or denigrating the good, giving it a futural status in fact elevates it and ensconces justice to come as the one idea that we cannot deconstruct — the ultimate or sovereign good.[25] Even in deconstruction, some idea of progress as a possibility must exist in order for the theorist to make any normative appeal whatsoever.[26]

But the inescapability of the idea of progress goes still further. It is not just the normative appeal that implies this idea; any system of thought, even one that confines itself to pure descriptions, inevitably points toward the possibility of progress. The act of articulating a system of thought implies the belief that a better world is possible and that the knowledge the system provides will assist in realizing this better world. If I didn't believe in the possibility of improvement, I would never bother to articulate any system at all. The very act of enunciating even the most pessimistic system attests to a fundamental optimism and hope for progress beyond the status quo. This is true for an extreme pessimist like Arthur Schopenhauer as much as it is for an avowed utopian like Charles Fourier. The position from which one enunciates the pessimistic system is the position invested in the idea of progress, even when the enunciated content of the system completely denounces the idea. Though the good may be impossible to realize, it is also impossible to abandon entirely. The production of knowledge itself points, often despite itself, toward a better future.

This link between knowledge and progress is the controlling idea of the Enlightenment. In his essay "What Is Enlightenment?" Kant emphasizes that Enlightenment requires a situation where one is free to gain knowledge, where one has "freedom to make *public use* of one's reason in all matters."[27] In the act of gaining knowledge through reasoning, subjects facilitate progress as they put this knowledge into use by restructuring society. Knowledge, for Kant and for all Enlightenment thinkers, has an inherently progressive leaning. It frees us from the tyranny of the past and from the drudgery of repetition. Progress is only possible because we have the ability to know the past and to learn from it.[28] The Enlightenment's belief in progress derives from its conception of the human subject as a subject of knowledge, a subject who fundamentally wants to know.

For psychoanalysis, the link between knowledge and progress dooms the possibility of progress. Rather than desiring to know, the subject desires not to know and organizes its existence around the avoidance of knowledge. In "Le séminaire XXI" Lacan states this straightforwardly: "There has been no desire for knowledge but . . . a horror of knowing."[29] The knowledge that we avoid is knowledge of the unconscious because this knowledge confronts us with the power of the death drive and the inescapability of repetition. What we don't know — our particular form of stupidity — allows us to move forward, to view the future with hopefulness. Without this fundamental refusal to know, the subject simply could not continue.[30]

Freud's great revolution in the history of thought stems from his conception of the subject as a subject of desire rather than as a subject of knowledge. Where thinkers from Plato to Kant consider an inherent striving to know as essential to subjectivity, not only does Freud envision a different essential drive, he contends that the subject wants not to know in order to continue to desire. The subject acts not on the basis of what it knows but on the basis of how it desires. We might imagine linking these two ideas of the subject if we could link the act of knowing and the act of desiring.

But knowledge and desire are at odds: the subject doesn't want to know what it desires or how it enjoys. Its knowledge remains necessarily incomplete, and the gap within knowledge is the trigger for the subject's desire and the point at which it enjoys. The unconscious emerges out of the subject's incapacity for knowing its own enjoyment. Conscious knowledge is not simply unable to arrive at the knowledge of enjoyment and its traumatic origin; it actively functions as a barrier to this knowledge. Conscious knowledge thwarts access to the unconscious, and, as a result, the conscious effort to know continually defeats itself.

Psychoanalysis attempts to fill this fundamental lacuna in the project of knowledge by demanding that the subject abandon the project in its traditional manifestation. It constructs a space that brackets conscious knowledge in order that the subject might discover the unconscious. The fundamental rule of psychoanalysis — one must reveal not what one knows but the words that come to mind — aims at bringing to light what the subject doesn't want to know. A gap exists between what the subject knows and what it says. In the act of speaking, the subject says more than it consciously knows, and this excess is the unconscious — a knowledge that the subject has without knowing it. The paradox of this knowledge is that one can access it only when *not* seeking it and that once one has it, one has lost it.

Adherence to the fundamental rule of psychoanalysis insofar as it is possible allows subjects to recognize what they don't know when it surprises them. But it doesn't thereby permit subjects to make progress through the acquisition of knowledge. The recognitions that one makes in psychoanalysis do not have the status of knowledge in the traditional sense of the term; instead, they mark an irreducible gap in the field of knowledge. One recognizes oneself in an unconscious desire that remains foreign, and one takes responsibility for it despite its foreignness. By doing so, one does not change or progress as a subject but becomes what one already was. One sees the death drive as the truth of one's subjectivity rather than as an obstacle that one might try to progress beyond in order to reach the good.

Interminable Repetition

If we accept the contradictory conclusion that some idea of progress inheres in every system of thought and that the psychoanalytic concept of the death drive shows the impossibility of progress, this leaves psychoanalytic thought — and especially a psychoanalytic political project — on difficult ground. It might explain the seemingly absolute pessimism of the later Freud, Freud after 1920, who appears to have abandoned his belief in the efficaciousness of the psychoanalytic cure. One of his final essays, "Analysis Terminable and Interminable," written in 1937 (just two years before his death), lays bare Freud's doubts concerning our ability to break from the power of repetition. Here, Freud conceives of subjects' refusal to abandon castration anxiety and penis envy as emblematic of the intractability of repetition. He notes: "At no other point in one's analytic work does one suffer more from an oppressive feeling that all one's repeated efforts have been in vain, and from a suspicion that one has been 'preaching to the winds,' than when one is trying to persuade a woman to abandon her wish for a penis on the ground of its being unrealizable or when one is seeking to convince a man that a passive attitude to men does not always signify castration and that it is indispensable in many relationships in life."[31] That is, the repetition that centers around traumatic loss acts as a barrier that we cannot progress beyond.

In light of this barrier, the formulation of a psychoanalytically informed political project demands that we dissociate politics from progress as it is usually conceived. We cannot escape progress, and yet the traditional conception of progress always runs aground. This paradox must become the foundation of any authentic psychoanalytic politics. It demands that rather than trying to progress toward overcoming the barrier that separates us from the good society, we begin to view identification with the barrier as the paradoxical aim of progress. The barrier to the good society — the social symptom — is at once the obstacle over which we continually stumble and the source of our enjoyment.[32]

The typical politics of the good aims at a future not inhibited by a limit that constrains the present. This future can take the form of a truly representative democracy, a socialist utopia, a society with a fair distribution of power and wealth, or even a fascist order that would expel those who embody the limit. But the good remains out of reach despite the various efforts to reach it. The limit separating us from the good society is the very thing that constitutes the good society as such. Overcoming the limit shatters the idea of the good in the act of achieving it. In place of this pursuit, a psychoanalytic politics insists on identification with the limit rather than attempting to move beyond or eliminate it. If there is a conception of progress in this type of politics, it is progress toward the obstacle that bars us from the good rather than toward the good itself.

Identification with the limit involves an embrace of the repetition of the drive because it is the obstacle or limit that is the point to which the drive returns. No one can be the perfect subject of the drive because the drive is what undermines all perfection. But it is nonetheless possible to change one's experience within it. The fundamental wager of psychoanalysis — a wager that renders the idea of a psychoanalytic political project thinkable — is that repetition undergoes a radical transformation when one adopts a different attitude toward it. We may be condemned to repeat, but we aren't condemned to repeat the same position relative to our repetition. By embracing repetition through identification with the obstacle to progress rather than trying to achieve the good by overcoming this obstacle, the subject or the social order changes its very nature. Instead of being the burden that one seeks to escape, repetition becomes the essence of one's being and the mode through which one attains satisfaction.

Conceiving politics in terms of the embrace of repetition rather than the construction of a good society takes the movement that derails traditional political projects and reverses its valence. This idea of politics lacks the hopefulness that Marxism, for instance, can provide for overcoming antagonism and loss. With it, we lose not just a utopian ideal but the idea of an alternative future altogether — the idea of a future no longer beset by intransigent limits — and this idea undoubtedly mobilizes much political energy.[33] What we gain, however, is a political form that addresses the way that subjects structure their enjoyment. It is by abandoning the terrain of the good and adopting the death drive as its guiding principle that emancipatory politics can pose a genuine alternative to the dominance of global capitalism rather than incidentally creating new avenues for its expansion and development. The death drive is the revolutionary contribution that psychoanalysis makes to political thought. But since it is a concept relatively foreign to political thought, I will turn to various examples from history, literature, and film in order to concretize what Freud means by the death drive and illustrate just what a politics of the death drive might look like.

The chapters that follow trace the implications of the death drive for thinking about the subject as a political entity and for conceiving the political structure of society. Part 1 focuses on the individual subject, beginning with an explanation of how the death drive shapes this subjectivity. The various chapters in part 1 trace the implications of the death drive for understanding how the subject enjoys, how the drive relates to social class, how the drive impacts the subject as an ethical being, and how the subject becomes politicized. The discussion of the impact of the death drive on the individual subject serves as a foundation for articulating its impact on society, which part 2 of the book addresses, beginning with the impact of the death drive on the constitution of society. Part 2 then examines how the conception of the death drive helps in navigating a path through today's major political problems: the inefficacity of consciousness raising, the seductive power of fantasy, the growing danger of biological reductionism and fundamentalism, the lure of religious belief, and the failure of attempts to lift repression. The two parts of the book do not attempt to sketch a political goal to be attained for the subject or for society but instead to recognize the structures that already exist and silently inform both. The wager of what follows is that the revelation of the death drive and its reach into the subject and the social order can be the foundation for reconceiving freedom.

The recognition of the death drive as foundational for subjectivity is what occurs with the psychoanalytic cure. Through this cure, the subject abandons the belief in the possibility of finding a solution to the problem of subjectivity. The loss for which one seeks restitution becomes a constitutive loss — and becomes visible as the key to one's enjoyment rather than a barrier to it. A political project derived from psychoanalytic thought would work to broaden this cure by bringing it outside the clinic and enacting on society itself. The point is not, of course, that everyone would undergo psychoanalysis but that psychoanalytic theory would function as a political theory. Politically, the importance of psychoanalysis is theoretical rather than practical. Politically, it doesn't matter whether people undergo psychoanalytic therapy or not. This theory would inaugurate political change by insisting not on the possibility of healing and thereby attaining the ultimate pleasure but on the indissoluble link between our enjoyment and loss. We become free to enjoy only when we have recognized the intractable nature of loss.

Though psychoanalytic thought insists on our freedom to enjoy, it understands freedom in a counterintuitive way. It is through the death drive that the subject attains its freedom. The loss that founds this drive frees the subject from its dependence on its social environment, and the repetition of the initial loss sustains this freedom. By embracing the inescapability of traumatic loss, one embraces one's freedom, and any political project genuinely concerned with freedom must orient itself around loss. Rather than looking to the possibility of overcoming loss, our political projects must work to remain faithful to it and enhance our contact with it. Only in this way does politics have the opportunity to carve out a space for the freedom to enjoy rather than restricting it under the banner of the good.

I

SUBJECTIVITY

1

The Formation of Subjectivity

The Importance of Losing

The politics of the death drive begins with the revolutionary idea of subjectivity that Freud uncovers: his understanding that the subject doesn't seek knowledge but instead desires. Following from this idea, the traditional notion of progress becomes untenable, and the subject becomes self-destructive. On the one hand, earlier thinkers like Arthur Schopenhauer and Friedrich Nietzsche anticipate Freud's revolutionary turn from the subject of knowledge to the subject of desire. Schopenhauer and Nietzsche emphasize how our quest for knowledge serves as a guise for a more fundamental quest for satisfaction, and in this way they overturn the traditional philosophical conception of subjectivity.[1] But on the other hand, both Schopenhauer and Nietzsche fail to grasp the significance of the human animal's entrance into the field of knowledge or language. For both, will exists on one side and knowledge (or representation) on the other, and will is nothing but a biological fact. Freud's conception of desiring subjectivity recognizes that the subject is the result of instinct being deformed through its submission to the realm of knowledge. Though we act on behalf of desire rather than knowledge, we do so, paradoxically, because our instincts are mediated by knowledge. Freud's subject, in contrast to Schopenhauer's and Nietzsche's, never experiences pure biological instincts but rather a desire that remains unconscious.[2]

Authentically prioritizing desire requires an idea of the unconscious not simply as the site of a will or instinct associated with human animality but as a radically different psychic scene fundamentally irreducible to consciousness.

For Freud, the subject doesn't know its unconscious desire not because of its failure to grasp its continued animality but because unconscious desire gives birth to the subject and always remains in front of every project of knowledge. Freud's revolution is a genuine one — tied to a unique vision of how subjectivity emerges.[3] The political implications of psychoanalytic thought begin with its understanding of the genesis of subjectivity, an understanding that sets psychoanalysis apart from other political theorizing of all stripes. The foundational status of loss for the subject entails a politics centered around the repetition of loss rather than the achievement of the good. Psychoanalytic thought sees us as condemned to the repetition of loss, but it aims at freeing us to take up a new relation to this repetition. This new relation is the emancipatory project of psychoanalytic politics.

Initially, as Freud conceives it, the human animal is an autoerotic being that has no object world. The distinction between self and other (or subject and object) is not a fact of birth but a psychical achievement. The infant's autoerotic mode does not yet differentiate between itself and objects, and the being finds some degree of satisfaction in its undifferentiated existence. This autoeroticism is not yet even narcissism. The narcissistic relationship of the subject with its own ego requires the formation of an ego, which can only form through a break in the autoerotic circuit. As Freud puts it in "On Narcissism: An Introduction," "A unity comparable to the ego cannot exist in the individual from the start; the ego has to be developed. The auto-erotic instincts, however, are there from the very first; so there must be something added to auto-eroticism — a new psychical action — in order to bring about narcissism."[4] Because the ego is just a special sort of object (one that competes with other objects for the subject's libido), it can form and the subject can become narcissistic only after the subject has created the division between subject and object. This creative act — what Freud calls "a new psychical action" — produces a division out of the undifferentiated autoeroticism of the human animal.

The subject as such emerges through the experience of loss. It is the loss of a part of the subject — an initial act of sacrifice — that creates both subject and object, the object emerging through this act as what the subject has lost of itself. The subject takes an interest in the object world because it forms this world around its lost object. As Jacques Lacan notes, "Never, in our concrete experience of analytic theory, do we do without the notion of the lack of the object as central. It is not a negative, but the very spring for the relation of the subject to the world."[5] The loss of the object generates a world around this loss to which the subject can relate.

Obviously, no one literally creates objects through an initial act of sacrifice of an actual body part. This would be too much to ask. But the psychical act of sacrifice allows for a distinction to develop where none existed before and simultaneously directs the subject's desire toward the object world. In his breakthrough essay "Negation," Freud describes this process as follows: "The antithesis between subjective and objective does not exist from the first. It only comes into being from the fact that thinking possesses the capacity to bring before the mind once more something that has once been perceived, by reproducing it as a presentation without the external object having still to be there. The first and immediate aim, therefore, of reality-testing is, not to *find* an object in real perception which corresponds to the one presented, but to *refind* such an object, to convince oneself that it is still there."[6] Though Freud doesn't use terms from linguistics, it is clear that he is making reference to the subject's alienation in language and that he sees this alienation as the key to the emergence of both the subject and the object.

When the subject submits to the imperatives of language, it enters into an indirect relation with the object world. The speaking being does not relate to books, pencils, and paper but to "books," "pencils," and "paper." The signifier intervenes between the subject and the object that the subject perceives. The subject's alienation into language deprives it of immediate contact with the object world. And yet, in the above passage from "Negation," Freud conceives of the subject's entrance into language — its "capacity to bring before the mind once more something that has once been perceived, by reproducing it as a presentation without the external object having still to be there" — as the event that produces the very distinction between subject and object. This means that the indirectness or mediation introduced by language deprives the subject of a direct relation to the object world that it never had.

Prior to its immersion in the mediation of language, the subject had no object at all — not a privileged relation to objects but a complete absence of relationality as such due to its autoeroticism. In this sense, the subject's willingness to accede to its alienation in language is the first creative act, a sacrifice that produces the objects that the subject cannot directly access. Language is important not for its own sake but because it is the site of our founding sacrifice. We know that the subject has performed this act of sacrifice when we witness the subject functioning as a being of language, but the sacrifice is not an act that the subject takes up on its own.

Others always impose the entry into language on the subject. Their exhortations and incentives to speak prompt the emergence of the speaking subject. But the subject's openness to alienation in language, its willingness to sacrifice a part of itself in order to become a speaking subject, suggests a lack in being itself prior to the entry into language. That is, the act through which the subject cedes the privileged object and becomes a subject coincides with language but is irreducible to it. The subject engages in the act of sacrifice because it does not find its initial autoeroticism perfectly satisfying — the unity of the autoerotic being is not perfect — and this lack of complete satisfaction produces the opening through which language and society grab onto the subject through its alienating process. If the initial autoerotic state of the human animal were perfectly satisfying, no one would begin to speak, and subjectivity would never form. Speaking as such testifies to an initial wound in our animal being and in being itself.

But subjectivity emerges only out of a self-wounding. Even though others encourage the infant to abandon its autoerotic state through a multitude of inducements, the initial loss that constitutes subjectivity is always and necessarily self-inflicted. Subjectivity has a fundamentally masochistic form, and it continually repeats the masochistic act that founds it. The act of sacrifice opens the door to the promise of a satisfaction that autoerotic isolation forecloses, which is why the incipient subject abandons the autoerotic state and accedes to the call of sociality. But the term "sacrifice" is misleading insofar as it suggests that the subject has given up a wholeness (with itself or with its parent) that exists prior to being lost.

In the act of sacrifice, the incipient subject gives up something that it doesn't have. The initial loss that founds subjectivity is not at all substantial; it is the ceding of nothing. Through this defining gesture, the subject sacrifices its lost object into being. But if the subject cedes nothing, this initial act of sacrifice seems profoundly unnecessary. Why can't the subject emerge without it? Why is the experience of loss necessary for the subject to constitute itself qua subject? The answer lies in the difference between need and desire. While the needs of the human animal are not dependent on the experience of loss, the subject's desires are.

It is the initial act of sacrifice that gives birth to desire: the subject sacrifices nothing in order to create a lost object around which it can organize its desire. As Richard Boothby puts it in his unequaled explanation of the psychoanalytic conception of the emergence of desire, "The destruction and loss of the object ... opens up a symbolic dimension in which what was lost might be recovered in a new form."[7] He adds: "Sacrifice serves to constitute the very matrix of desire. The essential function of sacrifice is less *do ut des*, I give so that you might give, than *do ut desidero*: I give in order that I might desire."[8] The subject's desire is oriented around this lost object, but the object is nothing as a positive entity and only exists insofar as it is lost. This is why one can never attain the lost object or the object that causes one to desire.[9] The coming-into-being of this object originates the subject of desire, but, having no substance, the object can never become an empirical object of desire. We may see an object of desire as embodying the lost object, but whenever we obtain this object, we discover its emptiness. The lost object is constitutively rather than empirically lost.

Eating Nothing

In this light, we can see the anorexic as the model for all desiring subjectivity. Most cultural critics justifiably see anorexia as the product of oppressive definitions of femininity that abound in contemporary society and force women to starve themselves in order to fit the ideals of feminine beauty. According to Naomi Wolf's classic popular account in *The Beauty Myth*, the ideal of thinness became a way of controlling women — disciplining their bodies — after the idea of natural female inferiority began to evanesce.[10] The anorexic embodies female victimization: she has internalized a patriarchal ideal and does violence to her own body in order to live up to this ideal.

But the problem with this analysis is that the anorexic doesn't just try to embody the ideal of feminine beauty.[11] She goes too far in her pursuit of thinness and comes to inhabit a body far from the ideal. Even when everyone tells her that she no longer looks good, that she is too thin, the anorexic continues to lose weight. It is for this reason that many feminists have seen her as a subversive figure. As Elizabeth Grosz puts it, "Neither a 'disorder' of the ego nor, as popular opinion has it, a 'dieting disease' gone out of control, anorexia can, like the phantom limb, be a kind of mourning for a pre-Oedipal (i.e., pre-castrated) body and a corporeal connection to the mother that women in patriarchy are required to abandon. Anorexia is a form of protest at the social meaning of the female body."[12] Grosz accounts for the excessiveness of anorexia by aligning it with feminist resistance to patriarchy rather than obsequious submission to it. But she aligns the anorexic with wholeness and the maternal bond rather than with the lost object. In this sense, she misses the true radicality of the anorexic, a radicality that stems from the power of the anorexic's desire.

The anorexic doesn't simply refuse to eat but eats nothing, the nothing that is the lost object. While all positive forms of food fail to address the subject's lack, nothing does speak to the subject's desire and allows that desire to sustain itself. The anorexic starves not because she can't find, in the mode of Kafka's hunger artist, any food that would satisfy her but because she has found a satisfying food, a food that nourishes the desiring subject rather than the living being. The logic of anorexia lays bare the hidden workings of desire that operate within every subject. Subjects believe that they pursue various objects of desire (a new car, a new house, a new romantic partner, and so on) and that these objects have an intrinsic attraction, but the real engine for their desire resides in the nothing that the subject has given up and that every object tries and fails to represent. Objects of desire are desirable only insofar as they attempt to represent the impossible lost object, which is what the anorexic reveals. Still, the anorexic is exceptional; most nonanorexic subjects imagine that their lost object can be found in something rather than nothing.

Despite its resonances with the structure of desire, anorexia cannot be dissociated from the imposition of the ideal of thinness as a mode of controlling female subjectivity. Though this ideal distorts the anorexic's relationship to her own body, it also renders the nature of desire itself apparent. The impossible ideal of perfect thinness allows the anorexic subject to avow, albeit unconsciously, the structural impossibility of desire itself. Unlike male subjects (or other female subjects who manage to distance themselves from the ideal), the anorexic cannot avoid confronting the impossibility of her object. The oppressive ideal of perfect thinness allows the anorexic to bear witness with her body to the truth of desire.[13]

Understanding the impossible nature of the lost object — what the anorexic makes clear — allows us to rethink the nature of the political act. Rather than being the successful achievement of some object, the accomplishment of some social good, the political act involves insisting on one's desire in the face of its impossibility, which is precisely what occurs in the death drive. The key to a politics of the death drive is grasping, in the fashion of the anorexic, the nothingness of the object and thereby finding satisfaction in the drive itself. But the subject's relationship to its object inherently creates an illusion that makes this possibility almost impossible.

Though the lost object that initiates subjectivity has no substance, its status for the subject belies its nothingness. For the subject, the originary lost object is *the* object that seems to hold the key to the subject's very ability to enjoy. Subjects invest the lost object with the idea of their own completion: the loss of the object retroactively causes a prior state of completion to arise — a state of completion that never actually existed — and the object itself bears the promise of inaugurating a return to this imaginary prior state.[14] In short, it promises to fill in the subject's lack and answer its desire. As a result of this investment on the part of the subject, the initial lost object becomes the engine for all the subject's subsequent desiring.

Without the initial act of sacrifice, the would-be subject neither desires nor enjoys but instead suffocates in a world of self-presence, a self-presence in which one has no freedom whatsoever. Through the loss of the privileged object, one frees oneself from the complete domination of (parental or social) authority by creating a lack that no authority can fill. Ceding the object is thus the founding act of subjectivity and the first free act. Every subsequent effort by authority to give the subject what it lacks will come up short — or, more correctly, will go too far, because only nothing can fill the gap within the subject. For this reason, dissatisfaction and disappointment are correlative with freedom: when we experience the authority's failure to give us what we want, at that moment we also experience our distance from the authority and our radical freedom as subjects.

Suffering as Ideology

The potential problem with identifying freedom and loss is that ideology often operates through this same identification. The apotheosis of suffering is one of the fundamental modes that ideology adopts in order to convince subjects to adapt to the demands of the social order. This is nowhere more apparent than in Christianity, which tells subjects that they must accept earthly suffering in order to gain the enjoyment of a heavenly paradise. The subjects who accept this exchange endure their misery quietly rather than revolting against it and toppling the oppressive ruling class. One of Marxism's primary claims is that there is no virtue in suffering under the yoke of capitalist oppression, that there is no otherworldly paradise awaiting those who suffer the most here. For Marxism, any attempt to privilege suffering necessarily aligns one with the oppressing class rather than the oppressed class. Liberation means first of all liberation from unnecessary suffering.

But Marx does allow that we cannot completely overcome what he calls the realm of necessity. Even in a socialist society, there will always be some necessary suffering that we must endure, though it will undoubtedly be minimal. As Marx puts it in the third volume of *Capital*, "The true realm of freedom, the development of human powers as an end in itself, ... can only flourish with this realm of necessity as its basis."[15] Nonetheless, suffering, in Marx's account, represents what we strive to avoid. The entire effort of his thought consists in enhancing the realm of freedom at the expense of the realm of necessity. The pleasure that we will experience in a socialist society is a pleasure opposed to suffering, not an enjoyment inseparable from it.

Though it clearly departs from Marx, the psychoanalytic idea that our enjoyment is linked to an initial experience of loss and that we derive enjoyment when we repeat this experience has little in common with Christian ideology or with any ideology that privileges suffering. Privileging loss as the source of our enjoyment means, if one can put it this way, that loss is its own reward. We don't experience loss now in exchange for pleasure later but instead enjoy loss because it allows a privileged object to emerge. In his landmark study *The Philosophy of Money*, Georg Simmel makes exactly this point about the value of objects. He claims: "Value is determined not by the relation to the demanding subject, but by the fact that this relation depends on the cost of a sacrifice."[16] We can value only what costs us some sacrifice because sacrifice — of money, of time, of possessions — produces desirability. Though we may need objects that don't require sacrifice, we cannot desire them.

This is why it is impossible to enjoy objects that are given away for free. The act of paying money imbues the objects purchased with sacrifice and loss, and this gives them their value.[17] The problem with free objects is not that one gets what one pays for — though this is often the case — but that they inevitably appear as simply empirical objects rather than as objects imbued with the elevating quality of the privileged object, which is a product of the association with loss. Loss is the creative act, the source of value.[18]

It is as if psychoanalysis accepts the Christian notion of original sin without the corresponding idea of a future recompense. It is *Paradise Lost* without *Paradise Regained* and with an understanding that the loss is also salvation. According to this homology, original sin would be at once the source of our suffering and our reward. Traumatic loss hurts, but it hurts in a way that we enjoy (or, at least, can enjoy). The ideological gesture — whether Christian, capitalist, or whatever — does not consist in proclaiming the necessity or the virtue of suffering but in holding out the promise of future respite or in mobilizing that suffering around an idea that redeems it.

Ideology develops in order to convince subjects that loss is not absolute and that it can become profitable.[19] No subsequent acquisition or reward can redeem the loss of the privileged object that founds subjectivity; it is a loss without the possibility of recompense. And yet, ideology proclaims that every loss has a productive dimension to it. In this sense, ideology is singular: all ideologies are nothing but forms of ideology as such. According to Christian ideology, our suffering on earth finds its reward in heavenly bliss. According to capitalist ideology, our labor today has its reward in tomorrow's riches. According to Islamic fundamentalist logic, our suicidal sacrifice results in an eternity in paradise.

No ideology can avow a completely unproductive loss, a loss that doesn't lead to the possibility of some future pleasure, and yet an unproductive loss is precisely what defines us. One challenges ideology not by proclaiming that loss or sacrifice is unnecessary that we might live lives of plenitude but by insisting on the unproductivity of loss.[20] Once a subject grasps that no future gain can redeem the initial loss, ideology loses its ability to control that subject. In this sense, one of the great anti-ideological works of philosophy is Hegel's *Phenomenology of Spirit*.

Hegel dedicates the entirety of his *Phenomenology* to illustrating the idea that loss is its own reward. The *Phenomenology* traces various philosophical positions as they undermine themselves through following their own logic to its endpoint. In each case the philosophical position tends toward its own annihilation. Hegel shows that loss or self-sacrifice is engrained in the logic of every philosophy (and hence of every subject). Rather than being a contingent outcome, loss becomes the center around which the position organizes itself. This is evident in the first attitude that Hegel interrogates — sense certainty, or the belief that our immediate sense experience is the ultimate truth.

By immersing himself in the logic of this position, Hegel demonstrates that despite sense certainty's protestations on behalf of the value of immediacy, it actually relies on a complex web of mediation in order to articulate its truth claims. In short, in the process of putting forward its truth claims, sense certainty undermines itself as a coherent philosophical position. This self-sacrifice is not, according to Hegel, a contingent problem within sense certainty but the necessary center of every type of philosophy. Whatever stability one finds in a philosophical position marks a retreat from the position's own fundamental logic, a retreat from the position itself. When one takes up a philosophical position, one must simultaneously grasp its self-destruction and identify oneself with this loss.[21]

But according to the standard reading of Hegel, this insight into other philosophical positions reaches a dead end in Hegel's own philosophy, especially in what he calls absolute knowledge, which is the position that concludes the *Phenomenology*. Absolute knowledge, as most commentators see it, marks the victory over loss, the point at which Hegel himself redeems loss, renders it productive, and achieves mastery of it. But this reading, perhaps misled by the term itself, fails to pay attention to how Hegel actually characterizes absolute knowledge. He concludes the *Phenomenology* with absolute knowledge in order to indicate the inescapability of a founding sacrifice.

To reach absolute knowledge is to come to this insight. As Hegel puts it, "The self-knowing Spirit knows not only itself but also the negative of itself, or its limit: to know one's limit is to know how to sacrifice oneself."[22] When one reaches absolute knowledge, one recognizes that loss is constitutive of whatever position one holds. This recognition allows one to embrace loss for its own sake and to enjoy it rather than retreating from it or trying to overcome it. Contrary to what even his own proponents say, Hegel's achievement of absolute knowledge marks philosophy's victory over the attempt to master loss, not the final step in the process of that mastery. Hegel leads philosophy to the position at which it can resist ideology's effort to recuperate loss and convince subjects that the status of loss is empirical rather than constitutive.

As it offers an image of the recuperation of loss, the ideological manipulation of human suffering also locates the source of suffering and loss externally: the violence and scarcity of the world produce the suffering of the individual subject. Cold War American ideology, for instance, envisioned the Soviet Union as the external force that necessitated sacrifice. Today Islamic fundamentalism plays a similar role. The threat of Islamic fundamentalism justifies the sacrifices of civil liberties that Americans make, and this justification takes on a broader resonance as it transforms how Americans relate to all their suffering. Locating the source of one's suffering in an external threat functions precisely like imagining a future recompense for that suffering. In both cases, loss becomes a contingent fact that one might overcome rather than the foundation of one's subjectivity. To avow the structural necessity of loss would deprive ideology of its most powerful incentive, which is why no ideology takes up this relation to loss. Or, to put it in other terms, what no ideology can acknowledge is the death drive. A psychoanalytic politics of the death drive produces a thoroughgoing critique of ideology in all the forms that it takes up, and a closer examination of the death drive will lay out precisely how it leads to this critique.

The Joy of Not Surviving

The death drive, despite the implications of the term itself and Freud's own suggestions in this direction, is not a drive to die and thereby return to an inorganic state. Rather than the death that occurs at the end of life, the death drive comes out of a death that occurs within life. It is a drive to repeat the experience of the loss of the privileged object that gives birth to the desiring subject. This experience is death in life insofar as it marks the moment at which death installs itself in the subject and rips the subject out of the cycle of life. The loss of the privileged object derails the subject and distorts the subject's relationship to life itself.

From this moment on, rather than simply trying to survive or to increase its vitality, the subject will continually return to the loss that defines the structure of its desire.[23] This disruption of life that founds the subject as such renders insufficient any recourse to an organicist or biological explanation of subjectivity. The subject of desire is never just a living subject; it is a subject that holds within it a form of death, a loss that shapes every relation that it subsequently adopts to the world. In fact, this loss pulls the subject out of the world and leaves it completely alienated from its environment or lifeworld.

Because of the traumatic loss that founds subjectivity, the subject never has a world. It does not exist as a being-in-the-world in the way that Martin Heidegger describes. Heidegger, who rejects the idea of subjectivity, considers our being in terms of what he calls Dasein, or being-there. For Heidegger, Dasein is always a being-in-the-world and is unimaginable outside its worldliness. We cannot speak of subjectivity when talking about Dasein precisely because subjectivity implies a separation between Dasein and its world. Dasein experiences alienation from its world, but it remains fundamentally a part of that world: its world is the limit that contains Dasein and that Dasein cannot go beyond. But Heidegger assumes rather than deduces Dasein's worldliness and its relationship to objects.[24] In fact, Heidegger lampoons much of the history of Western philosophy for casting doubt on the existence of the external world and for suggesting that one might need to prove its being. Dasein's world did not come into being through an act of sacrifice; this world, according to Heidegger, is the horizon that accompanies and constitutes Dasein's very existence.

By privileging the foundational experience of traumatic loss, Freud attempts to apprehend the birth of this relationship between the subject and its world rather than taking it for granted. He implies that one can't simply assume that a world in which one can distinguish objects as distinct from oneself is given a priori. Rather than always experiencing a world, the subject as Freud conceives it begins in the unworldly state of autoeroticism, where distinctions do not exist. Without some act of negation — the initial sacrifice of nothing — objects cannot emerge out of this undifferentiated existence. But even after this primordial sacrifice, the subject does not attain the worldliness that Heidegger identifies with Dasein's experience. Because it is born through the act of loss, the subject never has — and never can have — a world. It remains alienated and out of touch from the world, relating to the world and the objects in the world through the mediation of the lost object. The subject, in other words, experiences the presence of the world through the absence of the privileged object. The empirical objects in the world cannot but dissatisfy the subject insofar as they fail to be *the* object. The lost object structures every relationship that the subject takes up with the world.

The experience of traumatic loss has such a hold on the subject — the subject continually returns to it, re-creates it — because this experience itself engenders desiring and the object of desiring. This foundational experience provides insight into the otherwise inexplicable structure of the celebrated fort/da game that Freud discusses in *Beyond the Pleasure Principle*. The analysis of the fort/da game is not simply one example of many concerning the pleasure principle going awry in the 1920 book. It is rather the key philosophical moment in all of Freud's work. Through the observation of the fort/da game, Freud recognizes the priority of loss in human activity.

As everyone acquainted even slightly with Freud's work knows, he recounts watching his grandson play a game with a reel on a string, a game that consists of throwing the reel so that it disappears (while saying "fort" [gone]) and then pulling the reel back (while saying "da" [here]). What surprises Freud about the game is that even though "there is no doubt that greater pleasure was attached to the second act . . . the first act, that of departure, was staged as a game in itself and far more frequently than the episode in its entirety, with its pleasurable ending."[25] The quandary that this game presents for Freud derives from its defiance of the pleasure principle: repeating the disappearance of the reel more often than its more pleasurable reappearance doesn't make sense according to Freud's own theoretical approach. Nonetheless, Freud tries at length to interpret the game in terms of the pleasure principle. He posits, for instance, that his grandson obtains a sense of pleasure from taking an active role in an event that he initially endured passively (the departure of his privileged object). Even though the actual departure of the object is unpleasant, repeating it actively allows the grandson a sense of mastery that pleases him. Though not fully satisfied with this explanation, Freud leaves the discussion of the fort/da game without going further.

Because Freud arrests his analysis of the fort/da game just after positing that the game provides his grandson with the pleasure of mastery through symbolization, most commentators see this as Freud's final word on the game. But as he works through other phenomena that seem to defy the pleasure principle like the fort/da game does, Freud eventually posits a drive beyond the pleasure principle. The negative therapeutic reaction, the resistance to the psychoanalytic cure, convinces Freud that repetition has a much stronger hold on subjects than the quest for pleasure. It is in this light that one must return to the fort/da game and reinterpret it (even though Freud himself does not). Pleasure is not the final word on this game; there is something more — the pull of enjoyment, or what Freud calls the death drive.[26]

Though it seems completely counterintuitive, the subject enjoys the disappearance of its privileged object; it enjoys not having it rather than having it because this experience returns the subject to the initial moment of loss where the subject comes closer to the privileged object than at any other time.[27] Since the object does not exist, one cannot recover it; one can only repeat the process through which it is lost. This fundamental link between enjoyment and loss renders enjoyment difficult to endure. The subject inevitably suffers its enjoyment.

As the example of the fort/da game shows, pleasure serves as an alibi allowing us to endure our enjoyment. This is what Freud is getting at when he claims in *Beyond the Pleasure Principle* that "the pleasure principle seems actually to serve the death instincts."[28] Precisely because enjoyment traumatizes us with a return to a foundational experience of loss, we seek the pleasure that accompanies the presence of the object as a way of hiding this trauma from ourselves. But this pleasure is also fundamentally deceptive; it has a wholly imaginary status. That is to say, the pleasure accompanying the recovery of the lost object appears as the ultimate pleasure when we anticipate it but diminishes exponentially when we realize it. When we look at pleasure in this way, Freud's grandson's lack of interest in the "pleasurable ending" of the reel's return becomes easier to understand — as does the consumer's lack of interest in the commodities that she or he has already purchased.[29]

We can also understand the appeal of tragedy as an art form. If we think about art only in terms of the pleasure it provides, the emergence of tragedy seems difficult to comprehend, though Aristotle does manage to think of it in a way that approximates Freud's pleasure principle. The pleasure principle necessitates that the subject rid itself of excess excitation: pleasure comes not from excitement but from a neutral state in which one lacks excitation. For

Aristotle, we are drawn to tragedy because it works "with incidents arousing pity and fear, wherewith to accomplish its catharsis of such emotions."[30] That is, tragedy allows us to rid ourselves of the excessive emotions of pity and terror, and this process accounts for the pleasure that tragedy provides. But this explanation seems to underestimate art's ability to augment our emotional state, to leave us with more emotional excitation than before having experienced the work of art. If the point of tragedy is the release of powerful emotions, Aristotle can't explain why it first must augment these feelings in the spectator prior to facilitating their release. Any explanation that thinks of art purely in terms of pleasure will undoubtedly run into similar difficulties when it comes to tackling our desire for tragedy.

Even if tragedy as an art form doesn't offer us much in the way of pleasure, it does provide an opportunity for us to enjoy. While watching a tragedy, we enjoy the repetition of the experience of loss. What's more, tragedy does not simply depict a random loss. The loss it highlights is always in some sense self-inflicted. Oedipus blinds himself; Antigone defies Creon in order to make her death inevitable; Hamlet chooses to confront Claudius even though he knows it will cost him his life; and so on. The tragic hero is at once the agent responsible for the experience of loss and the one who endures it. Even when tragic heroes are not initially responsible for their fall, like Oedipus in *Oedipus Tyrannus*, they assume responsibility, as if they had willed it, which has the effect of transforming the externally inflicted wound into a self-inflicted one.[31] Tragedy's focus on the self-inflicted loss returns us as spectators to our own initial loss of the privileged object — the primordial self-inflicted wound. The enjoyment that tragedy produces in the spectator occurs through the repetition of sacrifice.

Things Were Never Better

Even though loss is a constitutive experience that founds the subject in its relation to the object, this initial loss misleads us into believing that we have lost something substantial. We often fail to see that we have lost nothing and that our lost object is simply the embodiment of this nothing. The belief in the substantiality of the lost object fuels the prevalence of nostalgia as a mode of relating to our origins. We dream of recovering the object and restoring the complete enjoyment that we believe ourselves to have once had prior to the experience of loss. This enjoyment never existed, and the recovery of the object, though it may bring some degree of pleasure, always brings disappointment as well, which is why sustaining our feeling of nostalgia depends on not realizing the return to the past that the nostalgic subject longs for. By insisting that loss is constitutive for the subject, psychoanalytic thought works to combat nostalgia and its poisoning of contemporary politics.

Nostalgia permits us to avoid seeing the necessity of the link between enjoyment and loss. Seen in a nostalgic light, enjoyment gains a purity that it can never actually have. It becomes an experience that completes the subject and provides plenitude rather than an experience that derives from the subject's partiality and lack. The false image of enjoyment that nostalgia portrays is the source of its widespread appeal. As subjects, we constantly turn ourselves toward both our individual past and our collective cultural history in an attempt to find what we have lost.

The story of Eden, the origin myth of Judeo-Christian society, reveals dramatically the privileged place of nostalgia in our society. While the doctrine of original sin attempts to represent the necessity of an original loss, the account of humanity's expulsion from the Garden of Eden counterbalances this doctrine with an image of lost perfection. Prior to the act of eating the fruit from the Tree of Knowledge of Good and Evil, humanity had a direct relation to its privileged object. One could enjoy in the Garden of Eden without restraint. This particular origin myth has the power that it does because it ties in with the subject's self-deception that emanates from its experience of original loss. The very experience of loss prompts us to believe that we have lost something, and the Eden myth fills in the content of what we have lost. If we accept the Eden myth (even as a metaphor), we explicitly affirm ourselves as subjects of nostalgia, subjects who have lost something rather than nothing.

But this mode of subjectivity goes far beyond our ideas about creation. It manifests itself in the privileging of the words of the Founding Fathers in political discourse, the power of fashion trends that mimic earlier eras, and the popularity of historical dramas in the cinema. To take just the last example, spectators go to films like *Braveheart* (Mel Gibson, 1995), *Saving Private Ryan* (Steven Spielberg, 1998), and *Cinderella Man* (Ron Howard, 2005) because they depict the past as a heroic time when people had an ability to enjoy directly the privileged object. Even though William Wallace (Mel Gibson) dies in his fight for freedom in *Braveheart*, he nonetheless has the appearance of a nonlacking subject, a subject defined by his wholeness rather than his loss. The image of this wholeness on the screen appeals to spectators' nostalgia for what they believe they once had. Nostalgia reaches into almost every aspect of contemporary culture, even those places where it appears to be most absent.

The contemporary idealization of the child seems on the surface to indicate a rejection of nostalgia, an investment in the future rather than the past. In *No Future*, his superb account of this phenomenon, Lee Edelman criticizes the cult of the child for precisely this reason. He sees the privileging of the child as part of a heterosexist ideology oriented toward the future and toward the reproduction of an oppressive social order. He claims: "The Child has come to embody for us the telos of the social order and come to be seen as the one for whom that order is held in perpetual trust."[32] For Edelman, the image of the child predominates as a result of our need to believe in a better future. What he doesn't address fully is the psychic source of this image's power.

We idealize the child not simply because it embodies our hope for the future but primarily because it provides us with a look at what we believe we have lost. The innocent child appears to be nonlacking, not subject to loss. When we devote ourselves to the image of the child, we affirm an image of our own lost completeness. Belief in the purity of the child is the positing of our own lost purity. We find violence against children so much more abhorrent than violence against adults because of this association of childhood with a lost purity. In the United States, Megan's Law (rendering public the addresses of those convicted of sexual offenses with children), the Amber Alert (a public emergency broadcast in response to the abduction of a child), and many other similar programs have emerged out of the nostalgic belief that the child is a nonlacking being and that violence against the child thus represents the ultimate crime — the destruction of innocent wholeness.[33]

It is nostalgia that gives the image of the child the power that it has over us. As we bow down to this image, we avoid seeing the constitutive role that loss plays in the experience of even the youngest child. Through an illusion of perspective, the child appears uncorrupted by the trauma of existence.

We can believe in a complete satisfaction, which is what companies and charitable organizations offer us when they use the image of the child in their marketing campaigns. This image is successful as a marketing tool because it partakes in the nostalgia that defines our relation to loss.

The prevalence of nostalgia has perhaps its most obvious impact in the shaping of contemporary political programs. The entirety of the contemporary right-wing social and cultural agenda has its basis in the nostalgia for a time of plenitude. Nostalgia fuels the demand for school prayer, the opposition to gay marriage, the effort to eliminate abortion, the support for the death penalty, and so on. According to contemporary American conservatism, the abandonment of school prayer, for instance, has helped to bring about many of the social ills (teen pregnancy, school violence, incivility, etc.) that plague contemporary American society. Champions of school prayer see the epoch when students prayed in school as time prior to loss.

At this earlier historical moment, subjects enjoyed a direct relation with their privileged object and achieved a perfect satisfaction. We exist in the aftermath of a fall, and from the perspective of the fall, we can see the possibilities for complete satisfaction in the world we have lost. Similarly, eliminating the threat of gay marriage allows conservatives to imagine a time when marriage itself was a pure institution, a bond that permitted a direct link to one's object. Within the nostalgia framework that conservatism offers, loss has a place only as a limit to overcome through the return to a nonlacking past. Conservatism cannot admit the notion of a constitutive or necessary loss.

Though right-wing political activity is unthinkable without nostalgia, emancipatory politics often succumbs to its power as well. Within certain forms of environmentalism, the alternative medicine campaign, and the antiglobalization movement, we can see prominent examples of this. In each case, the leftist political goal — protecting the environment, providing people more health options, countering global capitalism — becomes intertwined with the idea of a return to an earlier epoch and to a less alienated way of relating to the world. Implicit in this idea is the image of a nonlacking subjectivity, and this image stains the political goal with the tint of nostalgia.

Those who argue for a return to harmony with nature, for privileging non-Western and homeopathic forms of medicine, and for forsaking global capitalism by supporting only local producers all take up a politics of nostalgia. The idea that we might return to a stable relation with the natural world posits a prior time in which this stability existed, a time lost with the onset of subjectivity. By appealing to the inherent nostalgia of subjects, the forces of emancipation undoubtedly gain adherents. Many people drawn to the idea of "buying local" would not otherwise find common cause with emancipatory projects, for instance. But the long-term cost of this strategy is not worth the supporters that it wins for the emancipatory politics. Though conservatism doesn't have a monopoly on nostalgia, nostalgia does have an inherently conservative structure to it.

Nostalgia is fundamentally conservative insofar as it works to obscure the gap within the social order. It posits the possibility of an order that works without interruption and thus leaves no room for subjectivity itself. The freedom of the subject depends on the imperfection of the social order, its inability to achieve completion or harmony. A political philosophy that represses this failure also inherently represses the opening through which freedom emerges. In effect, the nostalgic subject longs to access a past prior to its subjectivization. To retreat into nostalgia is to flee one's own freedom. In order to accomplish this and to close the gap within the social order, nostalgic projects necessarily rely on a strong authority figure who promises to reinvigorate the lost past rather than on the freedom of the subject.[34] The emancipatory goal placed in a nostalgic appeal loses touch with the overall emancipatory project of freeing the subject from its submission to authority figures. What's more, nostalgia works only in theory, not in practice.

Nostalgic appeals always create disappointment in the last instance. We long for a time before loss, but this time only comes into existence with its loss: the birth of subjectivity retroactively creates the object that it loses. The politics of nostalgia involves never actually following through on the nostalgic promise, as contemporary conservatism's social politics makes evident. In contrast to their vigorous pursuit of a conservative economic program, Ronald Reagan and George W. Bush (the two great proponents of a politics of nostalgia in the last fifty years) did not actively try to enact their social agenda. For Reagan and Bush, the dream of a return has a political effectiveness that an actual return could not have. If school prayer again became the norm in public classrooms, the nonexistence of the former wholeness would be revealed. If the threat of the gay lifestyle were really eliminated, the banality of heterosexual marriage would once again show itself. Nostalgia remains a useful political tool only insofar as one doesn't effectuate it. This is the limit of its power.

Enemies Within and Without

While nostalgia locates the ultimate enjoyment in the subject's own past, paranoia locates it in the other. Paranoia thus offers the subject not just the image of the ultimate enjoyment (like nostalgia) but also an explanation for its absence. Nostalgia and paranoia usually operate side by side in order to provide the subject a way of figuring its missing enjoyment. On its own, nostalgia as a mode of subjectivity seems to have limited political consequences. Groups may use nostalgia as a political weapon, but its political weight is diffused to some extent because it involves the subject's relation to itself rather than to an other. The same cannot be said for paranoia, which is why finding a way to counter paranoia represents an urgent political task.

Paranoia is political in its very structure. It views the other as a threat and produces hostility toward the other. The paranoid subject usually adopts one of two possible attitudes toward the other. According to the first, paranoia serves to explain the loss of the privileged object. If I take up a paranoid attitude toward the other, I see her/his enjoyment coming at the expense of mine. The other enjoys the lost object that is rightfully mine. The other, having stolen my enjoyment, bears responsibility for my existence as a subject of loss. This type of paranoia removes the burden of loss from the subject and places it onto the other, and in addition it functions, like nostalgia, to convince the subject that having the object is a possibility. According to the second attitude, however, paranoia represents an attempt to convince ourselves that we have not lost the privileged object. We are paranoid not that the other has stolen the privileged object but that it plans to do so. The imagined threat that the other poses reassures us that we have the ultimate enjoyment and that this is what the other targets. By imagining a threat, we fantasize the privileged object back into existence despite its status as constitutively lost.

At first glance, it is difficult to see how paranoia might function as an attractive attitude for subjects to take up. The paranoid subject must endure a constant menace that has no tangible or definitive presence. Everyone that this subject meets is a potential enemy in disguise threatening to steal or already having stolen the subject's privileged object. In terms of the subject's own identity, paranoia does not provide security or stability. In fact, it uproots all sense of security that the subject has concerning its identity. But its appeal does not lie in how it transforms subjectivity; its appeal stems from its ability to close the gap in the social field of meaning, its ability to be a guarantor that authorizes our social interaction.

Paranoia develops in response to the inherent inconsistency of social authority.[35] There are authorities but no Authority, and a decisive Authority would be necessary to provide subjects a sense of foundation, a sense that there is solid ground underneath their feet. Social proclamations and regulations place the subject in an impossible position: one simply cannot believe and obey every edict emanating from social authorities without being torn apart in the effort. These contradictions occur on all levels of social pronouncements. One hears, for instance, about the dangers of eating too much fat, and then one hears about the cancer-preventing power of chocolate. Parents tell their children not to fight and at the same time tell them to stand up for themselves. George W. Bush claimed that the Iraq War was waged to prevent the spread of weapons of mass destruction and later claimed that its purpose was to liberate the country from a cruel dictator. Such inconsistencies are not merely contingent developments within our particular society but necessarily follow from the ultimate groundlessness of the social order itself. There is no final authority that calls all the shots in society and guarantees the consistency of the social order. It is instead a structure in charge, and this structure functions through its very misfiring.

The inconsistency of social authority—the gap in the social field of meaning—provides it with an openness to difference. If social authority was a closed circuit that operated without a hitch, it would have no way of incorporating the subject into its fold. The subject invests itself in social authority precisely because this authority gives the subject contradictory demands. Faced with these incongruous imperatives, the subject cannot readily decipher what the social authority wants from it. Beneath the inconsistency, the desire of the authority remains a mystery. The subject begins to desire in response to this unknown desire of the social Other: the inconsistency of the social authority has the effect of attracting the subject and constituting the desire of the subject as the desire of the Other. A thoroughly consistent social authority, while logically unthinkable, would not draw the desire of the subject in this way. It might force individuals into obedience, but it would not create the investment in the social order that the inconsistent social authority creates.

Confronting the inconsistency of social authority is not an easy task for the subject. Many try to sustain a belief in its consistency through an imaginary construction that represses contradictory ideas. The problem with this solution is that these ideas become more powerful through their repression, and the result is some form of neurosis. Another possibility is the paranoid reaction. Rather than trying to wrestle with the problem of the gap in authority, the paranoid subject eliminates it by positing an other existing in this gap, an other behind the scenes pulling the strings. As Slavoj Žižek explains it, "Paranoia is at its most elementary a belief into an 'Other of the Other,' into an Other who, hidden behind the Other of the explicit social texture, programs what appears to us as the unforeseen effects of social life and thus guarantees its consistency: beneath the chaos of market, the degradation of morals, and so on, there is the purposeful strategy of the Jewish plot."[36] The comfort that paranoia provides for the subject derives solely from this guarantee. For the paranoid subject, the surface inconsistency of social authority hides an underlying consistency authorized by a real authority whom most subjects never notice. Paranoia simultaneously allows the subject to sense its own superiority in recognizing the conspiracy and to avoid confronting the horror of an inconsistent social authority.

As with nostalgia, paranoia is primarily aligned with a right-wing political agenda. Its suspicion of the other nourishes a nationalistic politics and energizes the call for a return to traditional social arrangements. Just as much of the investment in the Cold War struggle derived from paranoia, it fuels the contemporary war on terror. The exemplary right-wing political formation, Fascism, has its basis in paranoia, seeing the Jew or some equivalent as secretly controlling the social order to the detriment of all law-abiding citizens. The idea of an other operating behind the scenes serves to justify restrictions on civil liberties, racism, police violence, and so on. A paranoid populace is a populace ready to embrace a Fascist regime.

Despite the inherent link between paranoia and conservatism, leftists employ paranoia to a vast extent, far more than they do nostalgia. Paranoid theories about the secret brokers of power who decide the fate of the capitalist world are widespread on the Left. It is common sense among leftists that big oil companies have suppressed the development of alternative energies, that the CIA assassinated Kennedy, and that major drug companies control the Food and Drug Administration, just to name a few of the more well known conspiracy theories. The truth or falsity of these theories has nothing to do with their function for the subject who accepts them. The paranoid subject is often correct in its various speculations, but paranoia nonetheless provides a way for the subject to avoid confronting the inconsistency of social authority. For the paranoid subject, conspiracy theories don't simply explain a single event; they solve the problem of the social order as such. According to this thought process, all loss stems from the conspiracy, which has derailed the social order and upset its balance.

The paranoid subject cannot accept the necessity of loss, and the conspiracy theory works to render loss empirical rather than ontological. This is evident in Oliver Stone's *JFK* (1991), a film in which Stone posits a vast conspiracy that resulted in the death of Kennedy. Of course, Stone is probably correct that this conspiracy existed, but the film goes astray primarily through its apotheosis of Kennedy, an apotheosis that reveals what's at stake in all paranoia. According to the film, had he remained in power, Kennedy would have prevented the horror of the Vietnam War and thus spared the United States the psychic wound that this war created. With Kennedy, one can imagine an American social order existing without strife and loss. The conspiracy theory allows Stone this image, which testifies to the avoidability of loss.[37]

But Stone is not the only leftist to turn to paranoia. Many do so in order to confront forces that they otherwise couldn't identify. Among those who suffer from political oppression, paranoia and conspiracy theory serve as vehicles for thinking through systems of control and even mobilizing action against those systems. As Peter Knight points out, "Conspiracy thinking has played an important role in constituting various forms of African American political and cultural activism."[38] When it directly produces activism, the political valence of paranoia seems to tilt more clearly to the left than it does in the case of Stone's film.[39]

Marxist Fredric Jameson focuses on a related aspect of paranoia as he analyzes the paranoid film in *The Geopolitical Aesthetic*. In this work, Jameson aligns conspiracy theory with what he calls cognitive mapping — the attempt to think the global capitalist system in its totality. The diffuseness of global capitalism prevents the kind of cognitive mapping that was possible in earlier epochs. Today, in order to think the totality at all, subjects must resort to the idea of a conspiracy. As Jameson points out in his analysis of *All the President's Men*, "The map of conspiracy itself... suggests the possibility of cognitive mapping as a whole and stands as its substitute and yet its allegory all at once."[40] Jameson's statement reflects his ambivalence about conspiracy theory and paranoia — even though it allegorizes cognitive mapping, it also substitutes for it — but he nonetheless sees its usefulness as a strategy for the Left, especially when facing the global capitalist leviathan.

The problem is that even when it works to mobilize subjects to fight against an oppressive system, paranoia has the effect of depriving subjects of their agency. By eliminating the gap in social authority and filling in this gap with a real authority who effectively runs the show, paranoia deprives subjects of the space in which they exist as subjects. The subject occupies the position of the gap in social authority; it emerges through and because of internal inconsistency in the social field of meaning. The extent to which paranoia allows the subject to experience social authority as a consistent field is the extent to which it works against the subject itself. Even if it manages tangible political victories, emancipatory politics that relies on paranoia undermines itself by increasing the power of authority in the thinking of subjects and decreasing their freedom. What's more, it doesn't actually work.

Like nostalgia, paranoia can never constitute a successful strategy for the subject dealing with its fundamental condition. It will never provide the enjoyment that it promises the subject. Uncovering and eliminating the hidden real authority will bring not the ultimate enjoyment but horrible disappointment. This is why the paranoid mindset cannot admit to itself that the hidden other has been vanquished. The enjoyment that paranoia does provide requires the continuing existence of the threat, even though it imagines an enjoyment that would come with the threat's disappearance. Paranoia runs aground due to its failure to admit the connection between enjoyment and loss. It allows the subject to imagine that loss is the contingent result of a secret malevolent force that we might conquer. By implicitly positing the avoidability of loss, paranoia leaves subjects unable to locate and recognize the nature of their own enjoyment.

Targeted Violence

Freud himself flirted with paranoia as he was creating psychoanalysis, and it took the form of the seduction theory. When Freud made his first theoretical breakthroughs in psychoanalytic thinking, he believed that hysteria had its ultimate cause in a sexual assault — the parent's premature introduction of sexuality to the child. According to this thesis, parental seduction was a vast conspiracy responsible for the prevalence of hysteria. But in an 1897 letter to Wilhelm Fliess, Freud concludes that "the unexpected frequency of hysteria" would force him to surmise that almost all fathers were actual sexual predators, and he contends that "surely such widespread perversions against children are not very probable."[41] Here, Freud jettisons the seduction theory because it would require him to see sexual abuse as the norm. Though Freud concocted the idea of the death drive in 1920, the major step he made in this direction occurred a little more than twenty years earlier when he abandoned the seduction theory.

Many leftist critics have taken Freud to task for precisely this leap. Where a popular figure like Jeffrey Masson accuses Freud of turning away from the truth of actual parental cruelty and criticizes psychoanalysis as a whole for its complicity with child abuse, psychoanalytic theorists like Jean Laplanche and Walter Davis rethink psychoanalysis by formulating seduction as the inescapable fact of childhood. Laplanche embraces the theory of seduction because it "affirms the priority of the other in the constitution of the human being and of its sexuality."[42] Davis sees in the seduction theory a way to affirm the primacy of "the cruelty human beings do to one another" in forming the subject's psyche.[43] For Masson, Laplanche, Davis, and many others, the abandonment of the seduction theory marks Freud's abandonment of the radicality inherent in the psychoanalytic project itself. Without the seduction theory, psychoanalysis seems to lose the dimension of social critique that attracts many on the left to it. But the turn away from the seduction theory also marks Freud's initial grasp of the nature of the violence that gives birth to the subject.

The conceptual breakthrough involved with the abandonment of the seduction theory paved the way for the discovery of the death drive because it permitted Freud to consider violence not as primarily coming from someone else but as what the subject itself fantasizes about. After this development in his thought, it would make theoretical sense to conceive of an original violence that the subject does to itself as the genesis of subjectivity and the death drive, which is the move that Freud makes in 1920. Of course, many other factors arose during the intervening years to either facilitate or delay Freud's discovery, but he laid the groundwork for it at the moment when he turned away from the idea of a generalized seduction.

The seduction theory would have prevented Freud from recognizing that subjectivity has its origin in violence that the subject does to itself — the violent sacrifice of the privileged object that begins desire. The death drive, the structuring principle of the psyche, engages the subject in a perpetual repetition of this violence. Both nostalgia and paranoia try to flee the subject's original self-inflicted violence. But even the attempt to avoid violence leads back to it. Nostalgia and paranoia lead almost inevitably to violence directed toward the other who appears as a barrier to the subject's enjoyment.

For many subjects, external violence — either fantasized about or actually realized — is the chief way of coping with the exigencies of the death drive. As Freud points out in the *New Introductory Lectures on Psycho-analysis*, "It really seems as though it is necessary for us to destroy some other thing or person in order not to destroy ourselves, in order to guard against the impulsion to self-destruction. A sad disclosure indeed for the moralist!"[44] Violence against the other attempts to replace violence against the self; this type of violence attempts to repeat the subject's initial moment of loss on the cheap, so to speak. It seeks repetition while sparing the subject itself the suffering implicit in this repetition. Aggressive violence toward the other tries to separate the enjoyment of repetition (which it reserves for the subject) with the suffering of it (which it consigns to the other). Understood in terms of the death drive, one can readily see the appeal of aggressive violence. It provides a seemingly elegant solution to the troubling link between enjoyment and suffering.

The problem with aggressive violence as a solution to the problem of the death drive stems not just from the cycle of violence that it will undoubtedly inaugurate. Aggressive violence is nothing but a detour or prolongation of the path toward self-inflicted violence. In this sense, the other's violent act of vengeance in response to the subject's own violence is precisely what the subject unconsciously hopes to trigger when committing a violent act in the first place. The other's violent response allows us to experience the loss that we have hitherto avoided. Violence directed to the other does not satisfy the subject in the way that violence directed toward the self does. In order to accomplish the repetition that the death drive necessitates, external violence must finally lead back to violence directed at the self.

The power of repetition in the psyche leaves the subject no possibility for escaping self-inflicted violence. This is what psychoanalytic thought allows us to recognize and to bring to bear on our political activity. The only question concerns the form that this violence will take. Will the subject use the other as a vehicle for inflicting violence on itself, or will it perform this violence directly on itself? By recognizing the power of unconscious repetition, we can grasp the intractability of the problem of violence, but we can also see a way out of aggressive violence that doesn't involve utopian speculation. Rather than trying to avoid violence, we can restore to it its proper object — the self. The more the subject engages in a violent assault on its own forms of symbolic identity, its own ego, its own deepest convictions, the more the subject finds an enjoyable alternative to the satisfactions of aggression.

2

The Economics of the Drive

I Can Get Satisfaction

The political dimension of psychoanalysis comes into better focus when we understand it as an economic theory. Though Freud at times puts ideas in economic terms, he doesn't make the economics of psychoanalytic thought fully explicit. But economics is nonetheless present and awaiting explication in the fundamental tenets of psychoanalysis. The economics of psychoanalysis emphasize, in contrast to the economics of capitalism, an ability to find satisfaction in our drive rather than seeking the ultimate satisfaction elsewhere. It is an economics that renounces any form of accumulation or attainment. Finding satisfaction in our drive frees us from the dissatisfaction associated with trying to comply with social demands, whatever form they assume. Sometimes social authorities demand that we obey or conform, while at other times they demand that we consume or express our individuality. In any case, such demands and our adherence to them lead inevitably to dissatisfaction. We try to acquire in this way an object or a sense of recognition that is impossible to obtain. What's more, this pursuit leaves us dependent on the social authority that issues the demands. In this way, the economic structure of capitalism and the endless pursuit of accumulation that it compels correspond with the subject's dependence on the power of social authority.

Psychoanalysis envisions a break from accumulation and from dependence. The political project of psychoanalysis envisions a turn away from searching for the ultimate satisfaction located elsewhere — from accumulation — and toward enjoyment, a turn made possible by rethinking where our enjoyment lies. According to psychoanalytic economics, enjoyment is located in what disturbs us rather than in what we might obtain, and when we grasp this, we change the nature of our political subjectivity. The obstacle to our enjoyment is at once the source of our enjoyment, not what we must eliminate in order to discover the ultimate satisfaction.

An idea of the economics of the psyche underlies Freud's work throughout his career, but it becomes most explicit in a very early work, the unfinished *Project for a Scientific Psychology* of 1895.[1] In this manuscript, Freud attempts to account for psychic processes according to a completely mechanical model, a model that marginalizes the effects of consciousness almost completely. Though for many psychoanalytically informed thinkers the physiological nature of Freud's theory at this point severely restricts its pertinence for understanding the psyche, one can translate Freud's physiological theory into a psychic one.[2]

In the *Project*, Freud sees the psyche as a system designed to discharge psychic energy that is transmitted through neurones. Energy bombards the psyche from both inside and out—through endogamous forces and external stimuli. At this point in his thought, Freud believes that the aim of psychic life involves returning to a zero level of excitation, an aim that he later aligns with the pleasure principle. By warding off excitation, the psychic processes free the psyche from unpleasure and return it to a state of satisfaction.

Once Freud conceived of the death drive in 1920, his conception of satisfaction underwent a fundamental shift. Whereas in the vision of the *Project* and his other pre-1920 work (which views the psyche in terms of the pleasure principle) satisfaction is a state that the psyche arrives at through the discharge of excitation, after the discovery of the death drive in *Beyond the Pleasure Principle* satisfaction will consist in the movement of the drive itself, not in the aim that it attains. Nonetheless, what remains constant in these two different economic models is the absolute psychic primacy of satisfaction. The psyche strives above all to sustain its satisfaction, and it is successful at doing so.

Satisfaction occurs in the operations of the psyche because, as Freud sees it in 1895, the discharge of excitation always occurs. Though there are infinite differences among individual subjects, we can say that all subjects are satisfied subjects insofar as they partake in the process of discharging excitation. For every subject, this process finds a way to occur successfully, even if it encounters a circuitous path in the psyche. Individual difference manifests itself in different psychic paths, but not in the fundamental fact of discharging excitation.

That is, what the psyche does is universal, but how the psyche goes about doing this varies in each particular case. The universality of what the psyche does allows Freud to recognize that the economy of the psyche produces satisfaction for every subject, even if the subject is unaware of its own satisfaction. This remains true when Freud turns from the 1895 model of the psyche to the later one centered on the death drive, though in the later theory satisfaction derives from the drive's constant force rather than from a discharge of excitation. The drive provides an inescapable satisfaction by never letting up.

When we think of therapy of any kind, including psychoanalysis, we usually think of a trajectory moving from dissatisfaction to some degree of satisfaction. Subjects enter therapy with a psychic ailment causing dissatisfaction, and if the treatment succeeds, they leave with the ability to lead a more satisfying existence.[3] If subjects didn't feel dissatisfaction, they wouldn't enter into any therapy, and if they didn't attain some satisfaction as a result, therapy would cease to be a viable practice.

But despite its commonsensical appearance, this model does not apply to psychoanalytic therapy — or, rather, psychoanalysis is not therapy in this sense. Rather than effectuate a qualitative change in the subject by transforming dissatisfaction into satisfaction, psychoanalysis attempts to intervene — and finds the justification for its intervention — on a quantitative level. Rather than attempting to cure dissatisfied subjects, psychoanalysis confronts subjects who are satisfied but who spend too much psychic effort or who take a path that is too circuitous for the satisfaction they obtain. In this sense, psychoanalysis is fundamentally an economic theory of the psyche.

The death drive and the repetition that it installs in the subject follow a self-satisfying course. The death drive finds a path to satisfaction or enjoyment despite — or because of — whatever obstacles the external world might erect. The satisfaction of the subject is the one constant in psychoanalytic thought, and it leads Freud to postulate the existence of the drive as the source of that satisfaction.[4] The satisfaction that the death drive produces stems from its circular structure: rather than trying to attain satisfaction through an external aim, the drive produces that satisfaction through the process of the repeated movement itself.

The self-satisfied quality of the drive differentiates it from physiological need: needs undergo fluctuation from a state of dissatisfaction to one of satisfaction when they achieve their aim. The drive, on the other hand, never fluctuates.[5] Unlike biological need (which might be satisfied or not, depending on whether it discovers its object), the drive (which has an absent object) always involves satisfaction. Thus, psychoanalysis, a practice oriented around the drive, cannot intervene by way of offering a missing satisfaction or providing a helping hand to those down on their luck.[6]

The psychoanalytic intervention must be strictly economic, that is, involving the quantity of psychic effort expended by the analysand. The aim of the psychoanalyst — the analyst's desire — must be to remove the detours that the analysand has placed along the path of the drive in order to allow the analysand to take up completely her or his position in the drive. In *Seminar XI*, Lacan lays out the situation confronting the analyst: "What we have before us in analysis is a system in which everything turns out all right, and which attains its own sort of satisfaction. If we interfere in this, it is only in so far as we think that there are other ways, shorter ones for example."[7] In submitting to analysis, the analysand submits, albeit unknowingly, to this desire for shortening or economizing the path of the drive. This shortening is the analytic cure, and Freud first comes to understand it as such in the 1895 *Project* where he emphasizes the costs of psychic detours that the subject erects to the flow of psychic energy.

The Secret of the Symptom

Typical neurotics enter into analysis believing in their dissatisfaction. They complain of a symptom — insomnia, say — that functions as a barrier to their enjoyment. They view the analyst as a subject supposed to know, that is, as a subject who knows the secret of the symptom. Through the transmission of this knowledge, neurotics hope to overcome their symptom and become able to freely enjoy themselves without this hindrance. Through the duration of a neurosis, symptoms serve as a source of satisfaction for the neurotic. Analysis emerges as a possibility only when this satisfaction becomes too troublesome, when the symptom begins to debilitate the neurotic and intrude on all aspects of the neurotic's life. What neurotics don't see, however, is the satisfaction that the disruptiveness of the symptom offers. The goal of analysis does not consist in eliminating this disruptiveness but in changing the subject's relationship to it. Rather than seeing the disruptiveness of the symptom as the barrier to a truly satisfying life, the subject must come to grasp this disruptiveness as the source of the subject's satisfaction.

The relationship between psychoanalytic thought and the symptom marks the former's most dramatic point of rupture from forms of healing (including both other kinds of therapy and medicine). When patients come to their doctors exhibiting a symptom, doctors ideally attempt to treat the underlying illness in order to eliminate the symptom. The symptom is valuable for the doctor insofar as it provides an indication of the underlying illness that can be addressed. For psychoanalytic thought, the symptom is the indication of an underlying disorder, but at the same time it coalesces the subject's psychic existence.

The symptom is the disruption of the circuit that the death drive follows, but its disruptiveness constitutes the circuit. Without the symptom's disruption of the circuit, there would be no drive at all; we would have a living organism rather than a desiring subject.[8] The symptom marks a point of excess at which the subject cannot conduct business as usual. It emerges out of the subject's failure to realize its desire: the subject develops a symptom — aphasia, say — in response to an unfilled lack, an inability to say the right thing to a love object.

Though the failure marks the point at which the subject misses something, it becomes the point through which the subject enjoys itself. Because there is no possibility for success in relation to the object, the subject can find satisfaction only through its specific mode of failure. Through the symptomatic failure, the subject relates to its lost object, and this failure is the only possible vehicle for doing so. It is not as if the symptom is a poor substitute for a true relation to the object. The subject's failure is its form of success, and the trouble that the disruptiveness of the symptom gives the subject defines the subject as such.

Every subject has a fundamental symptomatic disruption that serves as the foundation for subjectivity itself.[9] The elimination of this disruption would not produce a normal subject able to enjoy itself but would result in the annihilation of the subject itself (and its capacity for enjoyment). By simultaneously showing the subject that the disruption of the symptom is not the barrier to enjoyment but the source of it and that there is no normal symptomless path to enjoyment, psychoanalysis frees the subject to find satisfaction through the subject's symptomatic disruption rather than continuing to view the disruption as the obstacle to the ultimate satisfaction that the subject is constantly missing.

This is not to say that psychoanalysis simply condemns the insomniac to perpetual sleeplessness that must be enjoyed rather lamented. Instead, with the aid of psychoanalysis, the obsessional who views insomnia as the barrier to a satisfying life comes to recognize the satisfaction that it actually offers. The subject realizes that it will not lose the satisfaction attached to this disruption if it falls asleep, because the disruption is constitutive of the subject's very subjectivity. As a result, the subject can begin to enjoy while once again getting to sleep. By facilitating this transformation, psychoanalysis economizes the trajectory of the death drive.

A similar kind of economizing is at work in almost all of Toni Morrison's novels, though it is especially pronounced in later works like *Love*.[10] In this novel Morrison depicts two women who have lived together most of their adult lives despite hating each other. Christine and Heed are related through their bond with Bill Cosey, who is Christine's grandfather and Heed's husband, though Christine and Heed are the same age. Heed's marriage to Bill when she was eleven years old drove a permanent wedge between Christine and her, though they had been close friends. After the marriage, each experiences the other as a symptom, as the barrier to satisfaction, an indication that she has failed to have Bill Cosey for herself. After Bill's death, the women continue to live together in his house because each provides enjoyment for the other through her role as symptom, though neither can recognize this.

At the end of the novel, Christine and Heed return to an abandoned hotel that Bill owned and that they hadn't visited for years. While they are investigating it, Heed falls down some stairs and mortally injures herself. As she lies dying, she and Christine transform in each other's eyes. They both begin to see the other as the source of their enjoyment rather than as a barrier to it. Or they are able to see that they enjoy the barrier to the desired object rather than the desired object on the other side of the barrier. In the final moments of Heed's life, she is able, like Sethe in *Beloved*, to embrace and enjoy her symptom, thereby passing through a transformation akin to the one offered by psychoanalysis. Finally expressing her affection for Christine, Heed begins to economize the path of the drive and to recognize her mode of enjoyment as her own instead of fleeing from it.

Like the individual symptom, the social symptom also appears as a barrier to enjoyment while in fact marking the very possibility of it. As many theorists have noted, for capitalist society, the figure of the Jew is the symptom that appears to throw the capitalist system out of balance. (Because it is a figure above all, any social identity can occupy the symptomatic position that the Jew usually occupies. Though historically it was primarily actual Jews who were in this position, one of the great ironies of contemporary society is that the Palestinian can serve as the figure of the Jew, though it is most often the immigrant.) According to Slavoj Žižek, "The anti-Semitic capitalist's hatred of the Jew [is] the hatred of the excess that pertains to capitalism itself, i.e., of the excess produced by its inherent antagonistic nature."[11] The excesses attributed to the figure of the Jew are the excesses of the system itself, but the belief nonetheless arises that capitalism without excess is possible. This belief in capitalism without excess finds its political expression in Fascism, which attempts to eliminate the excess embodied by the figure of the Jew.

Fascist ideology singles out the figure of the Jew for its opprobrium not as a matter of historical contingency but because this figure is the symptom of capitalism itself. The figure of the Jew is capitalism run amok, and Fascist ideology posits that the removal of this figure will restore balance to the capitalist system and make possible the coexistence of the constant innovation of capitalist development and the stability of traditional society. Of course, the Fascist program for the elimination of the figure of the Jew stumbles over the inherent imbalance within capitalism. The successful extirpation of this figure doesn't create a balanced capitalism, and the result is that the Fascist project can never succeed and can never end. Fascism cannot countenance the elimination of the figure that it works to eliminate.

The enduring nature of the figure of the Jew — its persistence even after the eradication of actual Jews — testifies to the role that this figure plays in the subject's enjoyment. The Fascist subject sees the figure of the Jew as the ultimate barrier to its own enjoyment, which creates the exigency behind the project of eliminating this figure. What psychoanalysis makes clear is that, as in the case of the neurotic, the Fascist actually derives enjoyment from this barrier. Rather than blocking enjoyment, the figure of the Jew enables it. As the symptom of capitalism, the excess point in the structure, the figure of the Jew embodies the enjoyment of the system itself.[12]

By pursuing the destruction of this figure, the Fascist is actually accessing this enjoyment and taking part in it. The only reason that the destruction of the figure of the Jew provides enjoyment for Fascists is the position that this figure occupies as a symptom of capitalism. But like neurotics, Fascists take an indirect route to their enjoyment. They are unable to see the figure of the Jew as the source of their enjoyment rather than as an obstacle to it. They are satisfied subjects, but they give themselves too much trouble for their satisfaction.

Freud finds in the neurotic not dissatisfaction but a satisfaction that comes with too much trouble. In *Seminar XI* Lacan claims that this is, in fact, the driving force behind the entire psychoanalytic project: "It is this *too much trouble* that is the sole justification of our intervention."[13] In other words, the intervention has nothing to do with alleviating dissatisfaction but with changing the way in which the analysand relates to her or his satisfaction. Neurotics come to Freud believing themselves dissatisfied. But this is a reflected dissatisfaction: they are, though they usually aren't aware of it, dissatisfied with their satisfaction. They are seeking some other way of arriving at it, because they fail to recognize it as satisfaction. In response, Freud attempts to produce a change in position relative to this satisfaction.

The neurotic mistakes the experience of the death drive for the experience of desire, and psychoanalysis attempts to reveal the drive where the neurotic mistakenly sees desire. We misrecognize satisfaction as dissatisfaction because we imagine, in our present state of lack, that we once had a completeness that we have now lost. That is to say, we believe that our privileged object once had a substantial existence and fail to see that it became a privileged object through the very act of being lost. This misrecognition allows us to continue to believe in a previous and possible future completeness. Though it is neurotic, this misrecognition is inherent in the very nature of desire, and it is through this fundamental misrecognition that desire first begins and later sustains itself. Desire constantly seeks out the object that would satisfy it, but this object always eludes it — or, to be more precise, desire eludes the object, keeping desire perpetual (and perpetually dissatisfied). Desire, in other words, doesn't attempt to achieve satisfaction but to sustain itself as desire, to keep desire going. This is why desire constantly seeks out a satisfying object and yet never quite gets it. It leads us to see ourselves as dissatisfied and to fail to see the satisfaction we obtain from the circulation of the drive. Desire is nothing but a misrecognition of the death drive.[14]

Capitalism contra the Death Drive

Capitalist ideology aims at producing subjects who experience their existence as dissatisfied and simultaneously invest themselves completely in the ideal of happiness or complete satisfaction.[15] This idea manifests itself not just in the everyday workings of capitalism but in its most serious theorists — from Adam Smith and David Ricardo to Friedrich Hayek and Milton Friedman. According to Adam Smith, society can attain the satisfaction of true prosperity as long as it unleashes humanity's natural propensity for accumulation. He writes: "The natural effort of every individual to better his own condition, when suffered to exert itself with freedom and security, is so powerful a principle, that it is alone, and without any assistance, not only capable of carrying on the society to wealth and prosperity, but of surmounting a hundred impertinent obstructions."[16] The desire to accumulate enables capitalist subjects to overcome barriers and obtain happiness. For Smith and others, there is no question of an insurmountable barrier and no possibility of enjoying the barrier itself.

Capitalism survives on the basis of the same misrecognition that plagues Freud's neurotic: the mistaking of desire for drive, the inability to see satisfaction in the act of *not* getting the object. Without engendering this collective misrecognition, capitalism could not sustain itself as capitalism. Capitalist subjects structurally fail to see their own inherent self-satisfaction, and it is this failure that keeps them going as capitalist subjects. Freud's thought reveals this, and it reveals that there is a beyond of the capitalist subject — a beyond that is the death drive. The emancipatory politics of psychoanalysis is thus inherently anticapitalist insofar as the functioning of capitalism depends on the idea of obtaining the object.

Capitalism feeds off of desire's perpetual dissatisfaction. This dissatisfaction leads to efforts to accumulate more capital, attempts to increase productivity, and the introduction of new commodities into the market — in short, every aspect of capitalist economics. Marketers in capitalist society are bent upon producing desire in subjects and blinding them to the drive. In the *Grundrisse* Marx describes the way capitalism perpetuates desire through the production of needs: "Production not only supplies a material for the need, but it also supplies a need for the material. . . . The need which consumption feels for the object is created by the perception of it. The object of art — like every other product — creates a public which is sensitive to art and enjoys beauty. Production thus not only creates an object for the subject, but also a subject for the object."[17] Capitalism functions by sustaining — and even increasing — a sense of dissatisfaction commensurate with desire.

This explains capitalism's infatuation with the new. Capitalism constantly seeks out and embraces what is new, because the new keeps desire going by helping to create a sense of lack. The new holds the promise of a future enjoyment that will surpass whatever the subject has experienced before. This promise is the engine behind capitalism's creation of ever more needs. The more represents a constant lure, the next more — at least from afar — always seems to be *it*, the object that would provide the elusive enjoyment.

A portrayal of the inherent dissatisfaction that capitalism requires even among the wealthy occurs near the end of Roman Polanski's *Chinatown* (1974). In the film's penultimate scene, Jake Gittes (Jack Nicholson) reproaches Noah Cross (John Huston) for continuing a pattern of ruthless accumulation despite having already obtained a vast fortune. Their conversation makes clear the insatiable nature of the imperative to accumulate. Jake asks, "How much are you worth?" Cross, sensing the possibility of buying Jake off, says, "I have no idea. How much do you want?" But Jake doesn't want money; he wants to know what keeps Cross going. Jake continues, "No, I just want to know what you're worth. Over ten million?" Cross responds, "Oh my, yes." Then Jake asks, "Why are you doing it? How much better can you eat? What can you buy that you can't already afford?" Cross gives an answer emblematic of the capitalist subject: "The future, Mr. Getz [sic], the future." Cross's appeal to the "future" indicates that he believes in the promise of capitalism — that the future holds the lost enjoyment that always eludes us today. Despite his millions, his emphasis on the future demonstrates that Cross cannot recognize his own inherent satisfaction.[18]

Capitalism leaves individual subjects with a constant sense of their own dissatisfaction, but it also holds out the lure of future enjoyment, which prompts both the capitalist to create a new commodity and the consumer to buy it. Just as the capitalist hopes that every newly created commodity will be *it*, so does the consumer. However, no new commodity can ever provide the lost enjoyment for either the capitalist or the consumer, no matter how successful the commodity is, because the enjoyment has only an imaginary status. Once the commodity is realized for each (put on the market, in the case of the capitalist, or purchased, in the case of the consumer), it necessarily loses its enjoyment value.

In this sense, capitalism depends upon the dynamic of the child at Christmas time. On Christmas Eve all the presents under the tree offer the promise of a future enjoyment, but by afternoon on Christmas Day the child ends up bored and desiring once again, not having found the elusive enjoyment in any of the opened packages. This boredom isn't just the sign of the child's narcissism or that it has been spoiled by overindulgent parents; it is, rather, a structural necessity within the desiring world of capitalism. The cycle of the promise of future enjoyment and then the inevitable dissatisfaction that follows can only perpetuate itself as long as capitalist subjects continue to hope, that is, to believe in the promise that the new commodity holds out. More than anything else, hope keeps capitalism going. Giving up hope — and yet continuing on, enjoying continuing on — moves us from desire to the drive. This type of transformation also entails the end of the capitalist subject: capitalist subjects without hope are no longer capitalist subjects.

What holds us back from this possibility is our inability to discover a way of finding satisfaction satisfying. This failure, perhaps even more than its human costs, is what most disturbs Marx about capitalism. The points in *The Economic and Philosophic Manuscripts* at which Marx seems to slip into humanism as he recounts the effects of capitalism are the points at which he tries to articulate, though he wouldn't put it this way, the capitalist system's resistance to the death drive: capitalism doesn't allow us to find satisfaction in our satisfaction. Its logic is one that Marx calls "self-renunciation." As he puts it in perhaps the most famous passage from the *Manuscripts*, "The less you eat, drink and buy books; the less you go to the theater, the dance hall, the public house; the less you think, love, theorize, sing, paint, fence, etc., the more you *save* — the *greater* becomes your treasure which neither moths nor dust will devour — your *capital*. The less you *are*, the less you express your own life, the greater is your *alienated* life, the more you *have*, the greater is the store of your estranged being."[19] What Marx describes here as "alienated life" is not a life made unnatural by capitalism but a life where satisfaction is not satisfying, a life stuck within the capitalist logic of desire.

The alternative is not, as Marx seems to imply, an immediate satisfaction involved with eating, drinking, and buying books; rather, it is the ability to achieve a mediated satisfaction, becoming satisfied with the satisfaction that is already ours. The key, in other words, is not what we do so much as how we do it. It is on the level of this "how," rather than a "what," that capitalism alienates its subjects from their satisfaction. It fosters this type of alienation through its unrelenting demand for accumulation.

Accumulation is the superegoic imperative apropos of capitalism. That is, within capitalism, accumulation has the status of a moral obligation, and the capitalist subject inevitably hears an internal voice urging her or him on for "more." In the first volume of *Capital*, Marx captures perfectly the superegoic dimension of capitalism's command for accumulation. The voice proclaims, "Accumulate, accumulate! That is Moses and the prophets!"[20] Here, Marx reveals the way in which the call for accumulation functions as law and formally as a command. Despite whatever efforts we might make at obedience, we can never quiet this voice or sate the superego's appetite: no amount of accumulation is ever enough, either for the individual capitalist subject or for the capitalist society on the whole. The debt to the superego, in other words, is infinite. The more we accumulate, the more we see there is for us to accumulate.[21] Once we surrender to the demand for accumulation, we only get sucked further and further in by it.

The fundamental project of capitalist ideology involves identifying accumulation with enjoyment. This is why the capitalist subject can understand, if not identify with, the actions of the character Trina in Frank Norris's naturalist novel *McTeague*. In the most memorable scene of the novel, Trina goes to bed with the gold she has hoarded and derives an intensely sexual pleasure from this experience. Norris writes: "One evening she had even spread all the gold pieces between the sheets, and had then gone to bed, stripping herself, and had slept all night upon the money, taking a strange and ecstatic pleasure in the touch of the smooth flat pieces the length of her entire body."[22] Though Norris presents this sexual encounter between Trina and her gold as a perversion, it nonetheless resonates strongly and seems true to most readers because of the seemingly natural link between accumulation and enjoyment. The sexual nature of the gold in this scene stems from its ability to package and contain an enjoyment that would otherwise remain ungraspable.

Most of us do not have sex with gold or other monetary forms. But we do accept the link between accumulation and enjoyment that leads to the actions of a character like Trina. Most often, the apotheosis of accumulation manifests itself in purchasing commodities that seem to embody future enjoyment. One buys the newest clothes, the trendiest music, or the latest technological gadget in order to access the enjoyment that these commodities promise. But under the sway of capitalist ideology this attitude extends even to relationships: one chooses friends, albeit unconsciously, who will advance one's own social status, and one hopes to find a romantic partner who will do the same. The most private forms of enjoyment in capitalist society have their basis in the idea of accumulation and are unthinkable outside of it.

It follows from this that the primary line of social critique launched against capitalist society would focus on society's failure to live up to its ideology. It is a truism of Marxist analysis — especially after the Frankfurt School — to suggest that capitalist ideology uses the image of successful accumulation in order to hide the lack of accumulation that most subjects endure and thereby produce docility. According to this position, images of enjoyment, such as Hollywood films, create a false or illusory pleasure that helps to satisfy otherwise dissatisfied subjects. While entranced by the romantic bond between Humphrey Bogart and Ingrid Bergman or between Ashton Kutcher and Natalie Portman, capitalist subjects do not think about their position within the capitalist order of things. These subjects invest themselves in the image of enjoyment rather than in the real thing. This is why Theodor Adorno claims that "all mass culture is fundamentally adaptation."[23] The promulgation of the image of enjoyment, for Adorno and the Frankfurt School, becomes capitalist ideology's way of creating subjects who believe that they are enjoying themselves while existing within the intractable dissatisfaction of capitalism.

In the face of capitalist ideology's proliferation of such images, the task for the critical thinker becomes one of tearing them apart, exposing the lack of enjoyment at the heart of them and showing how, as Adorno and Max Horkheimer make clear in their *Dialectic of Enlightenment*, capitalism and its ideological handmaiden, the culture industry, never really deliver.[24] According to this view, capitalist subjects aren't really enjoying themselves despite feeling that they are. Such subjects actually exist in a state of perpetual dissatisfaction, and Adorno and Horkheimer hope to expose this dissatisfaction for what it is in order to create a revolutionary consciousness akin to their own. For Marxist thinkers like those of the Frankfurt School, the chief problem with capitalism is that it promises an enjoyment without ever delivering on that promise (even to those who seem taken care of by the capitalist system).

But there is a further problem that this critique doesn't touch — the alignment of accumulation and enjoyment. Few Marxist thinkers have questioned this link. In fact, the primary aim of the Marxist project seems to be expanding or equalizing accumulation while retaining it as the source of enjoyment. This attitude stems in large part from Marx's own privileging of production and his vision of the Communist revolution as an unleashing of the means of production. In contrast to capitalism, in which the restricted relations of production erect a barrier to the expansion of the unrestricted means of production, Communism would lift all such restrictions and allow for excess production without restraint — and thus enjoyment without limit.

The ideal of enjoyment without limit is visible in the politics articulated by many recent and contemporary thinkers influenced by Marx. One can see it in Gilles Deleuze and Félix Guattari's call for decoded flows, Alain Badiou's plea for more development of technology, and Paolo Virno's embrace of dissolved boundaries.[25] These visions of the future involve accepting the fundamental premise of capitalist ideology — its privileging of accumulation — but there is a countervailing movement within Marx's own thought that hints at a more radical critique of the capitalist system. By examining this other dimension of Marx's thought, we can see the relationship between enjoyment and pleasure as it operates within capitalist society and observe how a politics of the death drive would intervene in this relationship.

Finding Our Lost Enjoyment

At times, Marx indicates how the capitalist mode of production transforms the driving force of human activity, and he implicitly envisions Communism as a corrective to this transformation. The drive to accumulate, in this view, ceases to be a drive inherent in human subjectivity itself, and an alternative becomes visible. In the second volume of *Capital*, Marx almost articulates the position of psychoanalytic emancipatory politics directly when he says, "For capitalism is already essentially abolished once we assume that it is enjoyment that is the driving motive and not enrichment itself."[26] Here, the distinction between enjoyment and enrichment as motives for action divides capitalism from other unmentioned economic systems. The alternative to accumulation is satisfaction — or, more specifically, the recognition of our satisfaction. The fundamental problem with capitalism is this: it doesn't allow us to recognize our enjoyment or even to grasp enjoyment as what drives us. It's not that capitalism deprives us of the satisfaction involved with thinking, loving, theorizing, singing, painting, and fencing (to use Marx's examples cited above) but that it doesn't allow us to view satisfaction as a possible motive for our acts. We can think of the drive for enjoyment or a drive centered around enjoyment as a possibility existing outside of the capitalist system. This drive — the death drive — would have no purpose other than enjoyment, which is to say that it would operate in contrast to the accumulative logic of the capitalist drive. The capitalist drive to accumulate represents a distortion of the death drive, a rewriting of it that changes its structure.

But the capitalist drive to accumulate does not simply do away with enjoyment. As a rewriting of the death drive, it continues to provide the enjoyment that this drive does, though this drive to accumulate makes it more difficult for subjects to identify the site where they enjoy. Our investment in capitalism doesn't occur through a complete neglect of our enjoyment but depends in a fundamental way on its ability to deliver enjoyment. If capitalist subjects weren't actually enjoying themselves at all, they would not continue to be capitalist subjects. We really do enjoy ourselves within the capitalist universe — the death drive continues to function — but we don't enjoy in the way that capitalist ideology tries to convince us that we do.

Political struggle is not simply a struggle over the right to enjoy certain goods and the distribution of this right. It is also — even predominantly — a struggle over how we identify and locate our enjoyment. Capitalist ideology is triumphant today because it has won this struggle. As capitalist subjects, we must define enjoyment in terms of accumulation: one enjoys insofar as one accumulates objects of desire. This definition has become ubiquitous: according to the prevailing logic today, even the enjoyment that derives from romance comes from acquiring one's object of desire. But this is not the only way of figuring enjoyment. One of the most important political tasks for emancipatory politics today consists in transforming our way of thinking about enjoyment — breaking the link that capitalist ideology has forged between accumulation and enjoyment.

At every turn, capitalist ideology works to persuade subjects that their enjoyment derives from acquiring and having objects of desire. As a result, popular fantasies place most of their focus on the moments when subjects obtain these objects. Rather than emphasizing the points at which a couple struggles through the quotidian aspects of their relationship, the typical Hollywood romance stresses the moment of the couple's union. The entirety of *Sleepless in Seattle* (Nora Ephron, 1993) builds to the climactic embrace of the long-separated couple, and this embrace, according to the logic of the film, provides us as spectators with the ultimate enjoyment. The final embrace is the high point (the point at which each lover has the love object), and we leave the theater convinced that this embrace, this union, is the source of our enjoyment. In this way, the very structure of popular fantasies today underlines the link between acquisition and enjoyment.

The problem with this stress on the enjoyment of accumulation is not simply that it tends to produce a destructive society with egoistic subjects (though it certainly does) but that it doesn't really work. When we watch a film like *Sleepless in Seattle*, our enjoyment — if we have any at all — does not in fact derive from the moment when the lovers obtain their love objects. To understand where to locate our enjoyment of the film, we must observe the rigid distinction between enjoyment and pleasure. Pleasure occurs, for Freud, with a release of excitation, when we are able to overcome the barriers in the way of realizing our desire for this release. While pleasure provides a good feeling and a sense of well-being, enjoyment uproots us and disturbs our well-being. We have pleasures, but enjoyment, in some sense, has us. Though the proper spectator clearly experiences pleasure at the conclusion of *Sleepless in Seattle*, she or he does not enjoy at this point. Instead, this marks the moment at which our enjoyment dissipates. We enjoy the events leading up to the denouement — the struggles of each character with the absence of the object — not the acquisition of the object itself. The moment of acquiring the object represents the end, not the beginning, of our enjoyment, though it does mark the point at which we experience the most pleasure.

There is a link between Freud's conception of the pleasure principle as the motivating force of human activity and the capitalist drive to accumulate. In both cases, the focus is on the end point — either the psyche ridding itself of stimulation and achieving pleasure or the subject obtaining capital and commodities in order to have things to enjoy without worry. But what distinguishes them is their different ways of envisioning the end point: according to the logic of the pleasure principle, the subject works to eliminate excitation, and according to that of the capitalist drive, the subject tries to increase excitation through the acquisition of more and more commodities. We might reconcile the two positions by thinking of acquisition as a way of calming psychic excitation while enhancing the possibilities for physical excitation. If one has enough capital, one might avoid disturbing thoughts about losing it. But sustaining the homology between the psychoanalytic conception of motivation and the drive to accumulate becomes impossible when we turn from the pleasure principle to the death drive as the fundamental psychoanalytic category.

Before 1920 Freud identifies enjoyment and pleasure; he sees enjoyment as the product of the activity of the pleasure principle. As he puts it in "Instincts and Their Vicissitudes" in 1915, "The aim [*Zeil*] of an instinct is in every instance satisfaction, which can only be obtained by removing the state of stimulation at the source of the instinct."[27] Satisfaction or enjoyment results from eliminating stimulation, which is precisely what the pleasure principle demands. After writing *Beyond the Pleasure Principle*, however, Freud ceases to credit the pleasure principle with being the primary explanatory category for human activity.[28] He retains pleasure as a category, but the death drive dislodges it from its foundational place. Rather than explaining human activity itself, the pleasure principle begins to function as a supplement to the death drive as an explanatory category.

Pleasure supplements the death drive by providing a lure for consciousness. The subject actively takes up the path of the death drive — a drive that uses the subject and produces enjoyment at the cost of the subject's well-being or self-interest — because moments of pleasure render it bearable and even attractive. But this pleasure can only be imaginary: it is more the image of a future pleasure to be obtained than an actual pleasure experienced. This is the fundamental problem with the logic of accumulation and the would-be pleasure that derives from enrichment.

Every capitalist subject has experienced the dissatisfaction that inevitably results from actually obtaining the desired commodity. As an absent object, the object of desire appears to embody incredible pleasure, but when this object becomes present, it devolves into an ordinary object. In the act of obtaining the object of desire, we deprive this object of its very desirability. The pleasure embodied in the object exists only insofar as it remains out of reach for the subject. Because we desire the object as absent, actually obtaining the object provokes disappointment rather than pleasure. No matter how pleasurable the presence of the object is, this presence never offers us what we desired in the object. The great lie of capitalist ideology is its insistence that one can enjoy the act of accumulation itself. This act inevitably produces disappointment in the subject who buys into it, and this disappointment is never more acute than just after what promised to be the most satisfying acquisition.

For capitalist subjects, the disappointment that follows acquisition of a treasured commodity is not a reason to abandon the process of accumulation. In fact, it suggests to such subjects that they simply haven't taken accumulation far enough, that they need more. In this way, capitalist ideology feeds off the disappointment that it produces. If it actually produced the ultimate enjoyment for subjects that it promised them, they would no longer feel compelled to enter into the process of accumulation. After a little accumulation, subjects would become satisfied and thereby cease to be capitalist subjects, properly speaking. Capitalism needs dissatisfied subjects, but it also needs subjects who believe that the ultimate satisfaction is possible. This is accomplished by locating the ultimate satisfaction in the act of accumulation.

Subjects invest themselves in capitalist ideology because they accept its map of enjoyment. The key to combating this ideology lies not in undermining the fantasies that it proffers but in revealing where our enjoyment is located, in proffering a different map. Rather than enjoying the process of accumulation, we enjoy the experience of loss — the loss of the privileged object. Accumulation allows us to have objects, but it doesn't allow us to have *the* object in its absence. This is why accumulation always leads not to satisfaction with what one has but to the desire to accumulate more and more. Loss, in contrast, permits us to experience the object as such. Through the act of losing the privileged object, we in effect cause this privileged object to emerge. There is no privileged object prior to its loss. Understood in this way, loss becomes a creative act. The loss of the object is the foundation of our enjoyment because this act elevates an object above the rest of the world and embodies that object with the power to satisfy us.

Through the loss of the object, we are able to enjoy the object in its absence, which is the only form in which the object can motivate our desire. When we enjoy in this way, we enjoy nothing rather than something. This seems to offer, at first glance, an inferior mode of enjoyment. Why would anyone settle for the enjoyment of an absent object rather than a present one? Because this type of enjoyment — the enjoyment of absence — is the only type of enjoyment available to us as desiring beings. When we actually have the object, it loses the quality that renders it enjoyable. We can enjoy the object, but we can enjoy it only through its absence. The subject who recognizes this link between the absence of the object and enjoyment — at the moment of this recognition — ceases to be a subject invested in capitalist ideology. This ideology has a hold over us only insofar as we believe in its image of the ultimate enjoyment that it attaches to accumulation.

This is not to say that subjects who recognize that enjoyment is dependent on loss will become completely ascetic beings, enjoying the iPods, widescreen televisions, and luxury cars that they don't have. Instead, they will take up a different relationship to their objects of desire, which will be enjoyable for the loss and sacrifice that they embody. One cannot accumulate such objects because they have no positive value attributed to them. They arrive without the promise of the ultimate future enjoyment attached to them, and in this sense, they do not function as commodities. The commodity depends on the invisibility of the labor that produces it, and the subject who recognizes loss in the object renders labor, which is the loss that gives the object its value, visible. Those who are able to locate their enjoyment in loss ipso facto value the sacrifice made by society's producers and align themselves politically with this group. This transformation results not so much from a change of activity as from a change of perspective.

We might think of this change of perspective in terms of the way that athletes and fans view their devotion to sports. The increasing importance of sport in the contemporary world testifies in one sense to the dominance of commodity logic and its narcotizing effect. Sports figures and their fans associate the ultimate enjoyment with victory, and their focus on victory provides an escape from the dissatisfaction that inheres in everyday life under capitalism. But the focus on victory hides where the real enjoyment lies both for the athletes themselves and for the fan. Though one finds fleeting pleasure in winning, enjoyment derives from the sacrifice of time and the effort that go into making victory possible.

Both the athlete and the fan make this sacrifice to different degrees — the athlete through long hours of difficult training and the fan through giving up free time to follow the trajectory of the individual athlete or team — though the prevailing commodity logic obscures the role that this sacrifice plays as the source of enjoyment in both cases. According to this logic, the pleasure of the victory justifies the sacrifice, when in fact pleasure functions as an alibi for the enjoyment of sacrifice. Psychoanalysis allows us to turn the tables on commodity logic and to place the emphasis on the act of sacrifice. One strives for or roots for victory only in order to sustain the sacrifice that makes it possible. This shift in emphasis represents a radical transformation that stems from recognizing how we already enjoy, not from changing the nature of our enjoyment.

Though a simple shift in emphasis hardly seems likely to transform society in a fundamental way, this is precisely what Giorgio Agamben suggests in a stunning passage from *The Coming Community*. Agamben cites a story that Walter Benjamin purportedly told to Ernst Bloch describing the kingdom of the messiah. In the messianic kingdom, Benjamin says, "everything will be as it is now, just a little different."[29] Agamben sees the image of the halo as the indication of this slight difference that Benjamin identifies, but we might equally view the halo as a different way of approaching the commodity — a capacity for seeing the commodity as an object of sacrifice rather than as an object of accumulation.

Though capitalist ideology focuses the attention of subjects on the process of accumulation and on having the object rather than experiencing it as lost, capitalism as a mode of production continually forces subjects to endure the object in its absence. In this sense, capitalist ideology and the practice of capitalism are completely at odds with each other, and this discrepancy is crucial for the functioning of capitalism. The accumulative logic doesn't allow one to recognize oneself as a subject of loss or identify one's enjoyment with the object's absence. But nonetheless capitalism delivers enjoyment to the subject through a process of securing this absence.

This contradiction is pivotal for the reproduction of capitalist relations of production. The satisfaction that capitalism provides sustains subjects, while the desire that capitalist ideology provokes pushes them to expand the system, which is what it requires in order to survive. Because capitalism forces subjects to endure perpetually the absence of the privileged object, it does offer enjoyment to the subjects who invest themselves in its ideology. However, this ideology never allows these subjects to locate the actual source of their enjoyment. Through the act of relocating our enjoyment — of exposing the link between enjoyment and loss or absence — we undermine the ability of capitalist ideology to seduce contemporary subjects.

The Ego as Detour

One of the primary targets in the political effort to relocate (or to properly locate) our enjoyment is the ego. Since life within capitalism leaves subjects constitutively unable to enjoy their enjoyment, modes of accommodation arise, the most powerful of which is the ego. The self-help industry earns billions of dollars a year encouraging subjects to strengthen their egos. Believing themselves dissatisfied and in need of a sturdier ego identity, subjects turn to books, courses, videos, and other media in hopes of finding the solution to their dissatisfaction. The problem with whatever solution they find in this domain is that the introduction of the ego and its inhibitions to the psyche produces additional detours for the death drive. As a result, the ego can never lead the subject to the point where it will find its satisfaction satisfying.

Almost thirty years before he developed the idea of the ego as one of three distinct structures in the psyche, Freud theorized the ego's role in relationship to the flow of psychic energy in the 1895 *Project for a Scientific*

Psychology. Already at this point in his thought, Freud sees the ego as itself a mechanism of defense, as a way of protecting the psyche against trauma. As an attempt to ameliorate the unpleasure that the psyche experiences in trauma, the ego acts as a barrier to the direct flow of psychic energy. In the *Project* Freud notes: "If an ego exists, it must *inhibit* psychical primary processes."[30] The ego enacts this inhibition through the creation of what Freud calls side-cathexes. The side-cathexes provide alternate paths that diffuse the excitation resulting from a traumatic experience (or the memory of one). Rather than following a direct path to its release, which would lead to unpleasure, the excitation becomes caught up in the side-cathexes of the ego, which ultimately lessen the amount of unpleasure that the subject experiences. But the problem is that the detours of the ego — its side-cathexes — produce dissatisfaction at the same time that they dull the impact of trauma.

The more the subject develops a strong ego, the more it short circuits the drive and leaves the subject with the sense that it is missing out on its satisfaction. This is why the project of boosting self-esteem is an infinite one that never produces any victories. It is self-defeating in its very conception. As the subject's ego strengthens and the subject gains a more developed self-image, one would think that this would allow the subject to find its enjoyment enjoyable, but the opposite occurs. The development of a strong ego means that the path of the death drive has been largely short-circuited, and this is a process that alienates the subject from its own satisfaction. The strong ego of the subject causes the subject to experience its own enjoyment as alien — as the enjoyment of the other. This is why a strong ego is no defense against racism but in fact makes the subject receptive to racist appeals that focus on the excessive enjoyment of the other.

The very formation of the ego illustrates the source of its limitations. The subject develops its ego not out of itself but on the basis of an image of its fellow being. This image, like all images, conveys wholeness and thereby obscures the fragmentation of the subject's actual body when the subject adopts the image as its own bodily ego. By adopting an ego, we succumb to an illusion, but at the same time, we experience the failure of this wholeness in the fragmentation of the body. On one level, the ego provides the subject with a sense of identity and stability, but on another, it reminds the subject of its constant failure to be equal to this identity. And because the ego is modeled on the image of the perfect other, it leads us to link our failures with the other's successes.[31] The other's wholeness comes at the expense of our lack. The other's identity stems from the theft of ours.

The dissatisfaction and paranoia that a strong ego produces are evident in the figure of Captain Ahab in Herman Melville's *Moby Dick*. Melville imbues Ahab with a strong sense of who he is and of his mission in life. His rage at the white whale stems not just from the injury that the whale gave Ahab's body but also — and primarily — from the relationship of the injury to his bodily ego. The loss of his leg leaves Ahab's body fragmented, and he measures this fragmentation against the wholeness of his bodily ego. A fundamental dissatisfaction results, and in order to explain this dissatisfaction to himself, Ahab posits the whale as the barrier to his complete satisfaction, as the thief of his wholeness. Of course, the whale did actually take Ahab's leg, but it did not take Ahab's wholeness, which was never anything but imaginary. *Moby Dick* is structured around Ahab's dissatisfaction and quest for restoring a lost satisfaction. He believes that destroying the whale will accomplish this, but the quest only accomplishes his own destruction.

Ahab's determination to restore a satisfaction that he believes he has lost renders him an unattractive character. But his unattractiveness does not imply that he lacks a strong ego. It is the strong ego — his sense that he really is a whole, that he is identical with a certain image of himself — that fuels Ahab's dissatisfaction and is the source of his unattractiveness. Through Ahab, Melville reveals in the starkest terms the political and existential limitations of a strong ego. Here, we see directly what a strong ego looks like: it leaves the subject unable to recognize its own satisfaction and constantly searching for the source of its dissatisfaction in order to remedy it. In this sense, the strong ego is the perfect psychic modality for capitalist subjectivity, which is why the promotion of a strong ego proliferates throughout capitalist society.[32]

Miserliness and Excess

Much of the appeal of capitalism derives from its relationship to excess. Those who champion capitalism appreciate its capacity for demanding, bestowing, and utilizing excess. One capitalist subject works excessively today in order to enjoy tomorrow; another gains excessively as the result of a daring investment; and another uses excess capital to create additional jobs by opening a new factory. Capitalism's penchant for excess provides the basis for its link to individualism. Unlike socialism, which tolerates no excess and reduces individual economic difference to sameness, capitalism depends on the excesses of individual difference flourishing.

Capitalism doesn't simply mobilize excess to its own ends. It has its basis in the capitalist's appropriation of an excess created by workers. As Marx explains, the capitalist pays workers fairly for their labor, giving them money in exchange for the value they produce. But what the capitalist doesn't pay for — what the capitalist appropriates without any compensation — is the surplus value that workers create through their labor. This appropriated surplus value, a pure excess created by the way that labor functions in the capitalist system, is the source of the capitalist's profit, though the capitalist cannot recognize this.[33] Without this excess at its core, there would be no capitalist system.

The problem with capitalism's relation to excess is not just a moral one. If the capitalist's appropriation of surplus value had the effect of producing excessive enjoyment for the capitalist or for others (like those who might enjoy the end product), we might say that this end justifies the means and that the initial act of appropriation is worth it. We could use John Rawls's test for a just society — adopting a "veil of ignorance" and examining the desirability of the society without regard for our position within it — and imagine that we might opt for capitalism even if we didn't know for certain that we would be successful capitalists ourselves. In other words, the opportunity for great enjoyment might be worth the risk of poverty if one fails to achieve it. But even when capitalism produces excessive enjoyment, it never allows subjects to find satisfaction in it. Capitalist subjects remain necessarily alienated from their own enjoyment and experience instead the dissatisfaction that derives from positing the ultimate enjoyment in the future or in the other — always somewhere else.

The enjoyment that capitalist subjects experience is limited because they take too much trouble for this enjoyment. Capitalism's excessiveness imposes multiple detours on the death drive, and this engenders miserliness in the subjects' relationship to their enjoyment. The death drive produces satisfaction through the repetition of its trajectory, and this repetition occurs regardless of the detours it must navigate. But the detours cut into the subject's ability to find this satisfaction satisfying, and capitalism produces detours in the death drive through its deferral of enjoyment. Because the capitalist subject always locates the ultimate enjoyment elsewhere, this subject's own satisfaction is always unsatisfactory. Capitalism's excessiveness in attempting to derail the death drive results in a system lacking in excessive enjoyment.

Capitalism is a system of excess, a system functioning by appropriating the excess that workers produce, and yet it systematically erects barriers to the subject's experience of excess. Because capitalist economy inherently orients itself toward the future, it demands that the subject invest itself (psychically and economically) in the future. One must never enjoy excessively without regard for one's future enjoyment: there must be no expenditure without reserve. The problem with this capitalist ethos is its betrayal of the very nature of enjoyment. The subject cannot conserve its enjoyment or save it for tomorrow because enjoyment only exists outside the order that one would impose on it. Enjoyment is an experience of infinitude that overwhelms the subject's ability to reduce it to a calculus, which is precisely what the capitalist economy forces on the subject.

In contrast, economy in the drive results in an excess of enjoyment through the enjoyment of excess. When subjects eliminate the detours that sidetrack the death drive, they experience this enjoyment of excess. This is the kind of excess that one cannot find within the capitalist system. Capitalism uses excess in order to create thrift; the economy of the drive uses thrift to unleash excess. This dialectical relationship between thrift and enjoyment becomes apparent in Freud's analysis of the economy of the joke, an analysis that leads to the conclusion that the ultimate problem with capitalism is that it isn't funny.

In *Jokes and Their Relation to the Unconscious* Freud makes clear that the satisfaction coming from a joke derives from an act of saving or economizing. Puns exemplify this saving process: the pun makes a direct connection between two disparate ideas, ideas that otherwise we would be able to connect only indirectly, through a circuitous path of related signifiers. By shortening the path, by eliminating the excessiveness of the detours leading from one idea to another, the pun creates an economical path between two ideas. This saving in turn manifests itself as an excess enjoyment in the response to the pun. If I say, for instance, that "Jerry Garcia is now among the dead," I link two different senses of the word "dead" — not being alive and being a member of the band the Grateful Dead. We have the capacity for laughing at this type of pun (even if we don't actually laugh) because the pun has economized through the connection it makes apparent.

Other jokes also work according to the logic of the pun, allowing us to connect what would otherwise be disparate or to grasp connections that we didn't otherwise see. When Babe Ruth said that he had a better year than the president after being confronted with the fact that he earned more than the country's leader, people laughed because the joke linked the presidency, an occupation that we typically consider above comparison, with another occupation, that of a baseball player, that we think of as insignificant in the larger scheme of things. It also made evident the underlying connections at work in the economic system itself, revealing how this system links everyone. Connections such as these are at the root of our ability to enjoy the joke as such. As Freud says, "Enjoyment is . . . to be attributed to economy in psychical expenditure."[34] Because it economizes the unconscious connections in psyche, the joke produces an excess or remainder, which is precisely what the subject enjoys.

Though Freud himself never did, we can translate Freud's analysis of the joke back into the terms of the death drive. The joke functions to shorten the drive's path: it allows us to abandon the detours or side-cathexes that interrupt the direct path of the drive. When we laugh at the joke, it is as if we are momentarily recognizing our satisfaction and escaping the sense of dissatisfaction that stems from these detours. But capitalism lacks a sense of humor and works at every turn to minimize joking — or at least the economic effect of the joke.

The joke is anathema to capitalism because its functioning depends on severing connections between ideas rather than facilitating them.[35] For proper capitalist subjects, amoral behavior in the marketplace has nothing to do with private life at home; the products we buy have no relation to the labor that created them; and there is no link between economic hardship and politics. Of course, jokes proliferate within the capitalist system, and many capitalist subjects tell jokes constantly.[36] But in its essence the joke performs a function — connecting ideas that appear quite different — that in general subverts the functioning of the capitalist economy. Capitalism demands thrift in matters of enjoyment, but it abhors the thrift that facilitates connections and clears the path of the drive. Only by insisting on this type of thrift can we escape the sense of dissatisfaction that hides the underlying satisfaction of the death drive.

Psychoanalytic thought can't offer a precise prescription for a particular form of social organization beyond the capitalist one. But it can reveal the importance of embracing the economics of the joke. By doing so, one economizes in order to enjoy rather than economizing in order to accumulate (and enjoy in the future). The economic model of the psyche that psychoanalysis develops points toward the possibility of enjoying our excess instead of profiting from it. A society in which we enjoyed excess would not be the Promised Land, but it would be a place where enjoyment occurred without so much trouble precisely because we recognized the trouble for what it was. Our trouble is what we enjoy.

3

Class Status and Enjoyment

Freedom and Injustice

Almost all criticism of class society and capitalism from the left centers around the injustice perpetuated by the continued existence of social classes. This focus on injustice is the ethical basis of Marxism and its fundamental point of departure. In the preface to *Transcritique on Kant and Marx*, Kojin Karatani affirms the inseparability of Marxism and ethics when he links Marx's thought to Kant's: "If we think about it, from the beginning, communism could not have been conceptualized without the moral moment inherent in Kant's thinking."[1] As Karatani sees it, Marx argues for socialism on the basis of its historical necessity but also because of the terrible injustices within capitalist, class-based society. In the midst of his theoretical analysis of capitalism's structure, Marx often breaks out into terms that indicate moral condemnation as he describes the exploitation of workers or the ceaseless accumulation of the capitalist. These moments appear not just in Marx's early or polemical works (like *The Economic and Philosophic Manuscripts* or *The Communist Manifesto*) but even in the mature and sober analyses of the three volumes of *Capital*.[2]

The critique of capitalism for its injustice is not confined to Marxism. Most on the left, even moderates, tend to echo it despite their appreciation for the freedom that capitalism helps to engender. Someone like Richard Rorty, who distances himself from Marxist politics, nonetheless insists that within a capitalist system "the rich will always try to get richer by making the poor poorer, that total commodification of labour will lead to the immizeration of the wage-earners."[3] The fundamental problem with capitalism, according to this line of critique, is its structural resistance to egalitarian justice. Though the process of commodification eliminates qualitative distinctions between objects and thereby levels hierarchical difference, a countervailing pressure toward accumulation prevents this leveling process from facilitating genuine social equality. As objects within capitalism become more equal, subjects become less so, and this is the injustice that both Marxism and liberalism target in their critiques.

In contrast to Marxism and left-wing theories, which take justice as the point of departure in arguing against class society, psychoanalysis begins with freedom — or, more precisely, with the lack of freedom that exists under capitalism. In other words, psychoanalysis shares with Marxism a critical attitude toward capitalism (though this is predominantly implicit in the former), but psychoanalytic thought sees the problems that capitalism engenders in other terms than Marxism does. It poses a different critique, and, as a result, it implies a different response, a response that insists on freedom as the fundamental value rather than equality. Political philosophers constantly wrestle with the seemingly opposed poles of freedom and justice. Isaiah Berlin famously characterizes freedom and justice as positions that must constantly be measured against each other in order to construct a good society. He claims: "The extent of a man's, or a people's, liberty to choose to live as he or they desire must be weighed against the claims of many other values, of which equality, or justice, or happiness, or security, or public order are perhaps the most obvious examples. For this reason, it cannot be unlimited."[4] Most political philosophers who stress freedom (John Locke, Thomas Jefferson, Friedrich Hayek, and so on) are implicitly or explicitly procapitalist, or at least antisocialist, because socialism demands a restriction on individual liberty.

The thinkers who reject capitalism in the name of freedom, like Friedrich Nietzsche and Martin Heidegger, most often do so from the right rather than the left; they yearn for freedom from the leveling tendencies of capitalist reification that produce an equality of spirit if not of material wealth. They advocate for aristocratic figures who transcend merely mercantile relations and achieve self-overcoming or authentic being-toward-death, states of being that the relative equality of capitalism works to prevent. According to our usual way of thinking, to stress freedom rather than justice is to acquiesce to at least some degree of class division.[5] This becomes especially true if the freedom that one espouses is individual freedom, as seems to be the case with psychoanalysis. In short, because psychoanalysis places itself on the side of individual freedom, it would appear also to be de facto on the side of the kind of laissez-faire thinking we see in proponents of capitalism or the aristocratic thinking visible in its right-wing opponents.

But what we encounter with psychoanalysis is something wholly different: rather than insisting that individual freedom requires class division, psychoanalysis demonstrates how class society itself deprives subjects of freedom. Its criticism of class society is founded on its criticism of capitalism's restriction of freedom. One's class status is the badge of one's unfreedom. In order to distinguish oneself in terms of class, one must sacrifice freedom. This holds not just within capitalist relations of production but for the aristocratic ideal promulgated by Nietzsche and Heidegger as well. In a certain sense, on a theoretical level the entire psychoanalytic project targets the problems generated by a class structure in society, and the implicit ideal guiding psychoanalytic treatment is that of a classless society.[6] We can even see this opposition to class society inherent in the genesis of psychoanalysis.

Psychoanalysis emerges as such at the conjunction of the success and the failure of the Enlightenment project. The fundamental impulse of the Enlightenment is the insistence on subjects breaking from reliance on authority and becoming free. As Kant puts it in his essay "What Is Enlightenment?," "The motto of enlightenment is therefore: *Sapere aude!* Have courage to use your *own* understanding!"[7] On the one hand, psychoanalysis represents the continuation and extension of this project to the unconscious. In order to be authentically free, the subject must confront not just its conscious subjection to authority but its unconscious subjection as well. Insofar as it promotes this aim, psychoanalysis is of a piece with the Enlightenment project as Kant describes it. On the other hand, however, the emergence of psychoanalysis stems from the failure to put this project into action.

Despite the Enlightenment's rejection of external authority and its insistence on the subject's freedom, the dominance of this authority and the absence of freedom persist in the post-Enlightenment epoch. Authority continues to hold sway over the subject, but at the same time, the enlightened subject comes to believe in its own freedom from such authority. In its foundation, psychoanalysis addresses itself to the persistence of unfreedom in a time when freedom appears readily achievable. It is this contradiction that gives birth to psychoanalysis, which is an effort to solve it, to help the subject gain the freedom that the Enlightenment promises.

Social authority continues to restrict the subject in the wake of the Enlightenment precisely because post-Enlightenment society never achieved the Enlightenment ideal of equality. The continued existence of class division and of the inequality of class society sustains the unfreedom of subjects. While Marxism shows the economic and social costs of class exploitation for the exploited classes, psychoanalysis emphasizes the psychic costs of capitalism for the whole society, including those that most directly benefit from the capitalist system, the upper and middle classes. Its concern is not the suffering that social or environmental conditions explain but the suffering that appears inexplicable, the suffering endured by those who, when one regards their situation from the outside, should be happy. Psychoanalysis arises in response to the psychic costs demanded by capitalist, class-based society.[8] Ironically, upper-class subjects pay these costs disproportionately and thus suffer in their own way from the inequities of the capitalist mode of production. Of course, no one wants to lament the misfortune of the poor little rich kid or try to generate sympathy for the suffering of Bill Gates. The point is rather to emphasize the unfreedom and lack of enjoyment that haunt the beneficiaries of capitalism and all class society. Even those who win in the capitalist game lose, and this provides what is perhaps the ultimate indictment of the capitalist system. It is in this sense that we should revisit the status of the analysands that psychoanalysis treats.

Analyzing the Rich

Many Marxist thinkers consider psychoanalysis as a superstructural element within the class society of capitalism, and this critique often draws attention to the upper-class status of the average psychoanalytic patient. This line of attack is right, but for the wrong reasons. Psychoanalysis tends to focus on subjects in the upper and middle classes because these subjects are almost necessarily more invested in class privilege. The more one invests oneself in class privilege, the more one sacrifices one's freedom to enjoy. This is why, in his essay "On Beginning the Treatment," Freud even considers the possibility that lower-class subjects "are less easily overtaken by neurosis" and hence less in need of psychoanalysis.[9]

From the beginning of the discovery of psychoanalysis, Freud recognized that class status is a burden to psychic functioning.[10] As a result, or so Freud initially believed, the upper-class subject is likely to be more subject to repression than the lower-class subject. Class privilege itself demands repression in exchange for the social advantages that it offers. Freud finally rejects the idea that lower-class subjects have no need for psychoanalysis, but he never abandons the fundamental insight. What he comes to see is that, while upper-class status demands a psychic investment in class privilege, lower-class subjects can also easily partake of this psychic investment. Even those who find themselves on the losing side of the class struggle in capitalist society can identify with those on the other side and thereby psychically invest themselves in class privilege — sometimes even more fully than those who actually have class privilege.

We can see a profound example of this in the widespread opposition to the estate tax in contemporary American society. This tax would affect only the wealthiest 5 percent of Americans, and yet a majority of Americans oppose it. According to a March 2005 poll, 85 percent favor the reduction or elimination of the tax, and the opposition did not vary at all according to the income level of those polled.[11] Even when respondents were informed that this tax would affect neither their own family nor family farms nor any others than the richest Americans, the opposition to the tax remained firm. Such a staunch majority of people oppose it because they identify with the class status and privilege of the wealthiest 5 percent. It is not so much that the nonwealthy imagine that they will themselves become wealthy but that they want to sustain the image of untrammeled wealth not subject to taxation. Nonetheless, there remains some relationship between the analysand's class status and his or her need for psychoanalytic treatment. Unlike lower-class subjects, those in the upper class cannot avoid the psychic investment that their very social position rests on. The upper-class subjects who give up their investment in class status ipso facto cease to be upper class in material terms.[12]

We can return to the example of jokes from the previous chapter in order to make clear the way that repression accompanies class status. In *Jokes and Their Relation to the Unconscious* Freud contends that class has a profound bearing on the nature of jokes, and this leads him to describe the trajectory of jokes in terms of social class. According to Freud, among the lower classes (those without a privileged status in class society) the true sexual or smutty nature of jokes can be openly revealed. One can tell a dirty joke in the most direct fashion. As one rises in class status, however, the joke, in order to remain acceptable, must undergo more and more deformation and repression, so that its original sexual dimension appears only obliquely or indirectly.

In both cases, we enjoy the same thing, but in the latter our path to enjoyment must be more circuitous. As Freud points out, "When we laugh at a refined obscene joke, we are laughing at the same thing that makes a peasant laugh at a coarse piece of smut. In both cases the pleasure springs from the same source. We, however, could never bring ourselves to laugh at the coarse smut; we should feel ashamed or it would seem to us disgusting. We can only laugh when a joke has come to our help."[13] Because the upper classes have made more of a sacrifice of enjoyment than the lower classes, they cannot publicly experience the joke in its original, smutty form. Class status involves forgoing more enjoyment and living more strictly according to the dictates of the social law that commands its sacrifice. Even the most reprobate members of the upper class have undergone this sacrifice in exchange for the recognition that their class status provides. For psychoanalysis, class privilege is a bad bargain, and the ideal of a classless society represents the possibility not only for justice but also for an increased freedom to enjoy.

Of course, one can also enjoy one's sacrifice of enjoyment, and this is the primary mode of enjoyment that the upper class experiences. The self-satisfied nature of the death drive renders it impossible to abandon enjoyment altogether without producing additional enjoyment through the process of abandoning it. This is what occurs in the case of upper-class subjects who cannot enjoy jokes in their original smutty form. When they encounter the smutty joke, their way of enjoying it involves an experience of outrage or disgust. It is an unrecognized enjoyment, but an enjoyment nonetheless. But enjoyment in the form of outrage or disgust is a case of enjoyment that occurs with too much trouble. The upper-class subject who enjoys its superiority takes a circuitous route to find its satisfaction, and this circuitous route is the inevitable product of upper-class status. Though wealth and social recognition make material life easier, they elongate the path of the drive and thereby deprive the subject of the ability to embrace its own mode of enjoying.

The point is not to take a vow of poverty and attempt to live without any commodities at all but to transform one's relation to the commodity. The commodity does provide enjoyment, but only insofar as one doesn't have it. Class status serves as a vehicle for enjoyment when we experience it not as a goal toward which to aspire but as a burden to throw off. As psychoanalytic thought shows, every commodity is fool's gold, and class privilege is not a privilege in any other sense than the material one. Neither allows the enjoyment that it promises, even for those who accumulate the most commodities and reach the highest echelons of class.

Thus, psychoanalysis reveals a new approach to the critique of capitalism. The problem with capitalist society, according to what psychoanalysis lays out, isn't that it pays too much attention to decadent enjoyment and not enough attention to what's really important, which is one standard leftist critique. Such a critique might, for instance, attack capitalist society for focusing on titillating events, like the travails of Britney Spears, in lieu of more substantial events, like the Mideast peace process. Though we tend to think that capitalism — especially global capitalism, with its characteristic "pathological narcissism" — is enjoyment run amok, it is in actuality a socioeconomic system in which we cannot avow our enjoyment. Hence, when we voice a critique of capitalism, our rallying cry shouldn't be less enjoyment but more, though we must articulate this knowing that there is no direct access to this enjoyment.[14] More enjoyment — that is, the recognition of our satisfaction — is only possible insofar as we abandon the imperative to accumulate. This is the essence of Freud's critique of capitalism, as made implicitly in the joke book and elsewhere. He shows us how dearly we pay — with our pound of enjoyment — for each rung we take up capitalism's socioeconomic ladder.[15]

The cost in enjoyment for class status is illustrated in an almost programmatic way in David Fincher's *Fight Club* (1999). The film begins by chronicling the extreme dissatisfaction of Jack (Edward Norton), the film's narrator. He lives in an upscale apartment filled perfectly with expensive and trendy furniture purchased through chic mail-order catalogs. He takes great care in outfitting his apartment and believes that he will find enjoyment through this activity, but he ends up constantly dissatisfied. His consumption and class privilege lead to insomnia and depression rather than enjoyment. His life changes only when he blows up his apartment and goes to live in a dilapidated house with Tyler Durden (Brad Pitt), a man he seems to have met on an airplane but who turns out to be Jack's double. Whereas Jack is restrained and uptight, Tyler is free to enjoy himself. But after Tyler appears, Jack's enjoyment becomes more evident as well. The film links his increased enjoyment directly to the destruction of his apartment and the class status it embodies.

The fight club that Jack starts is unimaginable as an upper- or even middle-class phenomenon, which is why he can no longer continue to work at his middle-class job after having begun it. The fighting takes place in the basement of a grungy bar, and the ethos of fight club runs in the opposite direction of one concerned with class status. Joining fight club involves allowing one's face to become disfigured during fights, and the goal is receiving blows rather than delivering them. The recognition that accompanies social class rewards those on the top of the class struggle — those who fight and win — but fight club privileges the ability to receive blows and continue to fight, an ability that it associates with the absence of class status. Leaving his middle-class existence behind allows Jack to enjoy fight club and even to experience (as Tyler) a relationship with Marla Singer (Helena Bonham Carter) that he could not have had while living a middle-class lifestyle. While developing fight club, Jack moves to an abandoned and broken-down house in the poor part of town, a house that he enjoys much more than his old apartment despite the material inconvenience tied to living there. As the film illustrates, the pursuit of enjoyment through class status is a fruitless endeavor. It is only when one blows up one's class possibilities that the opportunity for real enjoyment appears.[16] Enjoyment requires sacrifice, but not the sacrifice of one's time for the sake of accumulation. It demands the sacrifice of accumulation itself.

A similar dynamic is at work in the character of Rose (Kate Winslet) in James Cameron's *Titanic* (1997). She begins the film attempting to secure her status in upper-class society through marriage and ends it by abandoning her rich fiancé and her family name (the only source of social value that she possesses, since, as her mother points out, the family has no more money). Through her relationship with Jack (Leonardo DiCaprio), Rose descends in class status in order to gain access to the enjoyment made inaccessible through her connection to wealth and privilege. Rose is drawn to Jack not simply out of love but because he offers her the freedom to enjoy. In fact, in the film Jack is nothing but a tool for her to use to escape the unfreedom of class privilege, which is why she can discard him into the depths of the ocean just after proclaiming that she would never let go of him.

For psychoanalysis, as for *Fight Club* and *Titanic*, class status represents a fundamental barrier to enjoyment. It alienates us from our own enjoyment even as it provides a compensatory enjoyment through this alienation. In trying to advance their own interests and rise in class status, subjects retreat from the burden of enjoyment. In fact, if we listen to what psychoanalysis has to say about the relationship between class society and enjoyment, we might even posit that the post-Enlightenment world has not come closer to the ideal of a classless society precisely because of our refusal to face the enjoyment implicit in such a realization. Nonetheless, psychoanalysis remains firmly on the side of enjoyment against class privilege.

The Cost of Recognition

When subjects enter into society, the social order confronts them with a demand. This demand for the sacrifice of enjoyment offers them social recognition in return. Recognition grounds the subjects' identities and allows them to experience themselves as valuable. The socially recognized subject has a worth that derives solely from recognition itself. Popular kids may believe that their sense of worth is tied to an activity — playing football, obtaining good grades, being a cheerleader — but in fact it depends on the recognition that an anonymous social authority accords those who engage in these activities. Though we might imagine the football player fully enjoying himself and his popular status, the recognition that comes with this status renders enjoyment impossible insofar as popularity adheres to the social authority's demand rather than its unarticulated desire.[17]

The demand that confronts the subject entering the social order is directly articulated at the level of the signifier. Social authority says to the subject, "Act in this way, and you will receive approval (or recognition)." But the demand conceals an unconscious desire that is not articulated on the level of the signifier. What the authority really wants from the subject is not equivalent to what it explicitly demands in signifiers. This desire of social authority or the Other engenders the subject's own desire: the subject's desire is a desire to figure out what the Other wants from it — to solve the enigma of the Other's desire and locate itself within that desire. The subject becomes a desiring subject by paying attention not to what the social authority says (the demand) but to what remains unsaid between the lines (the desire). The path of desire offers the subject the possibility of breaking from its dependence on social authority through the realization that its secret, the enigma of the Other's desire, does not exist — that the authority doesn't know what it wants. Such a realization is not easy to achieve, but adopting the attitude of desire at least makes it possible. For the subject who clings to the social authority's demand, dependence on this authority becomes irremediable and unrealizable.

This is the limitation of pseudo-Hegelian political projects oriented around garnering recognition. They necessarily remain within the confines of the order that they challenge, and even success will never provide the satisfaction that the project promises. Full recognition would bring with it not the sense of finally penetrating into the secret enclave of the social authority but instead the disappointment of seeing that this secret does not exist. The widespread acceptance of gay marriage in the United States, for instance, would not provide a heretofore missing satisfaction, because the social authority that would provide the recognition is not a substantial entity fully consistent with itself. Even though institutional authority can grant a marriage certificate to gay couples and the majority of the population can recognize the validity of the marriage, there is no agency that can authorize such a marriage that is itself authorized. Social authority, in other words, is always unauthorized or groundless, and this is the ultimate reason why the pursuit of recognition leads to frustration.

Those who seek social recognition structure their lives around the social authority's demand, and recognition is the reward that one receives for doing one's social duty. For instance, in order to gain popularity, one must adhere to the social rules that lead to popularity. This involves wearing the proper clothes, hanging out with the right people, playing the approved sports, and talking in the correct fashion. Too much deviation from the standard dissolves one's popularity. Even those who disdain popularity most often align themselves with some other source of recognition and thereby invest themselves in another form of it. The outsider who completely rejects the trappings of the popular crowd but slavishly obeys the demands of fellow outsiders remains within the orbit of social recognition. This devotion to social recognition is more apparent, though not more true, among the young; the adult universe employs strictures with a similar severity.[18] Following the path of desire — going beyond the explicit demand of the social authority — has a cost in terms of social status.

Those who restrict themselves to the authority's demand do not necessarily evince more obedience to actual laws than others do. In fact, the social authority's demand often conflicts with laws because it demands love, not just obedience. Criminals who flaunt the law for the sake of accumulating vast amounts of money are among those most invested in this demand. There is no inherent radicality in criminal behavior, and most criminals tend to be politically conservative.[19] The object of the demand is the subject's complete sacrifice for the sake of the social authority, not simply adherence to a set of laws.

By imposing a demand that requires subjects to violate the law, the authority creates a bond of guilt among those who follow this demand. For instance, contemporary capitalist society demands the unrestricted accumulation of capital, even if this requires bypassing ethical or legal considerations at some point. Those who adhere to this demand to such an extent that they break the law or act against their own conscience find themselves all the more subjected to the social authority than if the demand didn't include the dimension of transgression. The guilt that the demand engenders in them seals their allegiance. This is the logic of the hazing ritual, which always necessitates a violation of the law or common morality. The demand aims to redirect subjects away from their own enjoyment and toward social productivity. This turn is unimaginable without guilt, which is the fundamental social emotion.

Subjects who sacrifice enjoyment for the sake of recognition do so with the expectation that this sacrifice will pay off on the other side, that the rewards of recognition will surpass the enjoyment that they have given up. This wager seems to have all the empirical evidence on its side: every day, images of the most recognized subjects enjoying themselves bombard us. We see them driving in the nicest cars, eating in the finest restaurants, wearing the most fashionable clothes, and having sex with the most attractive people, among other things. On the other side, we rarely see the enjoyment of those who remain indifferent to the appeal of recognition. By definition, they enjoy in the shadows. What's more, the apparent misery of those who do not receive recognition is readily visible among the social outcasts we silently pass every day. To all appearances, the sacrifice of enjoyment for the sake of recognition is a bargain, as long as one ends up among the most recognized.

The problem with this judgment stems from its emphasis on visibility; it mistakes the display of enjoyment for the real thing. Someone who was authentically enjoying would not need to parade this enjoyment. The authentically enjoying subject does not perform its enjoyment for the Other but remains indifferent to the Other. As Joan Copjec notes, "Jouissance flourishes only there where it is *not* validated by the Other."[20] Enjoyment consumes the subject and directs all of the subject's attention away from the Other's judgment, which is why one cannot perform it and why being a social outcast doesn't bother the enjoying subject. One immerses oneself completely in enjoyment, and the enjoyment suffices for the subject. In contrast, recognition, though it offers its own form of satisfaction, ultimately leaves the subject eager for something else. No matter what level of recognition subjects receive, they always find it insufficient and seek more. Unlike enjoyment, recognition is an infinite struggle.

But no one can make a direct choice of enjoyment instead of recognition. The initial loss of enjoyment, the initial sacrifice, is inevitable. As I have insisted in earlier chapters, this enjoyment only exists insofar as it is lost: there is no way for the subject to avoid altogether the loss of enjoyment for the sake of recognition. But what the subject might avoid is the perpetuation of this abandonment of enjoyment through the embrace of recognition. One can't initially reject recognition, but one can subsequently revisit the original acceptance of the social demand and refuse it by becoming indifferent to recognition's appeal.

Everything in society works against this indifference. The social order receives the energy for its functioning from the enjoyment that subjects sacrifice for the sake of recognition. It continues to operate thanks to a constant influx of enjoyment from those subjected to it. When subjects embrace their own enjoyment rather than readily sacrificing it, they do not contribute to the process of production or reproduction in the social order. Enjoyment has no use value for society, though it organizes and sustains the subject's existence. (The subject who can no longer enjoy loses the will to live altogether.) The goal of the social order as such and the goal of capitalism in particular is the harnessing of the uselessness of the subject's enjoyment and rendering it useful. In order to tighten the social bond and perpetuate the ruling order, society attempts to redirect enjoyment into productivity, but in order to do so, it must convince subjects to sacrifice their enjoyment, to offer it as a tribute for social recognition, which functions as a kind of social cement.

In *The Parallax View,* Slavoj Žižek notes that the image from Andy and Larry Wachowski's *The Matrix* (1999) of human beings as metaphorical batteries feeding the computer system that controls them illustrates perfectly the relationship between the subject and social authority. He explains this in a passage worth citing in its entirety for its suggestiveness:

> Why does the Matrix *need* human energy? A solution purely in terms of energy is, of course, meaningless: the Matrix could easily have found another, more reliable source of energy which would have not demanded the extremely complex arrangement of a virtual reality coordinated for millions of human units. The only consistent answer is: the Matrix feeds on human *jouissance* — so here we are back to the fundamental Lacanian thesis that the big Other itself, far from being an anonymous machine, needs a constant influx of *jouissance.* This is the correct insight of *The Matrix*: the juxtaposition of the two aspects of perversion — on the one hand, the reduction of reality to a virtual domain regulated by arbitrary rules that can be suspended; on the other, the concealed truth of this freedom, the reduction of the subject to an utterly instrumentalized passivity. And the ultimate proof of this decline in quality of subsequent installments of the *Matrix* trilogy is that this central aspect is left totally unexploited: a true revolution would have been a change in the way humans and the Matrix itself relate to *jouissance* and its appropriation. What about, for example, individuals sabotaging the Matrix by refusing to secrete *jouissance*?[21]

The enjoyment that the subject sacrifices feeds social authority, but there is nothing permanently necessary about this sacrifice. The sacrifice is tied to recognition — which is to say, to class status — but one can opt out of the struggle for class status. By opting out of the struggle for class status, one enters into class struggle proper, which as Marx always insists is the struggle for the elimination of social class. But this is an impossible fight.

Class operates in some sense as the original sin of civilization itself, and it prompts Freud to consider that social life is perhaps not worth the suffering that it engenders. In *Civilization and Its Discontents* he notes: "We come upon a contention which is so astonishing that we must dwell upon it. This contention holds that what we call our civilization is largely responsible for our misery, and that we should be much happier if we gave it up and returned to primitive conditions."[22] When we recognize the psychic costs that the social order enacts on us as subjects in the way that Freud does here, it becomes clear that class privilege is not the privilege that it seems to be. The higher that one rises in class status, the more one invests oneself in an order that demands the sacrifice of enjoyment. There is no way around this exigency: subjects cannot simply opt for wealth or class privilege without the corresponding sacrifice of enjoyment that accompanies them because subjects make this sacrifice unconsciously.

If society cannot finally get over social class, we can take up a different relationship to it. Rather than being an ideal to be sought, class status can become a necessary encumbrance that we work to avoid. We can view social recognition in the same way that we view the most thankless tasks that society must perform. But this position becomes all the more difficult in capitalist society, where the investment in recognition infects all social strata, not just the ruling class. This represents the decisive break that capitalism introduces into history, and it marks the fundamental barrier that it erects on the path to adopting a different relation to social class and recognition.

Mastery versus Capitalism

A fundamental difference exists between traditional, precapitalist (and premodern) society and capitalist society in terms of how they deal with enjoyment.[23] Traditional society is structured around a strict division between those who are recognized as members of the society and those who do the work — between master and slave. Though capitalism sustains a difference between the capitalist class and the working class, it levels out the distinction between master and slave so that it no longer signifies ontological difference. The capitalist and the worker both exist within the social structure, while the master's position, in contrast, depends on a more radical exclusion of the slave.

In his analysis of the master/slave dialectic, Hegel sees prestige — what I have called recognition above — as the reward for mastery. What is important in the master/slave relationship for Hegel is not so much who works and who doesn't but the effects of the slave's submission and the master's independence. By agreeing to submit to the dictates of the master, the slave constantly recognizes the master's sense of mastery and thereby provides the master with prestige. The master has a sense of identity that the slave does not have because the service of the slave has the effect of validating this identity, making it concrete rather than abstract, proven rather than merely articulated. As Hegel puts it, "The lord is the consciousness that exists *for itself*, but no longer merely the Notion of such a consciousness. Rather, it is a consciousness existing *for itself* which is mediated with itself through another consciousness."[24] The mediation that the slave provides recognizes the master in her or his mastery, but the master does not reciprocate. The position of the slave is one that lacks symbolic identity.

All that the slave has, according to Hegel's version of this relationship, is work (though this work will eventually become the key to the transcendence of the master/slave relation). The slave's labor, because it is completely done for the master (unlike the labor of the worker under capitalism, which is only partially done for the capitalist), offers no rewards for the slave. No one in this position can hope to find either recognition or enjoyment through labor that belongs to an other. The slave works, and the master enjoys the fruits of this labor.

In fact, Hegel sees the master's enjoyment of the object that the slave produces as the purest type because someone else endures all the toil necessary for it. The problem with such a conclusion stems from its failure to acknowledge how recognition functions as a barrier to enjoyment. In the struggle for recognition, the master wagers her or his enjoyment precisely because it has no value for the master. Unlike the slave, the master finds no satisfaction in her or his own enjoyment, which is why she or he can risk it — with life itself — for the sake of prestige. As a result, the master may eat, wear, or hold what the slave produces, but she or he cannot enjoy it. In assuming the position of mastery and acquiring the recognition that accompanies it, the master makes a fundamental sacrifice of enjoyment that obtaining an object from the slave cannot redeem. The slave, on the other hand, remains free to enjoy, which is what, as Jacques Lacan points out, Hegel fails to see.

Hegel's image of the enjoying master and the working slave misses both the master's lack of enjoyment and the slave's capacity for it. The slave, as Lacan notes in *Seminar XVII*, is "the sole possessor of the means of *jouissance*."[25] Though the master demands work from the slave and appropriates the product of this labor, the master does not steal the slave's enjoyment. The master doesn't try to draw the slave into the prevailing symbolic structure but tries only to keep the slave working. Lacan adds: "[The master] has deprived the slave of the disposal of his body, to be sure, but this is nothing, he has left him his *jouissance*."[26] Not every slave enjoys, but, unlike the master, the slave at least has the possibility for doing so.

While the master invests in the idea of symbolic status and derives an identity from it, the slave can more easily adopt an attitude of indifference toward symbolic identity because this identity in the case of the slave is valueless. Some in the position of the slave identify with the master and retain a sense of identity from that of the master. These types of slaves experience the recognition that the master receives as if they receive it themselves. By doing so, they take the master's path, opting for recognition at the expense of enjoyment. But others, through the attitude of indifference to the master's recognition, are able to enjoy. The slave sacrifices, but this sacrifice, unlike the master's for the sake of prestige, does not preclude the possibility of enjoyment.

Of course, no one would opt for the slave system or a feudal economy over capitalism.[27] The development of capitalist relations of production liberates the slave and the serf from their direct bondage. But there is a cost for this liberation. Unlike the slave, the proletarian loses the capacity to remain outside the master's purview and outside the master's sacrifice of enjoyment. Capitalism eliminates explicit relations of domination — the capitalist and the worker encounter each other as ostensibly free agents, each with something to offer — but it also eliminates the outsider position that the dominated slave occupies.

The continual and unending sacrifice of enjoyment is a structural feature of the capitalist system. Capitalism functions through the capitalist's appropriation of the surplus value that the worker creates. The capitalist pays workers enough to reproduce themselves as a labor force, and though their work creates more value than this, they receive no wages for the labor that creates this additional value. As Marx frames it, workers spend a certain number of hours each day engaged in necessary labor, labor performed to reproduce themselves and the existing social arrangements, and they spend additional hours each day engaged in surplus labor. The sale of commodities produced by necessary labor is used to pay the workers, while the sale of commodities produced by surplus labor is used to enrich the capitalist.

Necessary labor time, for Marx, is the amount of labor we must perform in order to reproduce ourselves. One can think of necessary labor time on an individual level or a societal level. In each case, it constitutes the investment of time necessary for sustaining existence as it is. Surplus labor time, in contrast, is done for the sake of progress. It involves sacrificing time in the present for the sake of creating a better future. There is, in this sense, nothing necessary about it. In the act of performing surplus labor, one spends time working that might otherwise be spent enjoying; one works excessively at the expense of one's enjoyment, which is itself excessive.

The surplus value that surplus labor creates is the way that sacrificed enjoyment manifests itself in the capitalist system, and the universality of the appropriation of surplus value renders this sacrifice inescapable. The process that creates surplus value, as Marx notes, is purely structural: neither the capitalist nor the worker can simply opt out of the production and appropriation of surplus value. No matter the degree of class consciousness that workers develop, as long as they remain within the capitalist system they will continue to produce surplus value, and surplus value is nothing other than the point at which the worker's sacrificed enjoyment manifests itself.

Unlike the slave of antiquity, the worker within the capitalist system necessarily sacrifices enjoyment along with the capitalist. In order to generate surplus value, capitalism requires a sacrifice of enjoyment: surplus value is the manifestation of surplus enjoyment, which is the result of its original sacrifice. Rather than enjoy, the worker enters into the system of capitalist exchange and seeks out recognition through exchange. This system holds out the promise not just of sustenance (like the ancient system did for the slave) but of enrichment — or class status — even for the worker.

Anyone can be a capitalist, and the system demands that everyone act like one in order to get by. It is almost impossible to work within capitalism while remaining detached from the capitalist project of accumulation, and the capitalist system itself constantly offers incentives (such as, perhaps most obviously, retirement plans for workers that require investment in the stock market) to lure workers into a psychic investment. The structural process of the appropriation of the surplus value that the worker generates has a psychic equivalent. Witnessing this appropriation, workers invest themselves in the capitalist process, hoping to recuperate for themselves their lost enjoyment. In the capitalist's profit, workers see their own alienated surplus enjoyment functioning to enrich someone else, and this generates the idea of recovering this value for themselves.

But in the form of surplus value, enjoyment ceases to be enjoyable. Surplus value marks the transformation of enjoyment into a value that one can accumulate. Whereas enjoyment itself resists accumulation because it involves a pure expenditure, an expenditure without reserve, surplus value provides the basis for capitalist accumulation. When workers invest themselves in the idea of reappropriating the surplus value that they have created, they have already abandoned their enjoyment. Whereas the slave remains qualitatively different from the master, capitalism transforms workers into fledgling capitalists; it does not leave them outside the system but includes workers inside through the category of surplus value.

This structural elimination of the outside position within the system betokens an elimination of a site for enjoyment that existed in earlier sociohistorical systems not formed around the appropriation of surplus value. But the transformation does not entail the elimination of enjoyment as such. In fact, it offers a possibility for enjoyment not readily apparent in precapitalist epochs — or a possibility for reconceiving the very idea of enjoyment. The relationship between the master and the slave clearly divides recognition from enjoyment and assigns each to opposing subject positions. As a result, the enjoying subject can enjoy without confronting any internal limit on that enjoyment. Slaves experience a limit to their enjoyment, but this limit is always external, appearing in the form of the master's prohibitions and commands to work.

This situation creates a misleading idea of enjoyment for the slave — its infinite structure appears as only a potential infinite rather than a fully realized one. That is, for the slave, the partiality of today's enjoyment points toward a future enjoyment that would no longer be partial. The slave inevitably recognizes the partiality of enjoyment created by the limit that the master imposes, but she or he envisions a future in which this limit will be lifted, allowing enjoyment to proceed without restriction. This future enjoyment always only exists on the horizon. Within a master/slave economy, enjoyment is an infinite project that one remains within but never realizes. It is potentially infinite, but one doesn't reach this infinite.

Within the capitalist system and its universalization of recognition, no one can continue to enjoy according to this model of the potential infinite. All subjects exist as capitalist subjects, structurally implicated in the demand for recognition (through the appropriation of surplus value). Within capitalist society, recognition becomes that which no one can avoid — a universal that structures subjectivity. If one becomes an enjoying subject, one can do so only by passing through and then rejecting the lure of recognition and class status. One can enjoy only after having initially sacrificed enjoyment in search of recognition. This process reveals the true nature of enjoyment, obscured in precapitalist societies. Enjoyment is never direct but always based on a prior loss or sacrifice. One enjoys through this loss, and thus one enjoys partially.

We can return to Rose in *Titanic* to see an instance of a subject rejecting recognition and opting for enjoyment. After she has been rescued near the end of the film, Rose sits among fellow survivors, whom rescue workers attempt to identify. One asks Rose her name, and she responds, "Rose Dawson," giving the surname of her deceased lover rather than her own. This gesture takes on increased importance in light of our knowledge that her formerly aristocratic family has no money left and only its name as a source of value. By sacrificing this name, by unmooring herself from the social status attached to it, Rose gives up recognition for the sake of enjoyment. Identifying herself with the signifier "Dawson" paradoxically provides a way for Rose to break from the constraints of signification. She enjoys through her sacrifice, and she attains the freedom that would otherwise be impossible within the capitalist system.[28]

After capitalism, we can see that the partiality of today's enjoyment does not point toward a future enjoyment that would be complete. Its partiality is based on an internal necessity: without the loss of its object, the subject cannot enjoy; it enjoys the object only in its absence. This enjoyment, like that of the precapitalist epochs, has an infinite quality to it. But it is a fully realized infinite, an infinite that includes its limit — the necessity of the prior loss — internally, rather than continually moving toward this limit and never reaching it.[29]

On the one hand, capitalist society creates a trap that initially allows no one to escape, but on the other, it creates an opening through which anyone might pass. Amid all the inducements with which the capitalist system bombards the worker, it is structurally almost impossible not to invest oneself initially in the project of accumulating capital and trying to rise in class status. And yet, this is not the path to enjoyment. To give in to the temptation of recognition and class status is to continue to sacrifice one's enjoyment for the sake of the production and reproduction of the social order. The path to enjoyment is much more difficult. It involves resisting the image of enjoyment that social recognition uses to sell itself and focusing on an enjoyment that can't be imagined. This is the real enjoyment that the subject endures rather than performs. It is an enjoyment that generates anxiety and suffering; it is rooted in loss. But at the same time, it is the only enjoyment that leaves the subject satisfied rather than continually seeking a richer experience elsewhere.

4

Sustaining Anxiety

The Paradox of Recognition

Though recognition leaves the subject dependent on social authority and bereft of enjoyment, it nonetheless serves as the means through which subjects invest themselves in the social bond. When the subject seeks the recognition of others, this action bespeaks the rejection of the psychotic alternative, which involves the foreclosure of the social bond and the refusal of the binding restrictions that other subjects accept. In this sense, we might consider recognition a good. Perhaps the pursuit of recognition, despite its unseemliness and despite the sacrifice it involves, has an ethical dimension. It allows subjects to transcend merely private enjoyment and concern themselves with the well-being of others in the society.

Subjects seeking recognition are constantly trying to improve their social status, but they are also trying to find ways to please others. Though their motivations are not pure, they do bring others some degree of happiness. For instance, when a student compliments a professor on his sense of fashion, the professor knows on some level that the student's comment has its genesis in the quest for recognition, but it still has the ability to make the professor feel some amount of pleasure.[1] By emphasizing the cost of recognition for the subject seeking it, psychoanalysis seems to overlook its positive effect. Recognition involves submission to the symbolic authority, and this submission forges a connection.

There is a certain reading of Hegel that aligns his moral philosophy with the celebration of recognition. In the *Phenomenology of Spirit* Hegel affirms the role of the other's recognition in the emergence of subjectivity.

Without this recognition, the subject remains caught up in an illusory sense of its own isolation and unable to find a satisfying identity.[2] This is why the struggle between the master and the slave, where the stake is nothing but prestige (or recognition), marks a significant advance for the subject. In this struggle, the subject realizes its dependence on the other's recognition, even though the master and slave cannot properly recognize each other. In the later stages of the dialectic, recognition finds a form adequate to it in the spiritual community, and at this point, subjectivity arrives at its ethical terminus.

For a liberal thinker like John Rawls, Hegel's conception of the ethical role that the quest for recognition plays is the key to his worth as a moral philosopher. Hegel's great contribution, his advance beyond Kant, lies in his ability to link recognition — that is, social conformity — to ethical duty. He conceives of a social rather than an individualist ethical program. As Rawls says, "Hegel wants us to find our moral compass in the institutions and customs of our social world itself, as these institutions and customs have been made part of us as we grow up into them and develop habits of thought and action accordingly."[3] By seeking recognition, Rawls contends (or believes that Hegel contends), we initiate ourselves, perhaps even unconsciously, into the ethical position that best corresponds to our social world. Rather than marking an ethical nadir (our desire to give up our autonomy and become dependent on social authority), seeking recognition forms the basis for our ethical subjectivity.[4]

The problem with this reading of Hegel (which is in no way confined to Rawls and is in fact nearly the dominant reading) stems from its inability to come to grips with Hegel's insight into the ultimate failure of recognition.[5] Though the search for recognition inaugurates subjectivity, recognition can never apprehend the subject in its singularity. Recognition reduces the subject to a symbolic identity — I am recognized as a professional, as a parent, as an American, and so on — and thus completely misses the subject's uniqueness, what in the subject is irreducible to determinate symbolic coordinates, even if this uniqueness is finally nothing more than a fantasy (or the subject's singular mode of fantasizing).

The failure operates in the other direction as well: the subject who seeks the other's recognition does not address itself to the real other but only to a symbolic entity that exists only as a construction of the signifier. Even when we seek the recognition of an actual person, what gives value to this recognition is its authorization by social authority, which is itself wholly unauthorized. The search for recognition cannot have any ethical status whatsoever because it involves submission to an entity that exists only through the act of submitting to it.[6]

When the subject seeks recognition, it devotes itself to becoming someone in the eyes of social authority, and the search for recognition validates this authority. But at no point does the subject actually encounter the real other, the other as such. Encountering the real other, the other that several thinkers have christened the "neighbor," requires turning away from social authority and abandoning the project of recognition.[7] At the point where the subject does not experience social recognition, it discovers the neighbor. As Kenneth Reinhard explains, the neighbor "materializes an uncanniness within the social relationship, an enjoyment that resists sympathetic identification and 'understanding.'"[8] The experience of recognition obscures this uncanniness and mediates the other's enjoyment in order to render it more palpable for the subject. But in the process, recognition allows the subject to avoid the neighbor or the real other.

The encounter with the real other is the key to the subject's ethical being and to the subject's enjoyment. Psychoanalysis allows us to see the foundational link that exists between ethics and enjoyment, where other approaches erect a clear divide between the two. Ethics, for most ways of thinking, involves a sacrifice of my own enjoyment for the sake of someone else's. Rather than lying to get ahead at work, I tell the truth to help create a more pleasant workplace atmosphere. Rather than devoting all my free time to watching pornography, I spend part of it working at the food bank. For Spinoza in his *Ethics*, I become ethical when I cease thinking from my own private perspective and approach an *Amor intellectualis Dei*, or "intellectual love of God," in which I can think in terms of the whole of creation rather than simply view isolated events from my limited perspective. This movement from the private and self-interested to the public and concerned for the whole defines almost every ethical project. But psychoanalytic thought does not conceive of ethics in this way. It is through enjoyment itself, not the sacrifice of it, that I genuinely encounter the other. An insistence on enjoyment is at the same time an insistence on ethical subjectivity.

The neighbor or real other is the enjoying other. The other's mode of enjoyment marks the other as absolutely singular. Everything else about the other — emotions, thoughts, desires, achievements, and so on — can be understood and communicated through the order of signification or language. We can share all these experiences through the mediation of the signifier, which informs them in their very origin. The other's enjoyment, unlike everything else about the other, disturbs us when we encounter it because it does not take us into account. While the other's symbolic identity includes us as the source of the look that validates it, the other's enjoyment not only ignores us but seems to go so far as to occur at our expense. When we encounter the enjoying other, we experience our own isolation, our own absolute insignificance for the other.

The encounter with the enjoying other occurs at moments when a radical cut emerges between the other and the subject. Events such as basketball games and rock concerts allow spectators to identify with the enjoyment that they see and thereby to avoid the trauma of the encounter with the other's enjoyment. In contrast, the shared laughter of people speaking a foreign language, the rumor of an orgy at a secret society, or the strange noises that a toddler hears behind the closed door of the parental bedroom do not provide any opening to the outsider. One hears the enjoyment without any possibility of partaking in it through the act of identification, and one almost inevitably imagines that one's exclusion is part of the enjoyment. The distinction between an enjoying other enjoying itself at my expense and an enjoying other indifferent to me becomes negligible. The pertinent fact is the other's enjoyment that doesn't include me.

Beyond the Demand

In traditional social arrangements, societies confront subjects with demands, and subjects respond by attempting either to follow the demands or to seek the desire of the social authority that the demand hides. The former path is the neurotic one: by sticking to the authority's demand, the neurotic hopes to gain its recognition. The problem is that what the authority demands is not what it necessarily desires. As we saw in the last chapter, there is no demand that doesn't conceal — or seem to conceal, which for the subject amounts to the same thing — a desire. The project of securing the social authority's recognition always runs aground on the ineffability of its desire and the irreducibility of this desire to an articulated demand. The irreducibility of desire to demand leaves subjects confronted by a social demand with the choice between these two paths.[9]

This fundamental choice that defines our subjectivity has almost fully disappeared in contemporary capitalist society. While many of the dramatic changes that have recently taken place (the Internet revolution, the globalization of the economy, the emergence of hybrid subjectivities) create illusory movement and leave underlying social structures intact, the turn away from the dialectic of demand and desire represents a substantive transformation in the way that subjects experience their social existence. Subjects today do not encounter a clear demand from social authority, and consequently they also do not confront the secret of the authority's desire beneath this demand.[10]

Instead of a clear demand prohibiting the subject's private enjoyment and exhorting a contribution to the public good, the subject receives inducements to enjoy itself from a variety of authority figures. Authority's demands are no longer demands in the traditional sense, and they do not appear to conceal anything. Rather than hiding its desire, authority publicly flaunts its enjoyment and encourages the subject to do the same.[11] From Charlie Sheen's rants about his status as a "winner" to Nicolas Sarkozy's marriage to a supermodel to Silvio Berlusconi's open displays of corruption, figures of authority today parade their enjoyment and issue an implicit imperative for others to do the same. As a result, the subject does not face a choice between sticking to the explicit demand or seeking the hidden desire but rather the choice between trying to obey the imperative to enjoy or searching for the missing demand hidden somewhere in the social fabric. This is the choice between the position of the pathological narcissist and that of the fundamentalist, and it defines our era.

In contrast to the traditional social structure founded on the demands of a strong paternal authority, today's structure utilizes a new form of paternal authority, and this new authority has clear consequences for our relationship to enjoyment. This transformation bears directly on the ability of paternal authority to shield subjects from enjoyment. Traditional authority figures ruled through prohibition: they demanded that subjects sacrifice their enjoyment for admittance into the social order. This type of paternal authority governs through the establishing of distance — distance between the authority figure and the subject, as well as distance between the subject and enjoyment. The new authority, however, abandons distance for the sake of proximity. Rather than confronting us with an impenetrable demand that remains out of our comprehension, he assaults us with displays of his enjoyment.

The new authority rarely appears in the guise of an authority, but this, ironically, garners all the more power for him. As Slavoj Žižek points out, "Today's boss or father ... insists that we should treat him as a friend; he addresses us with intrusive familiarity, bombarding us with sexual innuendos, inviting us to share a drink or a vulgar joke," and as a result, "we are deprived even of the private space of irony and mockery, since the master is on both levels: an authority as well as a friend."[12] The proximity of the contemporary paternal authority deprives the subject of any space for private respite, and at the same time, it confronts the subject with its own obscene enjoyment.

What results is not a traditional subject of desire, a subject struggling with lack, but a subject wrestling with a disturbing presence. This is why, according to Eric Santner, contemporary anxiety is an anxiety "not of absence and loss but of overproximity, loss of distance to some obscene and malevolent presence."[13] Authority has become too close, and its obscenity has become visible. The transformation of paternal authority — a turn from the prohibition of enjoyment to a command that subjects enjoy themselves — fundamentally alters the subject's relation not just to authority itself but to the other as such.

Whereas prohibition creates a social authority that exists at a distance from the subject — or that installs distance within all of the subject's relationships — the absence of an explicit prohibition leaves the contemporary subject in the proximity of a real other. The social field of prohibition is a terrain stripped of all enjoyment where everyone is reduced to the form of symbolic identity. Without this terrain (which is the contemporary situation), one encounters the other beyond its symbolic identity, the enjoying other. It is others listening to music with their headphones, talking loudly on a cell phone, eating excessive amounts of food, communicating in an unknown language, or emitting an unusual odor.[14] Public displays of enjoyment occur with increasing frequency today because the dominant form of authority does not function through prohibition. Rather than violating the ruling social imperative, the public display of enjoyment heeds it. The result is rampant anxiety. Without the distance from the other requisite for desire, one experiences the anxiety produced by its presence.

Though a contemporary society that bombards us with the enjoying other is markedly different from traditional societies that prohibit public displays of enjoyment in order to sustain a public bond, there is a sense in which the current situation represents the truth of traditional societies. Just as Marx sees capitalism as revealing the truth of all hitherto existing social forms (specifically the structuring role that economy played), the society ruled by the imperative to enjoy lays bare the truth of all previous societies ruled by prohibition.

Through restrictions on enjoyment, these societies covered over the real encounter between the enjoying subject and the enjoying other. Nonetheless, even when the symbolic relation mediates this real encounter, it continues to mark the ultimate stake in social relations insofar as it occupies the limit point of all social relations, the point that social relations cannot include. In traditional societies, just as in contemporary society, the fundamental question remains the same for the subject, and it concerns the relationship that the subject takes up to anxiety.[15] The ethical position, for psychoanalysis, necessarily involves the embrace of this anxiety — and this is at once the path to enjoyment.

Taking a Short Cut

As the public presence of the enjoying other has become more prevalent, a series of films has appeared to document the transformation. These films depict multiple lives interacting through numerous apparently random encounters. The encounters take place without the mediation of a public world or symbolic structure, so that characters experience the encounters as violent shocks involving the enjoying other. The interactions that these films depict make clear the problem of the enjoying other and its tendency to produce anxiety in the subject. Paul Thomas Anderson's *Magnolia* (1999) and Paul Haggis's *Crash* (2004) are part of this new type of filmmaking, but Robert Altman's *Short Cuts* (1993) inaugurated the form and remains its exemplar.

The primary aim of Altman's film is to perform a rudimentary version of what Fredric Jameson calls cognitive mapping.[16] Through cognitive mapping, we transcend our individual isolation and gain a sense of the socioeconomic terrain on which we find ourselves. The connection between our seemingly independent activity and the activities of others becomes evident. Altman accomplishes this in *Short Cuts* through the contingent encounters between characters that reveal the underlying social bonds linking them together. Here, contingency functions as the form in which necessity appears: the film asks us to reread our contingent encounters in order to identify the necessity that underlies them. By doing so, we might break through the trap of our individual isolation and see the connection between our activity and that of others.

But if spectators are able to make this break, few of the characters in the film do. The connection to the other remains invisible to the characters in the film because almost every encounter with the other is an encounter with the enjoying other. The bond that unites the characters on the level of their subjective experience is the proximity of the real or enjoying other. This manifests itself when Gene (Tim Robbins), a motorcycle police officer, tries to seduce Claire (Anne Archer) during a routine traffic stop; when Gordon (Buck Henry), Vern (Huey Lewis), and Stuart (Fred Ward) repeatedly ask their server, Doreen (Lily Tomlin), for butter so that they can look up her skirt as she bends over; and when a drunken Andy Bitkower (Lyle Lovett) makes threatening phone calls to Ann Finnigan (Andie MacDowell) as her son lies unconscious in the hospital, to name just a few. The specter of the enjoying other colors almost every interaction in the film, and it has the effect of creating a level of anxiety that few can bear.

The encounter with the enjoying other in *Short Cuts* occurs both in public interactions and intimate ones within the domestic sphere. By depicting these encounters taking place everywhere in contemporary society, Altman reveals that the family is not what Christopher Lasch calls a "haven in a heartless world" but rather a redoubling of that heartless external world. At the very moment when characters want to retreat from the pressure of the enjoying other into a domestic space free of anxiety, they find the enjoying other appearing in an even more inescapable form. This becomes most apparent through the character of Gene, the motorcycle cop. At home, we see him constantly bombarded by screaming kids and a yapping dog, but when he leaves home to be with his lover, Betty (Frances McDormand), he must struggle with the enjoyment that she seems to be having without him.

Wherever he turns, the real other lurks, and his own illicit enjoyment — his affair — never seems equal in his mind to that of the other.

Altman not only tries to show the unbearable nature of the enjoyment of the other for other characters within the film but also confronts the spectator with the image of the enjoying other in all its overwhelming presence. This occurs throughout the film, but most pointedly in two key scenes. In the first, Paul Finnigan (Jack Lemmon) recounts at length his infidelity with his wife's sister, which led to his estrangement from both his wife and his son, Howard (Bruce Davison), to whom he tells the story. Having not seen his son for twenty-five years, Paul shows up at the hospital where Howard's son — Paul's grandson — lies unconscious after being hit by a car. Paul wants to explain the estrangement to Howard, but it is clear that Howard has no desire to hear the explanation. Not only does Paul continue to tell his story despite Howard's lack of interest, but he describes the sexual encounter with Howard's aunt in great detail, including the fact that Howard's mother found them in bed together. Altman films most of this narrative with long takes of Paul speaking in close-up. He only cuts in order to show an occasional reverse shot of Howard, and each of these shots emphasizes Howard's discomfort through his expressions or gestures. With Howard, the spectator must endure Paul's display of his enjoyment (in both the content of the story and its form — the inappropriate telling of it).

In the second such scene, Altman films a lengthy shot of Marian Wyman (Julianne Moore) arguing with her husband, Ralph (Matthew Modine), while she wears a top but no skirt or underwear. As is the case in the scene with Paul and Howard, here Marian is confessing an infidelity, and the spectator experiences the confrontation with her enjoyment just as Ralph does (who is having his suspicions confirmed for the first time). But Marian's state of undress adds an intensity to the production of anxiety in this scene. She spills a drink on her skirt and removes it in order to clean it. As she does, Ralph recognizes that she isn't wearing underwear, even though they have guests coming. In the extended shot in the middle of her explanation, Marian is wearing just a top that comes down each leg, exposing and even framing her pubic hair. Though the shot doesn't eroticize Marian's nudity, her nonchalance about it — and the fact that she isn't wearing underwear — adds to the sense that she is teeming with enjoyment, and

Altman gives the spectator, like Ralph, no respite from it. Altman depicts the exposed Marian offering the explanation for her illicit enjoyment in a long take, so that the spectator must endure her inappropriate nudity and her uncomfortable revelation simultaneously.[17]

Though *Short Cuts* focuses on the anxiety-provoking effects of the encounter with the enjoying other on the subject, it also reveals that the subject's experience of the other's enjoyment is quite often deceptive. That is to say, subjects believe they witness the other awash in enjoyment when in fact the enjoyment is nothing but a performance. One of the most memorable figures in the film, Lois Kaiser (Jennifer Jason Leigh), stands out because she reveals this distance between the appearance of enjoyment and the reality of her life. She works out of her home as a phone sex operator, and throughout the film, she provides phone sex service for her clients while working as a mother. In one scene, she describes performing oral sex on her client while she changes her daughter's diaper. Her sultry description of her completely imaginary sexual activity contrasts radically with what we see in the visual field. There is enjoyment here in word only, as we can't help but see.

The problem is that even when subjects become aware that the other is performing enjoyment, the suspicion remains that some real enjoyment nonetheless exists hidden in the performance.[18] This is why one could watch *Short Cuts* in the afternoon and call a phone sex hotline in the evening. This suspicion of a real underlying enjoyment is clearly evident in the case of Jerry (Chris Penn), Lois's husband, who sees her total lack of arousal in phone sex and yet believes that she must be experiencing some enjoyment in order to produce the words that she does. More than any other character in the film, Jerry feels the pressure of the enjoying other. His wife is a phone sex operator, his best friend, Bill (Robert Downey Jr.), is constantly making sexual comments to him, and he works cleaning swimming pools for clients much wealthier than himself. Unable to bear the anxiety that all this surrounding enjoyment produces, he finally strikes out with violence at the end of the film. After she resists his advances, Jerry brutally kills one of the girls that he and Bill have pursued while picnicking in the park. Altman reveals this act as the manifestation of the anxiety that the encounter with the enjoying other produces.

While most contemporary subjects don't smash rocks over the heads of those who provoke anxiety in them, the conclusion of *Short Cuts* is nonetheless revelatory. Much (physical and psychic) violence today occurs in response to the anxiety of the encounter with the enjoying other. Both the violence of the fundamentalist suicide bomber and the violence of the War on Terror have their origins in the experience of anxiety. Suicide bombers target sites of decadent Western enjoyment — bars, clubs, discos, the World Trade Center, and so on — in order to create a world where this enjoyment would return to the shadows and thereby cease to provoke anxiety. The true fundamentalist dreams about being able to desire once again with some respite from the proximate object and the anxiety it creates. But the actions of the suicide bomber, for their part, produce anxiety in the Western subject that leads directly to the phenomenon of the War on Terror.[19]

The anxiety that suicide bombers create does not stem from the purely existential threat that they pose. Unlike the Western subjects that they threaten, suicide bombers appear to enjoy through their belief. They believe so fervently that they are willing to sacrifice themselves: they have full confidence that they will receive an eternal reward of seventy-two virgins for their sacrifice. Confronted with this seemingly authentic belief, the cynical Western subject for whom belief is always belief at one remove almost inevitably experiences anxiety. After the September 11 attacks, the focus on the eternal reward that the suicide bombers believed they would receive indicates the relationship between anxiety about terrorism and anxiety generated by the encounter with the enjoying other. The suicide bomber enjoys — both through unquestioning belief and through the anticipation of the eternal reward — and it is this enjoyment that struck the towers on September 11, 2001. The War on Terror, which aims to wipe out all suicide bombers, has as its ultimate goal the elimination of this enjoyment and the anxiety that follows from it.

Both the suicide bomber and the perpetuators of the War on Terror make the same mistake that Jerry does in *Short Cuts* when he watches his spouse work as a phone sex operator. They see an enjoying other where there is nothing but the image of enjoyment. The suicide bomber sees Western women in revealing clothes and believes that the bare skin promises an opening to enjoyment, but this represents a failure to understand that enjoyment operates through limitations and barriers rather than through revelations and transgressions. One can never go far enough in the direction of transgression to reach real enjoyment. It is the veil, not the miniskirt, that is the true garment of enjoyment.[20] The enjoying Western other is the enjoying other of the suicide bombers themselves, not the enjoying other in itself. No number of successful attacks will dissipate this enjoyment because they can never hit its real source within the attacking subject itself.

The perpetuators and supporters of the War on Terror view suicide bombers as true believers in pursuit of the ultimate enjoyment. This is why the idea of the seventy-two virgins receives so much attention as the reason for the fundamentalists' willingness to die for their cause. Though the reward of the seventy-two virgins for the martyr has almost no basis in the Koran or in Islamic theology, people in the West repeat this justification for the suicide bombing because it fits within the fantasy of the enjoying other, a fantasy also furthered by the common perception that the Islamic fundamentalists, unlike most of us in the West, are true believers.

Belief constitutes the source of their danger and their enjoyment. But the act of blowing oneself up for a cause in no way testifies to the completeness of one's belief. As Pascal sees, acting as if one believes functions as a way of securing the belief of one who is not certain. The dramatic act is almost inevitably an attempt to prove to oneself that one believes rather than evidence for that belief. The subjects who have to sacrifice themselves for the cause most often have to do so in order to avoid losing faith in the cause. In short, the danger lies not in the true believer — the authentically enjoying other — but in the one who wants to believe but cannot. The violence of the War on Terror strikes out at the wrong target insofar as it aims at the true believer. The suicide bomber is not so different from the typical Western subject: both experience enjoyment assaulting them from the outside in the form of the enjoying other, and both seek ways of eradicating this enjoyment with violence before it becomes overwhelming.

The problem with violence as a solution to anxiety is not just that it would beget more violence and lead to a war of all against all but that it doesn't work. Violence can kill the other, but it can't destroy the other's enjoyment. In fact, often the death of the other has the effect of appearing to increase the level of enjoyment rather than destroying it, which is why violence never provides a definitive solution for the one who perpetuates it. Not only does the idea of the enjoying other persist for the subject after the other's death, but this same enjoyment often proliferates and manifests itself elsewhere. This occurs in David Lynch films such as *Lost Highway* (1997) and *Mulholland Drive* (2001), though it appears most pointedly in the *Twin Peaks* (1990–91) television series.

The series revolves around the mysterious death of Laura Palmer (Sheryl Lee), who is at once a prom queen, volunteer for Meals on Wheels, drug user, and prostitute. Laura's contradictory identity leads all the other characters in the show to see her as a cipher for their own ideas about enjoyment. She acts as the embodiment of the enjoying other. Inhabited by what seems to be a supernatural force, her father, Leland, kills her before the series begins. But Lynch (and cocreator Mark Frost) shows Laura's enjoyment returning in the figure of her cousin, Madeleine Ferguson (also played by Sheryl Lee). By having the same actor play both Laura and her cousin, Madeleine, Lynch stresses the continuity of the enjoyment that they convey. Leland must murder his niece in the same manner as his daughter, and the series gives no indication that this cycle of violence would ever end without his capture by the police. In fact, Lynch depicts Leland being inhabited by a supernatural force precisely in order to stress the insatiable nature of this type of violence.

The violence that targets the enjoying other is insatiable not just because the other's enjoyment cannot be destroyed but because the real goal of the violence is not eliminating this enjoyment but sustaining it. Suicide bombers attacking sites of decadent Western enjoyment do not want to eliminate that enjoyment any more than the perpetuators of the War on Terror want to put an end to the obscene enjoyment of Islamic fundamentalism. In each case, the violence has the effect of producing more outbursts of the enjoyment it professes to want to curtail. George W. Bush's invasion of Iraq made that country into a hotbed of Islamic terrorism, just as the September 11 attack aroused Western displays of violent enjoyment. If Bush and the fundamentalists were acting as enemy agents, they could not have been more effective at realizing the opposite of their stated goals. But these are not simply unwanted side effects of the violence. Violence directed at the enjoying other succeeds by failing: its failures to wipe out the enjoying other stimulate the other and thus produce even greater images of enjoyment.

But murderous violence directed toward the enjoying other is not, of course, the only alternative. Even within *Short Cuts*, Altman depicts several different responses to the experience of anxiety. Most often, we flee this experience through an attempt to reestablish the distance from enjoyment that social authority no longer provides. We see this effort to construct an alternate form of social mediation in many of the film's other characters. But there remains a third possibility: one might embrace the experience of anxiety as an ethical and political choice.

Anxiety as Ethics

It was Martin Heidegger who first conceived of an ethical dimension to the experience of anxiety. For Heidegger, anxiety differs from fear because it does not center on any particular object. Whereas the particular nature of all our fears allows us to eliminate them by eluding the object giving rise to them, anxiety allows for no such respite and thus reveals something constitutive about our existence. That is to say, the inescapable and universal quality of anxiety gives it its revelatory power. In "What Is Metaphysics?" Heidegger defines precisely what anxiety shows us when he insists: "Anxiety reveals the nothing."[21] In the experience of anxiety, the subject confronts the horror of nothing — the fact that there is no secure foundation for the subject's own being or for any beings in the world, that the subject remains "held out into the nothing."[22] As a result of its revelation of the nothing, anxiety creates an awareness of a fundamental openness that our ordinary experience closes off.

The ethical dimension of anxiety stems from its ability to expose the subject's radical independence and freedom — its lack of foundation in the social order and that order's own lack of foundation. The revelation of the nothing that occurs during the experience of anxiety frees the subject from its dependence on the social order, which is why Heidegger says that "without the original revelation of the nothing, no selfhood and no freedom."[23] If the nothing is the only basis for the subject, then this basis is only a nonbasis, and, in fact, the subject has no basis in any actual societal structure. Although the experience of anxiety does not bring the subject pleasure, it does reveal the subject's freedom because it involves this traumatic confrontation with the nothing. When one experiences anxiety, one ceases to be preoccupied with one's place in society or with the opinions of others.

Freud's definition of anxiety shares the same basic structure that Heidegger lays out, though Freud figures this structure in psychic rather than ontological terms. For Freud, anxiety primarily concerns castration: subjects experience anxiety when they enter a situation that confronts them with their lack, as the example of Little Hans illustrates. Little Hans developed a horse phobia in order to avoid encountering the castrating power of the father, which his neurosis relocated in the figure of the horse in order to render it avoidable. Castration is the nothing that generates the subject, and the encounter with it traumatizes the subject in the same way that the encounter with the existential nothing does.

There is, however, a different way of thinking about anxiety. Despite his kinship with Heidegger on so many points, Jacques Lacan defines anxiety in precisely the opposite way. For Lacan, anxiety does not involve a confrontation with absence — with what Heidegger calls the nothing — but with an overwhelming presence. Though the experience of castration establishes the scene where anxiety will play out, castration alone does not generate anxiety in the subject. The absence or nothingness that castration produces can have the effect of reassuring the subject: it provides the subject with a sense of distance from the other and breathing space for itself. The trauma of the rupture it occasions has a pacifying reverse side.

We experience anxiety when the absence that castration produces — the lost object, or *objet petit a* — ceases to be an absence. As Lacan puts it in his seminar devoted to the topic of anxiety, "It is this sudden appearance of lack in a positive form that is the source of anxiety."[24] We expect the absence that is the lost object, but we encounter a field of representation where this gap has been filled.

Social authority appears nonlacking and ubiquitous, never allowing the subject the space to desire. Lacan says, "The possibility of absence makes up the security of presence. What is most anxiety-provoking for the child is precisely when the relationship on which he sets himself up, the relationship which makes him desire, is disrupted; it is the most disrupted when there is no possibility of lack, when the mother is all the time on his back, and especially when she is wiping his ass, which is the model of the demand that cannot fail."[25] The total presence of the authority leads to anxiety because the child in this situation has no distance from the other's enjoyment. This situation proliferates from the parent/child relation to every social relation. The other's private enjoyment — its smell, its way of talking, its gestures — ceaselessly bombards the subject. This is an assault that occurs all the time in the contemporary social world.

During Clarence Thomas's confirmation hearing or Bill Clinton's impeachment trial, private enjoyment became a normal part of public discourse. The details of Thomas's alleged sexual harassment of Anita Hill and of Clinton's sexual involvement with Monica Lewinsky were a regular topic of discussion in newspapers, on the nightly news, and throughout the culture. At the time, one could find no respite from the obscene enjoyment of Thomas and Clinton, which had the effect of triggering anxiety — and calls for cleansing the public space by rejecting Thomas or impeaching Clinton — in large portions of the populace. But these celebrated cases only testify to a larger social phenomenon that occurs on a quotidian level today, though one can see it emerging even in the 1950s, the decade supposedly marked by strong paternal authority.

Though critics often dismiss the reductive Freudianism of Nicholas Ray's *Rebel without a Cause* (1955), it nonetheless exemplifies in a traditional way how the other's excessive presence produces anxiety.[26] The film stands as a cultural landmark for its expression of teen angst through the central character Jim Stark (James Dean). His anxiety stems not from an existential experience of nothingness but from the overzealous attention of his parents and the proximity of their displays of enjoyment. Jim's famous cry at the police station early in the film — "You're tearing me apart!" — represents his initial effort to escape the anxiety, but the final escape occurs during the film's denouement in a planetarium, where, with his friends, he finds freedom from anxiety at the site where earlier they witnessed a show on the vast nothingness and indifference of space. Rather than causing anxiety, nothingness in *Rebel without a Cause* functions as its cure.

The most common strategy for escaping the anxiety that inheres in today's subjectivity is the recourse to cynicism. The cynic adopts a posture of nonchalance toward the enjoyment of the other, seeing this enjoyment as nothing special. For the cynic, there is no such thing as real enjoyment, no object that has more value than any other. Cynicism allows the subject to see through the fiction of the impossible object and to see it as just another everyday object. For example, Diogenes, the parent figure of cynicism, masturbates in public in order to demonstrate that activities seemingly laden with enjoyment (like masturbation) are really just everyday affairs.

Through this transformation, the subject avoids the anxiety that emerges from its encounter with the enjoying other. To the extent that it works as it hopes to work, cynicism produces a world free of anxiety because it produces a world bereft of enjoyment.

But as theorists of contemporary cynicism have shown, cynical subjects don't really sustain a thoroughgoing cynicism relative to enjoyment. While they disbelieve in the possibility of enjoyment or authentic commitment, they do believe in belief. That is, they believe that there are others who really believe. Despite the cynical knowledge that this belief is false, the cynical subject does believe in the enjoyment that comes from belief, and as a result, cynicism doesn't offer the respite from anxiety that it initially promises.

Unlike cynicism, the opposite strategy — the attempt to restore prohibition and paternal law — involves an avowal of the lost object and its ability to deliver enjoyment. We try to create the requisite distance from enjoyment through our various efforts to resurrect prohibition, to return to the reign of traditional symbolic authority. These efforts most often take the form of various fundamentalisms. One of the chief appeals of fundamentalism is its promise to reintroduce a barrier to enjoyment into the experience of contemporary subjectivity. By reintroducing this barrier, fundamentalism promises to keep anxiety at bay, to allow us to attain some distance from the enjoying other.

But like cynicism, efforts to restore prohibition end up returning the subject to the situation of anxiety rather than providing relief. Contemporary fundamentalism derives its energy not from the idea of restricting enjoyment but from the idea of unleashing it. It promises increased enjoyment through restriction, and it delivers on this promise, though in doing so it produces even more anxiety. As fundamentalism restores prohibitions, it creates more intense sites of enjoyment. Whereas the cynical subject sees no enjoyment in the revelation of an almost-naked body, the fundamentalist subject sees enjoyment proliferating with the baring of a small patch of skin. In a world of anxiety, even the attempt to create distance has the effect of creating more enjoyment. Both cynicism and fundamentalism emerge in response to the contemporary subject's anxious proximity to the present object. Both see distance from the enjoyment of the other as the only possible solution to the experience of anxiety.

The alternative — the ethical path that psychoanalysis identifies — demands an embrace of the anxiety that stems from the encounter with the enjoying other. If there is a certain ethical dimension to anxiety, it lies in the relationship that exists between anxiety and enjoyment. Contra Heidegger, the ethics of anxiety does not stem from anxiety's relation to absence but from its relation to presence — to the overwhelming presence of the other's enjoyment. In some sense, the encounter with absence or nothing is easier than the encounter with presence. Even though it traumatizes us, absence allows us to constitute ourselves as desiring subjects. Rather than producing anxiety, absence leads the subject out of anxiety into desire. Confronted with the lost object as a structuring absence, the subject is able to embark on the pursuit of the enjoyment embodied by this object, and this pursuit provides the subject with a clear sense of direction and even meaning. This is precisely what the subject lacks when it does not encounter a lack in the symbolic structure. When the subject encounters enjoyment at the point where it should encounter the absence of enjoyment, anxiety overwhelms the subject.

In this situation, the subject cannot constitute itself along the path of desire. It lacks the lack — the absence — that would provide the space through which desire could develop. Consequently, this subject confronts the enjoying other and experiences anxiety. Unlike the subject of desire — or the subject of Heideggerean anxiety — the subject who suffers this sort of anxiety actually experiences the other in its real dimension.

The real other is the other caught up in its obscene enjoyment, caught up in this enjoyment in a way that intrudes on the subject. There is no safe distance from this enjoyment, and one cannot simply avoid it. There is nowhere in the contemporary world to hide from it. As a result, the contemporary subject is necessarily a subject haunted by anxiety triggered by the omnipresent enjoyment of the other. And yet, this enjoyment offers us an ethical possibility. As Slavoj Žižek puts it, "It is *this* excessive and intrusive *jouissance* that we should learn to tolerate."[27] When we tolerate the other's "excessive and intrusive *jouissance*" and when we endure the anxiety that it produces, we acknowledge and sustain the other in its real dimension.

Tolerance is the ethical watchword of our epoch. However, the problem with contemporary tolerance is its insistence on tolerating the other only insofar as the other cedes its enjoyment and accepts the prevailing symbolic structure. That is to say, we readily tolerate the other in its symbolic dimension, the other that plays by the rules of our game. This type of tolerance allows the subject to feel good about itself and to sustain its symbolic identity. The problem is that, at the same time, it destroys what is in the other more than the other — the particular way that the other enjoys.

It is only the encounter with the other in its real dimension — the encounter that produces anxiety in the subject — that sustains that which defines the other as such. Authentic tolerance tolerates the real other, not simply the other as mediated through a symbolic structure. In this sense, it involves the experience of anxiety on the part of the subject. This is a difficult position to sustain, as it involves enduring the "whole opaque weight of alien enjoyment on your chest."[28] The obscene enjoyment of the other bombards the authentically tolerant subject, but this subject does not retreat from the anxiety that this enjoyment produces.

Whose Enjoyment?

If the embrace of the anxiety that accompanies the other's proximate enjoyment represents the ethical position today, this does not necessarily provide us with an incentive for occupying it. Who wants to be ethical when it involves enduring anxiety rather than finding a way — a drug, a new authority, or something — to alleviate it? What good does it do to sustain oneself in anxiety? In fact, anxiety does the subject no good at all, which is why it offers the subject the possibility of enjoyment. When the subject encounters the other's enjoyment, this is the form that its own enjoyment takes as well. To endure the anxiety caused by the other's enjoyment is to experience one's own simultaneously. As Lacan points out, when it comes to the enjoyment of the other and my own enjoyment, "nothing indicates they are distinct."[29] Thus, not only is anxiety an ethical position, it is also the key to embracing the experience of enjoyment. To reject the experience of anxiety is to flee one's own enjoyment.

The notion that the other's enjoyment is also our own enjoyment seems at first glance difficult to accept. Few people enjoy themselves when they hear someone else screaming profanities in the workplace or when they see a couple passionately kissing in public, to take just two examples. In these instances, we tend to recoil at the inappropriateness of the activity rather than enjoy it, and this reaction seems completely justified. The public display of enjoyment violates the social pact with its intrusiveness; it doesn't let us alone but assaults our senses. It violates the implicit agreement of the public sphere constituted as an enjoyment-free zone. And yet, recoiling from the other's enjoyment deprives us of our own.

How we comport ourselves in relation to the other's enjoyment indicates our relationship to our own. What bothers us about the other — the disturbance that the other's enjoyment creates in our existence — is our own mode of enjoying. If we did not derive enjoyment from the other's enjoyment, witnessing it would not bother us psychically. We would simply be indifferent to it and focused on our own concerns. Of course, we might ask an offending car radio listener to turn the radio down so that we wouldn't have to hear the unwanted music, but we would not experience the mere exhibition of alien enjoyment through the playing of that music as an affront. The very fact that the other's enjoyment captures our attention demonstrates our intimate — or extimate — relation to it.[30]

This relation becomes even clearer when we consider the epistemological status of the enjoying other. Because the real or enjoying other is irreducible to any observable identity, we have no way of knowing whether or not the other really is enjoying. A stream of profanity may be the result of someone hurting a toe. The person playing the car radio too loud while sitting at the traffic light may have simply forgotten to turn down the radio after driving on the highway. Or the person may have difficulty hearing. The couple's amorous behavior in public may reflect an absence of enjoyment in their relationship that they are trying to hide from both themselves and the public.

Considering the enjoyment of the other, we never know whether it is there or not. If we experience it, we do so through the lens of our own fantasy. We fantasize that the person blasting the radio is caught up in the enjoyment of the music to the exclusion of everything else; we fantasize that the public kisses of the couple suggest an enjoyment that has no concern for the outside world. Without the fantasy frame, the enjoying other would never appear within our experience.

The role of the fantasy frame for accessing the enjoying other becomes apparent within Fascist ideology. Fascism posits an internal enemy — the figure of the Jew or some analogue — that enjoys illicitly at the expense of the social body as a whole. By attempting to eliminate the enjoying other, Fascism hopes to create a pure social body bereft of any stain of enjoyment. This purity would allow for the ultimate enjoyment, but it would be completely licit. This hope for a future society free of any stain is not where Fascism's true enjoyment lies, however. Fascists experience their own enjoyment through the enjoying other that they persecute. The enjoyment that the figure of the Jew embodies is the Fascists' own enjoyment, though they cannot avow it as their own. More than any other social form, Fascism is founded on the disavowal of enjoyment — the attempt to enjoy while keeping enjoyment at arm's length.[31] But this effort is not confined to Fascism; it predominates everywhere, because no subjects anywhere can simply feel comfortable with their own mode of enjoying.

The very structure of enjoyment is such that we cannot experience it directly: when we experience enjoyment, we don't have it; it has us. We experience our own enjoyment as an assault coming from the outside that dominates our conscious intentions. This is why we must fantasize our own enjoyment through the enjoying other. Compelled by our enjoyment, we can't do otherwise; we act against our self-interest and against our own good. Enjoyment overwhelms the subject, even though the subject's mode of enjoying marks what is most singular about the subject.

Even though the encounter with the enjoying other apprehends the real other through the apparatus of fantasy, this encounter is nonetheless genuine and has an ethical status. Unlike the experience of the nonexistent symbolic identity, which closes down the space in which the real other might appear, the fantasized encounter with the enjoying other leaves this space open. By allowing itself to be disturbed by the other on the level of fantasy, the subject acknowledges the singularity of the real other — its mode of enjoying — without confining this singularity to a prescribed identity.

The implications of privileging the encounter with the disturbing enjoyment of the real other over the assimilable symbolic identity are themselves disturbing. The tolerant attitude that never allows itself to be jarred by the enjoying other becomes, according to this way of seeing things, further from really encountering the real other than the attitude of hate and mistrust. The liberal subject who welcomes illegal immigrants as fellow citizens completely shuts down the space for the other in the real. The immigrant as fellow citizen is not the real other. The xenophobic conservative, on the other hand, constructs a fantasy that envisions the illegal immigrant awash in a linguistic and cultural enjoyment that excludes natives. This fantasy, paradoxically, permits an encounter with the real other that liberal tolerance forecloses. Of course, xenophobes retreat from this encounter and from their own enjoyment, but they do have an experience of it that liberals do not. The tolerant liberal is open to the other but eliminates the otherness, while the xenophobic conservative is closed to the other but allows for the otherness. The ethical position thus involves sustaining the liberal's tolerance within the conservative's encounter with the real other.

5

Changing the World

The Modern Critique of Normality

If an ethical subjectivity is possible, it would seem that this subjectivity would have positioned itself outside the straitjacket of normality. Normality represents, according to our usual way of thinking about it, a flight away from ethical and political responsibility with an embrace of mass unthinking passivity. Much of the energy of modern thought, art, and politics has been dedicated to the idea that normality is a prison that inhibits societal change or even simply individual flowering. According to this idea, the failure of intellectual, aesthetic, and political revolutions stems from the power that normality has for producing stasis. Capitalist society defeats revolutions and even the revolutionary impulse by producing normal subjects, subjects adjusted to the variegations of capitalist life and therefore not prepared to take up the radical alternative when it presents itself. Any impulse toward an alternative either is immediately suspicious or has its difference eliminated. As Adorno and Horkheimer put it in *Dialectic of Enlightenment*, within capitalist society where norms rule, "everything must be used, everything must belong to them. The mere existence of the other is a provocation."[1] Normality becomes the tool that suppresses otherness and thereby perpetuates the status quo.

The shared critique of the power of normality within modern society binds diverse lines of thought — Heidegger and Adorno, Sartre and Derrida, Foucault and Irigaray. Whatever their differences, each thinker wants to liberate some form of difference from the hegemony of the normal within modernity. To become a normal subject is to sacrifice one's difference for the sake of the functioning of capitalist society, and the project of thought — or political action — thus becomes one of finding a way to allow difference to survive. For Heidegger, this is accomplished through the experience of authentic being-toward-death; for Adorno, it arrives through the activity of critical thinking; for Sartre, it involves the subject recognizing its own nothingness; for Derrida, it emerges through the play of *différance* within signification. Though the normal seems all-encompassing and destined for dominance, each thinker imagines a mode of resistance to it, even if she/he thinks that this resistance represents a losing battle. The modern political imperative, if there is one, involves not allowing oneself to be subsumed within normality.

Though all would not put it this way, what most modern thinkers see in normality is reification, a process by which subjective activity takes on an objective status. In this sense, Heidegger and Georg Lukács represent the points of departure for the modern critique of normality. From a phenomenological and a Marxist perspective, they inaugurate the philosophical analysis of reification or some similar process. Reification renders everything the same by effacing the labor (and exploitation) that creates commodities and thereby endowing commodities with what Lukács calls "a 'phantom objectivity,' an autonomy that seems so strictly rational and all-embracing as to conceal every trace of its fundamental nature."[2] Through reification, the normal glazes over its own becoming and in this way presents itself as permanent and not subject to questioning. Normal subjectivity appears to be a stable and already achieved identity, not a process requiring constant reconstruction. The fundamental lie of normality is this appearance of stability. Combating it means exposing the fissures that this appearance belies.[3]

This identification of normality and a stultifying world of pure objectivity becomes most evident in the thought of Alain Badiou. According to Badiou, the situation, which is his term for the realm in which normality predominates, renders would-be subjects into objects and prevents their emergence as subjects. From the perspective of the situation, one cannot recognize the site of the event, and the event marks the key to both politics and subjectivity. The event is a rupture with the stasis of the status quo; it provides an occasion for subjects to emerge through their fidelity to its rupture. As he puts it in *Being and Event*, "The paradox of an evental-site is that it can only be recognized on the basis of what it does not present in the situation in which it is presented."[4] Recognizing the event and becoming a subject require that one grasp what the normal situation militates against grasping. Normality is for Badiou a stabilizing force, which is why one must constantly remain on one's guard against it.[5]

Ideology produces normality by establishing symbolic identities for subjects to embody. In fact, the fundamental gesture of all ideology is the construction and perpetuation of symbolic identity. Symbolic identity offers the subject a stable answer to the question of identity that emerges with subjection to the signifier. With an identity, the subject can feel itself at home within the inherently alienating structure of the social order and relieved of the burden of its own existence. This is why Jean-Paul Sartre links any affirmation of identity to bad faith. In the act of identifying myself with a symbolic identity, I become who ideology wants me to become and thereby deny my freedom — that I am never identical to what I am. Bad faith accepts symbolic identity as accurately defining the subject, and thus it produces a subject without any awareness of its own role in constituting and taking on this identity.

But as Sartre notes in *Being and Nothingness*, true bad faith is impossible. No subject can perfectly inhabit its symbolic identity. That identity inevitably remains an answer that doesn't fully satisfy the subject. My symbolic identity confronts me as an object that I am not. According to Sartre, "If I represent myself as him, I am not he; I am separated from him as the object from the subject, separated *by nothing*, but this nothing isolates me from him. I can not be he, I can only play *at being* him; that is, imagine to myself that I am he."[6] No matter how much I try to become one with a symbolic identity, I cannot traverse the barrier of nothing — that is, the barrier of my own activity — in order to achieve identification. Every symbolic identification is a failed symbolic identification.

This failure of symbolic identity is not simply a logical failure. It is also necessary for the ideological role that symbolic identification plays. Ideology needs symbolic identity to fail in order to produce subjects oriented toward the process of symbolic identification and concerned with completing this identification. This is the essential paradox: while symbolic identity marks the subject's immersion into ideology, this immersion must remain incomplete if it is not to undermine itself and produce a subject free from ideological pressure. If symbolic identification were successful and the subject were to immerse itself completely in the identity, the subject would cease to experience this identity as a problem to be worked through. Fully assuming a symbolic identity subverts the ideological work that identification does. The subject's abnormality — its failure to coincide perfectly with its identity — is the very thing that keeps it tied to normality.

If normal subjectivity requires a degree of abnormality in order to function, this complicates both the critique of normality and the celebration of deviations from the norm. The norm doesn't dominate through impressing its stamp of sameness on everything but through allowing for some degree of difference. Deviations from the norm do not subvert its power; they enhance it. To celebrate these deviations is ipso facto to succumb to the very logic that one hopes to oppose. Depicted in this way, there seems to be no way out of ideology's trap. If ideology, as Robert Pfaller claims, needs "a gesture of negation for it to function," one inevitably plays into its hands.[7]

No one has done more to reveal how deviations support the norm rather than subvert it than Michel Foucault. By conceiving power as productive and not simply restrictive (the usual idea of power), Foucault reshapes all thinking about how one challenges oppressive norms. For instance, he sees the subversion of puritanical ideas about sex and the emergence of a new discourse around sexuality in the twentieth century as indicative of the expansion of control over sex rather than as a genuine subversion of sexual norms. When we become free to talk about sex openly, our talk has the effect of enhancing the regulation or normalization of our sexual activity. As Foucault theorizes the problem, there seems to be no way out, no possibility for creating an effective subversion that would allow for resistance to the hegemonic power of normality.

Despite his insight into the link between subversion and the expansion of ideological control, Foucault nonetheless takes up a political position that clings to the model of subversion. He advocates resisting the discourse of sexuality altogether and insisting instead on "bodies and pleasures."[8] By doing so, Foucault believes, we successfully subvert the expansion of normality and insist on our individual specificity. But even though Foucault locates resistance in a register different from that of other modern thinkers — the unsignified body itself — he continues the modern celebration of subversion while he envisages its blind spot. He does so because his conception of the normal allows no other course. In the face of a completely oppressive conception of normality, subversion becomes the only palatable alternative.[9]

What separates psychoanalysis from almost all other modern thought is the attitude that it takes to normal subjectivity. Rather than seeing normality as a barrier to authentic change, it sees normality as the ability to act and to change the world. For psychoanalysis, pervasive abnormality, not pervasive normality, ensures the perpetuation of capitalist society. We are trapped not by our failure to subvert normality but precisely by our success in doing so. The norm dominates through being transgressed, not in spite of being transgressed. This is why Freud's work focuses on neurosis: it is much more widespread than normality, and we almost never find normality without a neurotic underside. The psychoanalytic challenge to modern thought's critique of normality forces a rethinking of the problem of conformity and the barriers that it erects to political activity.

Freud's primary claim is that what we perceive as the normal is actually rife with abnormality. For this reason, neurotics provide the key to the analysis of what seems to be normal subjectivity. In the *Introductory Lectures* Freud claims: "Neurotics merely exhibit to us in a magnified and coarsened form what the analysis of dreams reveals to us in healthy people as well."[10] Most "healthy" or normal subjects, like neurotics, supplement their experience of the world with a fantasmatic reserve that they keep separate from the world and that renders it bearable. This process of supplementation allows subjects to exist functionally within society, but it also prevents them from authentically acting. The failure to be normal dooms the subject to existing within the structures of ideology through the very activity of struggling against those structures. By becoming a normal subject, one gives up the insistence on one's own difference, an insistence that paradoxically serves to eliminate it.

The normal subject, conceived in the properly psychoanalytic sense, has no external entity by which to measure its own deviation from the norm. In this sense, to become a normal subject is to recognize that there is no authorized social authority, no guarantee for normality. Psychoanalysis, as Sheila Kunkle points out, "realizes that normality is really just a special form of psychosis."[11] The social authority that would define the normal is itself groundless and thus incapable of providing a genuine norm. But normality is not just psychosis but precisely "a special form" that enables a recognition that psychosis proper inhibits. It is not that this absence of an external norm allows the subject to recognize something like "I'm okay, you're okay" but more that the absence makes visible that no one is okay, that the fantasmatic deviation from the norm is part of the norm itself.

The Questionable Task of Analysis

This idea of psychoanalysis as an embrace and even celebration of normal subjectivity fits within a certain stereotypical image. The traditional leftist critique of psychoanalysis focuses on its role in adapting dissatisfied subjects to the exigencies of bourgeois normality.[12] The association of psychoanalysis with adaptation becomes most apparent in American ego psychology, where developing a healthy ego becomes the overriding goal of analysis. Heinz Hartmann, one of the parent figures in this movement, sees the production of the healthy ego as the key to the elimination of friction between the individual subject and the social order. He claims: "The aims of psychoanalytic therapy . . . [are] to help men achieve a better functioning synthesis and relation to the environment."[13] As the title of Hartmann's classic work *Ego Psychology and the Problem of Adaptation* suggests, psychoanalysis assists in the process of adaptation to the social order, even if it also helps the subject to influence this order in some way.[14] By doing so, it plays a role in the perpetuation of an oppressive normality in the mind of many leftists.

Defenders of psychoanalysis have been quick to claim that Hartmann and his followers are not representative of the psychoanalytic project as such.[15] But however one conceives it, psychoanalysis turns dissatisfaction into some degree of satisfaction — or at least into an ability to live without excessive dissatisfaction. It would not be able to survive as a mode of therapy if it instead made people feel worse in order to serve the cause of radicalism. Such a form of analysis might appeal to Marxists, but few would be willing to shell out hundreds or thousands of dollars just to augment their dissatisfaction and thereby become more politically engaged. What patients pay for is relief from their misery rather than its exacerbation. At the end of *Studies on Hysteria*, Freud and Joseph Breuer tell the hysteric, "You will be able to convince yourself that much will be gained if we succeed in transforming your hysterical misery into common unhappiness. With a mental life that has been restored to health you will be better armed against that unhappiness."[16] Even by fomenting "common unhappiness" as a substitute for "hysterical misery," psychoanalysis takes the edge off abnormality, thereby assisting in the process of normalization.

Even the most radical psychoanalytic thinkers see psychoanalysis as a response to human suffering and an attempt to alleviate some of that suffering. Jacques Lacan, for instance, sees this as the fundamental task of the analyst. Though Lacan does not want to adjust or normalize the subject — in fact, he criticizes American ego psychology for precisely this reason — he often singles out psychoanalysts as those committed to lessening human suffering, and any relief for individual suffering would appear to have the effect of increasing the stability of the society as a whole. Suffering is an engine for political action, and less suffering implies less political activity.[17]

Along these lines, theorists are often tempted to elevate the psychic disorders that Freud attempts to cure as incipient — or even almost fully developed — radical political positions. Almost every psychic disorder receives this treatment from some corner: Hélène Cixous celebrates the radicality of hysteria; Judith Butler praises the subversiveness of perversion; and Gilles Deleuze and Félix Guattari proclaim the revolutionary status of schizophrenia.[18] In each case, one must resist the idea of the cure. The radicality of the disorder stems from the challenge it poses to the hegemony of normality, with which the cure aligns itself. Hysteria questions where normal subjectivity accepts; perversion acts where normal subjectivity fantasizes; schizophrenia dissolves the coherence of the ego that normal subjectivity stabilizes. Freud himself, however, never gestures toward this kind of idealization of disorders, though he does see its appeal.

In his brief essay "The Loss of Reality in Neurosis and Psychosis," Freud makes it clear that he recognizes the rebellious nature of both neurosis and psychosis. He claims: "Both neurosis and psychosis are ... the expression of a rebellion on the part of the id against the external world, of its unwillingness — or, if one prefers, its incapacity — to adapt itself to the exigencies of reality."[19] The refusal that animates neurosis and psychosis indicates, in one sense, the strength of the subject's desire. Those who celebrate types of neurosis or psychosis focus on this refusal of the psyche to adapt itself to the social reality and the strength of desire it indicates. It is defiance rather than acceptance of symbolic identity and the restrictiveness that goes along with this identity.

The problem is that both neurosis and psychosis (and perversion, for that matter) remain rebellious without ever becoming revolutionary.[20] The changes that they inaugurate never affect social relations in a transformative way but stay confined to the internal dynamics of the psyche itself. In fact, they function only on the basis of *not* effecting any change in social relations and by sustaining an antagonistic social reality. Though neurosis and psychosis represent disparate psychic structures, they both effect a withdrawal from the public world and thereby mark a refusal to act. Each accomplishes this withdrawal in its own particular way: neurosis constructs a domain of fantasy, what Freud calls a "reservation," that exists separated from the public world, while psychosis simply creates an alternative world in place of the public world. In this sense, both substitute a private world for a public world, though psychosis does so more thoroughly.

Neurosis and psychosis leave the structure of the public world unchanged, despite their reaction against it. The withdrawal of psychic investment from the public world and the placing of it in the private alternative allow the subject to experience itself as rebellious and even radical but do not necessarily imply any actual radicality. Neurotics fantasizing about violations of societal norms feel themselves to be beyond those norms, even though the fantasy relies on these norms and leaves them intact. In this sense, the greatest barrier to becoming a radical subject is the belief that one already is a radical subject — the defining belief of the neurotic.[21]

Neurosis involves the subject's fundamental misrecognition of its own subjectivity because the subject accepts the private fantasmatic reservation as its true essence and avoids measuring it by its public manifestation. For the neurotic, the real me is the one that I hide, not how I manifest myself publicly. The neurotic's wholly private revolt not only fails to disturb the functioning of the society in which it exists; it helps to create a better subject for this society — someone always looking to secure her/his private enjoyment at the expense of others.[22]

Psychosis seems inherently closer to radical subjectivity than neurosis. It also rejects the public world, but it doesn't confine its rebellion to a fantasmatic reservation. The psychotic's alternative world would seem ipso facto to call into question the validity of the existing public world. Unlike the neurotic, the psychotic rejects the satisfaction that accompanies a socially constituted identity and therefore shatters the stability that the social order attempts to produce. For Deleuze and Guattari, the foundation-shaking capacity of psychosis is visible in the schizophrenic's relationship to capitalism. As they note in *Anti-Oedipus*, "The schizophrenic deliberately seeks out the very limit of capitalism: he is its inherent tendency brought to fulfillment, its surplus product, its proletariat, and its exterminating angel. He scrambles all the codes and is the transmitter of the decoded flows of desire."[23] The schizophrenic's lack of identity becomes in this vision a wrench in the functioning of capitalist relations of production.

But the psychotic is never psychotic enough. The psychotic subject tacitly acknowledges and accepts the existing public world by ignoring that world — and not recognizing its influence — in the creation of an alternative. Ironically, it is the very gesture of ignoring the existing public world that testifies to the psychotic's valuing of it. By ignoring it, the psychotic leaves it intact, though psychosis may cause a local disturbance within this public world. For example, when a psychotic like Jeffrey Dahmer eats someone, this clearly disturbs the person being eaten. But such an act doesn't disturb the workings of the social order itself. In fact, it helps this order to function insofar as it provides the image of a monster that encourages calls for more policing and surveillance. As with neurosis, psychosis runs aground on the essentially private nature of its rebellion.

Unlike neurosis and psychosis, perversion does not withdraw from the public world, which is why so many theorists celebrate perversion — or some parallel to it — for its political power. Like neurotics and psychotics, perverts insist on their private enjoyment, but they continually publicize it, thereby forcing the symbolic law to reveal itself through the oppressive stifling of this enjoyment. The pervert's humiliation of authority seems to undermine the power of that authority and to mark the pervert's radicality. But perversion is destined to remain always in the process of undermining authority and never having fully done so. The pervert never completes the radical act and topples the figure of authority, because perversion's enjoyment stems from the act of contesting itself. This is why one can say that the pervert acts out but never fully acts.

Freud defines normal subjectivity as the overcoming of this ineffectuality. In contrast to the perverse subjectivity, it doesn't just provoke authority but actually works to topple it. In contrast to neurotic and psychotic behavior, normal behavior involves an act, changing the public world rather than changing privately. Freud claims: "Expedient, normal, behaviour leads to work being carried out on the external world; it does not stop, as in psychosis, at effecting internal changes."[24] The normal subject, as Freud understands it, changes the world. It is certainly correct to view psychoanalysis as a normalizing endeavor, provided that one understands normality as the refusal to accommodate oneself to a dissatisfying public world and the consequent recognition that one must act to change it.

The Obscenity of Revelation

This definition of normality doesn't imply that it avoids recourse to fantasy altogether. Fantasy is unavoidable because the experience of social reality cannot be perfectly satisfying: as we've seen, ideological interpellation functions through failure, and this failure triggers the subject's turn to fantasy. As a result, the normal subject has a fantasy world like the neurotic does. The difference lies in the relationship between the fantasy and the public world: neurotics hold their fantasies as isolated reservations, as spaces apart, whereas normal subjects allow these two worlds to touch each other and to interact. The neurotic can suffer the dissatisfaction of the public world because retreat to the private sanctuary of the fantasy is always there as a present possibility. In the fantasy, the exigencies of the public world, if they exist here, become opportunities for the subject's enjoyment rather than working to stifle it. But for the normal subject, fantasy ceases to be this private respite and becomes part of the public world itself.

We might say that, for Freud, the normal subject is not the subject who has adapted itself to the social order but the subject who insists on its fantasy — or at least the enjoyment it provides — as a path for transforming the social order. As he puts it in the *Five Lectures on Psycho-analysis*,

> The energetic and successful man is one who succeeds by his efforts in turning his wishful phantasies into reality. Where this fails, as a result of the resistances of the external world and of the subject's own weakness, he begins to turn away from reality and withdraws into his more satisfying world of phantasy, the content of which is transformed into symptoms should he fall ill. In certain favourable circumstances, it still remains possible for him to find another path leading from these phantasies to

reality, instead of becoming permanently estranged from it by regressing to infancy.[25]

Though Freud here places the goals of psychoanalysis in very naive terms for the sake of a general audience, this does not disguise the fundamental direction that psychoanalysis takes. Rather than assisting subjects in accommodating themselves to a dissatisfying or unjust reality, psychoanalysis helps them to realize their own fantasmatic enjoyment.

This has the sound of a Nietzschean discharging of the subject's power on the world. Or even worse, it sounds like the advice that Donald Trump might give to aspiring executives just before firing them. Instead of accommodating oneself to the world, one dominates it. Instead of working in the mail room, one chairs the board. But for psychoanalysis, the path is not so simple. When Freud says that success involves turning one's "wishful phantasies into reality," the sense of this statement seems self-evident. Rather than toiling away in the mail room dreaming of being an executive, one takes steps — goes to night school, makes the proper connections, and so on — that will make it possible to live out this fantasy in the real external world. But what this initial reading of Freud's statement glosses over is the nature of the relationship between fantasy and external reality.

Fantasy and external reality cannot simply coexist in proximity. Though fantasy informs our picture of external reality and even provides essential coordinates of this reality, it does so from a safe psychic distance, shaping how we see but not visibly intruding on what we see. That is to say, we typically experience external reality through the lens of our fantasy but don't experience this lens itself as a part of that reality. When this distance shrinks and part of our fantasy becomes visible within external reality, the subject experiences the trauma of this proximity and loses its very grasp of reality. Confronted with one's fantasy, one is confronted not with the truth of one's being but with one's fundamental lie — the initial story one creates surrounding the encounter with an antagonism that resists all narrativization. This is why, as Slavoj Žižek notes, "the core of our fantasy is unbearable to us."[26] To realize one's fantasy is inherently traumatic because it involves exposing publicly the fundamental deception — which is to say, the mode of enjoying — that defines a subject's subjectivity.[27]

The romantic union that occurs at the end of so many Hollywood films seems to mark the point at which fantasy and external reality come together. The spectator watches nearly the entirety of a film like Frank Capra's *It Happened One Night* (1934) fantasizing about Peter Warne (Clark Gable) and Ellie Andrews (Claudette Colbert) becoming a romantic couple (as they themselves are clearly fantasizing within the film), and then the film concludes by allowing the spectator to witness the realization of their union. This union occurs without a traumatic dimension and allows one to feel good as a spectator.

What enables the film to avoid the trauma that occurs when fantasy and external reality come together is its failure to reveal fully the fantasy in all its disruptiveness. We fantasize about the romance because we see how each character exposes the other's fundamental lie: Ellie lays bare the imposture of Peter's masculinity, and Peter gives the lie to Ellie's illusion of independence. When they unite at the end of the film, however, each has learned to accept the other's lie; they accommodate themselves to each other, and this accommodation manifests the retreat from fantasy for the spectator. We can take pleasure in the concluding romantic union only because it represents a fantasy with the edges dulled.

The trauma that occurs when fantasy meets external reality is perfectly captured in Amy Heckerling's underrated *Fast Times at Ridgemont High* (1982). At one point, the film shows Brad Hamilton (Judge Reinhold) masturbating in his bathroom while imagining Linda Barrett (Phoebe Cates), who is swimming in the pool just outside, running toward him and taking off her bikini top. While Brad is masturbating, Linda walks in on him in the bathroom. While she is sickened by the sight, Brad feels completely humiliated, and the film forces the spectator to share in this humiliation. This — and not the seeming fantasmatic romantic union that concludes the typical Hollywood film — is the real coming together of fantasy and external reality.[28]

Fantasy defines a subject's subjectivity by providing it with a private narrative that explains the public loss of the privileged object.[29] This loss, as we have seen, gives birth to the subject: the subject and the object don't exist prior to the experience of loss but emerge through it. But when fantasy places the loss of the privileged object into a narrative structure — when it tells a story about how the loss occurred and what caused it — fantasy creates the illusion that the lost object had some substantial status prior to being lost. It is in this precise sense that fantasy functions as the primordial lie that the subject tells itself. Because fantasy imagines the lost object as substantial, it also envisions the possibility of recovering the lost object and recovering a lost satisfaction. Subjectivity is unthinkable without the fantasmatic lie. This lie gives the subject a reason for its suffering and permits the subject to endure its lack with the possibility of the restoration of fullness. Even psychoanalytic treatment doesn't enable the subject to overcome its inherent proclivity toward and reliance on fantasy (though psychoanalysis does permit the subject to become reoriented relative to its fantasy life). Without some recourse to fantasy, no subject could go on. Fantasy gives the subject a direction for its desire, a center around which to organize its enjoyment, and it always has an obscene quality to it.

The obscenity of fantasmatic enjoyment stems from its manner of short-circuiting the symbolic pact that constitutes the social bond. In our fantasies, we imagine ourselves pulling one over on society at large, enjoying in a way that no one else does. If ideology reduces all subjects to the same level, fantasy singles out the subject as the exception to every rule. The fantasmatic core of our subjectivity is the key to our uniqueness as subjects.[30] Fantasy produces enjoyment for the subject by bypassing the constraints that govern all our activity. Thus, when our fantasies become exposed, everyone can see the extent to which we are not a part of society, the extent to which we don't belong. And at the same time, everyone can see the purely imaginary status of our rebellion: rather than actually acting to break from the social bond, we have merely fantasized doing so. The subject with an exposed fantasy becomes visible as a pathetic would-be outsider. Realizing one's fantasy involves the ultimate shame.

To examine this dynamic in concrete terms we can return to the mail clerk who fantasizes about being an executive. One of the benefits of this example is its counterintuitive status: becoming an executive — unlike, say, being caught masturbating in one's bathroom — does not appear to expose anything other than a garden-variety ambition shared by almost everyone within capitalist society. The mystification here occurs because we assume that executives, or at least some of them, are former mail clerks who have realized their fantasies. But the fantasizing mail clerk never actually becomes the successful executive.[31]

The fantasy of the successful executive lies elsewhere than in being a successful executive. (Perhaps it involves being a lowly mail clerk.) Those who attain success in the business world or in any other domain are not those who fantasize about this success. They may plan their actions or envision goals being met, but these plans and visions are not, properly speaking, the domain of fantasy. Fantasy depends for its erotic power on a degree of unreality. It provides enjoyment for subjects because it allows them to cheat reality, and the enjoyment derives directly from this sense of cheating, of escaping the restrictions that bind others.

The sense of cheating a reality that others must obey forms the essential core of fantasy as such. It is for this reason that subjects hide their fantasies from public view. All fantasies share a formal hiddenness, and this hiddenness proclaims the subject's own belief in the fantasy's transgressive nature. It is not what the fantasy hides that threatens to traumatize the subject but the very fact of the hiding itself. The form of fantasy is shameful, not the content. No act is in itself shameful without hiddenness attached to it, which is why one of the most effective ways to avoid shame involves broadcasting one's potentially shameful acts — talking about one's interest in pornography, explaining one's tendency to sweat too much, and so on.[32] Self-exposure militates against having the fantasmatically charged act exposed by others and thereby revealed in its hiddenness. Exposing this hiddenness means exposing the subject's privileged and seemingly unique mode of obtaining enjoyment.

If the mail clerk who fantasizes about becoming an executive actually does realize this fantasy, the effect would be shattering for this clerk's erotic life and for her or his life as an executive. The erstwhile mail clerk would have no respite from this symbolic position — no hidden reservation where the "real me" could dwell. As a result, the clerk-become-executive would have to transform the position of executive itself, struggling against the very nature of this symbolic position. Realizing the fantasy traumatizes both the subject itself (depriving it of its treasured secret) and the social reality (depriving it of the underside it needs in order to function), and it leads to the transformation of both. It is in this sense that we should understand Freud's statement defining success as the realization of one's fantasies. It is far removed from how we usually define the word, and in fact, the subject who becomes what Freud sees as a success cannot be successful in the bourgeois sense of the term.

Psychoanalytic Success

What the social order demands from the subject above all else is sacrifice: one must sacrifice a part of oneself — a portion of one's enjoyment — in order to keep the social order, no matter what its make-up, functioning. This demand for sacrifice produces neurosis. The neurotic's repression is the manifestation of this sacrifice: rather than act for the sake of their enjoyment, neurotics repress, thereby adjusting themselves to the demands of the social order. The neurotic compensates for this sacrifice through recourse to fantasy, but this fantasy must remain private and thus can never intrude on the social order itself. Fantasy has the effect of keeping the neurotic working.

Though they don't involve sacrifice in the direct way that neurosis does, psychosis and perversion also function as ways of retreating from the truth of one's enjoyment. As we saw earlier, the psychotic subject seems much closer to a radical subjectivity than the neurotic. The psychotic specifically refuses the sacrifice that the neurotic undergoes and suffers from. And yet, psychosis marks a refusal to recognize the source of the enjoyment it generates. The psychotic ignores the symbolic law, finding enjoyment on its own terms rather than through the intermediary of the law. But this is the fundamental misrecognition that defines psychosis. In the act of bypassing the symbolic law, the psychotic tacitly acknowledges it, which is why no psychotic derives enjoyment from activities that the symbolic law does *not* in some sense prohibit. Psychotics cannot recognize their indebtedness to the very law that they ignore. Neither the psychotic nor the neurotic embraces the truth of his or her enjoyment; both deceive themselves as to the nature of how they enjoy.

In contrast, the failure of the pervert is especially instructive because this type of subject seems to embrace its own enjoyment in a completely public way. That is to say, perversion does not appear to involve a retreat from one's own enjoyment. But just like the neurotic and psychotic, the pervert never grasps the truth of how she/he enjoys. The pervert's public show of enjoyment is not an insistence on enjoyment for its own sake; the public show is an attempt to give rise to an authority who would lay down the law prohibiting that enjoyment. As Bruce Fink notes, "While it [perversion] may sometimes present itself as a no-holds-barred, jouissance-seeking activity, its less apparent aim is to bring the law into being: to make the Other as law (or law-giving Other) exist."[33] No pervert, of course, recognizes the truth of this mode of enjoying, that she/he derives enjoyment from the very effort to curb it. But perversion is fundamentally a provocation of social authority, and the enjoyment that it offers derives from the extent to which it arouses the authority, despite the pervert's inability to recognize this dependence. Even more than neurosis or psychosis, perversion represents a retreat from enjoyment.

Successful normal subjectivity, as Freud defines it, stands in contrast. The normal subject does not exist completely outside the domain of social authority, but this subject is able to enjoy in a way that neurotics, psychotics, and perverts cannot. Rather than keeping the subversion of social authority a private matter (in the manner of the neurotic), the normal subject publicly avows its fantasy. By insisting on its fantasies at the expense of social recognition, such a subject embraces its mode of enjoying.[34] This is the fundamental aim of the psychoanalytic process, and the subject who does this necessarily exposes its fantasy and enjoys in a public way.

By enjoying in a public way, the subject becomes what we might call a fool. The fool is a subject who ceases to court the social authority's approbation and becomes immune to the seduction of social recognition or rewards. Recognition has a value for the subject only insofar as the subject believes in the substantial status of social authority—that is, insofar as the subject believes that the identities that society confers have a solid foundation. The fool grasps that no such foundation exists and that no identity has any basis whatsoever. The only possible foundation for the subject lies in the subject itself—in the fantasy that organizes the subject's enjoyment. Such a subject becomes a fool because it constantly acts in ways that make no sense to the social authority. It acts out of the nonsense of its own enjoyment.

This does not mean that the fool acts at random. Nonsensical enjoyment is not arbitrary enjoyment but enjoyment irreducible to the symbolic world of signification. In fact, the fool, having embraced its own mode of enjoying, acts with considerable regularity. This type of subject clearly acts against its own self-interest and in defiance of any good at all. The paradigmatic instance of the fool is the subject pursuing the lost cause or the subject continuing to act when all hope has already been lost. The pursuit of the lost cause reveals that what motivates the subject is not a potential reward but purely the enjoyment of the pursuit itself. The authentic fool doesn't pursue the lost cause with resignation but with the knowledge that there is no other cause but the lost one. Rather than paralyzing the subject, this recognition emboldens it, as the example of Hamlet demonstrates.

When Hamlet receives his charge from his father's ghost and determines that he must kill Claudius in order to revenge his father's murder, he believes in the possibility of justice. For Hamlet at the beginning of Shakespeare's play, there is an order in the world that his act might restore, even though he laments that this burden has been placed on his shoulders. He tells us, "The time is out of joint. O cursed spite, / That ever I was born to set it right."[35] This couplet testifies to Hamlet's belief in distributive justice, which tacitly presupposes a social authority with a solid foundation that could distribute justice. This attitude undergoes a radical transformation, however, when he see Ophelia's grave. At this point in the play, Hamlet recognizes the groundlessness of all authority and the hopelessness of his own cause.

At Ophelia's grave, Hamlet confronts the power of death to dissolve every symbolic bond. Justice and honor become meaningless in the face of an all-conquering death. He realizes that even if he revenges himself on Claudius, nothing will be accomplished: order will not be restored, and the time will remain out of joint. And yet, it is precisely at this moment that Hamlet devotes himself to the completion of his project. He realizes his fantasy — avenging his father's death — when he grasps that it is its own end. Once his cause becomes a lost cause, Hamlet can act.

As long as Hamlet hopes that his act might accomplish something substantial, the moment will never be right for it. Once he ceases to believe in the possibility of restoring justice and understands the act only in terms of his own fantasmatic enjoyment, he frees himself from the search for the proper moment. Subjects who hope to make an impact on social authority never act because they cannot calculate how the authority will respond to the act. Such subjects, like Hamlet at the beginning of the play, spend their time probing the authority's desire and waiting for the moment when the act will make the proper impact on the other. But that moment never comes. When one adopts the position of the fool, the moment for the act is always at hand because the fool's act has nothing to do with the readiness of the social authority for it.

There is a danger in advocating the subjectivity of the fool, however. Many adopt the position of the fool as a symbolic identity that provides meaning for their lives. Such subjects perversely act out rather than accomplishing genuinely successful acts. The difference consists in how the subject relates to the position of the fool. The perverse fool acts in order to provoke the social authority into a response, while the genuine fool acts for the sake of its own enjoyment regardless of the authority's response. The former derives a sense of identity from the position; the latter does not.

The difference between the perverse subject and the authentic fool is visible within the character of Hamlet. After he first hears of his father's murder at the beginning of the play, Hamlet feigns madness; he literally plays the part of the fool. But he takes up this position in order to provoke authority, not in order to realize his own enjoyment. Hamlet uses his madness in an attempt to trigger a reaction in Claudius that will offer definitive proof of the latter's guilt. But even when Claudius reacts in the way that Hamlet wants to the performance of the provocative play that Hamlet has produced, Hamlet still does not act but continues to act out.

It is only well after the play ends, after he has realized the absence of any order in the world or any guarantee for his action in social authority, that Hamlet is able to act. When he acts, he acts not on the basis of laws or justice but on the basis of his own fantasy frame. In act 5 he becomes the authentic fool, one no longer playing to the crowd but determined to follow his fantasy regardless of authority's response. In so doing, he provides a model for successful subjectivity, for how the subject might act to change the world.[36]

Publicly insisting on one's fantasy hardly seems like a prescription for changing the world in any substantive fashion. If this is the political attitude advanced by psychoanalysis, the indictment of psychoanalysis on political grounds appears to have a great deal of merit. But this would be to move too quickly. We might think of the relationship between embracing one's own fantasy and politics as a twisted version of the line from the Talmud that characters repeat in *Schindler's List* (Steven Spielberg, 1993): "Whoever saves one life saves the world entire." Translated into our terms this would become: "Whoever publicly insists on her or his own fantasy opens this path for the world entire." By doing this, the subject institutes a fundamental change in the structure of its symbolic world.

When one subject opts for the nonsense of its own enjoyment over the blandishments of recognition, this act exposes the groundlessness of social authority — the emptiness around which the social order is structured. A collective awareness of the groundlessness of social authority would produce a different sort of social order, one in which subjects would be unable to rely on authority and would have to assume responsibility themselves for the social order. They would lose the sense of authorization for their acts. The freedom inherent in social existence would become evident in light of authority's evanescence.

II

SOCIETY

6

The Appeal of Sacrifice

A Shared Absence

It is impossible to divorce the question of subjectivity from the question of the structure of the social order. How one understands the relationship between the individual subject and society definitively marks one's theoretical position. This is true for psychoanalytic thought no less than for other theories. The understanding of this relationship almost inevitably exists as a theoretical presupposition or as a starting point for whatever theory one espouses. The two predominant positions on the interaction between individual and society see the isolated individual as the starting point on the one hand or the social organization as the starting point on the other. In modernity, the former derives from the tradition of British liberal philosophy, and the latter derives from the tradition of German dialectical thought.

For a liberal thinker such as John Locke, society doesn't form the individual; individuals come together to form society. In the tradition of thinkers from Thomas Hobbes to John Stuart Mill to Ayn Rand, Locke conceives the individual existing outside society as a clear and distinct being. According to Locke, one can analyze the situation of the individual removed from the fabric of societal construction. In this natural state, the subject is free. As he puts it, "The *Natural Liberty* of Man is to be free from any Superior Power on Earth, and not to be under the Will or Legislative Authority of Man, but to have only the Law of Nature for his Rule."[1] Locke can deduce the inherent freedom of the individual because he isolates the individual from the social production of identity. Individual identity emerges apart from the socialization process, which only affects it in an external fashion.

Society constrains the choices that the individual subject might make, but it doesn't create the will to choose itself within the individual. This is where someone like Karl Marx, coming from the opposed tradition, would see a fundamental blind spot in Locke's philosophy.[2]

Marx's critique of individualism is as vehement as Locke's endorsement of it. But rather than simply reducing the individual to the status of a social construction, as one might expect, Marx historicizes even the concept of the individual. Prior to a specific historical epoch (that of capitalist relations of production), the individual did not exist. Social forces constrain individuals to such an extent that they can produce worlds that have no individuals at all, which is how Marx envisions the precapitalist universe. In the *Grundrisse* he states this directly: "Human beings become individuals only through the process of history. . . . Exchange itself is a chief means of this individuation."[3] The very fact of a subject relating to itself in isolation from the social order is a result of social processes that owe nothing to the individual as such.

Beginning with either the individual or society, each position encounters a difficulty trying to account for the emergence of its opposite — society or the individual. Locke explains the societal impulse from the individual desire to protect property, and Marx deduces the development of the individual from structural changes in the means of production that form the basis of the social order. But each position runs aground on the power that the opposing force amasses and wields. Locke's liberalism cannot properly weigh the degree of social coercion in the individual's existence, and Marx's communism cannot fully address the conflict between the individual's desire and the social good.

In light of the limitations of the extreme positions, most thinkers take up a middle ground, seeing a struggle or tension in the relationship between the individual and the social order. For most, society shapes the individual profoundly, but individuality emerges through the way that each subject responds to this shaping. If, as Marx contends, there is no individual outside of society, there is also no society without the array of individual difference, and these differences can trigger changes in the social structure with which they interact. This is probably the dominant position today because it speaks to our sense that both the individual and society influence each other.[4] It is close to the position implicit in psychoanalytic theory, but psychoanalysis formulates the interaction between the individual and the social order in a very precise way that enables it to provide an explanation for why each comes into existence out of the other.

According to psychoanalytic thinking, neither the subject nor the social order exists independently but instead emerges out of the other's incompleteness. The subject exists at the point of the social order's failure to become a closed structure, and the subject enters into social arrangements as a result of its own failure to achieve self-identity. The internal contradictions within every social order create the space for the subject, just as the internal contradictions of the subject produce an opening to externality that links the subject to the social order. Failure on each side provides the connective apparatus and constitutes the bond between the subject and the social order.

To put it another way, the subject's entrance into a group or society depends on the originary loss that gives birth to its subjectivity. Without this loss and the desire that it produces in the subject, no one would agree to enter into a social bond, a bond that places a fundamental restriction on the subject's ability to enjoy. The psychoanalytic name for this foundational loss is the human animal's "premature birth," a condition that creates an undue dependence not present in other animals. But whether or not one wants to defend the idea of humanity's premature birth, the idea of a foundational loss is nonetheless essential for theorizing the emergence of subjectivity. Without loss, there could be no desire and no subjectivity. This loss leads the subject to society as the site where loss might be redeemed.

Once deceived by the lure of an imaginary complete enjoyment and disappointed with all the enjoyment it experiences, the subject is ready to agree to the entrance requirements of a society. The frustrated subject accedes to societal restrictions on enjoyment as she/he sees that others have also accepted these restrictions. A society circumnavigates the antagonisms between its members by promoting equality or justice among them all. This equality is an equality born through self-denial. As Freud points out, "Social justice means that we deny ourselves many things so that others may have to do without them as well, or, what is the same thing, may not be able to ask for them. This demand for equality is the root of social conscience and the sense of duty."[5] The subject's individual frustration with the inadequacy of every actual enjoyment measured against the anticipated enjoyment finds an outlet in the societal demand for equality, a demand that proscribes this enjoyment for all. The subject sacrifices a complete enjoyment that it never attains for the equality that derives from membership in society.

Shared Sacrifice of Nothing

Just as the sacrifice of what the subject doesn't have constitutes the subject as such, the shared sacrifice of an impossible pleasure gives birth to social living. The sacrifice that subjects make in order to enter society repeats the earlier sacrifice, but what occurs is repetition with a difference. While the initial sacrifice of the privileged object installs the death drive in the subject and thereby constitutes the individual as a subject, the repetition of this sacrifice marks an attempt to domesticate the death drive at the same time as it follows the death drive's logic. That is, the death drive leads us to this repetition, but the repetition attempts to solve the impossible bind that the death drive creates for us. Society is an attempt to solve the problem of subjectivity itself.[6]

Of course, the idea that subjectivity in the psychoanalytic sense exists prior to society is absurd, since subjectivity only becomes possible through the imposition of a societal demand on an animal being. But within society, the process of subjectivization occurs in two steps: an initial loss occurs that constitutes the subject, and subsequently the subject makes an additional sacrifice in order to commemorate the first loss and to join the social order. It is only through the repetition of loss that the social order really gets a hold on the subject because the second loss involves an investment through sacrifice in the good of the social order as a whole. In this sense, subjects do exist prior to their entrance into the social order, and properly socialized subjects are only those who have sacrificed for the sake of the social good. The subject who would refuse to make this sacrifice for the sake of society would not participate in the social bond and would exist as an outsider within the social order. This is the position that the psychotic occupies.

Because the originary sacrifice of the privileged object creates this object, we can never have what we've lost, which means that we desire an impossibility. The turn to society, however, allows us to envision possibility at the site of this impossibility. When we repeat the sacrifice in order to enter the social order, we do so in response to a demand made by social authority. Social authority prohibits the ultimate enjoyment, and this prohibition functions to disguise its impossibility. The transition from the initial sacrifice that constitutes subjectivity to its repetition that constitutes the social bond is the transition from impossibility to prohibition. We are willing to accept societal prohibition readily because it has the effect of making our impossible object seem possible. In this sense, joining society offers the subject the recompense of eliminating impossibility — replacing impossibility with a never- to-be-realized possibility.

But for the demand that society makes on me, the thinking goes, I would have the enjoyment that constantly eludes me. While the originary sacrifice involves the subject depriving itself of nothing, the repetition of the sacrifice when the subject enters society retroactively transforms this earlier sacrifice and allows the subject to believe that it has lost a substantial object rather than the embodiment of nothing. The socialized subject can no longer see the nothingness of what it has sacrificed. Thus, the turn to society is a deceptive turn. At its foundation, socialization imparts a lie to the subject. The social bond results from a shared lie and appeals to us because it permits a retreat from an unbearable impossibility to a frustrating prohibition.

We exist as members of a society and enjoy ourselves in this capacity through the shared sacrifice that gives us something held in common. What we hold in common is not a positive object; it is nothing but the act of sacrifice. For the subject itself, sacrifice provides a way of returning to its original genesis, and for society, sacrifice offers an opportunity for returning to the point at which the social order constituted itself. Organized rituals of sacrifice have an enduring place in society because they accomplish this type of return. To an extent that has not been adequately emphasized, psychoanalytic thought allows for a unique reappraisal of the origin and persistence of sacrifice within societies.

The prevalence of sacrifice presents a problem for political and social theorists because it is an act that seems to work against individual and social self-interest. The great thinkers of sacrifice have thus tried to reconcile it with an end that its appearance belies. For instance, Marcel Mauss sees sacrifice as the foundational form of the social bond. As he points out in his discussion of potlatch among the Indians of the American Northwest, "The purpose of destruction by sacrifice is precisely that it is an act of giving that is necessarily reciprocated."[7] Sacrifice engenders reciprocity (with another individual, another tribe, a god, or whatever), and it thus has the result of producing a bond where none had hitherto existed. Rather than constituting a loss for one sacrificing, the act redounds upon the one who performs it and bestows the profit of a desired relationship. By interpreting sacrifice (and gift giving) in this way, Mauss sidesteps its counterintuitive appearance and reveals how it remains within the realm of interested behavior. But by doing so, he also raises the question of why bonds or relationships require the act of sacrifice rather than mere verbal or contractual agreement. Sacrifice seems like too much trouble for societies to endure if they simply want to establish relations. In short, the excess implicit in the phenomenon of sacrifice remains despite the explanation that Mauss provides.

It is this excess that motivates the philosophy of Georges Bataille, perhaps the foremost thinker of sacrifice. Of all those who confront this mysterious phenomenon, Bataille is the one who does not try to reduce sacrifice to some form of interest. Instead, he accepts sacrifice as an act performed for its own sake. Societies sacrifice, according to Bataille, because sacrifice is essential to their functioning and because they enjoy it. He claims: "There is generally no growth but only a luxurious squandering of energy in every form! The history of life on earth is mainly the effect of a wild exuberance; the dominant event is the development of luxury, the production of increasingly burdensome forms of life."[8] Divesting itself of excess is the fundamental social operation, and this occurs most often through sacrifice. As society advances, it becomes more luxurious, sacrificing more and more, and this sacrifice is always its own reward, providing an enjoyment that derives from a process of unburdening.[9]

The problem with Bataille's theorization of sacrifice resides in the obscure ontology that informs it. For Bataille, there is an overabundance of energy in the world — represented most obviously by the sun, which is constantly burning off its excess — and the fundamental goal of existence is the elimination of this excess. All beings engage in efforts to rid themselves of their surplus energy, either through gifts, sacrifice, or simply destruction. Elimination in whatever form becomes, according to this theory, the primary fact, and accumulation occurs only in order to engender possibilities for sacrifice and destruction. While Bataille correctly sees the primacy of sacrifice as a social phenomenon, he links it to a theory of being as intrinsically excessive that is, at bottom, empirical (as evidenced by his argument about the sun). Where Bataille sees excess, one could just as easily see balance: a universe in which beings take in a certain amount of energy and then expel that same amount. But he sees excess in being itself because he begins with a philosophy of excess.[10]

Though psychoanalytic thought arrives at the same conclusion as Bataille — seeing sacrifice as a primary social fact not reducible to self-interest or a social good — it takes a different path to get there. It locates the impulse to sacrifice in the original loss that constitutes the subject and that entry in the social order repeats. Because loss creates society as such, societies tend inevitably toward reenacting it, most often in the form of sacrifice. Societies perform sacrificial rituals in order to allow subjects to experience and enjoy the social bond through an encounter with the nothing that they hold in common.

Such rituals appear explicitly in premodern societies, which consistently make public sacrifices of animals (or people) to please their gods. While sacrifices have the expressed intent of gaining good favor or warding off bad, their unconscious function consists solely in enacting the sacrifice itself. Any pleasure that follows from the sacrifice — such as abundant rainfall that produces good crops — is strictly secondary to the enjoyment of the sacrifice itself. Societies sacrifice for the sake of sacrifice, not for the end that it produces. This sacrifice for the sake of sacrifice doesn't end with the onset of modernity but instead continues primarily in a disguised form. What defines modernity isn't so much a degree of enlightenment and rationality as a fundamental refusal to avow the primacy of sacrifice.

Modernity replaces a regime centered around sacrifice and squander with one centered around utility and accumulation. Modern consciousness directs itself toward the useful: one justifies technological advances, medical breakthroughs, and economic progress through their utility.[11] Modern societies act with the conscious intention of making the world run smoother and with the utmost efficiency. And yet, at the same time, wasteful behavior endures — most conspicuously in the form of religion, which modernity's philosophy of utility has not succeeded in extirpating.

Even though modern religious observations tend for the most part to avoid animal or human sacrifices, they do nonetheless represent one of the predominant arenas in which social sacrifice occurs. Thought of in terms of the self-interest of participants or the larger social good, religion constitutes a massive sacrifice of time and resources. This is what renders it problematic for evolutionary biology. According to the tenets of this science, natural selection tends to eliminate waste rather than foster it.[12] The wastefulness of religion, combined with its continued wide appeal, forces evolutionary biologists to explain its existence and persistence as the by-product of another process that has evolutionary benefits (which is, according to most prominent evolutionary biologists, the tendency to trust authority figures). But what the evolutionary biologist cannot see, because this science does not take enjoyment into account, is the appeal of the sacrifice of resources for its own sake. Religious rituals persist in modernity — even if in a completely modified form, like the worship of a sports team — because they provide an opportunity for the repetition of the original shared social sacrifice.

Not only do religious observations allow subjects to repeat the original social sacrifice, but they also mask this sacrifice as the source of enjoyment. Religions tell their adherents that they must sacrifice freedom in their lifestyle choices, money that might be spent for pleasure, and time otherwise left for leisure. The reward for these sacrifices — most typically, an eternal life of pure enjoyment, or at least membership in a privileged community — serves to justify them. As a result, the sacrificing adherents of the religion can believe that they are sacrificing for the sake of the future reward rather than for the sake of the sacrifice itself. When we practice religious sacrifice, we don't see where our true enjoyment lies — we don't recognize the link between loss and enjoyment — and this deception is crucial for religion's attractiveness. We cling to our enjoyment, but we also cling to the illusion that it is something that we might have rather than a loss that we must endure.

Like religion, war continues in modernity, even though we understand and declaim its wastefulness. The typical modern subject can watch an antiwar film like Stanley Kubrick's *Paths of Glory* (1961) and feel convinced that war is hell and completely unnecessary. After leaving the theater, however, this same subject can come to believe that there is no alternative but to send troops to Vietnam to stop the potential spread of Communist aggression.

War appeals to even modern subjects because it mobilizes our enjoyment. Wars are not fought only for the sake of expanding or defending reigns of power but also in order to enact a social sacrifice. By fighting a war, a social order sacrifices its soldiers, and this sacrifice constitutes a great part of war's appeal. Supporting the troops necessarily implies supporting and celebrating their sacrifice, which is why antiwar movements that proclaim "Support the troops, bring them home" fail to arouse the masses to action. By bringing the troops home, one eliminates the possibility of their sacrifice, which is the source of the society's libidinal investment in them. Bringing the troops home renders it impossible to continue to enjoy them.

The problem with an antiwar film like *Paths of Glory* that depicts senseless sacrifice is that this sacrifice adds to rather than subtracts from war's appeal. This is why, as Sheila Kunkle has pointed out, every war film is a prowar film.[13] No matter how negatively a film depicts a war, the carnage inevitably links to war's hidden appeal. Of course, by showing war's utter meaninglessness, Kubrick's film impairs to some extent our ability to enjoy the sacrifice, but he doesn't eliminate it altogether.

A film like *Saving Private Ryan* (Steven Spielberg, 1998), on the other hand, shows the suffering of war leading to a meaningful end, which is why it is even more directly a prowar film. *Saving Private Ryan* allows us to enjoy the sacrifice of the soldiers in World War II and to dissociate enjoyment from sacrifice. We watch the film believing that we accept the sacrifice for the sake of the pleasure we experience in the end (with the rescue of Private Ryan or with the victory of the Allies) rather than for its own sake. We need a reason to sacrifice not because we otherwise aren't willing to sacrifice but because a reason allows us to disavow the traumatic nature of our own enjoyment. We can tell ourselves that we are sacrificing not for the sake of our enjoyment but for the sake of what we gain from that sacrifice. In this way, reasons for our sacrifices have the effect of accommodating sacrifice to the modern demand for utility.

An Absence of Final Causes

The widespread failure to see that sacrifice occurs for its own sake stems from the ubiquity of thinking from the perspective of the final cause. The final cause, as first defined by Aristotle, is the "end or that for the sake of which a thing is done."[14] It causes the action in the sense that it provides a motivating purpose or a result that the action will effectuate. When we analyze an action in terms of its final cause, we look for purposiveness. This type of analysis doesn't necessarily lead to an inability to identify other forms of causality. For Aristotle, of course, the final cause is but one aspect of an overall theory of causality that includes a formal cause, a material cause, and an effective cause.

One can, in short, sustain a pluralistic theory of causality in which the idea of the final cause does not eliminate other forms of causality. For instance, recognizing that the final cause for the American Civil War was the establishment of a unified industrial America with a basis in wage labor rather than slavery does not interfere with recognizing the development of modern war-making strategy as the formal cause, the military might of both sides as its material cause, and the decision to fire on Fort Sumter as the effective cause. But the dominance of the final cause over our thinking does obstruct our ability to grasp what we might call the immanent cause, the cause that inheres in an action done for its own sake rather than for a larger purpose.[15]

The perspective of the final cause dominates our thinking in the form of privileging the good that we might obtain. Whether we define the good as avoidance of harm, physical pleasure, mastery of others, knowledge, survival, self-interest, or material goods, we nonetheless almost inevitably see it as the final cause motivating our actions.[16] No one would act, so this thinking goes, in a way that did not aim at producing some good. Most contemporary subjects would conceive of the good in relative terms — Henry's good would not be Alexandra's good, and they might even be opposed to each other — but they would accept the privileging of the good itself.

The most common reigning conception of the good is identifying it with power. This line of thought, inherited ultimately from Nietzsche and popularized in the contemporary intellectual universe by Michel Foucault, analyzes actions in terms of the power that they provide for those who embark on them: the executive chases power in the form of capital; the lover chases power in the form of new romantic conquests; the minister chases power in the form of a psychically submissive congregation; and the parent chases power in the form of a high-achieving child. Though this seems like a radical subversion of the traditional idea of the good as the end that motivates us, the analysis of actions in terms of power simply replaces one idea of the good with another. Even those who morally question power as an end nonetheless think of it as the good — that is, the final cause — that motivates actions. Power analysis remains teleological in its conception of causality, and thus it suffers from precisely the same limitation as traditional thinking about the good.[17]

When we think from the perspective of the final cause or the good at which our actions aim, we miss the possibility that actions might be ends in themselves. To think of the actions of society in terms of the enjoyment that they provide is not to simply replace power or happiness or physical pleasure with another end. Enjoyment is not a result that actions pursue and allow us to obtain but instead inheres in the action itself. This is why, in contrast to power or any other good, no one can possess enjoyment. Enjoyment is irreducible to a good that one pursues because, rather than benefiting the society, it deprives the society of something. Enjoyment is expenditure without the possibility of recompense. While we might pursue pleasure, we never pursue enjoyment, though it can function as the immanent cause of our actions, as that which drives us rather than motivating us as a conscious goal.

When Freud discovered the death drive in 1920, he effectively theorized enjoyment as the immanent cause of our actions. But with the onset of the psychoanalytic method more than twenty-five years earlier, Freud began his break with the dominance of the final cause. The psychoanalytic method of free association takes as its point of departure an attempt to put the final cause, which governs our conscious interactions, to the side. When the analysand speaks, the analyst focuses on the signifiers themselves and what they say rather than on the meaning that the analysand intends to impart with these signifiers. The premise of psychoanalysis is that the analysand puts signifiers into play for their own sake and that these signifiers do in fact signify on their own, beyond the conscious intentions of the analysand. The conscious meaning behind them — what analysands believe that they are trying to communicate — functions precisely like the final cause. It is the translation into consciousness of an unconscious desire, and it obscures this unconscious desire just like the final cause obscures the immanent cause. Psychoanalytic treatment involves assisting analysands to arrive at the point where they can avow the immanent cause, where they can adopt a different relationship to their own enjoyment.

The Two Forms of the Social Bond

We might think of the ways that society relates to its own enjoyment in terms of the different types of logic articulated in sexual difference. Sexual difference has a privileged status within psychoanalytic thought. As Joan Copjec puts it, "Sexual difference is unlike racial, class, or ethnic differences. Whereas these differences are inscribed in the symbolic, sexual difference is not: only the failure of its inscription is marked in the symbolic. Sexual difference, in other words, is a real and not a symbolic difference."[18] The real status of sexual difference indicates that the sexual antagonism is the foundational antagonism within the social order. It creates a logical divide within society that no amount of reconciliation can bridge. But it also marks a point of political contention.

One of the most prevalent political critiques of psychoanalytic thought among contemporary theorists stems from its insistence on the priority of sexual difference over other differences (racial difference, class difference, sexual identity difference, and so on). Thomas Dipiero, for instance, explicitly attacks psychoanalytic theory on this point in *White Men Aren't*, where he contends that racial difference has an equal importance for identity formation.[19] The insistence on the priority of sexual difference seems at best arbitrary, a function of the particular structure of the psychoanalytic method rather than a response to subjectivity itself, and at worst ideological, minimizing the importance of class, racial, and ethnic divides. The focus on sexual difference affirms for critics the central oversight of psychoanalysis: its failure to think beyond the dynamic of the family and its inability to grapple with the problems posed by the social order at large.[20]

Ironically, it is precisely its insistence on the real status of sexual difference and on its primacy as an antagonism that gives psychoanalytic thought its social and political relevance. Unlike other differences, sexual difference underlies the fundamental structure of the social order. It provides two distinct though overlapping ways of organizing society in terms of enjoyment.[21] In *Seminar XX*, which he devoted to the problem of sexual difference, Lacan maps these two modes of organization with reference to set theory. The male side offers a familiar organization for society: it creates a social bond through the process of exclusion. Male sexual identity emerges through the exceptionality of the idealized primal father, a figure who, unlike all other men, is not subject to castration. This nonlacking figure provides a model for male subjects that they cannot possibly emulate — though they endeavor to do so ceaselessly — because he exists only as an exception. Nonetheless, this exceptional figure allows male subjects to constitute their identity by showing them what they aren't.

Male sexuation is a failure — no one achieves the ideal that he aims for — but it operates with a clear direction for male identity. Men cannot live up to the standard established by the ideal, but they can have a clear idea of what they're not accomplishing. In this sense, the situation of the male subject is not so bad: he has an unending project to animate his activity and provide some sense of purpose. But the role of the exception at the core of male sexual identity renders the project of male sexuation necessarily antagonistic with itself. Male subjects cannot simply pursue the ideal on their own without concerning themselves with others.

Because the ultimate enjoyment exists only in the position of exceptionality, the male subject must posit the existence of the exception in order to demonstrate that this enjoyment is possible. A society founded on the logic of male sexuation is a society at constant war with itself in the form of the exception. It targets the exception in order to access the enjoyment that this exception appears to be monopolizing. The goal for subjects constituted by male sexuation is either becoming exceptional (and thus enjoying as noncastrated exceptions) or eliminating the position of the exception (and thus accessing the exceptional enjoyment by destroying its exceptional status). Both possibilities require the targeting and conquest of the figure posited as the exception.

The social bond depends, according to the logic of male sexuation, on excluding a particular group in order to provide an enemy around which the collective identity of members of the society can form. The failure of legitimate members of the society to enjoy themselves finds its explanation in the illicit enjoyment of the enemy, which occupies the structural position of the exception. The enemy — either internal or external — surreptitiously plays the role of the idealized father for the society organized around the male logic. Here, identity forms only through opposition.

An insistence on the irreducibility of the friend/enemy distinction in social formations testifies to the dominance of a male logic that privileges exclusion as a way of constituting identity. This is perhaps most visible in the thought of political theorist Carl Schmitt, who cannot envision a political entity not organized around this distinction and the exclusion that it implies. The distinction trumps all others because it provides the basic organization for the social order as such. According to Schmitt, "The real friend-enemy grouping is existentially so strong and decisive that the non-political antithesis, at precisely the moment at which it becomes political, pushes aside and subordinates its hitherto purely religious, purely economic, purely cultural criteria and motives to the conditions and conclusions of the political situation at hand. In any event, that grouping is always political which orients itself toward this most extreme possibility. This grouping is therefore always the decisive human grouping, the political entity."[22] Schmitt cannot imagine a political grouping that would not revolve around the friend/enemy distinction because he cannot imagine identity without a clear opposition. This attests to his investment in the male logic of the exception.

It is not simply Schmitt's militarism and sympathy for Fascism — like Heidegger, he was an early supporter of the Nazi Party — that leads him to insist on the necessity of the friend/enemy distinction. In fact, he has concrete ethical reasons for this insistence. When this distinction disappears, the political as such disappears, and economics replaces it. Without the friend/enemy distinction, in other words, we become reduced to purely economic beings. According to Schmitt, this is precisely what results from the mass embrace of liberalism as a political philosophy, which is why he ardently opposes it. It also leads contemporary leftists like Chantal Mouffe to borrow this aspect of Schmitt's thought, despite his connection to the Right, and to incorporate it into a conception of radical democracy. Like Schmitt, Mouffe believes that we cannot overcome the we/they antagonism, and she contends that the attempt to do so has the effect of unleashing the reactionary populist politics of figures such as Jean-Marie Le Pen in France and Jörg Haider in Austria.

The friend/enemy distinction is so attractive to both the political Right and Left because it represents the mode of organizing the social bond that is the most accessible to consciousness. The figure of the enemy offers subjects within society an explanation for the loss that they experience as members of the society and as subjects. Trotsky provides a reason for the failure of the Five-Year Plan in the Soviet Union; the terrorist causes the insecurity of daily life in the United States; and Israeli hegemony produces the misery that the Palestinians experience. Of course, in some cases, the enemy really does contribute to the loss that occurs within a society, but no enemy bears responsibility for loss as such, which comes first with subjectivity and then with the social order itself. The enemy transforms an ontological phenomenon — loss within the social order — into an empirical one — instances of loss. Through the obstacle that it places in the way, the enemy facilitates the belief that the collective identity within the social order or an authentic social bond is something that we might have. The barrier transforms an absence of collective identity into the illusory possibility of having this identity, and the possibility of having is integral to the male logic of exception.[23]

Whereas male subjectivity is preoccupied with what it believes it has or should have, female subjectivity, as a structural position, involves an embrace of what one doesn't have. To adopt the feminine position is ipso facto to recognize that all having involves having nothing. This position is thus an indictment of the male illusion of the possibility of having. As Lacan's chief inheritor and son-in-law Jacques-Alain Miller notes, "A true woman . . . reveals to man the absurdity of having. To a certain extent, she is man's ruination."[24] When we grasp what Miller calls "the absurdity of having," we return to the initial experience of traumatic loss and face the nothingness of the object.

Female subjectivity does not orient itself around an ideal of noncastration. There is no figure of the primal mother who appears to have the ultimate enjoyment and to hoard this enjoyment for herself. Though various ideals of female subjectivity certainly exist and have an impact on female identity, there is not simply one ideal. Instead, there is a plethora of them, and they often contradict each other. This is why Lacan insists that "there's no such thing as Woman, Woman with a capital *W* indicating the universal."[25] The absence of the figure of Woman as an ideal creates a radically different structure of subjectivity for female subjects. While male subjects can define themselves in relation to the exceptionality that they can never themselves attain — for a man, the exception will always be someone else — female subjects must define themselves without such a reference point.

The result is that female subjectivity rests on a more tenuous ground: without the exception as a reference point that the male has, the female subject has no unified category within which to place herself. Because an exception is necessary to constitute the rule (or an outside is necessary to constitute an inside), there is no coherent category of female subjectivity. What results instead is a series of singularities without a clear rule defining them. As Kenneth Reinhard notes, "Unlike the case of men, for whom there *is* a unified category, 'all men,' that they are identified as being members of, women are *radically singular*, not examples of a class or members of a closed set, but *each one an exception*."[26] The absence of an exception defining the category of female subjectivity renders female subjectivity as such exceptional.

Male subjectivity always strives for the ultimate enjoyment that it posits in the unattainable position of exceptionality. Its enjoyment is always futural, and it depends on the act of obtaining or having its object. Female subjectivity provides enjoyment through what it doesn't have; one enjoys one's loss as a female subject. This type of enjoyment is not exclusionary in the way that the male form of enjoyment is. It is not confined to a few exceptions, because there is nothing but exceptions, according to the logic of female sexuation. The social bond involves both the female enjoyment of not-having and the male enjoyment of having, though it is the former that provides the only real enjoyment that subjects experience from the social bond.

The foundation of the social bond is a loss held in common, a collective sacrifice of nothing for the sake of the social order. This experience of collective sacrifice or loss provides enjoyment in the form linked to female sexuation. It is the enjoyment of a shared not-having, and it is the form that the social bond necessarily takes at first. Each subject sacrifices something in order to live together collectively, and through the shared sacrifice, subjects constitute the social bond. This bond is traumatic and shameful because its avowal places subjects in a position where their lack is completely exposed. When subjects experience the essence of the social bond — the moment of collective self-sacrifice — they simultaneously experience the humiliation of rendering their loss visible. The enjoyment of this bond comes with a steep price, and no society is willing to pay it for very long.

Consequently, every social order obscures the traumatic nature of the social bond, which operates according to the female logic of not-having, through recourse to a male logic of exception, manifested most directly in the friend/enemy distinction. This male logic is a logic of the all — a totality forged through the position of the exception — and it continually leaves subjects in a state of dissatisfaction, seeking a completeness that they will never attain. The female logic of not-having or universalized exceptionality is not a separate logic of the social order, a logic describing an alternative form of society. It is, rather, the hidden bond lying beneath the phallic order founded on exception. Every society has both logics simultaneously at work, but the underlying logic of the not-all is the one that societies find themselves unable to avow.

Neither Carl Schmitt nor Chantal Mouffe is able to think of the social bond in terms of the female logic of not-having. This logic has its basis in loss itself and the impossibility of overcoming it. Rather than viewing the social order in terms of friend and enemy, inside and outside, or rule and exception, the logic of the not-all posits that there are only enemies, only outsiders, and only exceptions. The point is not that everyone is a friend but that everyone is an enemy, including oneself. According to this idea of the universalized exception, we can't erect a firm distinction between inside and outside because those inside — friends — are defined solely in terms of what they don't have, and this renders them indistinct from those outside — enemies.

Our enjoyment of the social bond operates according to the logic of not-having: we enjoy the shared experience of loss. But the pleasure that we take in the social bond follows from the male logic of the all and the exception. We find pleasure in the possibility of having a collective identity that sets us apart from outsiders. This pleasure works in one sense to facilitate our enjoyment by hiding it from us. While most members of a society can accept the pleasure that derives from a sense of having a collective identity — almost no one objects to the affirmation of national unity embodied by a flag, for instance — few can embrace the idea that the social bond exists through a shared sense of loss. This is why the moments when the shared sense of loss becomes visible are often quickly followed by the attempt to assert a positive collective identity. Or, to put it in other terms, when enjoyment becomes visible, we retreat toward pleasure.

From Enjoyment to Pleasure

Nowhere is the retreat from enjoyment to pleasure more evident than in the American response to the attacks of September 11, 2001. The attacks immediately reinvigorated the social bond for a majority of Americans. The loss that they occasioned brought subjects back to the shared sacrifice that defines their membership in American society. Even as they were horrified by the image of the towers burning and then falling, most Americans, in the strict psychoanalytic sense of the term, enjoyed the attacks insofar as the attacks allowed them to experience once again their social bond with great intensity.

This is a bond that one suffers, just as one suffers from a terrorist attack. Even though it followed from an attack, this bond was not one formed through the male logic of friend/enemy, which is why the headline in *Le Monde* on September 12, 2001, could proclaim, "Nous sommes tous Américains."[27] The bond formed around the September 11 attacks was not initially a bond of exclusivity with a clear outside and inside. Any subject willing to accede to the experience of loss could become a part of American society at that moment. The not-all of the social bond occurs through the experience of loss, but the recognition of this type of bond is unbearable. One enjoys it without deriving any pleasure from it. It is, in fact, painful. Not only is it painful, but it also entails complete humiliation. The society experiences the shame of being a victim and enduring trauma — the shame of enjoyment itself.

In order to disguise this shameful enjoyment, the United States quickly turned to an assertion of power that would carry with it the promise of a restored wholeness — the recovery of an imaginary perfect security. The attack on Afghanistan brought pleasure to most members of American society. This pleasure had the function of rendering the enjoyment that emerged through traumatic loss bearable, but it could not fulfill its inherent promise. Enjoyment satisfies, and pleasure always disappoints. The disappointing nature of the attack on Afghanistan paved the way to the subsequent attack on Iraq in a further attempt to find an actual pleasure equal to what we anticipated. In terms of American society, these foreign wars serve as alibis for the enjoyment of the traumatic attacks themselves. Because we seek respite from the loss that binds us, we flee from the social bond despite our purported desire for it. The authentic social bond exists only in the shared experience of loss — that is, only according to the female logic of not-having.

But the attack on Iraq also illustrates the inescapability of the enjoyment attached to loss. The Iraq War clearly follows from the male logic of having and aims at producing the pleasure resulting from possession: the United States would conquer a recalcitrant dictator and obtain a firm ally in a globally significant region. This is both the stated justification for the war and the explanation offered by critics who see it as an exercise in American imperialism. For both the perpetuators of the war and its critics, the war concerns having, despite the different inflections they give this idea. But the result of the war is the failure of having and the renewed experience of loss. The pursuit of the pleasure involved in having returns American society to the traumatic loss involved in the September 11 attacks. Of course, no one fights wars with the express intention of losing them, but every war brings with it sacrifice and loss, which is ultimately the substance of the social bond and the source of our ability to enjoy that bond. The pursuit of the pleasure of having leads to the loss that inevitably accompanies this pursuit.

Imperial powers do not attempt to stretch their military and economic reach to the point that it breaks because of an inescapable will to power or a biological urge for infinite expansion. The conquering drive of empires has its roots in the search for what no amount of imperial possession can provide — the enjoyment of the experience of loss. Empires conquer increasing quantities of territory in order to discover a territory that they can't conquer. In this same way, the Afghanistan War disappointed the American leadership because it didn't provide even the possibility for loss. Donald Rumsfeld's lament that the country didn't have any targets to bomb points in this direction. Iraq, in contrast, promised a possible defeat, and if it hadn't, Syria or Iran would surely have come within the sights of the Bush administration. Whatever the proffered justification or hidden motivation, powerful societies ultimately go to war in order to reenact a constitutive loss and facilitate the enjoyment that this loss entails.[28]

This is the case not just with war but with any positive project that a social order takes up. Building a monument like the Eiffel Tower provided French society with a possession that allows for collective identification. But the work involved with the building involved a great sacrifice in time and in money. When we think of the Eiffel Tower, we rarely think of the sacrifice required for its construction; instead, we think of the sense of identity that it offers. It provides a positive point of identification for France itself as a nation, and French subjects can find pleasure through this identification.

Nonetheless, the enjoyment of the Eiffel Tower, in contrast to the pleasure that it offers, stems from the sacrifice required to construct it. Every finished societal product — such as victory in Iraq, the beauty of the Eiffel Tower, smooth roads on which to drive — promises pleasure, but this pleasure primarily supplies an alibi for the enjoyment that the sacrifices on the way to the product produce. These sacrifices allow us to experience the social bond by repeating the act of sacrifice through which each subject became a member of the social order. It is not so much that the pursuit of pleasure backfires (though it does) but that it is never done simply for its own sake. We embark on social projects not in spite of what they will cost us but because of what they will cost us.[29]

The dialectic of pleasure and enjoyment also plays itself out in the relationship that subjects in society have to their leader. According to Freud, all group members install the leader in the position of an ego ideal, and this ego ideal held in common furthers the bond among members of society. But the identification with the leader has two sides to it: on the one hand, subjects identify with the leader's symbolic position as a noncastrated ideal existing beyond the world of lack; but on the other hand, subjects identify with the leader's weaknesses, which exist in spite of the powerful image.[30] Both modes of identification work together in order to give subjects a sense of being a member of society, but they work in radically different ways. The identification with the leader's power provides the subject with a sense of symbolic identity and recognition, whereas the identification with the leader's weaknesses allows the subject to enjoy being a part of the community.

The identification with the leader's strength provides the pleasure that obscures the enjoyment deriving from the identification with the leader's weaknesses. The weaknesses indicate that the leader is a subject of loss, that she/he enjoys rather than being entirely devoted to ruling as a neutral embodiment of the people. The weaknesses are evidence of the leader's enjoyment, points at which a private enjoyment stains the public image. By identifying with these points, subjects in a community affirm the association of enjoyment with loss rather than with presence. But at the same time, the leader's weaknesses cannot completely eclipse the evidence for the leader's strength. The strength allows subjects who identify with the leader in her/his weakness to disavow this would-be traumatic identification and to associate themselves consciously with strength rather than weakness.

The trajectory of Bill Clinton's popularity during his presidency illustrates precisely how identification with the leader unfolds. When accusations of sexual impropriety with Monica Lewinsky first appeared, Clinton's public approval rating reached its highest levels. Most thought that Clinton was probably guilty of some private wrongdoing, but they also felt that his sexual peccadilloes should remain private. Though they infuriated his Republican accusers, his sexual weaknesses had the effect of enhancing his overall popularity. This trend continued until it became undeniably clear that Clinton really was guilty, when it became impossible to disavow his weakness. At this point, identifying with Clinton became inescapably apparent as identifying with Clinton in his weakness, which rendered it more difficult to sustain. The American populace could enjoy Clinton's weakness and form a social bond through this weakness only as long as it remained partially obscured.

The fundamental barrier to the establishment of an authentic social bond is the resistance to avowing the traumatic nature of that bond. We use the pleasure that accompanies the bombing of Afghanistan to disguise the shared enjoyment we experience through the traumatic experience of loss. But this pleasure inevitably disappoints us and triggers the belief that someone has stolen the complete pleasure that we expected to experience. This is why there can properly be no end to the War on Terror, no end to the list of countries that the United States plans to invade to attain complete security, no end to the number of terrorist leaders executed.[31] Complete security, like complete pleasure, is mythical. It attempts to bypass the one experience that cannot be bypassed — the foundational experience of loss — and it is this experience that holds the key to an authentic social bond.

The structure of society (which is the result of the structure of signification) is such that it blinds the subject to the possibility of shared sacrifice and the social bond that results from it. No matter how often children hear the ideology of sharing or how many times we repeat to them the gospel of fairness, they will inevitably believe that their sacrifice has enabled others to enjoy more than their proper share or unfairly. As Slavoj Žižek points out in *Tarrying with the Negative*, "We always impute to the 'other' an excessive enjoyment: he wants to steal our enjoyment (by ruining our way of life) and/or he has access to some secret, perverse enjoyment. In short, what really bothers us about the 'other' is the peculiar way he organizes his enjoyment, precisely the surplus, the 'excess' that pertains to this way: the smell of 'their' food, 'their' noisy songs and dances, 'their' strange manners, 'their' attitude toward work."[32] This belief — this paranoia about the other's secret enjoyment — derives from the signifier's inability to manifest its transparency.

In one sense, the signifier is transparent: the very possibility of psychoanalysis depends on the fact that subjects speak their unconscious desire even (or especially) when they try hardest to hide it. The signifiers that subjects choose reveal the truth of their unconscious desires. And yet, at the same time, the signifier does not avow its own transparency; every signifier appears to be hiding something, a secret meaning, a private intention, to which only the subject itself has access. Ludwig Wittgenstein spent the better part of his philosophical career attempting to disabuse fellow philosophers of the idea that the signifier could hide anything. When we believe that signifiers hide a private meaning, we fall victim to the deception of language as such. Hearing what someone says allows us to grasp all that there is to grasp. As Wittgenstein puts it, "To say 'He alone can know what he intends' is nonsense."[33] In fact, he goes so far as to claim that the subject can know the other's intention even better than its own. He notes, "I can know what someone else is thinking, not what I am thinking."[34] By recognizing the transparency of the signifier, we might fight against the paranoia that seems to accompany subjectivity itself, and all of Wittgenstein's thought participates in this combat.

Even though Wittgenstein's argument has undoubtedly found adherents among many philosophers and laypersons, paranoia about the other's hidden enjoyment has not disappeared in the years since this argument first appeared. One could even safely say that paranoia has grown more rampant. Is this simply the result of a failure to disseminate Wittgenstein's thought widely enough or of popular resistance to it? Or is it that paranoia is written into the structure of the signifier itself? The hidden meaning that the subject perceives beneath the signifier is the result of the signifier's apparent opaqueness, and no amount of inveighing against hidden meaning will stop subjects from believing in it.

The belief that the other holds a secret enjoyment that the subject has sacrificed renders the smooth functioning of collective life impossible. The force that allows human beings to come together to form a society in common — language — is at once the force that prevents any society from working out. The structure of the signifier itself militates against utopia. It produces societies replete with subjects paranoid about, and full of envy for, the enjoying other.

Though one might imagine a society in which subjects enjoyed without bothering themselves about the other's enjoyment, such a vision fails to comprehend the nature of our enjoyment. We find our enjoyment through that of the other rather than intrinsically within ourselves. Our envy of the other's enjoyment persists because this is the mode through which we ourselves enjoy. It is thus far easier to give up the idea of one's own private enjoyment for the sake of the social order than it is to give up the idea of the enjoying other.

This is why equality doesn't solve the problem of the social antagonism. Rather than eliminating the envy of the other's enjoyment, a sense of justice exacerbates it. The demand for equality and justice has its origins in envy of the other's enjoyment. According to Joan Copjec, "Envy is not simply an impediment, but the very condition of our notion of justice."[35] Because the idea of equality and justice is rooted in envy, each member of society has constant suspicions about the others and their commitment to forgoing pleasure for the sake of the social order as a whole. Suspicions continually emerge, revealing that the social antagonism remains in force in such a way that makes eruptions of violence inevitable.

The other is perhaps enjoying, but this is not an enjoyment that occurs in spite of loss. Like the subject's own, the other's enjoyment is the enjoyment of loss because there is no other kind. Recognizing the link between enjoyment and loss — that is, accepting the logic of female sexuation — allows subjects to emphasize enjoyment at the expense of pleasure. Those who achieve this experience the impossibility of having the object, recognizing that one can never have the object because it is nothing, existing only insofar as it is lost, and it is only in this form that it provides enjoyment for the subject.

As subjects of loss, there is no barrier to the establishment of an authentic social bond, one where envy does not play a key role. The antagonism between the society and the individual develops out of the envy that subjects experience when they believe other members of the society have greater access to the privileged object than they do. For the subject who grasps that this object only exists — and can only be enjoyed — through its loss, envy is no longer inevitable. The composition of nothing is such that no one can have more of it than anyone else; there can be no hierarchy of loss, because everyone alike loses nothing. The authentic society of subjects connected through the embrace of trauma would be a society that could recognize that nothing is something after all.

7

Against Knowledge

Rule by Experts

Psychoanalytic thought provides a way of understanding the role that enjoyment plays in structuring individual subjectivity and the social order. But it also allows us to see how enjoyment shapes the field of political contestation, which has undergone a fundamental historical shift in parallel with a similar shift in the location of authority. The onset of capitalism inaugurates a significant change not just in the structure of the economy and of social relations but also in the nature of social authority. As Michel Foucault and many others have documented, power relocates at the time of capitalism's emergence: diffuse networks of power replace a central social authority.[1]

The point is not simply that rule by royalty gives way to representative government, in which power is shared among a wider spectrum of people, but that the location and foundation of authority in society undergoes a revolution. Even when monarchs or despots persist in the capitalist epoch, they become fundamentally changed figures, no longer embodying the position of ultimate authority, which instead multiplies throughout the social fabric. A unified law becomes a hodgepodge of rules and recommendations.

Or one might say that the master controlling social relations from a transcendent position gives way to a variety of experts caught up within the very relations of power in which they exert their influence. In the absence of a central law uniting the social field, these experts provide rules to live by and guidance for the variegations of life. According to Anthony Giddens, what emerges is a universe ruled by "expert systems," which are "systems of technical accomplishment or professional expertise that organise large areas of the material and social environments in which we live today."[2] Knowledge, not mastery, becomes the source of social authority. The reign of expert systems is the denouement of the process that originates when, at the dawn of the capitalist epoch, "all that is solid melts into air, all that is holy is profaned."[3] This famous description of bourgeois society from the *Communist Manifesto* attempts metaphorically to chronicle the radical social leveling process that a capitalist economy entails.

An economy based on exchange, like that of capitalism, demands that the objects exchanged have an equivalent value. If the exchange did not involve equivalents or, to say the same thing, involved cheating on one side, the system could not sustain itself. A system of unequal exchange is not a viable system of exchange. The equivalence of all objects under the rubric of the commodity implies the equivalence of all subjects as well: if one entity is excepted from universal equivalence, the entire system would cease to function because its logic would no longer hold true.[4] One of Marx's great insights consists in recognizing the transformative effect of the dominance of universal equivalence that capitalist society necessarily institutes. But ironically, this process, as Marx and Engels describe it, ends up ultimately undermining the project that Marx and Engels themselves undertook to topple it.

Marx composed the three volumes of *Capital* and a multitude of other writings in order to supply knowledge about capitalist relations of production that leftist militants could use to change those relations. He fought capitalism with knowledge, with expertise, even as he hoped that it would not remain merely theoretical but become practical. Early on in his career, Marx tried to theorize in a practical way, to create a mode of thinking that actively engages in the world rather than reflecting on it (which is the position that knowledge, he claims, has historically occupied). This is apparent throughout *The Economic and Philosophic Manuscripts of 1844* and in the "Theses on Feuerbach." In the former, Marx claims: "The resolution of the *theoretical* antitheses is *only* possible *in a practical way*, by virtue of the practical energy of men. Their resolution is therefore by no means merely a problem of understanding, but a *real* problem of life, which *philosophy* could not solve precisely because it conceived this problem as *merely* a theoretical one."[5] Marx orients his theory toward praxis not because he is wary of knowledge's complicity with power (as Foucault is) but because he worries about its historical fecklessness. As the final thesis on Feuerbach indicates,

Marx wants to intervene and change the world rather than comment on it after history has already been made.

But the problem of knowledge in the epoch in which Marx wrote lies elsewhere. The danger isn't that knowledge will be powerless but that it will be too powerful and act as a form of social authority. As a purveyor of knowledge concerning how the capitalist system actually works, Marx cannot escape being an expert. And yet, within the process that capitalism unleashes, the expert functions as a figure of authority. In this sense, the transmutation of Marxism into Stalinism, though it is not inevitable, follows from the change in the structure of authority that capitalism triggers. Stalin is the ultimate figure of expert knowledge, tightly controlling Soviet society in order to develop its productivity to the maximum potential.[6] Stalin is the bureaucratic counterpart to Henry Ford, the expert of the free market. By establishing his doctrine as a system of expertise, Marx inadvertently succumbs to the logic that he aims to contest and makes someone like Stalin possible, though it is not clear that there is an alternate solution.

Marx is an Enlightenment thinker. At the beginning of the Enlightenment, knowledge was a force for liberation and revolution. Someone like Galileo represents a danger to the authority of the Catholic Church because this authority rests on the power of the master signifier rather than on the power of knowledge. In Bertolt Brecht's play depicting Galileo's recantation, the church's philosopher upbraids Galileo for seeking knowledge that might bring upheaval to the established order, but Galileo himself insists that the true scientist seeks knowledge without considering where it will lead. His advice to those thinkers who fear shaking the foundations of the church's authority is emphatic: "Why defend shaken teachings? You should be doing the shaking."[7] The position of the scientist or knowledge seeker, as Galileo sees it here, is unequivocal. The pursuit of knowledge involves one in a combat against the power of authority, and it represents a power that authorities fear, which is why the Inquisition targeted Galileo.

In actual history and in Brecht's play, Galileo's courage to defy authority wanes. He recants and capitulates to the power of the church, which deals a temporary blow to the Enlightenment project and its liberating potential. Descartes, for one, withheld the publication of his treatise *The World* out of fear that he might become a target of the Inquisition, as Galileo did. But the power of the Enlightenment and knowledge wins its historical struggle with the authority of the master signifier. When this occurs and knowledge becomes a source of social authority, knowledge loses its connection to the Enlightenment project of universal emancipation. Knowledge becomes a force for subjugation rather than freedom, and the Enlightenment is transformed into its opposite.[8]

When experts become the voice of authority, the political landscape undergoes a dramatic change, the ramifications of which have become increasingly visible in the last few decades. The transformation of authority that began in the seventeenth century realized itself at the conclusion of the twentieth, and the result has been a reversal of traditional political alignments. This social revolution strips the forces of social change of their favorite weapon — knowledge — because use of this weapon has the effect of turning subjects against social change, despite the fact that that change is clearly in their best interests.

In today's world, expert knowledge necessarily confronts the subject as an external imperative laced with the power of prohibition. The rise of the expert corresponds to the increasing complexity and treacherousness of everyday life; contemporary existence seems to demand expert analysis to render it navigable. In his account of the emergence of what he calls a "risk society," Ulrich Beck notices the politics of expert knowledge changing sides. He points out: "The non-acceptance of the scientific definition of risks is not something to be reproached as 'irrationality' in the population; but quite to the contrary, it indicates that the cultural premises of acceptability contained in scientific and technical statements on risks *are wrong*. The technical risk experts *are mistaken* in the empirical accuracy of their implicit value premises, specifically in their assumptions of what appears acceptable to the population."[9] Experts provide guidelines that allow subjects to navigate the contours of contemporary society, in which risk confronts us everywhere, but the experts perform this function with no proper sense of what the population desires. In this process, experts inevitably assume the role of authority figures. As Beck's statement above indicates, from the perspective of the general population itself, the relationship between the expert and the population is adversarial.

Through psychoanalytic thought, we can gain insight into the ramifications of the rise of the expert authority and the decline of the master. The emergence of the expert as the figure of authority fundamentally changes the political terrain, and our political thinking must adjust to this transformation. Psychoanalytic thought represents a privileged vehicle for making the adjustment. Combating the expert is much more difficult than combating the master: the knowledge that would subvert mastery becomes part of the power that the expert wields and thus loses its subversive power. A different political program — one that focuses on enjoyment rather than knowledge — becomes necessary because the master and the expert take up radically different positions relative to enjoyment.

Unlike the master, the earlier form of social authority, the expert not only prohibits enjoyment but also appears to embody this enjoyment through the act of laying down regulations. The expert enjoys informing subjects about the dangers they face or the ways they should alter their behavior, and it is this enjoyment that subjects rebel against. The enjoyment that the expert derives from providing counsel is the explicit focus of Peter Segal's *Anger Management* (2003), which finds comedy in the abuse that an anger management therapist heaps on his client.

The film recounts the travails of a timid businessman, Dave Buznik (Adam Sandler), who is sentenced to anger management therapy after a misunderstanding occurs between a flight attendant and him while he is traveling. His therapist, Dr. Buddy Rydell (Jack Nicholson), practices an aggressive treatment that involves intimidating Buznik, screaming at him, and even invading his personal life. At the end of the film, rather than helping Buznik, Rydell appears to have wooed Buznik's girlfriend away from him and basically destroyed his life. Here we see all the ways that the expert enjoys deploying knowledge, and this enjoyment occurs at the expense of the subject receiving the advice.

But in the last instance *Anger Management* remains fully ensconced in the regime of the expert, despite the comedy it tries to create at the expense of this regime. The film's ending reveals that Rydell has set up the entire experience — including the incident with the flight attendant and the sentencing by the judge — in order to impel Buznik to express himself, especially to his girlfriend. Rather than a course in anger management, Rydell has actually been offering a course in self-expression. This denouement transforms the film's (and the viewer's) relationship to the expert: rather than impugning the rule of expertise and knowledge, the film becomes an affirmation of it. The ending of the film doesn't simply spoil an otherwise trenchant critique of expert rule but infects the critique throughout the film. The critique — and the comedy, unfortunately — never go far enough because the idea that the expert really knows and really has the best interests of the client at heart informs the entirety of the film. The film's investment in the expert that it appears to critique portends the film's failure as both comedy and critique.

The rule of the expert has such a degree of hegemony today that it is difficult to think of any films, novels, and other artworks that attempt to contest it or expose the expert's enjoyment without ultimately partaking of it. On the other hand, the works that allow audiences to enjoy along with the expert multiply throughout the culture. Television shows such as *CSI: Crime Scene Investigations* and *House M.D.* display this dynamic in its most open form: the shows present a problem that appears utterly unsolvable to the viewer, and then they reveal the expert's genius at finding a solution. Expert knowledge — a knowledge not accessible to the ordinary subject — has all the answers and thus becomes the undisputable locus of authority. The popularity of these shows derives from their ability to allow audiences to share in the expert's enjoyment, an enjoyment that typically is the site of trauma for the subject.

Contact with expert authority has a traumatic effect on the subject because of the proximity of the expert. While the old master remained at a distance, the expert is always in the subject's face, like Dr. Buddy Rydell in *Anger Management*, never allowing the subject room to breathe. As *Anger Management* shows, this proximity has the effect of stimulating the subject. Under the rule of the expert, subjects experience what Eric Santner calls "a sustained traumatization induced by exposure to, as it were, *fathers who [know] too much* about living human beings."[10] Exposure to this type of authority, to "this excess of knowledge," produces "an intensification of the body [that] is first and foremost a *sexualization*."[11] Instead of emancipating the subject, knowledge traumatizes and plays the central role in the subjection of the subject to the order of social regulation.

The End of Class Consciousness

For emancipatory politics, the transformation of knowledge from a vehicle of liberation to an instrument of power has had devastating effects. Emancipatory politics has traditionally relied on knowledge in order to facilitate political change, and even today one of the primary operations of emancipatory politics is getting information out to citizens. In the minds of most people engaged in the project of emancipation, the fundamental task has been establishing class consciousness among the members of the working class. Class consciousness, according to this way of thinking, is the basis for substantive political change. As Georg Lukács puts it in *History and Class Consciousness*, "The fate of a class depends on its ability to elucidate and solve the problems with which history confronts it."[12] Political change depends, for someone like Lukács, on the knowledge that makes decisive action possible. As long as authority remains in the position of the traditional master, knowledge can have a revolutionary function. Historically, the primary problem for emancipatory politics involved access to education, which is why a key component of the communist program that Marx and Engels outline in *The Communist Manifesto* is universal access to public education.

There are those on the side of emancipation who continue to insist that knowledge will be the source for political change. According to this position, people side with conservative policies against their own self-interest because they lack the proper information. They are the victims of propaganda, and emancipatory politics must respond by providing the missing knowledge. If not for big media's control over knowledge, the thinking goes, subjects would cease to act against their self-interest and would begin to oppose contemporary capitalism in an active way. For those who adopt this position, political activity consists in acts of informing, raising consciousness, and bringing issues to light.

But today the failures of consciousness-raising are evident everywhere. Such failures are the subject of Thomas Frank's acclaimed analysis, *What's the Matter with Kansas?* Frank highlights the proclivity of people in areas of the United States like Kansas to act politically in ways that sabotage their economic interests. He notes: "People getting their fundamental interests wrong is what American political life is all about."[13] The Right's current success in the United States and around the world is not the sign that more people have become convinced that right-wing policies will benefit them. Instead, conservatism permits people a way of organizing their enjoyment in a way that today's emancipatory politics does not. Emancipatory politics may offer a truer vision of the world, but the Right offers a superior way of enjoying.

Traditionally, the primary advantage that emancipatory politics had in political struggle was its challenge to authority. When one took up the cause of emancipation, one took a stand against an entrenched regime of power and experienced enjoyment in this defiance. One can still see this form of enjoyment evinced in the revolutions of the Arab Spring in 2011. Though emancipatory activity always entailed a certain risk (even of death, to which the fate of innumerable revolutionaries attests), it nonetheless brought with it an enjoyment not found in everyday obedience and symbolic identity. In short, there was historically a strong libidinal component to emancipatory militancy that the risk it carried amplified rather than diminished. The liberating power of emancipatory activity is present in almost every political film. We see activists falling in love as they jointly embark on an emancipatory project or romance burgeoning as a fight for justice intensifies.

This dynamic, attesting to the enjoyment inherent in militancy against the oppressive ruling order, manifests itself in Warren Beatty's *Reds* (1981), Ken Loach's *Bread and Roses* (2000), and Gillian Armstrong's *Charlotte Gray* (2001), to name just a few of the many. In each case, the romance seems to spring out of the risk that militancy against an oppressive regime entails. The love that develops between Maya (Pilar Padilla) and Sam (Adrien Brody) in *Bread and Roses* sparks first at the moment when Maya helps Sam to elude corporate security agents at the office building where he is trying to help unionize the janitors. Maya risks losing her job as a janitor when she aids Sam, and this risk acts as the driving force for the eroticism between them.

Conservatism has not traditionally provided much enjoyment of this type, but it has had its own appeal. It took the side of authority and stability. Whereas emancipatory politics could offer the enjoyment that comes from defiance of authority, conservatism could offer the enjoyment that comes from identification with it. This is the enjoyment that one feels when hearing one's national anthem or saluting the flag. It resides in the fabric of the nation's military uniform that makes the fingers touching it tingle. This eroticism is not that of emancipatory politics — and it is perhaps not as powerful — but it is nonetheless a form of eroticism. It produces a libidinal charge. The struggle between conservatism and emancipatory politics has historically been a struggle between two competing modes of organizing enjoyment with neither side having a monopoly.

Despite the traditional emphasis that the forces of emancipation placed on knowledge, even in the past the struggle between emancipatory politics and conservatism centered on enjoyment rather than knowledge. In the political arena, knowledge is important only insofar as it relates to the way that subjects mobilize their enjoyment. If subjects see through ideological manipulation and have the proper knowledge, this does not necessarily inaugurate a political change. The knowledge that something is bad for us — a president or a Twinkie — does not lessen the enjoyment that we receive from it. It is not that we have the ability to enjoy while disavowing our knowledge but more that the knowledge works to serve our enjoyment. The enjoyment of a Twinkie does not derive from the physiological effect of sugar on the human metabolism but from the knowledge of the damage this substance does to the body. Knowing the harm that accompanies something actually facilitates our enjoyment of it, especially when we are capable of disavowing this knowledge. Enjoyment is distinct from bodily pleasures (which the Twinkie undoubtedly also provides); it depends on some degree of sacrifice that allows the subject to suffer its enjoyment. Sacrifice is essential to our capacity for enjoying ourselves.

There is a fundamentally masochistic structure to enjoyment.[14] It always comes in the form of an alien force that overcomes us from the outside. As Alenka Zupančič puts it, "It is not simply the mode of enjoyment of the neighbour, of the other, that is strange to me. The heart of the problem is that I experience my own enjoyment (which emerges along with the enjoyment of the other, and is even indissociable from it) as strange and hostile."[15] An initial experience of loss gives birth to the lost object around which we structure our enjoyment, and our subsequent enjoyment demands a return to the experience of loss.

Through sacrifice and loss, we reconstitute the privileged object that exists only as an absence. This is why actually obtaining the privileged object necessarily disappoints: when the lost object becomes present, it loses its privileged status and becomes an ordinary empirical object. Knowledge thus helps us to enjoy not in the way that we might think — that is, by showing us what is good for our well-being — but by giving us something to sacrifice: if we know, for instance, that cigarettes are unhealthy and could kill us, this elevates the mundane fact of smoking into an act laced with enjoyment.[16] With each puff, we repeat the act of sacrifice and return to the primordial experience of loss. The death that we bring on is not simply the price that we pay for smoking; it is the means through which we enjoy the act of smoking. In this sense, every cigarette is really killing the smoker. If it didn't, the act would lose its ability to provide enjoyment (though it may still produce bodily pleasure).[17]

Under the rule of the traditional master, prohibition sustains the possibility for this type of enjoyment: we can enjoy an act because it transgresses a societal prohibition. As Lacan notes in *Seminar VII*, "Transgression in the direction of *jouissance* only takes place if it is supported by the oppositional principle, by the forms of the Law. If the paths to *jouissance* have something in them that dies out, that tends to make them impassable, prohibition, if I may say so, becomes its all-terrain vehicle."[18] Prohibition makes our enjoyment possible by offering us the possibility for sacrifice. We sacrifice the good and violate the prohibition.

But prohibition no longer plays this role in contemporary society. No universal prohibition bars certain activities; instead, knowledge about the harm that activities cause begins to play the role that prohibition once played. We don't avoid smoking simply because it is wrong but because we know the harm that it causes. We don't refrain from extramarital sex because it is wrong but because we know the societal and physical dangers it entails. Even conservatives think and talk this way. When, for instance, conservatives argue for excluding information about condoms from sex education classrooms, they claim that we know condoms aren't 100 percent safe in preventing the spread of HIV. In each case, the authority is knowledge, not law. The libidinal charge in politics involved with challenging the master has largely disappeared today, and now that libidinal charge has attached itself to challenging the experts, who represent the new agents of authority.

An Oxymoronic Populism

Conservative populism — the most powerful form of right-wing politics today — owes its ascendancy to the development of this form of authority. The appeal of populist leaders consists in the relation that they take up to enjoyment. While the traditional master prohibits enjoyment, the populist leader liberates subjects from the restrictions on their enjoyment posed by experts. Though conservative populists often call for a return to traditional values (advocating restrictions on abortion, prayer in schools, and the like), they do not deploy these values in the service of prohibition. Instead, their rhetoric places traditional values in the position of liberation and freedom. The populist leader proposes to free subjects from constricting expert authority in order that they might freely embrace the traditional values that this new authority threatens to eviscerate. In this way, traditional values, despite their function as a source of prohibition, become transformed into their opposite — a source for apparent liberation.

This transformation clearly emerges in the debate in the United States surrounding the teaching of evolution and scientific creationism (named "intelligent design" in its latest manifestation). Creationism is a doctrine linked in its very foundation to authoritative rule and prohibitions on behavior. If God created humans, then it follows logically that humans ought to obey the restrictions that God places on them. But today the champions of creationism characterize themselves as rebellious challengers of authority rather than its acolytes. They fight for the freedom to believe and teach a doctrine that defies the ruling ideas laid down by expert authority — scientists who understand the complexities of evolutionary science that no layperson can master.

Advocates of creationism write rebellious-sounding books like *The Politically Incorrect Guide to Darwinism and Intelligent Design*, *Defeating Darwinism by Opening Minds*, and *Uncommon Dissent*.[19] Far from presenting themselves as the messengers of social authority, the proponents of teaching creationism characterize themselves as its most vociferous opponents. This sounds like a radical cause to take up, a way of refusing to believe just what we're told. The way in which proponents of creationism advance their case exemplifies the tactics of the contemporary populist leader.[20]

In the epoch of the expert authority, the figure of the master no longer appears as an onerous authority that one must toss aside. Unlike the authoritative master of traditional society, the contemporary master does not lay down prohibitions but rather offers ways around them. Prohibitions in the form of rules (or suggestions) for behavior come instead from the expert. Medical experts campaign for rules against smoking in public places or for stricter controls on the consumption of unhealthy foods (such as those containing unhealthy fats); environmental scientists propose regulations that would restrict how and what people drive; and parenting authorities try to place limits on the ways that parents can raise their own children.

The master, in the midst of this manifestation of authority, becomes a force for liberation and enjoyment. As Slavoj Žižek notes in the *Ticklish Subject*, "Although, on the surface, the totalitarian Master also imposes severe orders, compelling us to renounce our pleasures and to sacrifice ourselves for some higher Duty, his actual injunction, discernible between the lines of his explicit words, is exactly the opposite — the call to unconstrained and unrestrained *transgression*."[21] The contemporary populist master tells followers that they are free to smoke when they want to, to drive SUVs, and to discipline their children in whatever way they see fit. Rather than embodying authority, the master challenges the ubiquitous social authority of the expert.

But the figure of the master — best embodied by the Fascist leader — does not just simply unleash unrestrained transgression. Such figures also give this transgression the alibi of a return to genuine obedience. Those who, heeding the advice of some contemporary master rather than parenting authorities, beat their children with a belt can see themselves as the adherents of the true law (perhaps ordained by God). Followers can experience themselves as fully obedient (in contrast to the rest of society) while enjoying the satisfaction that accompanies transgression. This paradoxical position offers a way of maximizing the subject's enjoyment, despite its completely deceptive structure. The power of the figure of the master today derives from its ability to mobilize enjoyment in seemingly opposed ways: the follower simultaneously enjoys obeying *and* transgressing the law.[22]

Whereas the distribution of enjoyment once created a level playing field for the forces of emancipation and those of conservatism, the rise of expert authority tips the balance toward conservatism. Now both modes of enjoying — enjoying transgression and enjoying obedience — become the exclusive province of conservatism, and emancipatory politics is stuck with knowledge, which provides enjoyment only for the experts themselves (and those who identify with them). Former bastions of left-wing populism, like the Kansas that Thomas Frank analyzes, have retained their populist veneer while undergoing a seismic reversal of political valence. In the United States, leftist sympathies are strongest among the educated and among certain segments of the wealthy, not among the poor or working class, where one would expect to find them.

But leftist sympathies among the upper middle and upper classes can never be more than sympathies. They cannot be genuine convictions for change, since truly significant change would eliminate the very position from which the sympathies are expressed.[23] Upper-middle-class and upper-class subjects have a degree of satisfaction with the existing social arrangements that inheres in their very social position, and this satisfaction prevents them from passionately advocating for change unless they divest themselves psychically from their social position. They tend not to evince the commitment that inspires the participants in movements like the antiabortion Operation Rescue because their mode of enjoyment is not at stake. Conservative populists inspire subjects who are prepared to inaugurate social change, but they push these subjects in a reactionary direction. Their success is but a structural effect of the victory of expert rule and what Jacques Lacan calls "university discourse."

The Emergence of University Discourse

In the transition from the rule by the master to the rule by the expert and by expert knowledge, Lacan sees a change in the discourse that organizes social relations. For Lacan, a discourse is not simply an underlying mode of relating through language but the foundation of a social link. A discourse renders social interaction possible through the way that it structures the four fundamental elements at stake in social interaction: the master signifier, knowledge, enjoyment, and the subject. Each discourse deploys these elements in different ways, and the nature of the social link it creates depends on the specific arrangement of the elements. By turning to Lacan's theory of the discourses, we can examine the underlying structure of the regime of expert knowledge and discover what's at stake in this regime.

In *Seminar XVII: The Other Side of Psychoanalysis*, Lacan distinguishes between four discourses — those of the master, the university, the hysteric, and the analyst. The discourses share the same basic structure, which has four positions: (1) the agent within the discourse or the position of authority; (2) the other of the agent, which can either support or oppose the agent; (3) the product of the discourse, what the activity of the discourse produces; and, finally, (4) the discourse's truth, which is obscured within the discourse and visible only through an analysis of its structure. The four discourses vary in the ways that they distribute the elements of the social link (the master signifier, knowledge, enjoyment, and the subject) throughout these four discursive positions.

The theory of the four discourses is not first and foremost a theory of history, but it does permit the development of such a theory, which would involve primarily the discourse of the master and the discourse of the university. The master's discourse, which historically has provided the basis for the organization of society, has the master signifier in the position of the agent, the position that orients the discourse. It has knowledge in the position of the other, surplus enjoyment (or what Lacan labels a) in the position of the product, and the divided subject in the position of truth.

In societies organized around the master's discourse, the dominance of the master signifier serves to regulate possibilities and restrict activity. The master signifier provides the support for all the symbolic identities open to subjects; however subjects identify themselves, they remain within the dominance of the master signifier. And yet, this subjection does not come off without a hitch; the surplus enjoyment that the master's discourse produces has the capacity to animate revolt as much as compliance. It is a structure that relies on the enjoyment that stems from obedience but that is constantly endangered by an enjoyment associated with revolt. Knowledge supports this regime, but at the same time it threatens to turn against it, as occurs in the case of the Enlightenment.

The reason for the tenuousness of the discourse of the master is the position that the subject occupies within it. The subject is the truth of the master's discourse, which means that, despite the role of the master signifier as the agent, divided subjectivity is actually the driving force behind the discourse itself. The master's pronouncements and prohibitions represent an attempt to heal the rupture that the subject's division introduces into the social fabric. The subject divided against itself prevents the social body from becoming whole or harmonious. It is a bone stuck in the throat of society, a disorder in the middle of the social order. The master's discourse is constructed around this disorder in an effort to quell it and install an orderly regime through pure mastery alone. But the master's discourse fails at this task, which is what gives rise to the discourse of the university.

University discourse attempts to succeed where the master's discourse fails. It places knowledge in the position of the agent and surplus enjoyment in the position of its other, with the divided subject as its product.

University discourse and hysterical discourse emerge as historical responses to failures of the master. University discourse becomes the dominant social link, and hysterical discourse (which places the divided subject who is constantly questioning in the position of the agent and the master signifier who lacks the answers in the position of the other) becomes the chief form that oppositional social movements take up.[24]

The master's discourse cannot sustain itself in the capitalist epoch. Capitalism upsets the rule of the master's discourse by eliminating the space outside the circuit of exchange that the master occupies. The master's lack of exceptionality becomes readily apparent. As Mladen Dolar points out, "Capitalism is instated in conjunction with the university discourse, its twin and double."[25] Capitalist relations of production are revolutionary not only because, as Marx suggests, they introduce the ideas of equality and freedom but because they strip the master of the pretense that sustains this figure's authority. Without exceptionality, the master has no basis on which to make demands, and another authority with some other foundation must intervene in the master's stead. In this way, space opens up for the birth of expert authority.

Though the transition from the dominance of the discourse of the master to that of the university is a revolutionary transition, a key element remains the same. What Lacan's theory of the four discourses renders visible — this is the key to its importance as a theory — is the role that the master continues to play in the regime of expert authority or the discourse of the university. The rise of university discourse does not bring the rule of the master to an end. In fact, one might argue the opposite: the dominance of university discourse as a social link has the effect of installing the master in a position of near invulnerability, in clear contrast to the position that the master occupies within the master's discourse. By facilitating this change in position, the expert, whether intentionally or not, works in service of the master. Scientists, diet gurus, and world-renowned economists may appear to be calling the shots today, but they function as stand-ins for the concealed master.

This is a point that both Mladen Dolar and Alenka Zupančič insist on in their discussions of Lacan's four discourses. According to Dolar, "The whole point of Lacan's construction of university discourse is that this is another lure, that the seemingly autonomous and self-propelling knowledge has a secret clause, and that its truth is detained by the master under the bar."[26] In university discourse, the master signifier occupies the position of truth, which means that expert authority works ultimately in the service of mastery. For her part, Zupančič adds, "What Lacan recognizes in the university discourse is a new and reformed discourse of the master."[27] University discourse emerges in response to the failure of the discourse of the master, but it is not a radical social structure. It represents a retooling of the authority involved in mastery in order to allow that authority to cope with the exigencies of capitalist relations of production. As the truth of university discourse (and expert authority), mastery is hidden and all the more effective because of this obscurity within which it dwells.

The Form of the Superego

The change in the master's status makes itself felt through a corresponding change in the status of the superego, and this is a change that has distinct ramifications for political activity. One might understand this change in terms of the distinction between the way that Freud conceives the superego and the way that Lacan does. Though Lacan never claims to invent a new version of the superego and insists that he is merely elaborating on the Freudian concept, his account locates the emphasis differently from Freud's. In the move from Freud's theorization to Lacan's, the underlying structure does not change, but its form of appearance does.

Freud understands the superego as an internalized representative of the law. He describes it as an extension of figures of parental authority and sees the subject's relation to it in those terms. In *The Ego and the Id* he says: "As the child was once under a compulsion to obey its parents, so the ego submits to the categorical imperative of its super-ego."[28] The external authority of the law requires an internal supplement in order to function effectively, and the internal supplement ends up being a much more powerful agent of prohibition than the law itself because it is able to tap into the subject's own drives. Freud describes a close bond existing between the superego and the id, and this bond energizes the superego in its assaults on the subject. The superego is not simply a neutral authority but a thoroughly libidinized one.

Freud's vision of the superego emphasizes its role in prohibition. The superego restricts what the subject can think and do; it extends the power of mastery by placing an authority within the subject's psyche that is more demanding than any external master. Rational fear of punishment, Freud recognizes, is not sufficient for engendering properly docile subjects. An irrational force for obedience must supplement this rational fear, and the superego embodies such a force.

In his account of the superego, Lacan picks up on Freud's claim that the superego draws its energy from the reservoir of the id. The proximity of these two psychic registers in Freud's schema leads Lacan to dissociate the superego from prohibition and to align it with an imperative to enjoy. In his *Seminar XVIII* Lacan claims: "The order of the superego ... originates precisely ... in this call for pure enjoyment, that is also to say for non-castration."[29] Even when the superego bombards the subject with imperatives that appear in the guise of prohibitions, Lacan insists that these imperatives actually command enjoyment.

The superego, as Lacan understands it, constantly reminds the subject of its failure to enjoy, and it promulgates an ideal of the ultimate enjoyment as a measuring stick against which the subject can contrast its own failures.[30] No subject can obey the demands of the superego because the ideal it provides remains ever out of reach. The closer that the subject approaches to it through obedience, the faster it recedes. The superego enjoins an enjoyment that it never allows the subject to find.

In a sense, one might say that the superego only emerges as such with the rise of expert authority and the decline of the traditional master. No one theorized such an agency before Freud, and though this doesn't necessarily mean that the superego didn't exist before it was recognized, it does suggest that the superego didn't really makes its presence felt as a distinct and powerful agency. Under the regime of the master, the idiotic and purely despotic dimension of the law manifests itself in the figure of the master. The master lays down the law that must be obeyed not because it is justified or practical but simply because the master says so, and the master's authority derives from the nonsensical and completely random fact of birth or wealth.

This idiotic dimension of the law seems to disappear with the rise of expert authority. In every way, the expert's status and dictates have a justification that the master's don't. Education and training qualify the expert for the status of authority, and the expert's pronouncements never command obedience for its own sake. There is always a rational reason to obey: one should heed the expert's rules concerning diet for the sake of one's health; one should follow the expert's advice on dating because it will enhance one's romantic prospects; one should listen to the expert's counsel on the environment in order to save the planet; and so on. The irrationality of the law — its ultimate basis in the command "Obey because I said so" — is the foundation of every law, and yet expert authority leaves no space for it.

The result of the evanescence of the idiotic dimension of the external law is its reemergence internally in the form of the superego. Under the regime of the expert, the idiocy of the law migrates to the superego, allowing the superego to exert a power that it never had under the rule of the master. Thus, the proper birth of the superego occurs with the rise of expert authority and the evacuation of the external law's idiocy. Of course, precapitalist subjects experienced pangs of conscience and feelings of guilt, but they did not have to endure the insatiable and tyrannical demands of the fully developed superego, an agency that does not offer the subject any room to maneuver: the more one gives in to it, the more it demands. As the horror of external punishments abates — the practice of drawing and quartering criminals in public is no longer widespread, for instance — the internal horrors mount. This is a ramification of the rule of knowledge.

Taking the Side of Knowledge

The rule of knowledge places emancipatory politics in a difficult position. It cannot abandon the project of the Enlightenment without ceasing to be emancipatory, and at the same time it must find a way to incorporate enjoyment into its program. If emancipatory politics places itself on the side of knowledge, it abdicates its former position as a challenge to authority and becomes associated with the restriction of enjoyment rather than the unleashing of it. And as the representative of expert authority, emancipatory politics appears as the thief of enjoyment. The knowledge it forces on us produces a feeling of lost enjoyment.

Michael Moore provides a near-perfect illustration of the dilemma that contemporary emancipatory politics confronts, both in his successes and in his failures. When Moore succeeds as an activist filmmaker, he mobilizes the enjoyment of the spectator and works to align this enjoyment with increased freedom and equality. This is apparent in Moore's first two documentary features, *Roger and Me* (1989) and *The Big One* (1997). Both films allow the spectator to enjoy the opposition to big capital. In the former, Moore pursues General Motors CEO Roger Smith in order to secure an interview with him to discuss plant closings in Flint, Michigan. Moore's dogged pursuit of Smith shows Smith and General Motors not just as destroyers of workers' lives but also as the enemies of enjoyment, which spectators experience through the filmmaking project itself.

The Big One goes even further in this direction. At every turn, enjoyment inheres in the critique of capitalism. The film offers criticism of downsizing companies through the guise of a contest, in which Moore presents the worst offenders a large-sized symbolic check (like the kind given to actual contest winners) celebrating them as "Downsizer of the Year." Moore himself challenges Nike CEO Phil Knight to a footrace with opening an American Nike plant as the stake. The film depicts union organizing taking place clandestinely at night, which places union activity on the level of international espionage. Enjoyment inheres in the various critiques and efforts to undermine big capital, and big capital itself responds in the film with defenses rooted in knowledge.[31]

Moore's own presence in the films functions as an avatar of the enjoyment that derives from challenging the injustice of contemporary capitalism. His disheveled hair, his old baseball cap, his excess weight — all these aspects of his physical appearance attest to his personal commitment to enjoyment rather than propriety. He looks more like a bowling partner than an expert authority, and this look helps to link the cause of emancipation with enjoyment in his films. The link reaches its initial zenith in *Bowling for Columbine* (2002).

The genius of *Bowling for Columbine* is that it attributes American gun violence not, as one might expect going into the film, to the widespread availability of firearms in the United States but to the American retreat from the neighbor. Though the beginning of the film chronicles how easily one can obtain a gun in America — we see a bank giving guns away for opening an account, for instance — Moore concludes by contrasting the United States with Canada, where guns also proliferate but gun violence does not. The difference, the film suggests, is that Americans are animated by the specter of a threatening other in a way that Canadians are not. Moore visits a Toronto neighborhood and finds unlocked doors and a general lack of fear about the other. It is the absence of this attitude in the United States and the omnipresence of the idea that the other represents a threat to be guarded against that begets gun violence. The film's ultimate prescription is not fewer guns but fewer locks on doors.

The lock on the door is the synecdoche for the barrier to the other's enjoyment. By focusing on the locked door as the root of the problem of American gun violence, Moore associates this violence with the nation's retreat from its own enjoyment, which necessarily appears in the guise of the enjoying other. Guarding against the other's enjoyment is simultaneously guarding against one's own, and it is this attitude, *Bowling for Columbine* concludes, that produces massacres like the one perpetuated at Columbine High School. Like *Roger and Me* and *The Big One*, *Bowling for Columbine* manages to wrestle the terrain of enjoyment away from conservatism. But *Fahrenheit 9/11* (2004) marks a turn in the other direction. Here, Moore aligns himself with expert knowledge against the obscenity of enjoyment.

The explicit aim of *Fahrenheit 9/11* is breaking the identification that exists between the American people and George W. Bush. Moore sets about doing this by exposing the president's weaknesses and questioning his legitimacy. The problem with *Fahrenheit 9/11* is that its very structure precludes the political conversions that the film hopes to engender. On the one hand, the film gratifies leftist viewers by placing them in the position of authority. They can align themselves with Moore's voiceover as it chronicles Bush's moments of awkwardness and indifference, and they can feel justified in their position as the film chronicles his privilege and corruption. But on the other hand, *Fahrenheit* offers other viewers the possibility of identifying with Bush himself even at the moments when the film expends the most vitriol in denouncing him.

Throughout the first forty minutes of the film, we hear Moore's voice but rarely see him within the image. Perhaps Moore made this choice in order to allow the film to appear less subjective or partisan, believing that this would convince more viewers of its theses. But the result is the opposite: as a disembodied voice, Moore becomes a figure of authority. We see Bush enjoying himself, and we hear Moore condemning that enjoyment. We don't see Moore's physical presence, which tends to align him with enjoyment rather than knowledge.[32]

After recounting Bush's tainted victory in the 2000 election and its aftermath, Moore focuses on the Bush presidency prior to September 11, 2001. Specifically, he shows Bush vacationing and playing on his ranch rather than working at the White House. As a voiceover tells us that he spent 42 percent of his days before September 11 on vacation, we see a series of images of Bush fishing, boating, and hanging out at his ranch in Crawford, Texas. According to Moore's film, at least part of the blame for the terrorist attacks resides with Bush himself for spending too much time enjoying and not enough time attending to his job (and reading security briefings).

This critique comes to a climax at the moment when Bush hears about the September 11 attacks. We see him in an elementary school reading to children as he hears the news from his chief of staff, and Moore emphasizes Bush's lack of a demonstrable reaction. Moore's voiceover accompanies the shot of Bush in the classroom, and it articulates the indictment of him: "Not knowing what to do, with no one telling him what to do, and no Secret Service rushing in to take him to safety, Mr. Bush just sat there and continued to read *My Pet Goat* with the children." As Moore says this, we see Bush open up the book and begin to read. Moore places the time at the bottom of the screen: it says "9:07 a.m.," and after a dissolve it says "9:09 a.m.," then "9:11 a.m." after a dissolve to a shot of Press Secretary Ari Fleischer. Finally, after a dissolve back to Bush showing the time to be 9:12 a.m., the camera zooms out, and the voiceover says, "As Bush sat in that Florida classroom, was he wondering if maybe he should have shown up to work more often? Should he have had at least one meeting since taking office to discuss the threat of terrorism with the head of counterterrorism?" In this way, the film links Bush's failure to prevent the attacks and his failure to act decisively (or at all) when they occur to his lack of sufficient work. The authority of the voice hopes to break any identification with Bush as it reprimands him for enjoying too much.

The contrast between knowledge and enjoyment becomes clearest when Moore interviews Congressperson Jim McDermott of Washington. We hear Moore's voice and see McDermott as he answers questions about the Bush administration's use of fear as a political weapon. Moore uses clips from this interview to frame a seemingly incongruous scene where Bush talks with reporters on the golf course. Bush speaks into the camera and says, "We must stop the terror. I call upon all nations to do everything they can to stop these terrorist killers. Thank you." After a pause of two or three seconds, Bush adds, "Now watch this drive." The film cuts to a shot of him driving a golf ball and then returns to the interview with McDermott.

Moore shows us Bush's quick transition from combating terrorism to showing off his golf game in order to reveal his lack of effort in the former. The scandal of this scene derives from where Bush's attention lies: golf seems much more important to him than terrorism. It helps to undermine the authority that Bush has from the mere fact of his political office — the authority of the master. But as he undermines Bush's authority, Moore aligns himself with the authority of McDermott — not just a member of Congress but also a professional psychiatrist, as a subtitle informs us. Though the film blames Bush for the folly of the Iraq War and to a lesser extent for the September 11 attacks, it does not portray him as a responsible authority. His guilt stems from his obscene enjoyment.

Highlighting Bush's obscene enjoyment fails as a political strategy because the people who identify with Bush do so precisely because of this enjoyment, not in spite of it. If Bush doesn't read reports, skips meetings, vacations too much, or stumbles when talking to reporters, such failures provide possibilities for identification. Popular identification with a leader occurs on two distinct levels. On the one hand, we identify with the strength of the leader and see ourselves expressed in that strength. This identification affirms our ego and provides pleasure. On the other hand, we identify with the weaknesses of the leader. This identification is the key to our ability to enjoy the leader. The more *Fahrenheit* takes the side of knowledge against Bush's obscene enjoyment, the more it cements the identification between supporters and him through a shared enjoyment.[33]

Another film released around the same time as *Fahrenheit*, Morgan Spurlock's *Super Size Me* (2004), commits precisely the same error. The film depicts the damage that eating every meal at McDonald's for thirty days does to Spurlock's health and serves as an indictment against the fast food industry as a whole. Spurlock's doctor makes clear the precise nature of the health problems that ensue and identifies their cause in the fast food diet. *Super Size Me* gives us knowledge through expert testimony, but it never addresses the question of enjoyment. Instead, it continually renders this enjoyment visible within the image as we see Spurlock eating to excess. The film pronounces itself against fast food while at the same time revealing on the level of the image the intense enjoyment that this product delivers. Unlike in *Fahrenheit*, we see directly the enjoyment that knowledge facilitates.

What both *Super Size Me* and *Fahrenheit* have in common is their attempt to side with knowledge against enjoyment. Many figures on the side of emancipatory politics see the documentary as a valuable tool because it provides knowledge that traditional media outlets do not. It helps people to break from the ideological manipulation that dominates them. But as Hilary Neroni points out, the documentary form's obsession with the facts causes it to miss the role of enjoyment. Discussing documentaries that address the horrors that took place at the Abu Ghraib prison, she notes: "Pursuing the facts, then, leaves these documentaries to miss the most disturbing fact of the Abu Ghraib photos: the smiles on the faces of the torturers. And it is the enjoyment evident on their faces that gives us the most important clue to what underlies the ideology of torture: a certain kernel of nonsense is revealed that is at the heart of this ideology."[34] The focus of documentary form on revealing facts rather than facilitating enjoyment hinders its effectiveness as a political tool. It seems inherently to take the side of knowledge and thereby enable opponents to enjoy through disregarding what it teaches. This is the case even when a documentary presents an overwhelming need for dramatic action.

No political event on the American Left in the year 2006 received as much attention and acclaim as Davis Guggenheim's documentary film featuring Al Gore entitled *An Inconvenient Truth*. The success of the film catapulted Gore into the public eye and generated calls from all corners that he again run for president. Many saw it as a turning point in the fight against climate change. The film, which consists primarily of footage of Gore giving a slideshow on global warming, invests itself entirely in the authority of the expert. Speaking from a position of knowledge, Gore warns against excessive enjoyment — overuse of electricity, driving environmentally unfriendly vehicles, consuming without educating oneself, and so on. The entire film is an act of consciousness-raising and enjoyment-restricting. By seizing on Gore's film as a rallying point, the forces of emancipation again cede the terrain of enjoyment to conservatism, just as they did with the embrace of *Fahrenheit*.

Conservatism's most celebrated intervention into the global warming debate, in contrast, attempts to mobilize enjoyment against expert knowledge. Michael Crichton's novel *State of Fear* (2004) depicts the travails of global warming debunker John Kenner as he fights against environmental terrorist organizations desperate to create environmental disasters in order to prove their theses about climate change.[35] Crichton shows that these groups occupy the position of authority and power today. For instance, Kenner claims at one point: "Environmental groups in the U.S. generate half a billion dollars a year. What they do with it is unsupervised."[36] Kenner's struggle against the environmentalists consists in showing that they're wrong, but, even more importantly, he enjoys himself in a series of secret adventures.

He plays the part of James Bond in the fight against environmental terrorism, and his thwarting of the environmentalists' nefarious plans is at once an ideological victory and an emotional one. Of course, one cannot compare a documentary film with a popular novel. But this is precisely the point. While the emancipatory politics invests itself in the expert testimony given in a documentary, conservatism discovers a form that foregrounds enjoyment. The documentary as a form is designed to raise consciousness and to educate.

But for a documentary to be successful in really changing spectators, it must not simply provide them with additional knowledge. It must alter their way of organizing their enjoyment, which is what occurs in Moore's early documentaries and in *Sicko* (2007), the follow-up to *Fahrenheit 9/11*. If a documentary contents itself with providing knowledge, it will have the effect of contributing to the very problem that it attempts to eradicate. It must, in the manner of a film like Alex Gibney's *Enron: The Smartest Guys in the Room* (2005), identify expertise as the target of its attack rather than aligning itself with the authority of the expert. But in the last instance, investment in documentary as a mode of political activity and consciousness-raising, even in documentaries like *Enron* that try to combat expertise, represents a strategy guaranteed to fail because the form itself almost implicitly takes the side of the expert.[37] The commitment to the documentary form by the forces of emancipation testifies to their continued faith in the power of knowledge and their continued willingness to cede the terrain of enjoyment to conservatism.

Too Much Democracy

Psychoanalysis suggests that enjoyment will almost always triumph over knowledge, even — or especially — when this enjoyment occurs at the expense of our self-interest. But psychoanalysis does not simply offer political advice on the question of the relationship between enjoyment and knowledge. It represents an effort to mobilize our knowledge about enjoyment and its priority in order to make evident the identification of emancipation with enjoyment. Though conservatism marshals enjoyment in hopes of defeating emancipatory politics and defending authority, psychoanalysis reveals that enjoyment derives from emancipation from the power of authority.

As the existence of conservative populism shows, there is a conservative form of enjoyment, but this form borrows its structure from emancipatory politics. To be effective, conservative populists must convince their adherents that they are challenging social authority even at the moment when they cede themselves to it. They must consider themselves rebellious creationists, not obedient ones.

Enjoyment stems from an excess, from going beyond what social authority permits. If conservatism makes use of enjoyment, it always does so in a tenuous fashion, because enjoyment is proper to the forces of emancipation who work to free us from social constraints imposed by authority figures. In this sense, democracy is the social arrangement organized around enjoyment and its excess. This becomes disguised when democracy aligns itself with capitalism and with a parliamentary system that ensures the domestication of democracy's inherent excess.

But democracy has always been a signifier replete with enjoyment, an indication of an excess that no social structure can adequately contain. As Jacques Rancière puts it in *Hatred of Democracy*, "As a social and political form of life, democracy is the reign of excess. This excess signifies the ruin of democratic government and must therefore be repressed by it."[38] Democracy is excessive because it strips away all legitimacy justifying social authority. It signifies the absence of legitimate social authority, the fact that government is "based on nothing other than the absence of every title to govern."[39] In democracy, the people govern, but democracy entails the paradoxical recognition that the people as an entity does not exist. Democracy is thus an acceptance of a certain necessary illegitimacy and the enjoyment that accompanies it.

Early opponents of democracy like Plato and Aristotle countered democratic excess with the idea of balance and orderliness. For both Plato and Aristotle, the best form of government is not democracy but aristocracy, in which the best rule because they are best.[40] Unlike democracy, aristocratic rule operates from a vision of the common good. Under democratic rule, a social order will cease to pursue the common good and devolve into an anarchic state in which no limit restrains the advance of competing private interests. It signifies the eruption of too much enjoyment for the society to endure. Plato and Aristotle, these early opponents of democracy, advance a far better argument for it than its contemporary supporters.

Subsequent theorists of democracy have come to see it as an effective form for advancing the good of society, as precisely the mode of government that would provide stability and security. For figures such as John Locke, democracy becomes the best course for ensuring the good of all. Locke identifies the good with security of property; he claims that "the great and *chief end* therefore, of Men's uniting into Commonwealths, and putting themselves under Government, *is the Preservation of their Property*," and he sees rule by the majority as the best means to this end.[41] With the rise of capitalism, the scandal of democracy receded, and democracy became identical with the social good. Democracy proliferated, but at the cost of the betrayal of its essence and enslavement to an ideal it implicitly challenges.

For psychoanalysis, the good — even the impossible good that one can only seek without ever finding — does not exist. The idea of the good functions as a lure for thought. Seduced by it, we think about societal structures without considering enjoyment. We theorize that subject and societies act for the sake of the good or goods rather than for the sake of mobilizing their enjoyment. This leads to the practical problem that besets advocates of democracy in the capitalist epoch.

When we conceive democracy as a good, we have difficulty creating or even conceiving a desire for this good. Despite the fact that democracy seems to lie within subjects' best interests, it does not seem to have the power to mobilize subjects' enjoyment in the way that antidemocratic movements such as Fascism do. Fascism brings with it the promise of enjoyment that stems from its very excessive nature, and it is all the more attractive insofar as it demands that subjects act against their interest. As a follower of Fascism, one sacrifices the good, one sacrifices one's own interests, in order to enjoy. Thus, from the perspective of fascism, democracy becomes that which one sacrifices — the good that one destroys and enjoys destroying. Because Fascism facilitates the sacrifice of the good rather than holding itself up as an alternative good, it appeals to subjects in a way that democracy, conceived as a good, cannot, and this seems to leave the advocates of democracy with an insoluble difficulty. As long as one considers democracy as a good, one will never inspire subjects to pursue it, and one will always miss the nature of its universal appeal. The only possibility for identifying democracy with enjoyment lies in breaking the false link between democracy and the good. And thanks to recent developments in the global capitalist system, this link has become increasingly tenuous.

On the terrain of contemporary geopolitics, we can see a process of disconnection occurring between a capitalist economy and a democratic political structure. This is most clearly visible in autocratic China's emergence as a major capitalist power. In this case, we see a formerly unthinkable idea — capitalism without democracy — taking hold. Not only does capitalism function without democracy, but it seems to function better.[42] Freedom in China and within the contemporary capitalist universe is nothing but the freedom to sell one's labor and the freedom to appropriate surplus value — not the freedom to voice dissent and to participate politically in governance.

On the one hand, the disconnection of democracy from capitalism is an event to lament. In China it facilitates an increase in authoritarianism and a loss of the possibility for liberty. But on the other hand, this disconnection offers us the opportunity to reassess our idea of democracy and to return to the scandal of democracy. In fact, it reveals something remarkable about the status of democracy: democracy does not serve our interests. Capitalism delivers the goods — and the good — just as efficiently, if not more so, without democracy as with it. Increasingly, democracy itself functions as the excess of the capitalist system — not necessary to the successful working of that system and often a barrier to it.

Dissociating democracy from capitalism and understanding it as an excess of the capitalism system allows us to conceive of it in a new way. Rather than being a good that we strive to attain without ever fully attaining it (an impossible justice to come), democracy becomes the lost object animating our desire, an object that impels us to act against our interest. Democracy today does not help us to accumulate goods (or arrive at the good) but instead functions as a barrier on this path. Time spent insisting on freedom and equality, or even time spent engaged in democratic deliberation, is time that one cannot spend in the act of accumulation of goods. From the perspective of the service of goods, it is wasted time. In fact, democracy requires that we sacrifice our interests on behalf of it: we must put at risk and even abandon the goods that global capitalism offers us in order to achieve it. This demand for sacrifice, far from lessening the appeal of democracy, actually constitutes it as desirable.

The main thrust of Yannis Stavrakakis's *The Lacanian Left* involves forging the link between democracy and enjoyment. He sees that this is a link that most advocates of democracy — even radical democracy — have insufficiently emphasized because they fail to see the possibilities of an enjoyment derived from the experience of failure or of the not-all. He says: "Far from being antithetical to *jouissance*, democratic subjectivity is capable of inspiring high passions.... They mobilise a *jouissance* beyond accumulation, domination and fantasy, an enjoyment of the not-all or not-whole."[43] Democracy ceases to be antithetical to enjoyment, as Stavrakakis recognizes, when we sever it from the image of the social good to which it has been connected since the beginning of modernity.

Severing democracy from the image of the social good requires emphasizing its scandalous dimension — the location of power in an entity (the people) that does not substantially exist. Democracy emerges not through the expression of the popular will in institutionalized forms but when we experience the ultimate groundlessness of political power itself, when we experience the absence of any foundational social authority making itself felt. The democratic impulse is tied to the absence at the heart of the social order, but the association of democracy with capitalism and the good has had the effect of filling this absence with the myth of the sovereign substantive people. The contemporary geopolitical universe has broken this association and returned the scandal to democracy, placing it in the position of the lost object.

Of course, the simple act of theorizing democracy as a lost object instead of a good does not have the power to change the way that the idea of democracy functions practically. But we are already seeing the enjoyment that derives from contemporary invocations of democracy. The enjoyment that surrounded Barack Obama's presidential campaign and the enjoyment that the 2011 Arab revolutions evinced are but two examples of this phenomenon, which becomes possible when the status of democracy shifts from being central to the capitalist order to being excessive. This transformation is actually a restoration of democracy to its original status and to its original association with an enjoyment that doesn't fit properly within the social order.

Identifying democracy with enjoyment can also change the way that we articulate its appeal. We can make evident the contemporary disjunction between democracy and the good and emphasize the necessity of sacrificing the good for the sake of democracy and the enjoyment it provides. If democracy becomes recognized as a lost object among contemporary subjects and the advocates of democracy can marshal the enjoyment that it might engender, they will have a chance to triumph over the reign of the universalized service of goods that is global capitalism. The political project of psychoanalysis is fundamentally democratic, but it envisions democracy as an excess that we can enjoy, though we cannot reconcile it with our enlightened self-interest. It is not more knowledge that will bring about our emancipation but more enjoyment.

8

The Politics of Fantasy

Philosophy versus Fantasy

Shifting the emphasis of politics from the question of knowledge to the question of enjoyment requires a rethinking of the role that fantasy plays in political struggle. Fantasy is how subjects and societies organize their enjoyment. Even if fantasy tends to promise more enjoyment than it ultimately delivers, it provides the frame through which subjects locate the experiences that bring them enjoyment. But the political verdict on fantasy has been almost universally negative. Though utopian socialists use fantasies of a nonantagonistic tomorrow to motivate adherents, serious political thinkers, especially in the tradition of Marx, tend to emphasize the deleterious effects of fantasy on political awareness. Political thinkers have inherited this indictment of fantasy from Western philosophy itself, which has made the critique of fantasy in some form or other one of its central projects since Plato wrote *The Republic*. But psychoanalytic thought offers a way of redeeming fantasy while avoiding the progressivism that seems to inhere in the very structure of fantasy. This places it at odds with the political vision articulated throughout the history of Western philosophy and offers a new way of conceiving politics.

The great figures of Western philosophy, at least prior to Marx, are not known for their political radicality. If there is a politics of philosophy as such, it would seem to be some version of conservatism. From Plato onward, the history of philosophy is a history of justification for inequality in social relations. Plato begins this tradition by showing, according to Jacques Rancière, that "democratic equality is just the inequality of tyranny."[1] Near the other end of the tradition, Hegel insists on the philosophical necessity of the monarch — the pinnacle of inequality — in order for the people to constitute themselves as a people. The monarch acts as a form of punctuation mark, in Hegel's political philosophy, that provides a limit through which the state gains a definitive essence.[2] Like most Western philosophers, Hegel does not believe that a social order can survive without inequality, and he orients his political philosophy around this supposed fact.

Even the most philosophically radical thinkers in the Western tradition, those who challenge authority rather than trying to appease it, share what seems to be a philosophical bias against the people. Spinoza constructed the *Theological-Political Treatise* as an attack on the forces of repression and a call for freedom. But it does not, for all its antiauthoritarianism, champion the possibility of social equality. In fact, Spinoza inveighs against the "common people" as potential readers of his treatise. He even goes so far as to explicitly dissuade them from reading it: "I do not invite the common people to read this work, nor all those who are victims of the same emotional attitudes. Indeed, I would prefer that they disregard this book completely rather than make themselves a nuisance by misinterpreting it after their wont."[3] What's especially disturbing about the hostility toward the people that Spinoza evinces here is that it does not simply reflect a private prejudice that has no bearing on his philosophy but emerges directly from the philosophy as such.

For Spinoza, giving in to the power of emotion and subjecting rationality to emotion (rather than the reverse) constitutes precisely the problem that his philosophy tries to combat. Those, like the common people, who allow themselves to be led by emotion exist in the state of human bondage, whereas those who place the emotions under the guide of rationality exist in the state of human freedom. Though perhaps the most radical thinker in the Western tradition before Marx, Spinoza nonetheless partakes of the antidemocratic attitude that infects this tradition as a whole.

In spite of this avowed hostility to democracy among the philosophers of the West, there exists in this tradition a widely shared philosophical project essential to democratic emancipation. Even the most aristocratic thinkers — like Plato and Nietzsche — subscribe to the idea that the project of philosophy involves an assault on the distorting and debilitating power of fantasy. Perhaps the most widely shared idea in the Western tradition is that fantasy prevents both subjects and society alike from experiencing truth and thereby emancipating themselves.

The fight against fantasy animates the philosophical tradition from Plato and Aristotle to Quine and Derrida. For these philosophers, fantasy represents the great bogey in human experience. Though it would be difficult to find one philosopher who speaks directly of fantasy or even employs the term, the philosopher who doesn't direct her or his thought against a specific mode of being or experience that we can best characterize as fantasmatic is a rarity. To put it another way, the most widely shared political project of Western philosophy is that of combating the power of structures that operate on the subject in precisely the same way that fantasy does.[4]

To characterize Western philosophy as having a political project runs against what philosophers themselves tend to say. Wittgenstein, for instance, claims that "philosophy . . . leaves everything as it is."[5] This claim echoes similar statements in the work of Kant, Nietzsche, Heidegger, and others. But despite this explicit disavowal of philosophy's political dimension, the philosophical critique of fantasy-like thinking is implicitly political insofar as it pushes subjects toward an awareness of their position within the social totality. In short, to break the hold of fantasy over the subject is to politicize that subject in the process.

What's more, this philosophical challenge to fantasy has informed the way that we tend to think about politics and about generating political action. Even though few may have adopted, say, Kant's thought as a basis for political commitment, many have taken philosophy's critique of fantasy in general as a political starting point.[6] Political action has become, thanks in some part to philosophy, the project of fighting against the power of fantasy and fantasy's role as a supplement to ideology. The significant political innovation of psychoanalysis in this respect is that it allows us to see fantasy in another way. Psychoanalysis recognizes that the political valence of fantasy remains up for grabs; it is not, contra the Western philosophical tradition, ipso facto negative. With the aid of psychoanalysis, we can approach fantasy as a basis for political engagement rather than necessarily joining philosophy's critique of its hold over us. In this sense, the political task becomes not working to eliminate fantasy altogether or trying to create politically progressive fantasies but changing the way that we relate to fantasy by enabling us to see the radical dimension of fantasy's structure.

The assault on fantasy has its most famous expression in Plato's allegory of the cave, a discussion that locates ideological deception within the contours of the visual image. In the opening of book 7 of the *Republic*, Socrates describes a cave in which prisoners are held and forced to look only at shadows on the wall in front of them cast by puppeteers manipulating their puppets behind the backs of the prisoners. In this situation, Socrates contends, "the prisoners would in every way believe that the truth is nothing other than the shadows of those artifacts."[7] This is allegorically the situation of individuals within the social order when they succumb to the influence of the fantasmatic dimension of that order or what Socrates calls its "visual realm." The task of philosophy is that of facilitating emancipation, movement from the cave of shadows to the light of day, which is the good.

Socrates sees the potential for emancipation democratically distributed. He argues: "The power to learn is present in everyone's soul and . . . the instrument with which each learns is like an eye that cannot be turned around from darkness to light without turning the whole body."[8] Everyone can escape fantasmatic deception, but it requires a fundamental transformation of one's mode of existence. One must turn oneself away from the visual image and toward the realm of ideas, which ultimately provides the basis for the visual realm. By doing so, one sees how the image is produced and thereby eludes its power of seduction. This is Plato's conception of freedom, and it comes through the act of transcending the power of fantasy.

For many modern philosophers, fantasy involves a failure to think the full ramifications of the subject's insertion into language. The insertion into language necessarily leaves the subject alienated — the world of language is a world of words rather than things — but this alienation does not, as fantasy deceives the subject into believing, represent a fall from some original state of plenitude. The subject of language lacks, but this lack does not correspond to any loss on the part of the subject.

The role of fantasy is to convert the subject's traumatic experience of lack into a more acceptable experience of loss in order to produce the illusion that there is somewhere a satisfying object of desire, that there is a world of things that language obscures and hints at. Hence, fantasy's fundamental deception consists in its constituting an image of originary plenitude that the subject has lost. By providing the subject with such an image (and the narrative that explains its loss), fantasy blinds the subject to its own situatedness within language and society. Fantasy allows the subject to believe that it operates and experiences outside the confines of language — that these confines are not constitutive for the subject. Through fantasy, the subject can sustain its belief in a "real world" beyond its present world, and this belief blinds the subject to this present world. As a result of this fantasmatic deception, the subject never sees the limitations that its situatedness places on it.

We can see different versions of this critique of fantasy throughout modern philosophy, but perhaps no philosopher targets fantasy and its deception as clearly as Immanuel Kant in the *Critique of Pure Reason*. There, Kant aims to purge reason itself of its fantasmatic dimension and thereby establish definite limits beyond which philosophy cannot speculate. In the first *Critique*, Kant views philosophy as nothing but the act of exposing the limits of thought itself. As he puts it, "Philosophy consists precisely in knowing its bounds."[9] Philosophy informs us that our thinking cannot transcend our experience without falling victim to illusion. When we attempt to use our reason in a positive way and to think beyond the realm of experience — to speculate about, for instance, God, freedom, or immortality — we necessarily become involved in the lure of fantasy. Reason itself leads to fantasmatic deception, such as the ontological proof for the existence of God, which proves the existence of God on the basis of concepts alone. This kind of fantasmatic deception is not simply a philosophical error that Kant aims to emend; it has definite political consequences as well, which is ultimately why Kant wrote the *Critique of Pure Reason* as a corrective.

When a fantasmatic formulation such as the ontological proof seduces us, the political danger stems from the way in which this fantasy blinds us to the limits that actually govern our thought. In the fantasy scenario that pure reason provides, we can have certain knowledge about the deepest mysteries of the universe, even the existence of God. Pure reason thus provides the illusion of an unrestricted freedom — it imagines no limit to what we can think — but when we fall for this deception, we necessarily fail to see the restrictions inherent in our experience.

According to Kant, we can recognize our actual freedom only through the awareness of the a priori regulations that govern our experience. This is what leads Kant to claim that "pure reason, which initially seemed to promise us nothing less than an extension of our knowledge beyond all boundaries of experience, if we understand it rightly contains nothing but regulative principles."[10] Rather than employ reason to speculate in a fantasmatic way, philosophy teaches us to use reason solely to recognize the structural limitations of our positions. This, for Kant, is the position that philosophy must take up vis-à-vis the fantasmatic proclivity of reason itself.[11]

Despite Kant's effort to cleanse philosophy of its fantasmatic dimension, subsequent philosophers have repeated this theme, albeit with a new emphasis. For the two major movements of late nineteenth- and twentieth-century thought — phenomenology and analytic philosophy — the effort to cast fantasy aside requires jettisoning the prior philosophical tradition beginning with Plato and continuing through Descartes and Kant. Plato's critique of fantasy is not, according to these lines of thought, critical enough but actually participates in the most profound type of fantasy — the metaphysical fantasy. The metaphysical fantasy envisions an accessible realm of ideas and a subject that exists outside of time.

The project of phenomenology involves grounding philosophy in experience and thereby deflating the Platonic fantasy that governed the history of Western thought. Husserl urges philosophers to return to the things themselves and the experience of things because he believes that a transcendent realm of ideas represents a fantasmatic deception that does not actually exist. Any attempt to think outside of the experience of things results in the creation of an illusory world without any philosophical validity.

Within the tradition of phenomenology, thinkers criticize not only the history of philosophy but also each other for not going far enough in the direction of experience. Heidegger claims, for instance, that Husserl's retention of consciousness as the basis for understanding experience remains within the metaphysical fantasy of Western philosophy. He introduced the term "Dasein" in order to reduce subjectivity to being itself and thereby to strip away all fantasmatic elements from it. Dasein is nothing but the situatedness in time of a being that only exists in the experience of its temporality. The subject that animates Western thought from Plato onward continues to exist only as a fantasmatic illusion.

The analytic tradition is equally harsh with the history of philosophy, though it sees the proclivity to fantasy in a different realm — philosophy's tendency to resort to psychological explanations. At the beginning of the analytic tradition, Gottlob Frege attempted to cleanse philosophy of its tendency toward psychology. Frege does not want to reduce the subject to experience but rather to separate the rules of logic from the activity of the subject that arrives at these rules. As he puts it, "Never let us take a description of the origin of an idea for a definition, or an account of the mental and physical conditions on which we become conscious of a proposition for a proof of it. A proposition may be thought, and again it may be true; let us never confuse these two things."[12] Just as Heidegger attacks Western thought for its metaphysical attempt to discover an origin, Frege also sees the inquiry into the origin as a false step that has nothing to do with truth, which he wants to preserve. Though he has an end in mind vastly different from Heidegger's, Frege shares the project of dislodging truth from the metaphysical position that it has occupied in the history of Western philosophy. Both Heidegger and Frege aim at bringing philosophy back down to earth and thereby stripping it of its fantasmatic dimension.

In a related way, Wittgenstein envisions philosophy as a corrective against our inherent tendency as beings of language to believe in a world beyond language (that is, to fantasize). As he puts it in *The Blue Book*, "Philosophy, as we use the word, is a fight against the fascination which forms of expression exert upon us."[13] Our "forms of expression" fascinate us — they create a fantasmatic deception — insofar as they disguise our status as beings of language. They obscure our essential groundlessness and the groundlessness of our particular language game by providing an image of something prior to our insertion into language. This is why Wittgenstein says in *On Certainty* that "it is so difficult to find the *beginning*. Or, better: it is difficult to begin at the beginning. And not try to go further back."[14] On the basis of our fantasmatic illusions, we believe that we can go "further back" and access the foundations of our being that exist outside of language. Thus, our language game comes to seem as if it has roots in the very structure of reality, whereas it has no foundation whatsoever.

For Wittgenstein, the beginning of the language game represents an absolute beginning, and fantasy serves to disguise the absolute nature of the break that the language game introduces. He sees definite political consequences following from the turn to fantasy: duped by fantasy, subjects fail to grasp their own subjection to the determinants of the prevailing language game and take refuge in an illusion of freedom. They fail to see that they are always already playing a (language) game. It is this fantasmatic illusion of freedom that so much modern philosophy is intent on dismantling, if only in order to constitute an authentic freedom.[15]

Throughout the history of analytic philosophy, the opposition to fantasy is nearly ubiquitous, and this opposition often identifies fantasmatic thinking with Continental philosophy itself. According to this line of thought, Continental philosophy's habitual appeal to some sort of transcendence marks its investment in fantasy — and its failure to stick to experience. It is for this reason that so many analytic philosophers dismiss Continental philosophy as "poetry" or "theology." A. J. Ayer, for instance, contends that any appeal to transcendence removes one from the realm of logic. As he puts it, "The labours of those who have striven to describe [transcendence] have all been devoted to the production of nonsense."[16] Philosophy can save us from nonsense by exposing the lure of fantasmatic thinking and allowing us to gain some purchase on it.

Marx with the Philosophers

When it comes to fantasy's role in the subject's experience, Western philosophy seems to have a clear political content — and even a political program. This program involves stripping away the seductive lure of fantasy in order to acquaint subjects not with bare reality but with the way that reality is produced. This emphasis on critiquing fantasy in the name of production provides a clear link to Marx and Marxism, despite Marx's hostility to philosophy. As is well known, Marx attacks philosophy for its failure to become politically efficacious. His diatribe against philosophy finds its most straightforward expression in the eleventh of his "Theses on Feuerbach." Here Marx claims: "The philosophers have only *interpreted* the world, in various ways; the point, however, is to change it."[17] According to Marx, philosophers have failed in the central duty of thought: having a practical effect on the world rather than just arriving at a theoretical understanding of it.

Marx sees philosophy itself as the problem, and hence he sees the need to break from philosophy altogether if thought is to become politicized. In *The Philosophy of Marx* Étienne Balibar claims: "The *Theses on Feuerbach* ... demand a definitive exit (*Ausgang*) from philosophy, as the only means of realizing what has always been its loftiest ambition: emancipation, liberation."[18] But Marx's call for a "definitive exit" from philosophy comes to seem paradoxical when we consider the politics of philosophy in juxtaposition with the tenets of Marxist politics. Despite his attack on philosophy's failure to politicize itself, Marx himself actually adopts a version of philosophy's conception of politics. Marx's political critique of capitalist relations of production is at almost every instance a critique of the tendency of these relations to produce subjects entranced by fantasy and thus unable to see how the economic structure of capitalism actually functions.

The fundamental fantasy of the capitalist subject is that of an individual existence that owes nothing to the larger social structure in which it resides. Throughout his career as an analyst and critic of capitalism, Marx combated this fantasy, but nowhere more directly than in the *Grundrisse*. From the beginning of the first notebook in this work, Marx works to show that the individual is never an isolated monad but part of a larger social order that makes individual existence possible. The act of historicizing allows us, he claims, to give the lie to individual independence. As he puts it, "The more deeply we go back into history, the more deeply does the individual, and hence also the producing individual, appear as dependent, as belonging to a greater whole."[19] Historicizing renders visible the array of social forces that have enabled the individual to act in an apparently independent manner. Like the prisoners in Plato's cave, capitalist subjects believe in their own unfettered agency because they cannot turn their heads to see the forces holding them in place and controlling what they see. The ahistorical thinking that predominates under capitalism blinds individuals to their social dependence, and this blindness acts as an insurmountable barrier to proletarian class consciousness and the overthrow of capitalism.

The individualist fantasy that capitalism promulgates fails to think through its own implications, and Marx attacks the fantasy on this front as well. Just as fantasy as such owes its cogency to its lack of coherence, to its ability to exist in contradiction with itself, the individualist fantasy depends on restricting it to a few isolated individuals. Though the individualist believes that everyone is an individual and is capable of acting as a free agent, this status is implicitly denied to the majority. The fantasy envisions workers saving money and raising themselves up in this manner to the status of capitalists.

In this (almost universally accepted) account of things, capitalism is a meritocracy that rewards the industrious and penalizes the lazy. But as Marx points out, the fantasy unravels as soon as we imagine it being universally taken up. He says:

Only as an exception does the worker succeed through will power, physical strength and endurance, greed etc., in transforming his coin into money, as an exception from his class and from the general conditions of his existence. If all or the majority are too industrious (to the degree that industriousness in modern industry is in fact left to their own personal choice, which is not the case in the most important and most developed branches of production), then they increase not the value of their commodity, but only its quantity; that is, the demands which would be placed on it as use value. . . . An individual worker can be *industrious* above the average, more than he has to be in order to live as a worker, only because another lies below the average, is lazier; he can save only because and if another wastes.[20]

By thinking through the individualist fantasy to its endpoint and imagining what would happen if everyone adopted the policy of industriousness, Marx reveals the contradiction that proponents of the fantasy must simply ignore. All fantasizing obscures such contradictions, and this is the key to fantasy's power.

For Marx, fantasy is not just the product of capitalist ideology and the way of thinking it promotes; it is written into the very structure of capitalist relations of production. The capitalist judges the success of an enterprise solely by its profitability, and profit is — at least in the conscious mind of every successful capitalist — the reason for the production process. Profit occurs in the act of exchange, when a consumer purchases a commodity that the capitalist has produced. The location of profit within exchange rather than within production proper misleads everyone within the capitalist mode of production into believing that exchange itself produces the increase in value when in fact the source is labor — or, more precisely, the appropriation of surplus labor. All capitalists believe themselves to be in the business of producing profit, but Marx shows that they are actually in the business of producing (or facilitating the production of) surplus value. Surplus value, which the labor process creates, provides the basis for and determines profit, though those immersed in the system cannot recognize this.

Profit is, as Marx sees it, a capitalist fantasy allowing capitalists to blind themselves to the role that labor has in creating value and to their own pitiless appropriation of that value from those who created it. In the third volume of *Capital*, Marx claims: "Profit, as we are originally faced with it, is thus the same thing as surplus-value, save in a mystified form, though one that necessarily arises from the capitalist mode of production."[21] The mystification of profit does not result from conscious or even unconscious manipulation on the part of the capitalist class. It inheres in the capitalist system or "necessarily arises." But its structural necessity does not make it any less fantasmatic or mystifying, and Marxist political struggle consists in fighting against this fascination by exposing profit's basis in surplus value.

Those who recognize that the appropriation of surplus labor rather than advantageous exchange is responsible for the creation of additional value will be less invested in capitalist relations of production and ready to work for its political overthrow. Marx considered his theoretical work analyzing capital to have a directly political dimension because of its focus on eviscerating the mystification inherent in profit. One breaks through this mystification by gaining awareness of the underlying structure that produces it and that the fantasmatic nature of profit serves to obscure.

Marx's war on the mystification inherent in capitalism reaches its apogee with the critique of commodity fetishism. He sees commodity fetishism as the fundamental barrier in the way of proletarian class consciousness, and commodity fetishism has the precise structure of fantasy. Capitalist subjects treat the commodity in a fantasmatic way without any awareness that they are doing so. They interact on a conscious level with the commodity in a realist fashion, as if it were an ordinary object, without realizing that they are imbuing the commodity with transcendent significance.

In short, capitalist subjects caught up in the fetishism of commodities do not realize that they are fantasizing, and Marx's efforts in *Capital* consist in facilitating awareness of this. As Marx famously puts it in the first volume of *Capital*, "The commodity-form, and the value-relation of the products of labour within which it appears, have absolutely no connection with the physical nature of the commodity and the material relations arising out of this. It is nothing but the definite social relation between men themselves which assumes here, for them, the fantastic form of a relation between things."[22] The commodity becomes a fantasmatic object, completely divorced from the process of production — the social relations — that created it. The structural exigencies of capital demand that subjects interact with commodities as if they had a magical power, and this is what capitalist subjects do even when they remain consciously aware that commodities do not intrinsically have this power. In the very way that subjects buy and sell commodities, they implicitly deny the role that labor plays in the creation of commodity value.

By creating awareness about the fetishism of commodities, Marx hopes to render the fantasy conscious and thereby break its hold. This is why Marx and so many Marxists following him have given the analysis of commodity fetishism a central place in the critique of capitalism. Perhaps the key text of Marxist philosophy in the twentieth century, Georg Lukács's *History and Class Consciousness*, takes commodity fetishism as its point of departure in order to elaborate the concept of reification. The entire theoretical edifice of the Frankfurt School also rests on the edifice of commodity fetishism. It plays this foundational role because it appears to be the fantasy without which capitalist relations of production could not continue, and it is also the fantasy that acts as the most intransigent barrier to capitalism's overthrow.

Commodity fetishism is crucial in sustaining capitalist relations of production insofar as it, like the nature of profit, disguises the very existence of relations of production. It functions in this sense as a fundamental fantasy within capitalist society. In advancing a Marxist critique of fetishism, Laura Mulvey notices that the process of commodity fetishism "entails a fantasy disavowal. A commodity's market success depends on the erasure of the marks of production, any trace of indexicality, the grime of the factory, the mass moulding of the machine, and most of all, the exploitation of the worker. Instead, the commodity presents the market with a seductive sheen, as it competes to be desired."[23] The key to revolutionary change for Mulvey (and for Marx himself) consists in shattering this fantasmatic illusion and creating the proletarian class consciousness that it attempts to suppress.[24]

This political program, while more explicitly political than that found in the history of Western philosophy, nonetheless shares its fundamental structure with the politics of philosophy. Both positions recognize that fantasy disguises our status within society — hiding the *productive* dimension of our social relations. In doing so, it weds us almost inextricably to the ruling ideas in the society and, by extension, to the interests of the ruling class. According to this position, subjects must break the hold that fantasy has over them before they can take authentic political action and act according to their own class interests. Attacking fantasy thus becomes, for Western philosophy and for Marxism, the sine qua non of political activity.

The Psychoanalytic Embrace of Fantasy

Like philosophy and Marxism, psychoanalysis also has a history of opposing itself to fantasy. Its basic trajectory appears to involve curing the patient of an excessive investment in fantasy life. It seems as if neurotics come to psychoanalysts suffering from their fantasies and that the sessions allow the neurotics to gain some distance from these fantasies and thereby see them for what they are. Gaining purchase on one's fantasy life — or simply becoming aware that one is fantasizing — is one predominant image of the psychoanalytic process.

My own therapy, for instance, consisted in gaining awareness of the nonexistence of normal people. The analyst's unremitting silence in response to my questions about how everyone else would react in similar situations ultimately allowed me to recognize the obvious fact that there was no such thing as a normal reaction or normal person. I was invested in the fantasy of normality without realizing that it was a fantasy, and analysis laid this fantasy bare and thus facilitated a disinvestment in it. In this way, like so many patients I felt as if I was able to move beyond a barrier that I did not even know existed.

Many theorists who recognize the political importance of psychoanalysis do so because of its ability to combat fantasy. For example, this dimension of psychoanalysis leads Yannis Stavrakakis, in *Lacan and the Political*, to see the contemporary political task of psychoanalysis as one of "traversing the fantasy of utopian thought."[25] In the vein of the philosopher or the Marxist, Stavrakakis sees a danger in the way that fantasy hides the gap that haunts the symbolic order. As he notes, "Fantasy negates the real by promising to 'realise' it, by promising to close the gap between the real and reality, by repressing the discursive nature of reality's production."[26] Here, Stavrakakis sees the ideological dimension of fantasy, and psychoanalysis for him facilitates this recognition and provides a way to dissolve fantasy's power. This kind of psychoanalytic politics evinces the attitude toward fantasy that both modern philosophy and Marxism take up, and this attitude certainly seems faithful to psychoanalytic practice and its attempt to assist the subject in "traversing the fantasy."[27]

But despite the seeming antipathy directed toward fantasy in its very practice, for psychoanalysis the political valence of fantasy is not so unambiguous as it is for philosophy and Marxism. To unlock fully the political potential of psychoanalysis, we must turn our attention to the positive significance that psychoanalysis bestows on fantasy. Both philosophy and Marxism are, of course, right about the role that fantasy has in disguising our social situatedness. But the problem with this conception of politics is that, by focusing on what fantasy conceals, it fails to consider what fantasy reveals. It is at this point — the point of what fantasy reveals to us — that we can see the political significance of psychoanalysis. The value of psychoanalysis in relation to philosophy lies in the ability of psychoanalysis to grasp the political importance of fantasy in a way that philosophy and Marxism have been unable to do.

At the same time that fantasy disguises our subjection to the signifier and makes it difficult for us to experience this subjection, it also has the effect of making otherwise impossible experiences possible.[28] Fantasy offers the subject a transcendent experience, and this transcendence, despite its illusory quality, has a political content. It represents a moment at which the subject is no longer bound by the limitations of the symbolic structure that ordinarily constrain it. As such, this moment of fantasmatic transcendence poses for the subject a fundamental challenge to the authority of that symbolic structure. In fact, the radical import of fantasy is located in precisely the same feature that causes fantasy to further ideology: the illusions of fantasy keep subjects content with the ruling symbolic structure, but they also provide a venue for thinking beyond that structure. In contrast to modern philosophy and Marxism, psychoanalysis permits us to see this political complexity inhering within the structure of fantasy.

From the beginnings of psychoanalysis, this respect for fantasy makes itself felt. When it comes to the psyche of the subject in analysis, the fantasy has more significance than actual memories. For instance, Freud's early essay "Screen Memories" describes early childhood memories as screens for unconscious fantasies. The sexual content of the fantasy, Freud contends, can only appear through the vehicle of a genuine memory. He writes: "It is precisely the coarsely sensual element in the phantasy which explains why it ... must be content to find its way allusively and under a flowery disguise into a childhood scene."[29] Freud's point here is not that we must subtract the distortion of fantasy from the memory in order to discover what actually happened but that what actually happened has far less psychic importance than the fantasy it conceals.

The subject uses the memory of a genuine scene to access and at the same time disguise a fantasy. Fantasy distorts, but its distortion embodies subjectivity itself and transports the subject outside the constraints of actual experience, which is why Freud values it over memory. This valuation is part of the implicit political project inhering within psychoanalytic thought, and it distances the politics of psychoanalysis from other political projects rooted in the Enlightenment.

Because it allows the subject an experience of transcendence beyond the limits of the ruling symbolic structure, fantasy has tangible political benefits. These benefits can be characterized in three related ways: (1) through fantasy, we experience alternatives to the ruling symbolic structure that remain unthinkable within this structure; (2) fantasy facilitates an encounter with traumatic disruption that our everyday reality guards against; and (3) fantasy makes evident the link between loss and enjoyment, allowing us to conceive of a politics that embraces loss rather than attempting to escape it. These political dimensions of fantasy all manifest themselves in the thought of Freud and Lacan, even though neither conceives of fantasy (or psychoanalysis as a whole) in a political sense.

But the political viability of fantasy becomes even more evident when we look at works of art that are explicitly devoted to the exploration of fantasy, such as the science fiction novels of Ursula K. Le Guin. Obviously there are many artworks that display fantasy's political possibilities, but Le Guin's novels delve into fantasy in widely disparate ways, providing a field that is able to touch on all sides of fantasy's political power. By looking at three of Le Guin's novels — *The Left Hand of Darkness*, *The Lathe of Heaven*, and *The Dispossessed* — we can see the specific political dimensions of fantasy as they are dramatized. In each of these novels, Le Guin creates a world that unlocks an aspect of fantasy's potential political power and that makes clear the role that fantasy can play in the project of emancipation.

Making the Impossible Possible

While fantasy protects us from an experience of lack (as it disguises our situatedness within the social order), it also exposes us to possibilities that would otherwise remain concealed by ideology. This is the most basic political work that fantasy does. Fantasy not only offers the subject an opportunity for experiencing activity that the symbolic law prohibits but also stages scenarios that are not even thinkable in the everyday world, possibilities concealed to such an extent that no law explicitly prohibits them. This is a point that Freud makes in the *Introductory Lectures*, noting that "in the activity of phantasy human beings continue to enjoy the freedom from external compulsion which they have long since renounced in reality."[30] In the realm of fantasy, the subject has the freedom to explore the blank spaces in the symbolic structure. Fantasy has this power because it emanates from the unconscious desire of the subject, and this desire is drawn inexorably to the impossibilities that haunt the ruling symbolic structure. Through fantasy, desire seeks out that which the symbolic structure does not — and cannot — contain, that point of nonsense within the symbolic structure. In this sense, every fantasy is subversive in its very essence, directing the subject to a position of radical freedom from symbolic constraints.

For both the history of philosophy and Marxism, the freedom of fantasy is the worst kind of unfreedom because it serves to vitiate actual freedom. If subjects fantasize a scenario in which they escape the "external compulsion" that they endure in reality, they become much less likely to recognize or to revolt against that compulsion. Freedom on the level of fantasy thus supplements a material lack of freedom. This is why so many philosophers inveigh against the illusory freedom that fantasy provides. In attacking fantasy, they argue for recognizing the actual constraints that govern us. When we strip away the veil of fantasy, we can see our unfreedom. But stripping away the veil of fantasy does not allow us to see beyond our situatedness into other possibilities, and this represents the fundamental barrier that this kind of politics runs up against.

That is to say, the politics of attacking fantasy does not allow us to transcend the limitations that the prevailing ideology places on us. Through offering us an illusory image of transcendence, fantasy takes us beyond the limitations that the symbolic order places on us, and in doing so, it opens us to possibilities that were previously foreclosed. It is through fantasy that one sees the possibility of the impossible. If psychoanalysis allows us to see the political effectiveness of fantasy, it does so because it emphasizes how fantasy allows us to experience the impossible.

One of the chief ways that ideology sustains its hold over subjects is that it constrains what appears as a possibility. For instance, contemporary ideology has constituted capitalism as our very horizon of possibility. The idea of an economic organization beyond capitalism has become unthinkable. The unthinkable status of radical change represents *the* great victory of late capitalist ideology. But the terrain of fantasy is the weak point of this ideology. If we can't think about the possibility of capitalism's end, we can fantasize about it.[31] Ideology relies on fantasy to sustain its underside, to seduce subjects even in the most private region, but this reliance on fantasy itself testifies to ideology's fundamental vulnerability. Through fantasy, subjects today do envision the unthinkable: they play out possibilities — like the end of global capitalism's hegemony — that seem impossible. In this way, fantasy gives the lie to the limitations that seem most intractable for the contemporary subject.

This ability to transcend the ideological limits of the present animates the fantasy that Le Guin constructs in her novel *The Left Hand of Darkness*. Written in 1969, during the incipience of the consciousness-raising movement in American feminism, this novel envisions a world that reveals the ultimate contingency of all gender characteristics. Le Guin tells the novel's story through the character of Genly Ai, who is an alien envoy to the planet Winter (or Gethen, in the language of the inhabitants). In general, the inhabitants of Winter have no sexual identity. For twenty-two days of the month, the Gethenians exist in a state of sexual inactivity in which they are neither male nor female. During the remaining days of the month, they enter into a wholly sexual phase known as *kemmer*. In this phase, the Gethenians can take on either a male or a female sexual identity, but it is only during these few days of the month that they are sexed beings. Perhaps the most significant feature of this fantasmatic scenario is that it totally befuddles the perception of an outsider such as Genly Ai, the foreign envoy to Winter.

As a sexed being (a male), Genly Ai finds it difficult to perceive identity without the gender characteristics that he associates with sexual difference. He describes his own inability to perceive the people of Winter without ascribing them a gender identity: "Though I had been nearly two years on Winter I was still far from being able to see the people of the planet through their own eyes. I tried to, but my efforts took the form of self-consciously seeing a Gethenian first as a man, then as a woman, forcing him into those categories so irrelevant to his nature and so essential to my own."[32] This failure to see the Gethenian correctly indicates the power of gender-oriented thinking over human perception, but the novel also points toward another possibility, the possibility of depriving gender identity of the role that it has in our thought.

Through its depiction of a world that eschews gender definition while retaining sexual reproduction, *The Left Hand of Darkness* allows readers to see the groundlessness of gender as such. In the fantasy that Le Guin constructs in the novel, gender becomes not simply arbitrary but unattached to subjectivity, and this works to reveal its contingent and ultimately insignificant status. Through the imagining of a world that exists without male and female gender categories, Le Guin imagines what patriarchal ideology renders unthinkable and thereby defies its unthinkable status. In this sense, the fantasmatic dimension of Le Guin's novel functions as a political act, opening up possibilities that patriarchal ideology foreclosed.

As a result of the sexual structure on Winter, even our thinking about the activities that seem most naturally gender-identified, such as the association of women with child-bearing, become open to question. As Genly Ai notes, "The fact that everyone between seventeen and thirty-five or so is liable to be ... 'tied down to childbearing,' implies that no one is quite so thoroughly 'tied down' here as women, elsewhere, are likely to be — psychologically or physically."[33] Of course, Le Guin's novel can't accomplish a physiological miracle and allow men to bear children, but it can change the way that we think about the activity, prompting us to stop viewing the burden as uniquely feminine. This is one of the ways in which Le Guin's fantasmatic scenario allows subjects to think new possibilities. In doing so, it reveals a political power that exists implicitly within all fantasizing.[34] Not surprisingly, some feminists took up the fantasy of *The Left Hand of Darkness* and made it the basis for their political program.

An Express Path to Trauma

In addition to opening up the possibilities that ideology attempts to foreclose, fantasy also opens the subject to an experience of trauma that the social reality closes off. Subjects structure their everyday social reality around an avoidance of a traumatic kernel that nonetheless haunts that reality and continually upsets its smooth functioning. Our world appears "normal" insofar as this traumatic kernel functions in it only as an absence. In fact, the exclusion of the unknowable and traumatic kernel is what allows everyday reality to seem everyday.

If subjects encountered this trauma in their experience of this reality, the shock would deprive it of its everydayness. This is the power of ideology: it constitutes our reality as a terrain untroubled by the trauma that grounds this reality.[35] As long as we remain on the terrain of social reality, the trauma remains a present absence. It is only when we turn from reality to fantasy that it becomes possible to experience the traumatic kernel that functions as a necessary present absence within every social order.

Because it facilitates an otherwise impossible experience, fantasy places us on the path toward the traumatic kernel. Fantasy lures us toward the point at which ideology breaks down, and it allows us to experience this traumatic opening. Outside of fantasy, we resist any experience that calls ideology into question because we want to avoid the trauma that accompanies this experience. But within the structure of fantasy, things are altogether different. When the encounter with the trauma occurs in fantasy, we pursue rather than resist it because of the ultimate pleasure that fantasy promises. In the fantasy, recognizing the traumatic gap within ideology becomes a possibility.[36]

Though fantasy blinds us to the structure of the social order in which we exist, it also allows us to recognize the gap within this structure that represents the very possibility of political change. The gap within the social order marks the possibility of political change because it marks the point at which this order lacks: it is *the* point of vulnerability in any order. The subject employs fantasy in order to fill in this gap in the social order, but it is this very effort to fill in the gap that allows the subject to experience the gap in its traumatic dimension. Fantasy creates an imagistic narrative that explains what the symbolic structure can never adequately explain—its own origin.

The fantasy scenario stages the origin of the symbolic law—the moment at which plenitude and enjoyment are lost—and at this point, the real becomes evident in its evanescence. The fantasy scenario always points toward this real that it cannot include. As Richard Boothby points out in *Freud as Philosopher*, "Phantasy is always a picturing, an imaginal figuration, yet also aims toward something unimagable. What is most deeply sought by desire in the phantasy cannot be given in the register of the image."[37] That is, fantasy uses the image and the imaginary scenario in order to indicate the traumatic kernel that exists beyond the image.

The founding dream of psychoanalysis — the dream of Irma's injection — reveals fantasy's ability to facilitate an encounter with the traumatic gap in the social structure. Freud's dream constructs a fantasy scenario that exculpates both his close friend Wilhelm Fliess and himself for their errors in treating a patient. In this sense, the fantasy hides the pathological origin of psychoanalysis itself, obscuring the pseudoscientific practices out of which it arose.[38] But at the same time, the fantasy that Freud constructs in the Irma dream enables him to encounter a trauma that cannot be rendered meaningful despite the attempts that the dream makes in this direction.

As he looks into Irma's throat to investigate her ailment, Freud experiences this trauma. As Lacan describes it, "There's a horrendous discovery here, that of the flesh one never sees, the foundation of things, the other side of the head, of the face, the secretory glands *par excellence*, the flesh from which everything exudes, at the very heart of the mystery, the flesh in as much as it is suffering, is formless, in as much as its form in itself is something which provokes anxiety. Spectre of anxiety, identification of anxiety, the final revelation of *you are this — You are this, which is so far from you, this which is the ultimate formlessness.*"[39] Here, in the dream of Irma's injection, Freud encounters a traumatic kernel that completely subverts his secure position within the symbolic structure.

This trauma confronts Freud with the inside of the body, with the exposure of the subject's material being that no symbol can ameliorate. According to Lacan, it is specifically the fantasmatic nature of the dream that allows Freud to have an "abyssal relation to that which is most unknown, which is the hallmark of an exceptional, privileged experience, in which the real is apprehended beyond all mediation, be it imaginary or symbolic."[40] The fantasmatic scenario of the dream thus turns against itself, and instead of merely concealing the functioning of the social order, it facilitates an encounter that disturbs this functioning.

The encounter with the traumatic gap in signification is inherently a political event because it exposes the contingency of the symbolic structure and makes evident the fundamental symbolic lie. At the point of this encounter, the symbolic law's hold over the subject evaporates as its ultimate groundlessness and meaninglessness are revealed. Subjects invest themselves in and submit to the symbolic law insofar as they believe in its ability to confer meaning and identity, and this is precisely what the encounter with the traumatic gap gives the lie to. Thus, fantasy's ability to lure the subject toward the encounter with this trauma attests to the political importance of fantasy. Fantasy assists public ideology by obscuring the dimension of the trauma, but in this very act of obscuring it, fantasy stages an encounter with it. In this way, the qualities that allow fantasy to assist ideology allow it to subvert ideology as well.

In the fantasy scenarios that Le Guin's *Lathe of Heaven* depicts, we experience the world in its becoming, the formless real out of which the symbolic structure emerges. In this novel, the protagonist, George Orr, has the power to re-create the very structure of reality on the basis of his dreams, dreams that Orr calls "effective dreams" for their ability to effect actual change in the world. Because these dreams re-create the world anew, they strip away the symbolic fiction that structures the world and lay bare the traumatic and formless basis. By doing so, the effective dreams allow George Orr to encounter the trauma and show the reader how such an encounter occurs.

We don't need an effective dream to have an encounter with the trauma, but this type of dream has the benefit of making evident why the encounter can take place in the dream or the fantasy. In the act of re-creating the world, the effective dream returns the subject to the origin of the symbolic structure in order to build that structure in a new way, but this return to the origin is the trajectory that every dream and every fantasy follow. Fantasy is always a fantasy of origins, an attempt to stage the inaccessible onset of the symbolic law.[41] Every fantasy returns the subject to an imaginary time prior to the loss of enjoyment that occurred with symbolic castration, and then it stages the process of loss. The logic of the effective dream in *The Lathe of Heaven* is thus the logic of fantasy as such.

The novel begins with Orr feeling guilt about altering the world with his dreams. As a result, Orr uses drugs to stop his dreaming altogether, but soon the police discover his illegal drug use. His punishment for the drug use is a series of sessions with a psychiatrist named Dr. William Haber, but, unlike Orr, Haber feels no compunction about using Orr's dreams to change the world for the better (though each time he tries, the world changes for the worse). Eventually, Haber develops a machine that will allow him to produce effective dreams himself. During Haber's effective dream, Orr enters into the dream and experiences the world as it is in the process of re-forming under the influence of the dream.

Here, Orr confronts a radical discontinuity in the heart of existence. As the narrator of *The Lathe of Heaven* describes it, "The emptiness of Haber's being, the effective nightmare, radiating outward from the dreaming brain, had undone connections. The continuity which had always held between the worlds or timelines of Orr's dreaming had now been broken. Chaos had entered in. He had few and incoherent memories of this existence he was now in; almost all he knew came from other memories, the other dreamlines."[42] In the midst of Haber's dream, Orr encounters the basis of social reality without any means of symbolizing it. It confronts him with the ultimate groundlessness of his existence, and this encounter allows him to recognize the contingency of all symbolic structures. Hence, the encounter inherently politicizes the subject, creating the possibility of the subject's disinvestment from the symbolic structure and from symbolic identity. Fantasy opens the subject to an encounter with what doesn't fit, and this experience has tangible political benefits — allowing the subject to reshape the world.

Even the Losers

The third dimension of fantasy's political power is its most significant: fantasy dictates the way in which the subject enjoys. We fall for the deception that fantasy offers because of the enjoyment it produces. The role of fantasy in structuring our access to enjoyment complicates the struggle against it. To struggle against fantasy is to pit oneself against the very way in which subjects enjoy, as we can see when Marxism tries to convince subjects about the deceptions of nationalism. Nation is clearly a fantasmatic object that serves to disguise relations of production with an image of unity, and yet we are loath to abandon this fantasy because it would entail a loss of enjoyment. Neither Marxism nor philosophy has an answer on this point: both simply insist on the illusoriness of the fantasy and continue to argue against it.

Philosophy and Marxism fail to consider the enjoyment that subjects derive from their investment in fantasy because they focus on knowledge rather than on enjoyment. As we have seen, both advance political programs that share a fundamental structure. One of the key aspects of this structure is its impulse to correct the illusions of false consciousness. For both philosophy and Marxism, the act of correcting false consciousness represents the fundamental political project; it provides the basis for all subsequent efforts at political transformation. In this sense, both are on the side of consciousness and knowledge.

Philosophy encourages us to eliminate our investment in fantasy and pursue the truth of our situation within the symbolic structure, but it does not make clear the incentive for this kind of pursuit. According to the philosopher, we should pursue the truth... because it is the truth. The problem with this conception of politics is that it leaves out any consideration of the role of enjoyment in our activity. The subject falls for the fantasmatic deception not solely because of false consciousness but also because the subject is a subject of desire. Prior to seeking truth, the subject seeks the paths of enjoyment. The philosopher (Plato, Descartes, Kant, or whoever) encourages us to abandon the deception of fantasy but doesn't acknowledge the enjoyment that this deception provides for the subject. Philosophy asks us to reject fantasmatic enjoyment for the sake of the harsh truth of accepting our symbolic situatedness, and it holds up truth as its own reward.

Unlike philosophy, Marxism attempts to provide an additional motivation for discovering the truth of one's symbolic situation. This discovery can lead — ultimately — to a fundamental transformation of society, a transformation that will provide the enjoyment that current social arrangements make impossible. On occasion, Marxism offers a vision of what a socialist society will look like in order to illustrate to politicized subjects the ultimate end of their truth-seeking, to give them an image of the enjoyment they are pursuing. Marx and Engels themselves provide just such an image in *The German Ideology*: "In communist society, where nobody has one exclusive sphere of activity but each can become accomplished in any branch he wishes, society regulates the general production and thus makes it possible for me to do one thing today and another tomorrow, to hunt in the morning, fish in the afternoon, rear cattle in the evening, criticise after dinner, just as I have a mind, without ever becoming hunter, fisherman, shepherd or critic."[43] Marx and Engels chose this idealized image because of the distance between it and the prevailing conditions in which subjects exist.

With an image of the ideal future in mind, subjects can commit themselves to enduring the harsh truth of their present conditions without the veil of the prevailing ideological fantasy and can work toward bringing about the ideal. The nature of this political program follows the structure of the reality principle: sacrifice the (imaginary) enjoyment of fantasy now in order to ensure a greater enjoyment in the future. Even though Marxism offers the subject the image of a future enjoyment as an incentive for the pursuit of truth and the abandonment of fantasy, it shares with philosophy its call for the renunciation of enjoyment in the present. It is precisely this demand for renunciation that limits the political effectiveness of both philosophy and Marxism. Rather than advocating a sacrifice of enjoyment, politics must instead offer an alternate way of experiencing our enjoyment — and this is what psychoanalysis contributes.

If we look at fantasy and the scenario that it stages closely enough, it has the virtue of revealing to us precisely where we find the experience of enjoyment (which is not where we would first expect). We tend to think of fantasy as a way of satisfying desires that cannot be satisfied in our actual lives. Fantasy permits this because it allows us to bypass the restrictions that govern our material existence within the social order. And yet, this conception of fantasy fails to explain the structure of fantasy, a structure that never perfectly fulfills our desire. Fantasies never stage an Edenic scene of total bliss, free of any conflict. They always involve something going wrong for the subject.

In fact, a masochistic scene of loss at the hands of some figure embodying authority seems central to the structure of fantasy. In fantasy, we experience enjoyment not through the activity of acquiring the privileged object but through that of losing it. What the fantasy indicates to us is that there is something inherently counterintuitive about our relationship to enjoyment. Enjoyment manifests itself at the point in the fantasy where we would least expect it — the point of loss. We fantasize about the loss of the privileged object because it is through the act of losing it that we bring this object into existence and give it form. There is thus a productive power attached to fantasy: we fantasize the privileged object into existence through staging a scenario that depicts its loss. And it is only fantasy that allows us to recognize this link between loss and enjoyment.

If we recognize the proper location of enjoyment in the fantasmatic experience of the loss of the privileged object, this allows us to reconceive the basis for political action. We do not have to base our political action on the idea of a future reward but can base it on the enjoyment that the subject experiences in breaking from its symbolic and ideological constraints. Ironically, the turn to fantasy by psychoanalysis opens up the possibility of a politics not beholden to an imaginary enjoyment that the future promises. The key lies in recognizing where we find our enjoyment. This enjoyment resides in the moment of the loss of the privileged object, not in the image of its return. The return of the object is pleasing but not enjoyable. Fantasy is ultimately deceptive only in the sense that it induces us to equate enjoyment with the image of the return of the privileged object. But if we pay careful attention to the structure of fantasy — as psychoanalysis does — we can recognize the location of enjoyment at the moment of this object's loss/inception. This points us toward a politics with an appeal structured around our enjoyment rather than reality (as with philosophy) or an image of the future (as with Marxism).

Le Guin's novel *The Dispossessed* shows us what this idea of politics might look like. It is a novel of political activity. The novel's hero, Shevek, comes from a peaceful world of anarchists (on a moon named Anarres) that retains its way of life through isolation from other worlds. Shevek's political activity consists in reaching out to the rest of the universe and specifically to the moon's mother planet (Urras) with a revolutionary egalitarian philosophy. What is distinctive about Shevek is the motivation for his political activity. He doesn't act out of a desire to eliminate loss by constructing a better world in the future; instead, he acts out of an embrace of loss.

Unlike most revolutionary political figures, Shevek adopts a completely pessimistic view of existence. He is convinced of the utter hopelessness of the human condition. This sense of the necessity of loss animates Shevek as a political being. Shevek thus advances a political program that does not hold out the image of a future complete enjoyment. But if Shevek begins with the acceptance of loss and suffering, this doesn't lead him to deny the possibility of enjoyment altogether. In fact, Shevek aims to convince others that the secret of enjoyment lies in the embrace of loss, not in the promise of overcoming it. According to Shevek (and psychoanalysis), loss doesn't represent the end of enjoyment but the beginning.

Throughout *The Dispossessed*, Shevek works toward a more egalitarian society both on his home world of Anarres and on the mother planet, Urras, that he travels to. But he recognizes that they cannot achieve an egalitarian society through the idea of overcoming loss and achieving wholeness. This image of a complete enjoyment that we might attain in the future (in, say, a future socialist society) is necessarily illusory because it depends on some kind of exclusion in order to sustain it. The only way to break out of this exclusionary logic is through abandoning the image of a future completeness. Instead of holding out this image, Shevek offers the ideal of a shared embrace of loss. Through the fantasy that Le Guin constructs in *The Dispossessed*, we can see the link between enjoyment and the loss of the privileged object, and through recognizing this link, we can rethink politics.

Fantasy has the ability to foster a distinctive kind of politics, and psychoanalysis provides the key through which we can unlock fantasy's emancipatory potential. Psychoanalysis allows us to understand both sides of fantasy and its relation to politics. On the one hand, fantasy does hide our subjection to the signifier, but on the other, because of the way it hides our subjection, it allows us to militate against our very subjected status itself in ways unthinkable outside of fantasy. Through its revaluation of the status of fantasy, psychoanalysis enables us to see fantasy's fundamental political value in a way that neither philosophy nor Marxism can. Both the philosopher and the Marxist, because of their shared attitude toward fantasy, tend to remain stuck in attacks on the proliferation of false consciousness. Psychoanalysis allows us to rethink the way in which we conceive political activity: not as the triumph of the proper consciousness over the experience of enjoyment but as the embrace of the trauma inherent in real enjoyment.

The political task as it might be envisioned by psychoanalytic thought entails not attempting to eliminate fantasy but transforming our relationship to it. Fantasy functions in an ideological way when it works to cover over the structural necessity of absence within the social order, but fantasy appeals to us because it also conveys an experience of loss or absence that we can access nowhere else. One could say that we are never more inauthentic than when we fantasize but never more authentic at the same time. In order to provide the pleasure that comes from overcoming absence, fantasy must introduce and narrate loss. As it does so, it allows the fantasizing subject to experience the impossible loss that founds subjectivity itself. In every fantasy, this loss is enacted, whether implicitly or explicitly. The political task involves fostering the recognition that we enjoy our fantasies for their depiction of loss rather than for the illusion of return.

Accomplishing this task demands orienting ourselves and our societies around the enjoyment that fantasy provides. Rather than remaining a marginalized activity indulged in during sleep or while surfing for lewd Internet sites, fantasy must become central, the avowed basis of our social organization. We must count fantasy as worth more than our social reality because we already do. Though it always has a social and psychic centrality, we fail to recognize it, and the political project of psychoanalysis demands the recognition of fantasy's primacy and a consequent devotion to fantasy. Without this, we cannot grasp the possibilities for enjoyment that inhere in the trauma of the lost object.

9

Beyond Bare Life

Life versus Death

The contemporary geopolitical landscape is largely divided between those who privilege life and those who privilege death. This struggle pits the advocates of modernization and global capitalism against the fundamentalist alternative that seeks to resist the effects of modernization (if not modernization itself). The central idea of psychoanalysis — the death drive — reveals a path out of this seemingly intractable opposition. The insistence on the death drive marks a rejection of both the celebration of life and the apotheosis of death. The death drive represents the bringing together of life and death in a way that confounds the adherents of both sides.

As early as 1996, Osama bin Laden himself put the struggle between modernity and fundamentalism in the terms of life against death. In his fatwa of that year entitled "Declaration of War against the Americans Occupying the Land of the Two Holy Places," he tells his American enemy, "These [Muslim] youths love death as you love life."[1] In his statement after the September 11 attacks, bin Laden again framed the conflict in the same way, and commentators drew considerable attention to this formulation. Though Western leaders rejected almost the entirety of bin Laden's political philosophy, they almost universally accepted the way of framing the opposition between global capitalism and Islamic fundamentalism.

In doing so, they follow a tradition that prevails within much contemporary thought and even within psychoanalytic political philosophy. Erich Fromm, who tried to bring psychoanalysis and Marxism together in order to form a new political program, saw within psychoanalysis an embrace of the love of life and a struggle against the love of death. He called these phenomena "biophilia" and "necrophilia." As Fromm notes in *The Anatomy of Human Destructiveness*, "*Love of life or love of the dead is the fundamental alternative that confronts every human being. Necrophilia grows as the development of biophilia is stunted. Man is biologically endowed with the capacity for biophilia, but psychologically he has the potential for necrophilia as an alternative solution.*"[2] While we naturally love life, the interruption of this love leads to a devotion to death and a consequent aggressive bent. Later in *The Anatomy of Human Destructiveness*, Fromm identifies Hitler as a particularly obstinate case of necrophilia, and he would undoubtedly have done the same with bin Laden and the Islamic fundamentalists, had he lived to see them.

The problem with this opposition is the way that it constrains our thinking. On one level, recognizing an opposition between those who love death and those who love life represents an accurate appraisal of the contemporary political landscape, but it does not exhaust the political possibilities. If we look at things like this as George W. Bush would have us do, either we are with the capitalist West or we are with the terrorists. But psychoanalysis helps us to see the falsity of this opposition, to see that hidden between the contrast of life and death is a third possibility — death in life, or the death drive. An insistence on the death drive marks an option beyond what seems possible on the contemporary political landscape. The implications of this other path will emerge through the following examination of the widespread opposition of life and death.

On the level of common sense, this opposition is not symmetrical. What thinking person would not want to side with those who love life rather than death.[3] Everyone can readily understand how one might love life, but the love of death is a counterintuitive phenomenon. It seems as if it must be code language for some other desire, which is how Western leftists often view it. Interpreting terrorist attacks as an ultimately life-affirming response to imperialism and impoverishment, they implicitly reject the possibility of being in love with death. But this type of interpretation can't explain why so many suicide bombers are middle-class, educated subjects and not the most downtrodden victims of imperialist power.[4] We must imagine that for subjects such as these there is an appeal in death itself.

Those who emphasize the importance of death at the expense of life do so because death is the source of value.[5] The fact that life has an end, that we do not have an infinite amount of time to experience every possibility, means that we must value some things above others. Death creates hierarchies of value, and these hierarchies are not only vehicles for oppression but the pathways through which what we do matters at all. Without the value that death provides, neither love nor ice cream nor friendship nor anything that we enjoy would have any special worth whatsoever. Having an infinite amount of time, we would have no incentive to opt for these experiences rather than other ones. We would be left unable to enjoy what seems to make life most worth living.

Even though enjoyment itself is an experience of the infinite, an experience of transcending the limits that regulate everyday activity, it nonetheless depends on the limits of finitude. When one enjoys, one accesses the infinite as a finite subject, and it is this contrast that renders enjoyment enjoyable. Without the limits of finitude, our experience of the infinite would become as tedious as our everyday lives (and in fact would become our everyday experience). Finitude provides the punctuation through which the infinite emerges as such. The struggle to assert the importance of death — the act of being in love with death, as bin Laden claims that the Muslim youths are — is a mode of avowing one's allegiance to the infinite enjoyment that death doesn't extinguish but instead spawns.[6]

This is exactly why Martin Heidegger attacks what he sees as our modern inauthentic relationship to death. In *Being and Time* Heidegger sees our individual death as an absolute limit that has the effect of creating value for us. As he puts it, "With death, Dasein stands before itself in its ownmost potentiality-for-being. This is a possibility in which the issue is nothing less than Dasein's Being-in-the-world."[7] Without the anticipation of our own death, we flit through the world and fail to take up fully an attitude of care, the attitude most appropriate for our mode of being, according to Heidegger. Nothing really matters to those who have not recognized the approach of their own death. By depriving us of an authentic relationship to death, an ideology that proclaims life as the only value creates a valueless world where nothing matters to us.

But of course the partisans of life are not actually eliminating death itself. They simply privilege life over death and see the world in terms of life rather than death, which would seem to leave the value-creating power of death intact. But this is not what happens. By privileging life and seeing death only in terms of life, we change the way we experience the world. Without the mediation that death provides, the system of pure life becomes a system utterly bereft of value.[8] We can see this in the two great systems of modernity — science and capitalism.

Both modern science and capitalism are systems structured around pure life.[9] Neither recognizes any ontological limit but instead continually embarks on a project of constant change and expansion. The scientific quest for knowledge about the world moves forward without regard for humanitarian or ethical concerns, which is why ethicists incessantly try to reconcile scientific discoveries with morality after the fact. After scientists develop the ability to clone, for instance, we realize what cloning portends for our sense of identity and attempt to police the practice. After Oppenheimer helps to develop the atomic bomb, he addresses the world with pronouncements of its evil. But this rearguard action has nothing to do with science as such. Oppenheimer the humanist is not Oppenheimer the scientist.[10]

The same dynamic is visible with capitalism. As an economic system, it promotes constant evolution and change just as life itself does. Nothing can remain the same within the capitalist world because the production of value depends on the creation of the new commodity, and even the old commodities must be constantly given new forms or renewed in some way.[11] Capitalism produces crises not because it can't produce enough — crises of scarcity dominate the history of the noncapitalist world, not the capitalist one — but because it produces too much. The crisis of capitalism is always a crisis of overproduction. The capitalist economy suffocates from too much life, from excess, not from scarcity or death. Both science and capitalism move forward without any acknowledged limit, which is why they are synonymous with modernity.[12] Modernity emerges with the bracketing of death's finitude and the belief that there is no barrier to human possibility.[13]

The problem with the exclusive focus on life at the expense of death is that it never finds enough life and thus remains perpetually dissatisfied. The limit of this project is, paradoxically, its own infinitude. It evokes what Hegel calls the bad infinite — an infinite that is wrongly conceived as having no relation at all to the finite. We succumb to the bad infinite when we pursue an unattainable object and fail to see that the only possible satisfaction rests in the pursuit itself. The bad infinite — the infinite of modernity — depends on a fundamental misrecognition. We continue on this path only as long as we believe that we might attain the final piece of the puzzle, and yet this piece is constitutively denied us by the structure of the system itself.

We seek the commodity that would finally bring us complete satisfaction, but dissatisfaction is built into the commodity structure, just as obsolescence is built into the very fabric of our cars and computers. Like capitalism, scientific inquiry cannot find a final answer: beneath atomic theory we find string theory, and beneath string theory we find something else. In both cases, the system prevents us from recognizing where our satisfaction lies; it diverts our focus away from our activity and onto the goal that we pursue. In this way, modernity produces the dissatisfaction that keeps it going. But it also produces another form of dissatisfaction that wants to arrest its forward movement.

The further the project of modernity moves in the direction of life, the more forcefully the specter of fundamentalism will make its presence felt. The exclusive focus on life has the effect of producing eruptions of death. As the life-affirming logic of science and capitalism structures all societies to an increasing extent, the space for the creation of value disappears. Modernity attempts to construct a symbolic space where there is no place for death and the limit that death represents. As opposed to the closed world of traditional society, modernity opens up an infinite universe.[14] But this infinite universe is established through the repression of finitude. Explosions of fundamentalist violence represent the return of what modernity's symbolic structure cannot accommodate. As Lacan puts it in his seminar on psychosis, "Whatever is refused in the symbolic order, in the sense of *Verwerfung*, reappears in the real."[15] Fundamentalist violence is blowback not simply in response to imperialist aggression, as the leftist common sense would have it. This violence marks the return of what modernity necessarily forecloses.

Progress or Value

Historically, the opposition between those who privilege life and those who privilege death has coincided with the opposition between the forces of emancipation and those of conservatism. The emancipatory project works to liberate life from the restrictions that the oppressive and hierarchical social order places on it, while conservatism tries to sustain a life-denying order because it views order as the source of all value. Conservative thinkers defend their abridgement of life's possibilities in the name of order and civilization. Without the restrictions that we place on life, according to this line of thought, we would lose everything valuable.

Perhaps the greatest literary account of this opposition occurs in Willa Cather's masterpiece *Death Comes for the Archbishop*. Cather's 1927 novel describes the lives of two missionary priests, Father Latour and Father Vaillant, whom the Catholic Church has sent to New Mexico. Though the two are friends, an antagonism develops between them concerning an elaborate church that Latour wants to build. For Vaillant, the money spent on an elaborate cathedral could be better spent feeding the hungry and impoverished people of the region. Latour, who is Vaillant's superior, ends up having the church constructed despite his friend's objections, consoling himself with the idea that the building will provide something more important than mere life.

The building will feed the souls of the poor and give them value, even if it implicitly takes literal food from them by diverting the Catholic Church's funds. The opposition between Latour and Vaillant represents the conflict between death and life. Latour insists on denying life — choosing to build a church rather than feed people — because he sees how the church brings value into the world. Vaillant, in contrast, believes that people must be alive and well fed before they can appreciate the worth that the church gives their lives. It is difficult for the left-leaning reader not to find Vaillant the far more sympathetic figure in the struggle.

The emancipatory project's promotion of life against death reached its apex in the 1960s. The student radicals of the 1960s fought for peace against war, for sexual exploration against repression, and for liberty of expression against artificial restrictions. At the heart of each of these struggles was a desire to free life from the limits that bourgeois society imposed on it. The Berkeley Free Speech Movement, for instance, sought to affirm the productive chaos of life itself and reject the life-denying restrictions represented by the police, the government, and the ruling class. Even the mode of resistance championed by this movement indicates its kinship with life: members would simply allow themselves to go limp and become figures of bare life when police tried to drag them away. The antiwar movement attacked not just the injustice of the war in Southeast Asia but rather the destructiveness of war in general. The imperative that one should "make love, not war" expressed a larger philosophical orientation beyond a specific struggle. The opponent was the warring mindset that denied the beauty of pure life.

The radicals of the 1960s were true to the basic tendency of Marx's thought. As is well known, Marx sees revolution as a progressive force that occurs when the means of production outstrip the relations of production. The means of production move society forward, while the relations of production act as a restraining force on this forward movement until the advent of socialism (at which time the relations of production will cease their conservative function and will finally be adequate to the means of production).[16] The revolution can topple capitalism when the capitalist relations of production — the capitalist's appropriation of the surplus value generated by the working class — become a brake on the economic system's productivity. By aligning the revolutionary impulse with the forward movement of the forces of production, Marx takes the side of life against death, of infinite striving forward against the limits of finitude. When death interferes with life's outward movement, this movement displaces and overcomes it.

Marx's view of the relationship between the forces of production and the relations of production actually places him within the logic of capitalism itself. As Slavoj Žižek and others have pointed out, the Marxian utopia of unrestrained forces of production is a *capitalist* fantasy. It would be capitalism unleashed, capitalism without the artificial political restraints on productivity that are currently built into the system. Marxism does not so much aim at combating the development of capitalism as pushing this development further — past the point at which it would remain within the orbit of capitalist relations of production. Marx wants more capitalism, more globalization, more technological development, not less. This is why all activists and theorists who advocate developing local economies or patronizing small businesses, despite their professed allegiances, have left the domain of Marxism and aligned themselves, at least indirectly, with the fundamentalist project. For Marx himself, the defeat of capitalism must come from within, from taking its own refusal of death seriously and seeing the socialist ramifications of this refusal.

The identification of the leftist project with life reaches its peak in the thought of Gilles Deleuze and Félix Guattari. More than any recent leftist thinkers, Deleuze and Guattari remain true to Marx's belief that the logic of capitalism is the friend of revolution and not the enemy. They define capitalism as a process of universal deterritorialization in which the flows that traditional societies hold in check are released. As a result, capitalism becomes the end point of every other society. As they put it, "If capitalism is the exterior limit of all societies, this is because capitalism for its part has no exterior limit, but only an interior limit that is capital itself and that it does not encounter, but reproduces by always displacing it."[17] For Deleuze and Guattari, as for Marx, the proper leftist strategy involves taking the deterritorializing logic of capitalism to its end point and eliminating the reterritorializations that accompany contemporary capitalism and restrain its own inherent tendency. The problem isn't too much capitalism but not enough. We need more of the life that capitalist productivity provides, and we need that life distributed more evenly.

Deleuze and Guattari's attitude toward capitalism remains vibrant today in the prevailing leftist conceptions of the struggle against global capitalism. For Michael Hardt and Antonio Negri, global capitalism — what they call empire — functions by tearing down barriers, dislocating people, and creating hybridity. This unleashing of life will become the engine that pushes through empire to socialism — a social structure that no longer needs to hold death over the heads of its subjects. According to Hardt and Negri, global capitalism presents the emancipatory project with new opportunities precisely because it liberates the forces of life to a hitherto impossible extent. But despite the novelty of their thesis, they belong to a long leftist tradition of attempting to defy the social order's invocation of death.

Conservative critiques of modernity inevitably involve an assertion of the priority of death over life. This is true, to take the two most prominent examples, of Fascism from the middle of the last century and of contemporary fundamentalism. Despite what Giorgio Agamben claims in his otherwise stunning account of the logic informing Nazism, this political movement is not so much the culmination of modernity's elevation of bare life into the ultimate political category as a reaction against it. It is a critique of the philosophy of life and of the elimination of all values in the flow of bare life. But in *Homo Sacer* Agamben claims: "The Jews were exterminated not in a mad and giant holocaust but exactly as Hitler had announced, 'as lice,' which is to say, as bare life. The dimension in which the extermination took place is neither religion nor law, but biopolitics."[18] Agamben sees a direct throughline from the elevation of life itself as the ultimate value to the concentration camps that reduced the Jews to the status of bare life. But the problem of the Jew for the Nazi was precisely her or his irreducibility to bare life — the excess of life, the surplus enjoyment, that she or he embodies. The humiliations and degradations of the camps were an attempt to isolate this excess — to discover the secret of Jewishness itself — and then to extirpate it.

What Agamben's otherwise compelling account of Nazism cannot explain is why there were two sets of camps — concentration camps and extermination camps. The concentration camps alone were sufficient to strip the Jews of everything but their bare life. Why was the mass extermination necessary? The Nazi project was at once isolating the essence of Jewishness and eliminating this excess. The two sets of camps corresponded to these two tasks, but the key to understanding the project lies in the extermination.[19] The pogrom aligns Nazism with death rather than life, with the creation of value through the destruction of excessive life.

The Nazis associated Jewish excess with modernity and the flow of capital. By eliminating Jewishness, they hoped not to eliminate capitalism — Hitler was no opponent of business — but to place a limit on its universal leveling process. Capitalism destroys all value, in the Nazi view, only when it goes too far, when it is infused with a Jewish element. Nazism wagers that one might have capitalism and, at the same time, retain the idea of value inimical to it. This desire reveals the contradiction at the heart of every attempt to restore value by embracing death. The ultimate aim of the partisans of death is to make life valuable. All their efforts on behalf of death betray a hidden faith that life itself can be redeemed, that a devotion to death could render life genuinely enjoyable. In this sense, we might say that even with Nazism the devotion to death doesn't go far enough in abandoning the ideology of life. This position fails to reconcile itself with our inescapable alienation from life — with our inability to enjoy pure life.

Fighting for Death in the Guise of Life

Despite American social conservatives' insistent claims on behalf of a culture of life, we should not take them at their word. In relation to life and death, there is little difference between Islamic fundamentalism and right-wing

Christian fundamentalism in the United States. Both assert the priority of death over life, though only the former expressly says so. By proclaiming its embrace of a culture of life, conservatism attempts to mold its advocacy of death into a package that would be acceptable for most contemporary people. On most issues, conservatism's allegiance to death and its insistence on an absolute limit are perfectly clear. Conservatism almost inevitably supports military aggression, the death penalty, a strong police force, restrictions of sexual education, and so on. When the issue is, say, the death penalty, one never hears an invocation of the culture of life.

But perhaps the most visible manifestation of American social conservatism's commitment to death was its enthusiastic support for Mel Gibson's *Passion of the Christ* (2004). What is truly shocking about the film is its complete lack of emphasis on the teaching of Christ or the Christian message. It is a 127-minute immersion in the beauty of sadistic torture and death. If one enjoys the film, one enjoys the long, grueling death itself; Gibson leaves the viewer no other option. Despite the film's brutal violence and the absence of any Christian teaching, fundamentalists ran to the film in huge numbers and often found themselves moved beyond words. What they found so powerful could be nothing other than the brutal sacrifice and death itself. Christ's death, a death that redeems the world and gives it meaning, stands out in contrast with the banality of life in modernity. Where modern life operates without value, Christ shows his willingness to die in order to create value.[20]

Conservatism found Gibson's film appealing for the same reason that it pursues what it calls "the culture of life." By looking at three contested issues, the politics of death will become visible beneath conservatism's claims about the culture of life. For the proponents of the culture of life, abortion is unquestionably the foundational issue. It is the issue concerning which conservative politicians are permitted no heresy. One could not even imagine a Republican presidential nominee, for instance, who accepted a woman's right to choose on the issue of abortion. Proclamations by antiabortion groups emphasize the importance of the life of the unborn and purport to value life above everything else (including the choice of the pregnant woman). But the life that these groups cherish is not the pure life of modernity; it is, in contrast, a life made valuable through death.

Conservatism privileges the unborn fetus only insofar as it remains not yet alive. Fundamentalists express little or no concern about the plight of babies born into extreme poverty or other dire circumstances. Why not? Is it simply a case of hypocrisy? It is more that the living baby is already lost in modernity's flow of pure life and thereby rendered valueless. Only the nonliving fetus — especially the aborted one — can act as a source of value. Even as they lament the practice that produces the aborted fetus, fundamentalists rely on its result as a source of value. Far from advocating a culture of life through their opposition to abortion, fundamentalists embrace the issue for its relationship to death.

It is in fact the culture that permits untrammeled access to abortion that is the culture of life. For this culture, the presence of the fetus and its claims cannot stop the movement of life. If a woman opts to terminate her pregnancy, she does so, according to this thinking, because the exigencies of life demanded it: there is no space in her life (whether for economic, emotional, or other reasons) for the presence of a child. The exigencies of life, for most of the prochoice movement, trump the claims of the not-yet-alive fetus. Most who are prochoice are not unsympathetic to the arguments made on behalf of the fetus, but they simply privilege the life of the mother.

The opponents of abortion object to the way that it permits a woman to continue her normal life despite having become pregnant. Their favorite term for legal abortion — "abortion on demand" — indicates this. By sanctioning abortion on demand, so the thinking goes, society allows life to run too smoothly (for the pregnant woman) and thereby tears down the limits that give life value. These limits, these disruptions in the flow of life, are concrete stand-ins for death. Every time we encounter a limit, we encounter a foreshadowing of death, which is the absolute limit. When one denies the pregnant woman the ability to choose abortion, one insists on a form of death for her. Even when it appears most securely on the side of life, fundamentalism remains devoted to the value-creating power of death, as is also apparent in fundamentalism's objection to evolutionary theory.

Those conservatives who dismiss evolution as theory rather than as fact — and thus equivocate on the term "theory," as numerous critics have pointed out — find evolution objectionable not because there is insufficient proof for it but because it contributes to the universal leveling undertaken by modernity. The idea of evolution doesn't eliminate human superiority: it posits humanity as the crowning achievement of an evolutionary logic, even if this logic relies on accident and circumstance. But it does eliminate human transcendence and difference. Humanity remains a separate species, but we can think of it in the same terms that we use for other animals. This leveling does away with the special value that a humanity created by God's volition would have. The widespread acceptance of evolution portends the flattening out of value, which is why it is inextricable from the project of modernity.

The evolutionist views life itself as proceeding without interruption. There is no moment at which death intrudes to break the cycle of life: the individual deaths that occur and even the deaths of whole species never constitute a break in life's forward movement. By insisting on the primacy of God's creative act, conservatism attempts to insert a gap into the movement of pure life.[21] Even though it doesn't take the form of advocating death, this position aligns itself with death through its attempt to erect a limit. The limit to the movement of life takes the form of God, who intervenes in the movement of pure life with a design. Though creationism or intelligent design seems like a positive position, fundamentalism adopts it for its negative power, for its ability to halt the unending movement of life. The idea of divine creation — and the limits that it introduces — enables us to say that each subject has a worth that goes beyond its bare life.

The intrinsic worth of each subject became the crucial issue in the case of Terri Schiavo. The Schiavo case was significant because it became a particular stand-in for the universal question concerning the right to die. Brain-dead for over a decade, Schiavo emerged as a cause célèbre for conservatives after the decision of her husband to remove the feeding tube keeping her alive. If ever conservatism seemed to be on the side of life against death, it was here. Right-wing columnists like Peggy Noonan accused those who opposed the reinsertion of the feeding tube of being, like bin Laden himself, in love with death. Speaking about those arguing for pulling the feeding tube, she asks rhetorically, "Why are they so committed to this woman's death? They seem to have fallen half in love with death."[22] Though she alludes to Keats and "Ode to a Nightingale," the real connection that Noonan attempts to make here is between those who advocate pulling the plug and those who perpetuate terrorist violence, which is why she ends the column with references to Columbine and Auschwitz. Those who want to discontinue feeding Terri Schiavo must be motivated by a secret love of death, the kind explicitly articulated by bin Laden.

But the dynamics of the issue were not so simple. Conservatives objected not to Schiavo's death but to the reduction of her living body to the meaningless cycle of life. By removing the feeding tube, her husband failed to see her transcendent uniqueness as an individual, a uniqueness — or so many visitors claimed — still visible within her eyes. Those who wanted to facilitate Schiavo's death denied that there was something more than mere life processes at work in her body. Ironically, by insisting that doctors keep Schiavo alive, conservatism takes the side of death in the sense that it champions an external limit on the mechanical process of life. The idea of life provides an alibi for conservatives in the Schiavo case, but they nonetheless remain on the side of death in opposition to the meaninglessness of pure life. To openly take up the side of death would require American conservatism to recognize its philosophical link to bin Laden, and this is not thinkable.

Those who argued for the reinsertion of Schiavo's feeding tube or who continue to argue against stem cell research (or cloning) want to establish limits on the power of human decision making. The introduction of the limit is an act of negation, an act of bringing death to life or of acknowledging the presence of death to negate life. According to this line of thought, when humans remove the feeding tube or destroy living tissue in stem cell research, they play God; they leave no territory sacred and eliminate all value. By insisting on the limit, fundamentalism attempts to restore the value lost through modernity. This value is inextricable from death because every value-producing limit — every act of negation — embodies death.

The link between the act of negation or of limitation and death becomes clear in Jean-Paul Sartre's analysis of the phenomenon in *Being and Nothingness*. For Sartre, negation would not be possible without an experience of what he calls "non-being." Ontology conditions the ability to judge, which means that every judgment carries with it a hidden ontology. He says: "Non-being does not come to things by a negative judgment; it is the negative judgment, on the contrary, which is conditioned and supported by non-being."[23] Every time we make a negative judgment and inject a limit into life, we affirm the priority of nonbeing, or death over life. The various fundamentalist campaigns often conducted under the cover of life — the opposition to abortion, to Darwinism, and to the right-to-die movement — all have their origin in this affirmation of death.

Death in Life

In the modern struggle between the forces of life and the forces of death, psychoanalysis doesn't take a side. The point is not simply that psychoanalysis stands on the sideline and analyzes the struggle (as seems to be the case at the end of *Civilization and Its Discontents*, where Freud wonders which adversary — life or death — will ultimately prevail). Though many thinkers and activists (like Erich Fromm) have seen psychoanalysis as a partner in the fight against repression and death, psychoanalysis in fact represents a third way. Rather than championing life against death or insisting on death as the necessary limit on life, it focuses on the death that remains internal to life. This death within life is what Freud calls the death drive.

Viewed from the perspective of the death drive, the uniqueness of a subject does not derive from the divine. As the earlier chapters have contended, that uniqueness is the product of a primordial act of loss through which the subject comes into being. The subject emerges through the sacrifice of a privileged object that the act of sacrifice itself creates. This act is correlative to the acquisition of a name, which allows the subject to enter into a world of meaning and signification — a world that brings with it an indirect relation with the world of objects and with its privileged object. With the acquisition of a name, the subject becomes a subject of loss. The entire existence of the subject becomes oriented around its lost object, even though this object only comes into being through the subject's act of ceding it. This death that founds the subject creates in it a drive to return to the moment of loss itself because the originary loss creates both the subject and the subject's privileged object. The only enjoyment that the subject experiences derives not from life nor from death but from the death-in-life that is the death drive.

The signifier writes itself on top of life and reifies life's supposed vitality in its death-laden paths. Every signifier is at bottom a stereotype, a rigid category for apprehending and freezing the movement of life. This is why Deleuze and Guattari attack signification itself and compare the signifier with the tyrant. They claim: "One will never prevent the signifier from reintroducing its transcendence, and from bearing witness for a vanished despot who still functions in modern imperialism. Even when it speaks Swiss or American, linguistics manipulates the shadow of Oriental despotism."[24]

For the champions of life, the signifier is on the side of the forces of death and repression, and the emancipatory project must involve contesting the signifier's hegemony. A liberated society, in this view, would be a society no longer bound by the vertical logic implicit in the signifier/signified relationship.

Though Deleuze and Guattari's attack on the signifier is an extreme case, the general suspicion of the signifier and its link to death is widespread among the forces of emancipation. This is why many revolutionary projects involve attempts to transform the prevailing status of signification. This is especially clear in Roland Barthes's *Mythologies*, an analysis of the relationship between ideology and the signifier. Barthes contends that ideology or myth is the product of a bourgeois conception of the signifier that fails to recognize the productivity inherent within the act of signification. Society after a working-class revolution would not eliminate the signifier but instead attune itself to the idea of signification as production. Barthes claims: "There is ... one language which is not mythical, it is the language of man as a producer: wherever man speaks in order to transform reality and no longer preserve it as an image, wherever he links his language to the making of things, meta-language is referred to a language-object, and myth is impossible. This is why revolutionary language proper cannot be mythical."[25] Barthes envisions a different manner of speaking in which signifiers would no longer have a link to static images (or myths) and would become genuinely productive. That is, signifiers in this utopia would cease to be transcendent interruptions of life and would enter into the process of life itself. Revolution would eliminate the seemingly unsurpassable distance between the signifier and life.[26]

The revolutionary attempt to sustain the project of pure life inevitably founders on the very act of embracing it. In order for theorists to champion the forward movement of life or production, they must take the side of death by resorting to the signifier. The form of the call for an embrace of life belies the content of the message: the theorist uses the instrument of death—the signifier—to inveigh against death. Even the argument for a transformation of the signifier like the one Barthes advances relies on the mode of signification it attacks. No matter how productive the signifier becomes, it will never access the flow of life itself and will always remain an interruption of that flow. When Marx writes about the liberatory power of society's productive forces, he implicitly abandons these forces in order to reflect on them. When Deleuze and Guattari champion decoded flows and deterritorialization in their books, they engage in an act that they themselves would have to condemn as a reterritorialization. When Barthes calls for a revolutionary language that would transcend myth, he does so in the language of myth. The very act of theorizing an embrace of pure life violates the theory in the process of constructing it.

The leftist advocates of life are either explicitly or implicitly the followers of Spinoza. Spinoza constructs a system that has no space for the negative. This is the essence of Hegel's critique of Spinoza's system in the *History of Philosophy*:

> For the moment of negativity is what is lacking to this rigid motionlessness, whose single form of activity is this, to divest all things of their determination and particularity and cast them back into the one absolute substance, wherein they are simply swallowed up, and all life in itself is utterly destroyed. This is what we find philosophically inadequate with Spinoza; distinctions are externally present, it is true, but they remain external, since even the negative is not known in itself. Thought is the absolutely abstract, and for that very reason the absolutely negative; it is so in truth, but with Spinoza it is not asserted to be the absolutely negative.[27]

Though Spinoza and his contemporary descendants make every effort to avoid death and the negative, this very effort has the effect of asserting the primacy of the negative in an absolute fashion through the construction of a necessarily abstract system. Though the avoidance of death never works, it does nonetheless distort one's system, as is visible with Spinoza, Deleuze and Guattari, and Michael Hardt and Antonio Negri.[28]

There is no system of pure life. In order to advocate a turn to life, one must take a detour through death. The philosophers of life conceive of the signifier as an evil that might be overcome. This conception of the signifier fails to account for the inseparability of negation and production.[29] The signifier does in fact kill; it does mortify the body. But this mortification is itself a productive act. Prior to the mortification of the body, the body is not vital and productive; it is simply stupid. The signifier writes itself on top of this stupid body and transforms it into a signifying body. But this transformation is not complete: there are points at which the body resists its signification, where it refuses to speak. The troubled passage from the living body to the signifying body reveals the antagonism between the subject and the social order that leads to the formation of psychoanalysis.

Hysterics originally came to Freud and Breuer because of the disjunctive relationship between the body and the world of signification. Part of the hysteric's body refuses to speak, to accept its integration into the symbolic order, and this refusal is symptomatic. The signifier deadens the entire body in order to make it signify, but part of the body resists the deadening process and becomes mute. This occurs literally in the case of aphasia, though every hysterical ailment follows the same pattern.[30] The muteness of part of the subject's body is the form that resistance to symbolization necessarily takes. One affirms one's subjectivity not through proclaiming it but through a certain mode of keeping silent.[31]

The psychoanalytic project involves helping the subject to recognize its symptom — the part of the body that resists full integration into the symbolic order — as the source of its enjoyment and its freedom. The part of the body that gives us trouble, that refuses integration, is the expression of our subjectivity, the kernel that negates or refuses what has been imposed on it. By identifying ourselves with our mute body part, we take up the death drive and affirm a value that transcends pure life.

Like the conservative project, a psychoanalytic political project rejects the mechanical flow of pure life and instead privileges the disruption of that flow. But like leftist politics, it refuses to adhere itself to that which transcends life and limits it from the outside — such as God or death. This does not mean that psychoanalytic politics represents a compromise between the Right and the Left, some sort of median position. Instead, it operates outside the confines of the established opposition and presents a political choice that transcends the philosophical limits inherent in both the Right and the Left.

The source of our enjoyment and the source of whatever value we find in existence is neither life nor death. It is a product of the collision between death and life, between the signifier and the body. The signifier's deadening of the body opens up the space for a part of the body that resists this deadening. It creates value not directly but through the bodily remainder that escapes its power. This remainder is not a present force but an object irretrievably lost for the subject.

If we locate the origin of the subject in the act where it loses nothing, this promises to revolutionize our thinking about the struggle between life and death or between Left and Right. Privileging an originary loss allows us to see how death, rather than acting as an external limit, inheres in life itself for the subject. There is no life for the subject that does not have its origin in death. The subject begins its life with a death — a loss of what is most valuable to it — and no subsequent loss or death will ever be the equal of this originary one (which occurs only structurally, not empirically). We do not have to seek out death in order to render life valuable; death is always already present within our lives and providing us value. We don't recognize it because we resist the notion that we originate as subjects through loss and that loss is the only vehicle through which we can enjoy. We can only give up the pursuit of death when we realize that we have already found it — or that it has found us at the moment of our emergence as subjects.

With the help of psychoanalysis, we might rewrite Heidegger's notion of being-toward-death. Rather than an attitude of resoluteness toward a future possibility that we cannot evade, it would be a grasp of our rootedness in a past loss. We would embrace loss itself as the key to our freedom and our enjoyment rather than trying to flee the experience of loss through having. Recognizing the creative power of loss for us as subjects would imply a political transformation as well. It would place us neither on the side of life nor on the side of death but would allow us to take a position that left this false choice behind. In light of such a position, we could reexamine the issues that we looked at above.

Conservatism equates abortion with the most brutal forms of murder because it involves the destruction of pure life. The innocence of the victim augments the barbarism of the crime. But if we recognize how loss constitutes the subject as such, the innocence of the fetus becomes an argument against prohibiting abortion. As a being of pure life, a being that has not yet experienced death in life, the fetus does not yet have the status of subject, while the pregnant woman does. One cannot murder a being that has not in some way murdered itself — made itself a subject through undergoing the foundational experience of loss, a loss that occurs with the trauma of birth. The point is not simply that the pregnant woman has the right to control her own body but that in the struggle between pregnant woman and fetus, subjectivity exists only on one side. Here, the concept of the death drive modifies the reasoning of the Left but not the conclusions. This changes when we look at the argument between evolution and creationism.

The problem with evolution, from the perspective of psychoanalysis, lies in its failure to see that existence cannot be reduced to adaptation. For the creationist, the gaps in evolutionary theory attest to the fictional status of the theory. For psychoanalysis, the untruth of evolution resides in precisely the other direction: it fails to leave a place for the disruptions in the forward movement of life. Far from being undermined by having too many gaps, evolutionary theory presents us with the illusion of an entirely natural history, a history without breaks.[32] In his *Seminar VIII*, Lacan puts the psychoanalytic critique of evolutionary theory like this: "It appears to me essential to return to its elisions, to show or to reopen the gaps that the theory of evolution leaves open inasmuch as it always tends to cover them over in order to facilitate the conceivability of our experience. If evolution is true, one thing nonetheless is certain, which is that it is not, as Voltaire said when talking about something else, as natural as all that."[33] If we can reconcile psychoanalytic thought with evolutionary theory, the latter must incorporate some conception of a break in the flow of life.

We cannot trace a through-line from the evolutionary development of animals to the emergence of subjectivity. Subjectivity emerges through a break, through a moment in which death is injected into life and thereby throws life off its course. But in order for this disruption to be possible, a fundamental gap in the evolutionary process must have already been there. That is to say, if the evolutionary process moved forward without a hitch, there would have been no space for the emergence of language and subjectivity. The very existence of a subject of the death drive—a being that doesn't desire its own good—testifies to a profound lacuna within evolutionary theory. This reveals that even the movement of life in the natural world has an unnatural dimension to it, or else the death drive as such could never emerge. The natural world harbors death within it as an excess that permanently disrupts its forward movement.

This conception of a death-infested life can also inform how we might look at the Terri Schiavo case. Though Schiavo became a subject through loss, her vegetative state attests to the disappearance of loss. She persists only as a living being, as bare life, and it is for this reason that we could freely allow her to die. Her merely living body no longer housed a subject of loss. What value it once had was lost, and all we could do was mark the loss of this loss through funeral rites. The Schiavo case reveals the precarious status of subjectivity. Neither its emergence nor its disappearance comes with any guarantee. It persists only as long as it sustains the experience of loss and continues to return to this originary experience.

To recognize the excessive presence of death in life would result in a fundamental transformation of the social order. It would create neither the pure productivity of the Marxist utopia nor the strict prohibitions (and resulting ultimate enjoyment) of the fundamentalist's dreams. The world in which we recognized death in life would contain at once more suffering and more enjoyment. We would see the trauma of loss as our only destiny, but we would also see loss as the site of our enjoyment.

10

The Necessity of Belief

Fighting against Faith

The question of the politics of life and death is inseparable from the question of God's existence. God's role in political struggle today is as pronounced as it ever has been. Contemporary fundamentalists of all stripes around the world fight for different forms of theocracy, and their secular opponents, the inheritors of the Enlightenment, argue vehemently for the necessity of atheism (or at least sustaining a laical social structure). The question of God's existence has once again emerged as a preeminent political question in our epoch. Psychoanalysis speaks not to the question directly but to the causes that inform its emergence. As such, it can provide a political intervention that goes beyond the Enlightenment insistence on atheism.

Concerning the ontological question of God's existence, psychoanalytic theory insists on a strict neutrality. Neither the actual existence nor nonexistence of God bears on the psychoanalytic project in itself because it would not fundamentally alter the problem of subjectivity. With or without God, the subject remains divided from itself and confronts a social order equally divided from itself. Furthermore, psychoanalysis recognizes that being as such is self-divided and that this self-division must reflect the nature of God, if such a being exists.[1]

But if psychoanalytic thought does not concern itself with God's ontological status, it does devote considerable attention to the phenomenon of religious belief. It shows us that the emergence of religious belief is neither a response to miraculous signs of God's presence nor an attempt to find solace in a cold universe. It is, instead, an effect of the structure of signification. As psychoanalytic theorist Pierre Daviot puts it, "The theory ruins the ineffable and transcendent character of the spiritual nebula by showing that it is governed by an immutable logic: that of the signifying articulation as it expresses itself across spoken language."[2] In this sense, religious belief is wholly necessary, and even the professed atheist shares in it, albeit in a disguised form.

At its foundation, religious belief is belief in the lack in the order of meaning — in the incompleteness of the field of signification that one confronts as a subject. By unraveling the nature of religious belief and revealing its structural necessity, psychoanalytic theory has the ability to make the implicit nature of belief explicit and thereby to eliminate the illusions that accompany its form of appearance. In doing so, it might lessen the political power of belief and help to fight against the theocratic impulse in contemporary politics. It reveals that the best way to counteract the power of religious belief is not overt struggle against it — arguing for atheism — but the insistence on the absolute necessity of faith.

At times, Freud himself is far from seeing religious belief as a structural necessity, and, in fact, he inveighs against belief in the strongest terms. Much of *Civilization and Its Discontents* and all of *The Future of an Illusion* are devoted to attacking the foundations of religious belief. For Freud, "a protection against suffering through a delusional remoulding of reality is made by a considerable number of people in common. The religions of mankind must be classed among the mass-delusions of this kind."[3] Here, Freud links religious belief with a form of psychosis, and he views it as one of the tasks of psychoanalysis to challenge this cultural form of psychosis. His focus on the believer's delusion obscures, however, the genuine insight that accompanies belief — its initial affirmation of the gap or failure within the field of signification.

To be sure, the believer fills in this gap with a transcendent and supernatural being (which is precisely what Freud objects to), but the religious impulse takes the gap itself as its theoretical point of departure. To insist on atheism in the manner that Freud does is to obfuscate this central religious insight, which is what constitutes the primary source of belief's appeal. That is, the devoted believe not so much because faith offers consolation in the face of the irremediable horror of existence but because faith provides a way of conceptualizing what is constitutively absent in the everyday world or signifying structure. Religious belief is a way of affirming that everything cannot be said and including this inherent incompleteness within language itself.

Nonetheless, one cannot leave belief in its prevailing form of appearance. Freud rightly combats manifestations of belief for the psychic toll that they take on the subject, and contemporary psychoanalytic theory must take up Freud's combat, albeit in a different guise. As belief in an ultimately unknowable God consciously intervening in the world, religious faith is a form of psychotic delusion, and it is delusional even if its basic contention — that God exists — is true. Whether God actually exists or not is entirely beside the point for the subject engaged in belief. The problem with the religious delusion lies elsewhere: like all forms of psychosis, it removes the subject from the fundamental problems of subjectivity and thereby depoliticizes it. Belief in its typical form is, as psychoanalysis allows us to see, incompatible with a properly politicized subjectivity or an authentically engaged existence. It interferes with the subject's ability to intervene in order to change the world. Belief is a barrier to the genuine political act.

This idea of an antithesis between belief and politics seems especially evident today as we see belief align itself with calls for a return to traditional social relations. The fundamentalist critique of modernity, though it often takes the form of right-wing politics, has its basis in the rejection of politics as such. Politics proper involves an embrace of an irreducible antagonism that defines the social field. As Alain Badiou notes in *Metapolitics*, "What true politics undermines is the illusion of the bond, whether it be trade unionist, parliamentary, professional or convivial."[4] Politics involves acting on the basis of the incompletion of the social order, on the basis of the realization that no omnipotent force determines the nature of social relations. When one becomes a politicized subject, one implicitly affirms the social antagonism, whereas fundamentalist militancy attempts to combat antagonism itself in the name of healing the social order and giving that order an abiding unity.[5] This is a fantasy that subtends not just fundamentalism but all religiously based attempts at politics, inclusive of progressive movements linked to even a vague conception of spirituality.

This is not to say that religiously based attempts at politics cannot effect substantive social change. This type of militancy has the ability to be quite successful in changing aspects of society. But the problem with these victories — even if they happen to appear to lead in the direction of emancipation — is their ultimately nefarious effect on both the subject and the social order. They leave us with the idea that the split in the subject and the split in the social order can be healed — and in this way they play a part in an ultimate depoliticization or in an eventual turn to Fascism. In this sense, social change motivated by religion cannot properly be seen as the result of political agitation.

Religious belief doesn't only affirm the gap in the field of signification; it also, in the manner of the paranoiac, posits an entity that fills this gap. In the gap of social authority, at the real point where society remains irreducibly unauthorized, the believer finds an other that authorizes and justifies it. Where the power of social authority breaks down, religion allows the subject to find an authority authorizing and thereby obscuring this breakdown.[6] The believing subject doesn't experience the utter groundlessness of social relations — and this means that responsibility for these relations is always external. While sustaining belief, one can never perform the radical gesture of accepting responsibility for one's desire. The distortion of being that is the result of desire itself remains the responsibility of the hidden (and not fully known) other, who is the object of the believer's faith, and not the subject itself.

But arguing against belief, a technique practiced since the Enlightenment, has had dubious results. Though Freud's imaginary dialogue in *The Future of an Illusion* may have convinced a few to abandon their belief, belief endures and even prospers in modernity. The arguments against belief almost inevitably have the effect of securing it rather than shaking its foundation. The centuries-long effort to reveal the irrationality of belief — an effort that continues today in the work of scientists and philosophers like Victor Stenger, Daniel Dennett, Sam Harris, Michel Onfray, and Christopher Hitchens — has been a monumental failure, despite the importance of the political stakes involved.[7] This failure stems from the way in which these arguments that adduce reasons for not believing end up providing more libidinal rewards for the believer. We can see the process taking place in one of the more polemical attacks on belief — Richard Dawkins's *The God Delusion*.

A Universe of Utility

Dawkins is admirably open with his readers from the beginning of the book. He states, "If this book works as I intend, religious readers who open it will be atheists when they put it down."[8] In order to prompt this transformation, Dawkins engages in a three-pronged strategy. He begins by demolishing the various proofs for God's existence, proceeds to locate the origin of belief through evolutionary biology, and finally demonstrates why the belief in God is unnecessary on every level (morally, socially, and existentially). Every aspect of Dawkins's argument derives from the sense of utility underlying his Darwinian approach, and in fact it is easy to speculate that belief's utter lack of utility motivated him to write the book in the first place.

This is a motivation that Dawkins shares with other contemporary critics of religion. Both Sam Harris and Victor Stenger see religion not just as a barrier to social utility but as having unambiguously deleterious effects that demand its elimination. According to Harris, "We should . . . recognize what a fathomless sink for human resources (both financial and attentional) organized religion is."[9] For Stenger, religion is "inimical to human progress."[10] It is, in the mind of these thinkers, a relic of humanity's barbaric past that must be jettisoned.

Religious belief arose as an unhealthy by-product of a useful tendency, which, according to Dawkins's speculation, was the proclivity for trusting authorities. Trust in authority had an evolutionary utility because it saved children from danger, but it had the secondary effect of facilitating religious belief (or the acceptance of religiosity when sanctioned by authorities). It is also a by-product of our tendency to see agency everywhere, which typically keeps us from harm but in the case of religion leads us into a self-destructive behavior. The falsity of belief might be redeemed by its usefulness in creating moral beings or providing comfort in the face of death, but Dawkins shows how it simply doesn't do these things that we tend to give it credit for. It is a behavior without any use at all, and we are better off without it.

Dawkins proceeds in his assault on belief in the precise manner that Noam Chomsky proceeds in his critique of contemporary capitalism. Underlying the arguments of both is the belief that if people simply had all the facts, they would abandon either their religious belief or their investment in the capitalist mode of production. But religious belief and ideological commitment are not reducible to knowledge. Both represent libidinal investments that provide adherents with a reward that no amount of knowledge can replace.

What Dawkins's argument against belief leaves intact — and what every argument against belief leaves intact — is the enjoyment that derives from believing. In fact, arguments that make clear the inutility of belief augment this enjoyment rather than detracting from it. Enjoyment has an inverse relationship to utility: we enjoy in proportion to the uselessness of our actions. If an activity such as belief is useful, we gain something from it. It might, for instance, provide us healing during a time of illness or bring a good harvest during a drought. When an activity is not useful, however, it results in no tangible or even immaterial benefit; pursuing it involves pure expenditure without any return and thus wastes time, energy, resources, and life itself. Religious belief is essentially waste and pointless sacrifice, which for critics augurs its eventual elimination. But when one examines religion from the perspective of human enjoyment, its wastefulness becomes the chief source of its attraction.

Looked at from one side, the sacrifice that religion demands is not wasteful but productive: the believer gives up something in this life (sensual pleasures, free time on the weekend, and so on) in order to gain a blissful life in the afterworld. Belief, in this sense, operates according to the logic of exchange, and the exchange accrues to the benefit of the believer, since almost everyone would sacrifice some immediate pleasure for the assurance of eternity in heaven. Even religions without a clear conception of the afterlife (like Judaism) nonetheless offer the believer tangible rewards — a sense of membership in a community, transcendent justification for one's actions, and so on. If this account of belief were sufficient to explain the phenomenon, the arguments against belief would have a cogency that they in fact lack. As Dawkins shows from the perspective of evolutionary biology and as Stenger shows from the perspective of physics, the probability that there is a God and that there is an afterlife is almost zero.[11] Given the odds, belief represents a poor investment and should attract very few adherents. But if the driving force behind belief is not eternal bliss but the very act of sacrifice itself — a wasteful rather than a productive act — the arguments against belief would lose all of their force.

Wasteful sacrifice appeals to us because we emerge as subjects through an initial act of ceding something without gaining anything in return. The creative power of the human subject stems from its ability to sacrifice. Through sacrificing some part of ourselves, we create a privileged object that will constitute us as desiring subjects, but this object exists only as lost or absent and has no existence prior to the sacrificial act that creates it. There is a fundamental dissatisfaction written into the very structure of subjectivity that no one can ever escape. But at the same time, the act of sacrifice allows us to create anew our lost object.

Through religious belief, the subject repeats the original act of sacrifice that constitutes its desire. Belief thus provides a foundational enjoyment for the believer, who, through the act of believing, wastes without recompense. The promise of a future reward in the afterlife is nothing but the alibi that religion provides in order to seduce the subject on the conscious level. But this is not where the real libidinal appeal of religion lies. The proliferation of religious belief is inextricable from its failure to deliver on its promises and from its status as a bad investment for the devout. Especially in the contemporary world, religious belief provides respite — an oasis of enjoyment — for the subject caught up in the capitalist drive to render everything useful and banish whatever remains unproductive.[12]

The more that the demands of capitalist relations of production imprint themselves on a social order, the more that subjects — or at least a subset of them — within that order will turn toward religious belief or some other form of pure sacrifice (such as sports fandom). Capitalism installs a regime of utility that demands productive accumulation and leaves little space for useless expenditure. As Marx points out in the *Grundrisse*,

> Just as production founded on capital creates universal industriousness on one side — i.e., surplus-labour, value-creating labour — so it does create on the other side a system of general exploitation of the natural and human qualities, a system of general utility, utilising science itself just as much as all the physical and mental qualities, while there appears nothing *higher in itself*, nothing legitimate for itself, outside this circle of social production and exchange. Thus capital creates the bourgeois society, and the universal appropriation of nature as well as of the social bond itself by the members of society.[13]

The social bond within capitalist society is one that unites all subjects and all objects in a general calculus of utility.

In the midst of this system, subjects increasingly carve out the space for useless acts, and religion provides a ready arena for them. Though the Protestant ethic may have initially paved the way for the development of capitalism, today it is capitalism and its ethos of general utility that provides the ground, albeit negatively, for religious belief.[14] Consequently, displaying the uselessness of religious belief or its wastefulness can only have the effect of highlighting its ultimate value for the believer.

Demonstrating the improbability of God's existence — one of the goals of *The God Delusion* and the other attacks on belief — allows believers who sustain belief in spite of this improbability to experience themselves as radicals. This is a great problem in contemporary society because the prevailing ideological mode of subjectivity is that of the rebel or outsider. Though religious belief involves bowing to authority, the contemporary believer also experiences the enjoyment that comes from defiance of earthly authority. In most societies today, there is simply no earthly authority inveighing against faith or even prohibiting it; there is no one to defy. But Richard Dawkins, Sam Harris, Christopher Hitchens, and the other contemporary critics of religion help to erect just such an authority. One might even imagine that their books were undertaken with the unconscious aim of allowing believers to enjoy their belief.

No Club to Join

Though Freud eagerly participated in this failed frontal assault on belief, psychoanalysis also points toward another strategy: rather than insisting on the irrationality or problematic nature of believing, we might instead maintain the impossibility of not believing. Religious belief has the power that it does over subjects because they are convinced that their belief is the result of an extraordinary act, a leap that places them among the elect and the truly enlightened.[15] This privileged status of the believer is one of the key motivations for belief. But psychoanalytic insights reveal that belief is not exceptional but the de facto attitude of the subject, the result of a structure in which the subject enters in order to become a subject. By exposing the structural nature of belief, we can attack it at its most vulnerable point — at the point of its very ubiquity.

When the subject enters into the signification, it encounters the senseless injunction of a master signifier, a signifier that requires unconditional obedience. Through the form of this initial signifier, the subject receives the social authority's demand. But this demand never acquires a sense, and the structure of justification remains incomplete because no binary signifier for the master signifier exists. The authority's injunction exists on its own, without any subsequent signifier that would provide completion and justification for the master signifier. The parent tells the child to obey, but no parent can ground this demand in an ultimate reason that would allow it to make sense. This is why, at some point, the parent must respond to the child's question "Why?" with the unsatisfying response "Because I said so." The ultimate justification for parental (and societal) authority is tautological. In the last instance, the child must obey simply because the parent says so, and this absence of a ground for the parental injunction is typically our first experience of the missing binary signifier that would provide a sense for the senseless master signifier.

The absence of a binary signifier, a signifier that would explain or justify the demand of the master signifier, creates an opening within the structure of signification. Signification begins with a master signifier, but there is no binary signifier that would close the signifying utterance definitively. Every stopping point remains a failed stand-in for the missing ultimate stopping point. The absence of a final stopping point or binary signifier unleashes the subject's desire, but it also molds the subject into a believer. Religious belief, in its essence, is not the result of human weakness (as Nietzsche would have it), an outdated evolutionary mechanism (as Richard Dawkins would have it), or ideological manipulation (as Marx would have it). Even Freud's contention that belief is the residue of an infantile relationship to the father and a desire for a nonlacking authority fails to grasp the real cause for the obstinacy of belief. While enlightenment and rationality might topple our belief in God qua master signifier, it cannot touch our belief in the God of the real, the God who occupies the position of the missing binary signifier and thus does not appear in the chain of signifiers.

Following Pascal, Lacan distinguishes between the philosopher's God, on the one hand, and the believer's God, on the other, and we can align these two versions of God with the master signifier and the binary signifier, respectively. The first version, the philosopher's God, acts as a present authority in the world. It is Aristotle's prime mover, or the first cause of the cosmological proof. Such a God acts as the starting point for the signifying system. Kant's demolition of the proofs for the existence of God in the first *Critique* targets precisely this God who functions as a master signifier.

What Kant shows, through his refutation of the ontological proof (and, by extension, of the cosmological proof and the argument from design, or physicoteleological proof), is that the master signifier, the starting point for signification, may be just a name rather than a being. The ontological proof relies on the fallacious idea that the existence of the master signifier requires a referent to which that signifier corresponds, which is why Kant's refutation consists in showing that one hundred imaginary dollars have the same signifying status as one hundred real dollars but that they do not have the same ontological status (because one cannot, unfortunately, buy anything with them!).

The Enlightenment assault on the God of the philosophers or the symbolic God leaves intact the other version of God — the God of the missing binary signifier. This is the God who acts in mysterious ways, who provides the answers that transcend causal explanations. This God never shows itself but always remains in the position of impossibility. One cannot argue away this God because it occupies a position outside all rationality and argumentation: the more successfully one refutes this God's existence, the more ardently the believer will cling to belief. This insistence is visible not just in backwater fundamentalists but even in a thinker as sophisticated as Kierkegaard, who contends that the strength of the arguments against the existence of God provide incentive for the leap of faith rather than discouraging it. But even Kierkegaard's belief is not the result of an existential choice made by the believer but is rather imposed on the subject by the nature of the symbolic structure itself.

In the act of speaking, we implicitly invoke the God of the real in the space of what is missing but nonetheless supports the field of the signifier. As Lacan puts it in *Seminar XX*, "The *dire* constitutes *Dieu*. And as long as things are said, the God hypothesis will persist."[16] He adds: "It is impossible to say anything without immediately making Him subsist in the form of the Other."[17] What one says includes an appeal to the missing real other, an appeal for the validation of what one says. This validation, in order to be effective, must emanate from a position beyond the signifier. Every validation that occurs on the level of the signifier simply suggests the need for further validation anchored somewhere beyond it.

Each act of speaking makes us aware of a field of the unsaid that does not exist prior to or outside of the act of speaking. The field of the unsaid, the field of the real other, is irreducible. No matter how many times we attempt to say the last word and to provide an ultimate ground for what we say, our act of speaking will open up this field of the beyond that no words can subsequently contain. The inescapability of the real other is at once the inescapability of the God of the missing binary signifier, who is nothing but the name for that which we cannot grasp through the signifier, even though the signifier structurally creates a place for it.

Such a claim seems to go too far. Despite the degree of religious belief in contemporary society (even in Western Europe, where organized religion no longer has a hold on the population), almost everyone can name an atheist among her or his acquaintances. Some subjects seem to be able to transcend the structural necessity of belief. The problem with many self-proclaimed atheists is that they can sustain their atheism only by substituting a different real other to replace God. Atheist Marxists appeal to History; evolutionary biologists appeal to Natural Selection; Nietzsche appeals to the fecundity of Life itself; and so on. Even though such figures reject the name of the God, they accept God as a structural position by filling in the missing space in the structure of signification with an explanatory guarantee.

The key to fighting against the nefarious effects of belief involves promulgating the recognition that we cannot but believe. Armed with this recognition that God is a structural necessity rather than a being in whom we might opt to believe, we transform the believer's conception of God. Though in one sense widespread acceptance of the necessity of belief wouldn't change much, it would allow this transformation in the nature of what is believed. The subject who grasps belief as a necessity and God as a structural entity recognizes that even God doesn't know — and this is the fundamental recognition inherent in every politicization. If psychoanalysis is atheistic, it is atheistic in the sense that it insists that even though there is God qua gap in the signifying order, there is no knowledge in this gap. Or as Lacan puts it in *Seminar XI*, "The true formula of atheism is *God is unconscious*."[18] To know that the other in the gap doesn't know or that God is unconscious is to understand that nothing grounds human existence. The recognition that nothing grounds human existence founds any genuinely emancipatory political project.

An Unconscious God

Both religious belief and atheism — what seem to be the two basic alternatives — have a recognizable face that has manifested itself throughout human history, but the form of appearance of a necessary belief that grasps itself as such seems less clear. How might the necessity of belief realize itself concretely in those who take it up? How might one reveal God as unconscious? Recognizing belief as necessary or God as unconscious requires an ability to see contingency at the point where explanations break down and where one typically posits the mysterious power of God. The place where the binary signifier is missing represents the place where the contingent resides. Of all the arts, the cinema has a privileged relationship with contingency. While the other arts can depict contingent encounters, the immediacy of cinematic viewership — the spectator is in some sense in the film while watching — makes it the most conducive to offering the experience of contingency itself. While viewing a film, one expects the unexpected, the encounter that defies calculation. By highlighting this aspect of the cinema, a film can thematize the contingent and work toward a revelation of the unconscious nature of God.

The first three feature films of Alejandro González Iñárritu depict events as if an unconscious God were the structuring absence informing them. *Amores Perros* (2000), *21 Grams* (2003), and *Babel* (2006) demand that the spectator experience the events that they show from the perspective of the subject who recognizes the necessity of belief and thereby sees contingency in the place of God. According to the taxonomy developed by Charles Ramirez Berg, these films employ the Hub-and-Spokes Plot, in which "multiple characters' story lines intersect decisively at one time and place."[19] For Berg, the radicality of the Hub-and-Spokes Plot stems from its ability to thwart the ideological conception of individual agency. He claims: "Thematically, they demonstrate the frailty of agency by presenting a world where happenstance prevails and best-laid plans come to naught. . . . If agency is illusory and self-actualization risible, then the notion of rugged individualism, a fundamental component of the American mythos, becomes quaint at best, dangerously delusional at worst."[20] Films like *Babel*, according to this account, undermine the ideological idea of self-determination and control over one's destiny. But subverting the idea of individual agency often goes hand in hand with locating agency in a hidden force, lurking behind nominal authority figures, that pulls all the strings, and this is what *Babel* avoids.

The central event in *Babel* — the hub — occurs when Yussef (Boubker Ait El Caid) and his brother Ahmed (Said Tarchani) use a powerful gun purchased by their father to shoot at a tour bus driving through the Moroccan desert. Shooting at extreme long range, Yussef hits the bus, and the bullet strikes Susan (Cate Blanchett), almost killing her. Iñárritu structures the film in a way that underlines the contingency of this central encounter between the Moroccan youth and the American tourist. *Babel* begins with a tracking shot of a man (later identified as Hassan [Abdelkader Bara]) walking through the Moroccan desert while carrying a large object wrapped in white cloth on his back. Hassan comes to sell a high-powered rifle to Abdullah (Mustapha Rachidi), a goatherd who gives the rifle to his sons so that they can shoot jackals that threaten the family's goats.

While the boys practice shooting the new gun, the white tour bus appears on a road in the valley below. Yussef shoots at it, but there is no intentionality behind this act. He is simply testing the gun, trying to prove his shooting ability and the gun's range, and the bus appears to be so far in the distance that it is difficult to imagine the bullet striking the target in a way that might do damage. Because Iñárritu films the bus from the perspective of the boys, it remains almost an unreal target for the spectator, just as it is for the boys.

By opening the film with Hassan's sale of the gun and the boys' experimentation with it, Iñárritu makes clear that, contrary to what American officials later believe, the shooting is not in any way an act of terrorism. It is not even a boyhood prank. A chain of causality leads to the shooting, but the film highlights the contingency at work through the causal chain. Neither a benign nor a malevolent force is at work behind the scenes, manipulating things in order to produce the event. The point is not that the shooting occurs at random but that nothing could account for it through any form of calculation. The event defies calculation and arrives in the form of an unexpected encounter for both Susan and the spectator.

After a sequence that occurs days later when Susan's husband, Richard

(Brad Pitt), phones home to report on the extent of Susan's condition to Amelia (Adriana Barraza), the woman who is watching Richard and Susan's two children, Iñárritu returns to the event from the perspective of those inside the bus. We see the white tour bus driving through the desert, followed by a close-up of Richard reading a book and a medium close-up of Susan sleeping with her head resting against the window of the bus. After ten seconds of this shot, the glass on the window abruptly breaks, and Susan slumps over with blood on her shirt. The film cuts to Richard asking what happened and then back to Susan looking dazed. As the other passengers realize that Susan has been shot, Richard screams, "Stop the bus! Stop the bus!" Whereas the beginning of the film shows the shooting from the perspective of the boys shooting the gun, this scene shows it from the perspective of the victim. From this perspective, the shot appears to come from nowhere and be unaccountable.

It is completely unexpected for everyone on the bus. But for the spectator who has seen the film's opening, this unexpected event stems from the activity of the boys. Even for those armed with this knowledge, however, the shooting remains a contingent encounter. Though the American officials try to interpret the shooting according to the logic provided by the War on Terror, the film's presentation of the narrative makes evident the folly of this interpretative gesture. Because Iñárritu allows the spectator to see the long prelude to the shooting prior to the actual event and because this prelude exposes the contingency of what happens, the spectator cannot interpret it as the American officials do.

Most films (and other works of art) that provide the background for traumatic events do so in order to reveal the necessity leading up to them. These works attempt to mediate events that people experience as immediate and thereby show the political actions that provide the background for the traumatic events. Gillo Pontecorvo's *La Battaglia di Algeri* (*The Battle of Algiers*, 1967) is perhaps the most celebrated example of this genre. By foregrounding the viciousness of the French army in Algeria, Pontecorvo shows the causes leading up to the bombings perpetuated by the National Liberation Front (or FLN) — bombings experienced simply as acts of terror by French civilians in Algeria. The view of *La Battaglia di Algeri* sees the necessity behind what appear to be contingent events. *Babel*, however, moves in the opposite direction.

Iñárritu does not begin the film with the purchase of and experimentation with the gun in order to emphasize the necessity leading up to the shooting. One might imagine a different leftist film constructed with this end in mind. It would begin not with Abdullah's purchase of the gun but with an illustration of American activity and influence in Morocco. Demonstrating the idea of blowback, it would reveal how American policies led to the shooting of an American tourist. But Iñárritu is not attempting to provide the spectator with a means for mediating seemingly immediate events; he is facilitating a contingent encounter. *Babel* aims to produce a spectator attuned to the foundational role of contingency in shaping our existence. At the point where the unexpected and the inexplicable occur, one finds the contingent, not God.

By constructing the film as he does, Iñárritu intervenes in the debate surrounding religious belief. Rather than stressing the godless nature of the universe or the inutility of faith, his film shows contingency operating at the point of the absent signifier, where believers would locate God. Instead of God connecting everyone to each other, *Babel* shows the contingent nature of the social bond. Contingency becomes the source of the link between disparate worlds, and the contingent encounter provides a possibility for the realization of this link.

As producer Jon Kilik tells it, Iñárritu began work on *Babel* with the idea, as the title suggests, that the exigencies of contemporary existence divide subjects from each other and produce individuals completely isolated from each other. But during the course of the shooting, it became a film about connection rather than separation.[21] This change forced itself on Iñárritu, we can hypothesize, because of the decision to focus on the contingent encounter as a device for narratively linking the four different stories: such encounters always provide an opportunity for recognizing an underlying connection. The contingent encounter forces the subject to confront a lack of knowledge concerning the other. One has no assurance about what the other desires, and no one can provide this assurance — not even the other itself.

In response to this encounter, one can react in the manner of the American officials who see terrorism in this unknown point. But this absence of belief represents an attempt to evade the contingent nature of the encounter. As *Babel* shows, the contingent encounter offers the subject the opportunity to act — to thrust itself toward the other without any guarantee concerning how the other might respond. In doing so, it brings the subject back to the moment of its entry into symbolization and the point at which belief first manifests itself.

The first act of belief that a subject undertakes has nothing to do with religion. It corresponds to the step that one takes into the signifying order. When subjects begin to speak, they accept on faith that words have the signification that the other (most often the parent) attributes to them. The child hears innumerable times the word "red" associated with a certain appearance of things and eventually comes to believe in this association. But this belief is ultimately a belief that others believe, and as such it has no ultimate ground or justification. Faith is a faith in the fidelity of others, not in God.

What connects speaking subjects is not, as Jürgen Habermas would have it, an underlying rationality that inheres in the act of a speaking, a communicative rationality but rather the act of belief in signification itself. Whereas Habermas finds a guarantee supporting every utterance that derives from the power of language, a psychoanalytic approach finds no foundation for speech, no fundamental agreement on the basis of which one could have certainty. Nothing guarantees signification except the belief of the other, and one can have no certainty concerning this belief. The social bond depends on the free act of the subject entering into it, and this free act is always an act of faith. The subject must act before knowing, without any assurance that its faith will be justified.

Worshiping Contingency

One of the most persuasive critiques of the contemporary attacks on faith focuses on the lack of a positive vision of the world offered by these critiques. They tear down belief, but they offer nothing in its stead. As reviewer Daniel Lazare puts it, "Atheism is a purely negative ideology, which is its problem. If one does not believe in God, what should one believe in instead?"[22] In addition to proclaiming what one is against, one must also proclaim what one is for. In the absence of faith or some new form of equivalent belief (such as Communism's future fully realized society), it is not clear what might offer an underlying coherence for societies and provide an aim for human existence.

One might see it as freedom — and perhaps this is how the atheists themselves would respond. Atheism appears to open up the space for human freedom that the idea of God had hitherto closed off. Without God, people could follow their own desires in a way hitherto unimaginable. This is the philosophy of Ivan Karamazov in Fyodor Dostoyevsky's *The Brothers Karamazov*. According to Ivan's way of thinking,

> were mankind's belief in its immortality to be destroyed, not only love but also any living power to continue the life of the world would at once dry up in it. Not only that, but then nothing would be immoral any longer, everything would be permitted, even anthropophagy. And even that is not all: . . . for every separate person, like ourselves for instance, who believes neither in God nor in his own immortality, the moral law of nature ought to change immediately into the exact opposite of the former religious law, and that egoism, even to the point of evildoing, should not only be permitted to man but should be acknowledged as the necessary, the most reasonable, and all but the noblest result of his situation.[23]

Though the absence of God seems to lead directly to Ivan's theory of complete human freedom — where "everything would be permitted" — it actually leads in the opposite direction.

Atheism is the road the unfreedom. The universe of contemporary atheism — and of atheism as such — is a universe in which all events can be explained according to a system of utility and interest. Entities within this universe behave in ways that aim at either their own good or the good of a larger organization to which they belong. In such a universe, there is no place for freedom. Freedom is nothing but the ability of a being to act against its own good or to reject what is in its self-interest.[24] Through the self-destructive act, the subject frees itself from the dictates of nature and ideology, dictates that almost always manifest themselves through the prism of utility. A universe dominated by the claims of utility has no conceptual space for freedom.

Despite their belief in a universe ruled by the claims of utility, those who write polemics on behalf of atheism presuppose some idea of freedom: to argue against belief implies that believers have the freedom to act on what they read and transform their lives. When proponents of the godless universe allow for freedom, as they must, they locate it within the structure of utility. In *Freedom Evolves*, Daniel Dennett gives this logic its most complete articulation. Human freedom develops, according to Dennett, precisely because it is a useful tool to have. He says: "Free will is real, but it is not a preexisting feature of our existence, like the law of gravity. It is also not what tradition declares it to be: a God-like power to exempt oneself from the causal fabric of the physical world. It is an evolved creation of human activity and beliefs, and it is just as real as such other human creations as music and money."[25] The freedom that Dennett affirms here is an empirical freedom, a freedom that evolution provides rather than a freedom written into the structure of subjectivity as such. One should not oppose freedom and the determinative laws of the universe but see freedom operating within those laws. In these terms, freedom perseveres, but in an attenuated form. Atheism is incompatible with a freedom that violates the laws of nature or that interrupts the claims of utility. In order to arrive at this type of freedom, one must have a place for God.

In his 2003 State of the Union address, George W. Bush identified the roots of human freedom with the benevolence of God. He famously proclaimed (as part of his justification for the Iraq War), "The liberty we prize is not America's gift to the world, it is God's gift to humanity."[26] Many commentators have attacked the theocratic impulse present in this formulation, but Bush's statement does in fact contain a kernel of truth, if we understand the God to which he refers in the proper way — that is, as unconscious. An unconscious God is the necessary condition for human freedom. Freedom depends on the signifying structure containing a point of nonknowledge. This point is the result of the absence of a binary signifier, a signifier of justification, that would complete any signifying utterance. The lack of a last word that closes the field of meaning — the position of absence occupied by an unconscious God — produces the free subject because it implies that no other has the ultimate responsibility for this field. In the absence of a binary signifier (a conscious God, a being behind the scenes pulling the strings), ultimate responsibility rests with the subject itself.

The freedom that derives from an unconscious God is not the freedom that neoconservatives attempted to unleash on Iraq in 2003 — and in this sense Bush's statement is totally misleading. Freedom does not mean lack of restraint. There is no contradiction between doing what one wants and slavishly following a natural or ideological structure.[27] Individual capitalists freely take up the project of the accumulation of capital without disturbing the structure of the ruling relations of production in the slightest. They want to accumulate, and the society leaves them free to do so. But there is no freedom present here in the transcendental sense because the social structure shapes the will to which it grants freedom. The subject of capitalist society is simply free to follow the dictates of the social structure willingly and without direct coercion.

If it is to break from these dictates, the idea of freedom must be dissociated from the usual conception of free will or absence of restraint. One must think of freedom in conjunction with restraint. As Jean-Paul Sartre recognizes in *Being and Nothingness*, freedom necessarily encounters limits and would be inconceivable without them, and these limits occur within the sphere of freedom, not outside of it. He claims: "It is therefore our freedom which constitutes the limits which it will subsequently encounter."[28] Sartre grasps the inextricable relation between freedom and its limit, but even this formulation fails to go far enough in articulating the dialectical nature of the relation between the terms. Freedom does not encounter limits but posits them, and it is in the act of positing a limit that a being affirms itself as free.

Rather than being the liberty to do what one wants, freedom is the capacity to limit oneself. Under theism, freedom appears to manifest itself in the limiting power of law and thus be necessary rather than contingent. By linking freedom to law as its limit, theism disguises freedom's radicality. Even when one sees law as the product of the subject's own self-positing and thus as ultimately groundless (as Kant does in the *Critique of Practical Reason*), one remains within the logical bounds of theism and sells freedom short. Law implies necessity and thus carries with it an implicit imbrication with a transcendent order that authorizes it. In other words, there are always legitimating reasons guaranteeing law. It cannot derive purely and simply from freedom itself, which is why Kant ultimately links the moral law back to the idea of God.[29]

If we recognize that contingency rather than God occupies the place of the absent signifier — or, which is to say the same thing, that God is contingent — we at the same time grasp the fundamental contingency of all limits. Limits do not come from God in the form of, say, the Decalogue; they derive from the way in which societies and subjects posit themselves.

The limit is the condition of possibility for the society and for the subject. This is the great insight of Fichte's philosophy of the self. As he puts it, "The self posits an object, or excludes something from itself, simply because it excludes, and on no higher ground; by means of this exclusion, the higher sphere of *positing in general* (regardless of whether the self or a not-self is posited) now first becomes possible."[30] The act of exclusion or of self-limiting constitutes the subject, but this act has, as Fichte emphasizes, "no higher ground" on which it is based. This means that the limit through which a subject defines itself and its freedom is, in the last instance, contingent. It might be something else. But what defines every subject and every society is the contingent limit that they establish for themselves.

Both atheism and traditional theology deny the radicality of human freedom by obscuring the fundamental absence that structures all social arrangements. In the space of this absence, one finds an unconscious God — a contingent moment that takes one by surprise and remains fundamentally inexplicable. By grasping religious belief as a necessary response to the structural primacy of contingency, we can take up a different relation to it. Rather than reducing contingency to a deeper necessity in the way of the believer or eliminating the space for it in a universe of utility like the atheist, we might avow the contingent as our unsurpassable limit and place it at the center of our conceptual and social universe. A universe structured around contingency is a universe of freedom.

ID

11

The Case of the Missing Signifier

The Political Deadlock

Perhaps the most important political problem of the last century concerns lifting repression. Even more than the obstacle of religious belief, repression represents a rigid barrier that has often been the focus of emancipatory politics. But as the history especially of the last half of the twentieth century has shown, lifting repression doesn't necessarily lead to political liberation. It can even, as the main thesis of the Frankfurt School has it, become the vehicle for further decreasing the freedom of the subject in the face of ideological control. As societies eliminate varieties of repression, some fundamental deadlock remains recalcitrant and stands as a political stumbling block.[1]

If the political project of lifting repression inevitably goes awry, then this confronts the project of emancipation with the question of what it can do. This is where the intervention of psychoanalytic thought makes itself felt. Psychoanalysis has historically functioned as a tool for the struggle against repression, but if the attempt to fight repression inevitably fails or even backfires, the engagement of psychoanalytic thought with politics today requires a new attitude. The key to the political project of psychoanalysis lies in the unexpected twist that it gives to the fight against repression.

According to this project, one must reenvision the deadlock that limits the political project of lifting repression. Rather than seeing the deadlock that projects for emancipation encounter as purely a stumbling block to be negotiated, one might embrace the deadlock as itself a political position. A properly psychoanalytic politics would transform it from an obstacle into a point of identification. By identifying with the symbolic deadlock that impedes liberation, one can transform the cause of past political failures into a source of success. But the cost of this transformation is a redefinition of success as clarifying and embracing a limit rather than transcending it. The ultimate contribution of psychoanalytic thought to politics is its ability to provide a basis for an emancipatory politics of the limit.[2]

The fundamental symbolic deadlock—the root of the disorder that plagues every signifying system—involves the binary signifier, or the signifier of the feminine. The absence of this signifier prevents the operations of the social order from running smoothly (and, as the previous chapter showed, prompts the belief in God). Nothing necessitates, of course, that the missing signifier had to be the signifier of femininity, as it is in patriarchal society: one can envisage a different structure with a different binary signifier, but we cannot conceive of a successfully completed signifying structure or a structure without a missing binary signifier.[3] There will always be a missing signifier, though it won't always be the signifier of the feminine.[4] The subtraction of this signifier marks the founding moment of the social order as such and thus is impossible for us to experience. It is, instead, a condition for the possibility of experience.

One can't restore this missing signifier through analysis or political activity. It marks a point of impossibility within the social structure, and thus it poses a political question for psychoanalysis. Most psychoanalytic thinkers envision a politics that merely respects and sustains the gap marked by the missing signifier. As one prominent Lacanian theorist notes, "The aim of psychoanalysis is best described as negative: it ought not to deteriorate into a system which presents itself as an answer to the lack of a signifier."[5] The problem with this purely negative psychoanalytic politics lies in its failure to appreciate the ontological status of the gap and to come to terms with the pervasive desire to fill it.

The appeal of codes, cryptograms, crossword puzzles, and so on derives from the absence of the binary signifier. Even though most people tend to think of them as merely private amusements, these are fundamentally political activities because they concern the gap within the signifying order. In working these word puzzles, one seeks the missing signifier that would complete the system of signification itself, but finishing the puzzle provides only a momentary completion, opening up to another puzzle and another and another. The infinite nature of the word puzzle attests to the impossibility of overcoming the problem of the missing signifier once and for all. There will always be another puzzle because whatever signifier one uncovers, whatever binary signifier one finds, will always be a piece of knowledge rather than *the* binary signifier. For us, knowledge replaces the missing signifier and functions in its stead, but it remains by definition incomplete.[6] There will always be more to know, whereas the recovery of the binary signifier would provide a definitive ending.

More sophisticated codes, such as the genetic code or the Bible code, attract lifetimes of devotion because they promise the definitive ending that no mere cryptogram or crossword puzzle can provide. Obviously, there is a world of difference between those committed to cracking the genetic code and those trying to solve the Bible code. The former are seeking a definitive scientific discovery, while the latter are searching for an explanation that transcends scientific inquiry. Nonetheless, there is an essential symmetry to these quests, which is why the idea of cracking the Bible code manages to attract genuine mathematicians and scientists. Both projects aim at a conclusion that would put to rest the trouble that the missing signifier stirs up, and this animates them with a political charge.

On the one hand, the absence of the binary signifier has a structural relationship to all injustice: it produces the imbalance that manifests itself in class society, racial difference, and male domination. But on the other hand, the absence of this signifier allows us to enter into the regime of language and escape relations of pure force. It results in an insurmountable injustice at the same time as it introduces the very possibility of conceiving justice. In *Specters of Marx,* Jacques Derrida articulates this dual character of the absent binary signifier when he says: "To be 'out of joint,' whether it be present being or present time, can do harm and do evil, it is no doubt the very possibility of evil. But without the opening of this possibility, there remains, perhaps, beyond good and evil, only the necessity of the worst."[7] The missing binary signifier leaves the subject and the social order out of joint, as Derrida puts it (following Shakespeare), but without this disjointedness there exists only simple domination by force — "the necessity of the worst" — and no possibility for just interventions against pure force.

In other words, without an absent signifier, there would be no politics, but the political act cannot simply involve the attempt to sustain its absence, since this absence produces injustice and evil. The fundamental political question concerns what relationship we should try to take up relative to the missing binary signifier, a signifier whose inaccessibility constitutes us as subjects. There are four possible attitudes toward the binary signifier: the first three (the fundamentalist, the positivist, and the hermeneutic) function ideologically to deliver us from the trauma attached to this signifier's absence, while the fourth (the psychoanalytic) is founded on an encounter with the trauma. Most often, one encounters these attitudes in amalgamated forms that obscure how each functions. The great merit of *The Da Vinci Code* lies in its ability to lay out clearly the three ideological attitudes and thus to suggest negatively the contours of the fourth.

What's Missing in *The Da Vinci Code*

Much of the popularity of *The Da Vinci Code* (both Dan Brown's novel and Ron Howard's film) stems from the relationship that it assumes to the missing binary signifier. The novel and film identify the signifier of the sacred feminine — or, more specifically, of Mary Magdalene, the wife of Christ and mother of his child — as the signifier absent in Western Christian civilization. This signifier has taken the form, unbeknownst to all but the initiated, of the Holy Grail. The absence of this signifier, according to the thesis proffered by *The Da Vinci Code*, led to the creation of a patriarchal religious structure and an oppressive society. As the hero, Robert Langdon, explains, "The *Holy Grail* represents the sacred feminine and the goddess, which of course has now been lost, virtually eliminated by the Church. The power of the female and her ability to produce life was once very sacred, but it posed a threat to the rise of the predominantly male Church, and so the sacred feminine was demonized and called unclean."[8] By demonizing the sacred feminine, the church threw the universe out of balance, and the novel and film thus enjoin us to uncover the sacred feminine in order to restore the lost balance.

It is tempting to simply dismiss *The Da Vinci Code* as barely worth our analysis not only because of its formulaic narrative but, more substantively, because of its investment in the fantasy of sexual complementarity.[9] It follows a line of popular fictions and self-help books that advocate restoring a balance in the universe that was lost with the onset of patriarchy or capitalism. If there is one position that psychoanalytic thought rejects without qualification, it is the idea that we can achieve sexual complementarity or balance in sexual relations. Our existence as subjects depends on not achieving it, which is what Lacan means: "What constitutes the basis of life, in effect, is that for everything having to do with relations between men and women, what is called collectivity, it's not working out. It's not working out, and the whole world talks about it, and a large part of our activity is taken up with saying so."[10] While there is nothing necessary about patriarchy, the imbalance in sexual relations — what Lacan describes as the nonexistence of the sexual relationship — represents a deadlock that we cannot move beyond. It is a stumbling block of sense itself, marking the two contradictory modes (called male and female) of entering into language. The image of transcending this deadlock always has an ideological function. Though *The Da Vinci Code* fantasizes sexual complementarity and thus partakes of a thoroughly ideological fantasy, its single-minded focus on the missing binary signifier practically guarantees its relevance for psychoanalytic inquiry and for an understanding of how psychoanalytic thought might inform politics.

The Da Vinci Code assumes a contradictory attitude toward the binary signifier, and this attitude reveals the role that this signifier plays in the functioning of contemporary ideology. In the beginning of the novel and film, the villains seem to be the representatives of the patriarchy who are committed to wiping out all trace of the sacred feminine — that is, the real identity of the Holy Grail — within Christianity. These figures from Opus Dei, specifically, Bishop Aringarosa and his henchman, Silas, are dangerous because they view the existence of the sacred feminine as a threat to the true church, which has a necessarily male-oriented structure.

But despite initial appearances, the real villain in *The Da Vinci Code* turns out to be Leigh Teabing, a proponent of the sacred feminine who uses Opus Dei to force the truth of the Holy Grail to public awareness. Teabing believes that the unveiling of the binary signifier would effect a fundamental transformation in the structure of the entire world and inaugurate a new era of social justice. According to the logic of the novel and film, the zealot championing the sacred feminine is far more politically dangerous than the forces of patriarchy themselves.[11]

Through the depiction of the fundamentalists trying to eliminate the binary signifier and the liberationist trying to reveal it to the world, two popular ideological positions become visible. The first of these two positions denies the existence of the absent signifier and attempts to constitute a social order through the unchallenged authority of the master signifier itself. Such a position appeals to the word of God as the absolute arbiter of all social questions and views this word as unambiguous. There is no gap in the chain of signification, no need for knowledge to compensate for the missing binary signifier. But because it rejects the very existence of a gap, fundamentalism must constantly struggle with the feminine, which marks the point at which the gap in signification manifests itself.

Both contemporary Islamic and Christian fundamentalists focus much of their political efforts on the elimination of any representation of feminine enjoyment because any such representation would attest to the failure of the master signifier to signify everything. They do not, of course, work to destroy all signification of the feminine. For Islamic fundamentalism, femininity can manifest itself under the burqa so that its potential disruptiveness does not threaten the authority of the master signifier and thereby expose a gap in the order of signification. The burqa represents an extension of the master signifier draping itself over the entirety of the female body and working to deny that this body troubles the system of signification in any way. The burqa attempts to transform the missing binary signifier of the feminine into a fully present signifier of chastity and moral rectitude.

While American fundamentalists do not insist on the burqa, they do focus an inordinate quantity of their political energy on the issue of abortion. Abortion is the key social issue for American fundamentalists because it asserts the feminine in a way irreducible to the authority of the master signifier. As many critics of the antiabortion movement have noted, the position has little to do with valuing life in all instances or with fighting against the suffering of innocents. Most who hold antiabortion views fully embrace the death penalty and support policies that result in impoverished children going without adequate health care and nutrition.[12] But the right to legal abortion, according to the fundamentalist position, allows women to have sex—to enjoy—without severe consequences. It permits the disruptiveness of feminine enjoyment to appear publicly, and this enjoyment is precisely what the master signifier cannot account for. If the woman's sexual act results in a child, however, she becomes calculable within the reign of the master signifier as a mother.

Signifying a woman as a mother—which is what both Islamic and Christian fundamentalism work toward—effectively eliminates the gap in the signifying structure that the missing signifier of the feminine marks. Whereas the woman enjoys unaccountably, the mother enjoys reproducing the social order through her children. This is why, according to Jacques-Alain Miller, "the truth in a woman, in Lacan's sense, is measured by her subjective distance from the position of motherhood. To be a mother, the mother of one's children, is to choose to exist as Woman."[13] That is, the mother is fully there as a signifier — she is Woman as a present identity — rather than existing as an absence within the chain of signifiers. Fundamentalism works to transform women into mothers because the mother figure, as the complement of the father or master signifier, heals the incompleteness in the social structure.

In *The Da Vinci Code*, Bishop Aringarosa and Silas go to extraordinary lengths to destroy any trace of the sacred feminine — the feminine as a disturbance within patriarchal control. They realize, like contemporary Islamic and Christian fundamentalists, that the widespread recognition of the missing binary signifier would have devastating effects on the efficacy of symbolic authority. The church, as an institution that functions through the power of the master signifier, would lose whatever dominance it has in the world. The awareness of the missing signifier — the encounter with the gap within signification — emancipates the subject from the authority of the master signifier, which rules through the semblance of being a complete authority. Fundamentalism is the effort to sustain the illusion on which that complete authority depends.

The other contrary position recognizes the existence of the gap within signification but views it as merely empirical and thus reparable. According to this logic, articulated by Leigh Teabing in *The Da Vinci Code*, uncovering the feminine signifier will restore harmonious social relations — and harmonious relations with nature — that have been lost under capitalism and patriarchy. Teabing unleashes a violent plot to expose the true nature of the Holy Grail, even going so far as to murder his own assistant, because he believes that the future society free of the repression of the missing signifier will redeem this violence. Embarking on this project, he espouses a positivism widespread among those invested in the power of scientific thinking and research to solve all the questions of our symbolic universe. Even though practically no scientific thinkers worry about the repression of the sacred feminine as Leigh Teabing does, they nonetheless share his attitude toward the missing signifier, treating its status as missing, to put it in Kantian terms, in an empirical rather than a transcendental way.

For the positivistic scientific inquirer, all questions are fundamentally scientific questions, not ontological ones. As a result, we can hope that one day we might close the gap within the chain of signification. This hope animates Richard Dawkins as a thinker and even provides the basis for much of his enjoyment of existence (as it undoubtedly does for many scientists). As he puts it, "I am thrilled to be alive at a time when humanity is pushing against the limits of understanding. Even better, we may eventually discover that there are no limits."[14] A symbolic universe without any limits on our understanding would be one without a missing signifier.

Though Dawkins expresses excitement about the possibility of closing the gap within signification, this closure, were it possible, would bring an end to excitement and enjoyment as such. Our enjoyment depends on the missing signifier, even in the way that it produces the scientific drive to eliminate it. By reducing the missing signifier to the status of any old signifier, the positivist thinker like Dawkins (or like Leigh Teabing) fails to see the constitutive role of the limit for the structure of our symbolic universe. In this precise sense, the fundamentalist and the positivist have a fundamental similarity: both positions refuse to sustain the gap that animates the system of signification.

Of course, there are many scientists, unlike Dawkins, who respect the difference between the empirical gap that science works to eliminate and the ontological gap that it cannot touch. In *Rock of Ages: Science and Religion in the Fullness of Life*, Stephen Jay Gould maintains an absolute distinction between the scientific realm and the philosophical or theological. Science, for Gould, concerns itself with filling the empirical gap — with understanding the natural world — and not with filling the ontological gap — with finding the final answer to the mystery of existence itself.[15] Though Gould does not resemble Robert Langdon any more than Richard Dawkins resembles Leigh Teabing, his attitude toward the limitations of scientific inquiry mirrors Langdon's position relative to the missing signifier.

The Hermeneutic Ethos

The attitude advocated by *The Da Vinci Code* appears to avoid the fundamentalist's and positivist's closure of the gap through the novel's commitment to respecting the missing signifier without trying to force it to appear.

Though *The Da Vinci Code*, on the one hand, seems to share Teabing's desire for the revelation of the missing signifier, on the other hand, it endorses an attitude that leaves this signifier in its transcendent status and refuses to reduce it to being just another signifier in the way the positivist does. Both the novel and the film stress that the absent signifier must be respected in its absence rather than made present, though this attitude becomes clearest in the concluding shot of the film.

After the actual location of the Holy Grail (the tomb of Mary Magdalene) comes to Robert Langdon (Tom Hanks) while he is shaving in his Paris hotel, he hurries to trace the Paris meridian, or what the text refers to as the Rose Line, which he follows to the Louvre museum. The Paris meridian was an alternate prime meridian to the one running through Greenwich, and this gives it a special significance. Like the sacred feminine, it represents a repressed alternative. It represents the possibility of the world being mapped and configured in an entirely different way.[16] When he arrives at the Louvre, Langdon recognizes the location of the tomb and kneels down on top of La Pyramide Inversée, which, as he noted earlier, is itself a symbol of the sacred feminine.

At this point, the film cuts to a spiraling shot traveling down through La Pyramide Inversée that finally arrives at the hidden tomb, which is located beneath the inverted glass pyramid. Though in the novel Langdon goes underground to access the missing signifier, in the film he simply kneels reverently above it and prays as the circling movement of the camera indicates the respectful distance that one must maintain relative to this signifier. Though it gives the spectator a look at the coffin, the film's final shot returns to the image of Langdon praying, an image that conveys the presence of the sacred feminine through its absence. The film thus captures even more fully than the novel the type of relationship to the missing signifier that the novel itself privileges.

But in both the novel and the film, Langdon refuses to broadcast the revelation of the missing signifier because he recognizes that being attentive to it in its absence is more important than causing it to appear. This is an attitude that receives reinforcement from the Priory of Scion, the organization that safeguards the Grail. As one of the leading members of this organization puts it to Robert toward the end of the novel, "The Priory has always maintained that the Grail should *never* be unveiled. . . .

It is the mystery and wonderment that serve our souls, not the Grail itself. The beauty of the Grail lies in her ethereal nature."[17] According to this line of thought (advocated most strongly by *The Da Vinci Code* as a text), one must appreciate and advocate for the sacred feminine, but one must not destroy the transcendent status of this signifier.

Robert Langdon is the hero of *The Da Vinci Code* because he recognizes and appreciates the binary signifier, while most of us do not. He is able to read what he calls the sacred feminine in both classical and contemporary texts where it has been encoded. While the novel displays this ability throughout, the film highlights it by introducing us to Langdon during a lecture that he is giving in Paris to promote his new book on the sacred feminine. The scene begins in a crosscut with the dying Jacques Saunière (Jean-Pierre Marielle), who is struggling against his own imminent death in order to leave a coded message that only Langdon will be able to decipher. The use of crosscutting between Saunière constructing the code and the beginning of Langdon's lecture makes clear the link between the code and Langdon.

In the lecture that follows this introductory sequence, Langdon puts on a display of hermeneutical skill. Through a slideshow presentation, he shows the audience how little they understand about famous symbols because they fail to interpret them properly. Langdon shows the audience slides of various symbols and asks what associations the symbols bring to mind. Each time an audience member volunteers the obvious response — linking white robes to racism and the Ku Klux Klan, for example — Langdon gives the real historical meaning of the symbol. His hermeneutical bravado culminates with an example that undermines the iconography of the Christian Church. He shows a picture of a mother with a child that occasions the expected reactions: members of the audience shout out "Madonna and child" and then "Faith . . . Christianity." Langdon enjoys debunking this misconception as he tells the audience, "No, no, it's the pagan god Horus and his mother Isis centuries before the birth of Christ." As he speaks, the camera pans over a gasping, shocked audience. In his subsequent speech, Langdon emphasizes the need to get beyond "historical distortion" in order to get to "original truth," and the primordial original truth is, for Langdon, the sacred feminine, which only becomes visible, like the non-Christian origin of the image he shows, through the act of interpretation. In the terms of *The Da*

Vinci Code, to interpret is to engage oneself ethically in the struggle against injustice.

The Da Vinci Code became a popular success precisely because it champions this hermeneutic ethos, an ethos that predominates today. While it impels us in the direction of uncovering the binary signifier, this position also recognizes that the process has an absolute limit and that, as a result, it can never succeed once and for all. The best that we can do is to continually seek the missing signifier armed with the knowledge that we will find only its traces, not the signifier itself. Even though Langdon does discover the location of the Holy Grail at the end of the novel and film, his refusal to publicize it testifies to an implicit endorsement of the idea that the signifier must remain missing. The interpreter must always leave others with more interpretative work to be done. We do not live under the control of a patriarchal order, like Opus Dei in *The Da Vinci Code*, that works toward the elimination of the binary signifier. Instead, contemporary ideology encourages us to assume an attitude similar to that of Robert Langdon — to be aware of and respect what has been primordially excluded while recognizing the impossibility of fully including it.

The attitude manifests itself in the ideology of diversity. One must respect the difference of, say, the American Indian culture lost with white conquest — and even learn about it, perhaps adopt certain aspects of it for oneself — but one must not work for a full return of this culture. One must respect Islamic religious practices, but one must not attempt to impose them universally, which is precisely what the real believer would do. The project of infinite inquiry into the missing signifier ensures that no disruption will occur. The hermeneutic subject never goes far enough to effect a foundational change.

This sort of political attitude finds its ultimate expression in the advocates of radical democracy. These theorists, as the title of an essay by Ernesto Laclau and Lilian Zac has it, work at "minding the gap," at sustaining the absent point within signification by resisting both the attempt to deny the missing signifier and the attempt to render it present.[18] Chantal Mouffe provides the clearest articulation of the logic behind this position: "A pluralist democracy contains a paradox, since the very moment of its realization would see its disintegration. It should be conceived as a good that only exists so long as it cannot be reached. Such a democracy will therefore always be a democracy 'to come,' as conflict and antagonism are at the same time its condition of possibility and the condition of impossibility of its full realization."[19] For Mouffe and other advocates for radical democracy, the political subject must simultaneously devote itself to the missing signifier and to preventing its appearance. This represents a translation into political terms of a hermeneutical attitude toward this signifier.

The problem with this attitude stems from the way it implicitly conceives the absence of this signifier. According to its logic, the binary signifier is at once a transcendent absence and just an empirical one. With its attempt to navigate between these two definitions, the hermeneutical attitude thus falls into the error of both the fundamentalist and the positivist. Here, the missing signifier doesn't just found the signifying system but exists in a register wholly different from that system. In this sense, it is a transcendent signifier. For someone like Jacques Derrida (who exemplifies this logic), the binary signifier — what resists thought, as he puts it — exists in an alternate temporality or on an alternate plane. He claims: "What remains to be thought: the very thing that resists thought. It resists *in advance*, it gets out ahead. The rest gets there ahead of thought; it remains *in advance* of what is called thought."[20] Derrida emphasizes the separation between what resists thought — the missing signifier — and all efforts of thought, but at the same time he conceives of the deconstructive project as an attempt to pursue the resistance of thought within thought.

The hermeneutic thinker constantly embarks on impossible tasks, tasks that she or he does not in fact want to realize. But the pursuit of the impossible task has the effect of reducing the missing signifier to an empirical absence within the chain of signification. If one really believed the missing signifier to be transcendent, one would not work toward the goal of revealing it. In *The Da Vinci Code* Robert Langdon has a clear idea about the nature of the missing signifier, and this idea informs his interpretative pursuit of it. The very pursuit itself testifies to a conception of the gap within signification as an empirical one. As a result, the hermeneutic thinker renders the missing signifier both transcendent and empirical when in fact it is neither one nor the other. The status of the missing signifier is transcendental. Its absence serves only to shape the signifying structure in the same way that Kant conceives the regulative ideas of reason shaping the structure of our understanding.

The Immanence of the Missing Signifier

The key to responding to the absence of the binary signifier lies in recognizing its presence within the signifying structure, or, to put it in Derrida's terms, in recognizing the immanence of what resists thought within thought itself. This signifier does not exist, even as a trace, which is what Lacan is getting at when he insists that "the Woman does not exist" or "the Other does not exist." Recognizing the nonexistence of this signifier changes the way we relate to the signifying structure and has clear political consequences.

Rather than respecting the gap in signification as the placeholder for the missing signifier, we should recognize that nothing exists in the gap and that nothing really is, for us, something. The gap marks the point at which senselessness itself is included in the world of signification. Nothing or senselessness is not a specter that haunts the system but the very basis of the symbolic system. The absence of the binary signifier constitutes the social order as such, which means that this missing signifier is not simply absent but present as an absence. The missing signifier is already here, already within the signifying structure, constantly making its effects felt on this structure.

When we recognize the transcendental status of the missing signifier, we can give up the impossible pursuit of it that dominates the contemporary popular and intellectual landscape. In *Seminar XI* Lacan distinguishes between hermeneutics and psychoanalytic interpretation. He says: "The way of developing signification offered by hermeneutics is confused, in many minds, with what analysis calls *interpretation*. It so happens that, although this interpretation cannot in any way be conceived in the same way as the aforementioned hermeneutics, hermeneutics, on the other hand, makes ready use of interpretation."[21] Hermeneutics embarks on an endless quest for the impossible signifier that it can never find — it is an unending process of seeking — but psychoanalytic interpretation finds without seeking.

In order to articulate just this point, Lacan alludes to Picasso: "Personally, I have never regarded myself as a researcher. As Picasso once said, to the shocked surprise of those around him — *I do not seek, I find.*"[22] To find, in the sense that Lacan uses the term here, signifies recognizing the missing signifier as a structuring presence. The endless seeking of the hermeneutic position functions as a barrier to genuine political engagement; it allows the subject to avoid the political act of identifying itself with the missing signifier. This identification is the result of the finding that Lacan mentions. The psychoanalytic position fully takes up the advocacy of the missing signifier, and it can do so because this signifier is not external to the signifying structure but ensconced within it as that which gives the structure its form, so that there is no risk that the identification will transform it into a full presence within the structure.

The missing signifier does not reside elsewhere, on a separate plane, but rather operates within the signifying structure. Even the most banal moments of everyday life center around the missing signifier, which animates them with whatever vitality they possess. Every aspect of the signifying structure takes the missing signifier as its point of departure because this gap marks the point at which the structure opens itself to the new and different. We affirm the missing signifier not just when we politicize ourselves through fidelity to the exceptional event that occurs in the space of the missing signifier or void but through all the variegations of our everyday lives.[23] Every aspect of the signifying structure is already informed by the gap. We can identify with the missing signifier in its absence, and this is the gesture that a genuine politics demands.

In the contemporary political landscape, the figure of the immigrant often occupies the position of the missing binary signifier. There is no legitimate place for the immigrant within the ruling symbolic structure, and this absence leads to calls for the deportation or elimination of immigrants. In response to the conservative push around the world for tough national policies against illegal immigration, leftists have responded by calling into question the idea of illegality with the slogan, "No One Is Illegal." Those who take up this position work toward a future world where illegality itself would be eliminated, where the absent binary signifier could be fully revealed, even though they remain aware that this future is impossible. The problem with this slogan and the political position informing it lies in its failure to grasp precisely how the missing signifier interacts with the signifying structure.

Because the missing signifier is present as an absence, it exerts a constant pressure. The more successful leftists are in promulgating the idea that we should not consider any immigrants as illegal, the more strenuously some other group will be located in the position of the missing binary signifier. The leftist fight against the idea of illegality, despite the good intentions of those involved, will inevitably backfire. No amount of political effort will eliminate the position of the missing binary signifier, nor will it succeed in vacating this signifier of any content. There will always be someone in the position of the immigrant, but the question concerns how we relate to this structurally requisite position. The only political solution lies in abandoning the quest for a solution. It involves identification with this signifier rather than in the effort to integrate it successfully. Instead of attempting to conceive of the missing signifier from the perspective of the signifying system, we must conceive of the signifying system from the perspective of the missing signifier.[24]

By doing so, we would see that the missing signifier, despite appearances, does not concern those who are not properly represented. It concerns the system of signification itself, the law itself. The absence in the law is the founding moment of the law, not an otherness that the law cannot accommodate. This means that the struggle against illegal immigration does not concern illegal immigrants outside the legal social structure, even though they are clearly affected by this struggle. It concerns, instead, the status of the upstanding citizen within the social structure. By responding on the level of the immigrant — or by responding to patriarchy on the level of the feminine — the political battle is already lost.[25] The missing signifier is not an opening to a mysterious otherness; it is the unacknowledged way that the symbolic structure manifests itself.

Rather than the slogan "No One Is Illegal," a politics of identification with the missing binary signifier would involve a slightly different one, something like "No One Is Legal." The missing signifier does not hold the key to the future full citizenship of all subjects; instead, it prevents the full citizenship of any subjects. The structure of citizenship itself depends on the absence of the signifier for the illegal immigrant, and, as a result, the legal citizen cannot avoid this absence. In order to be effective in the last instance, our political efforts must emphasize the missing signifier as an internal dislocation of the structure of legal citizenship, to continue with the example. Rather than working to include previously excluded subjects within the structure of signification, we must work instead to reveal how those inside are themselves already excluded: there is no inclusion that does not partake of the fundamental exclusion that defines the structure. Legal citizens must come to recognize that legality doesn't exist. Fostering this recognition is the essence of a psychoanalytic politics, even though it fails to provide the comfort of the more traditional slogan.

The Feminine Signifier Isn't

The Da Vinci Code presents itself as a feminist text despite the fact that the author of the novel, the director of the film, and the hero of both are men. One might object to its feminism, of course, on exactly these grounds: it envisions feminist politics from a fundamentally masculine perspective, a perspective unable to see the feminine as a radical alternative to patriarchy. But the error of *The Da Vinci Code* lies in the opposite direction. It fails to recognize how, as Simone de Beauvoir perspicuously points out, "the problem of woman has always been a problem of men."[26] That is, the missing signifier of the feminine has no existence outside the symbolic structure that defines it, and this signifier is important insofar as it undermines all identity deriving from that structure.

The signifier of the feminine trips up male identity from within, not from without, which is why it is the concern of men rather than women. Beauvoir's statement suggests that feminism should properly be a project for the male subject, though there are few capable of taking it up in a way that avows rather than elides the nonexistence of the feminine signifier. Although it moves in the direction of a feminism that concerns men, *The Da Vinci Code* finally refuses to contend with the internal abyss that the missing signifier marks, and it instead erects an ideal image of woman to attach to that signifier.

In contrast, Simone de Beauvoir grasps the abyssal status of the signifier of the feminine. She sees that insofar as it signifies an essential or sacred feminine, it signifies nothing. As she puts it, "Insofar as woman is considered the absolute Other, that is — whatever magic powers she has — as the inessential, it is precisely impossible to regard her as another subject."[27] As long as woman is associated with the binary signifier, she cannot accede to the alternate form of subjectivity that *The Da Vinci Code* attempts to posit in her. Instead, woman will remain an absolute void, an absence that cannot be integrated into the ruling symbolic structure.

In the last instance, Beauvoir's own political project involves working to eliminate the association of woman with the missing signifier and thus to constitute an egalitarian society in which no one bears the mark of exclusion. But as long as one remains attached to task of the including everything that is missing — even if one views this as an impossible ideal never to be realized, as Derrida and Robert Langdon do — one transforms the absent signifier into an actual one when in fact it is nothing but a certain necessary distortion within signification itself. Beauvoir recognizes the internal limit that the missing signifier marks and then attempts to overcome this limit through advocating for inclusion. Inclusion at once goes too far and doesn't go far enough.

One can neither elevate everyone to the status of the empowered (male) subject nor eliminate entirely the idea of the subject. But one can combat the idea of the subject as an integral whole. It is on this ground that one might struggle against the repressiveness of patriarchal society. When one opposes male and female in order to exclude the latter, one presupposes the wholeness of the male subject and fails to recognize the way in which the incompleteness of the signifying structure actually serves to constitute this subjectivity. The point is not simply the banal one that the concept of the male depends on the existence of its opposite but that the missing signifier is part of the concept: the barrier to "male" functioning as a complete identity is an internal one. The task of a psychoanalytic politics involves bringing conceptual location of the feminine — or the missing signifier — to light.

The missing signifier indicates the failure of any set to close itself as a whole. By emphasizing this failure through one's political activity, one works to effect a fundamental change in the relationship between inclusion and exclusion. As long as the logic of wholeness or success predominates, inclusion within a set will provide a certain symbolic identity for those who are included, and those who are excluded will experience the absence of this identity. The logic of the whole secures a stable barrier that creates vastly different experiences on each of its sides, but this stable barrier is always an illusory one. The logic of the failure of any closure does not eliminate the barrier between inside and outside or deconstruct the difference between inclusion and exclusion. Instead, it reveals the speculative identity of inclusion and exclusion. The two positions become visible as the same through their very difference.

With a basis in the logic of failed closure, political struggle in the psychoanalytic sense must involve an effort to change the terrain of the political as such without eliminating this terrain in the process of changing it. Politics requires the enemy or the outsider. It requires a gap within the signifying structure where there can be no understanding. But psychoanalytic thought allows us to relate to this gap — and to the enemy — in a new way. We cannot understand the gap, but we can identify with it as that which defines us, as that which produces our enjoyment rather than destroying it. This is, as Juan-David Nasio has it, the goal of the psychoanalytic process. He claims: "Before the analysis, the loss had been a badly healed scar, while at the end of analysis there is also a loss, but a loss carried out in the manner of a cut with creative effects."[28] The gap in signification becomes a fecund limit, a limit that we enjoy. This type of recognition is not confined, as Nasio's comment may suggest, to the psychoanalytic clinic. It is possible wherever we bring psychoanalytic thinking to bear on our situation. We can take the logic of the clinic and unleash it in our political practice. In fact, this logic is inseparable from any authentic politics.

When male subjects identify themselves with the feminine and begin to think of themselves in these terms, they do not, of course, immediately transform the material conditions that inform this identity. Actual women continue to live as second-class citizens. Many would object to such an identification for just this reason. But it does have the effect of reinventing subjectivity as such and, in this way, leading to the transformation of the material conditions of women. If men began to take up the identification with the feminine, we would not live in a world without divisions; instead, we would live in a world with an internal rather than an external division. The divide between male and female subjectivity would become what it already is: a division within the subject itself.

The recognition that the missing signifier operates within the signifying structure rather than outside deprives politics of the long-cherished ideal of total inclusion, an ideal that often animates concrete struggles, but it provides political action with a new form. Instead of working directly to expand the umbrella of rights to include more of those excluded, the political act would involve the refusal, on the part of those on the inside, to accept the benefits that insider status provides. Recognizing that the missing signifier is internal to the signifying structure, the male subject insists on taking up the relationship to the symbolic structure that the female subject bears.[29] The question of feminism becomes a personal question for every male subject. By personalizing the question, male subjects affirm their own failure to attain the status of real men and thereby testify to the void that undermines — and defines — every identity.

Because of its transcendental status, the missing signifier is the stumbling block that the attempt to lift repression continually comes up against. But psychoanalytic thought offers us a unique vision of this signifier as nothing but an internal torsion within the signifying structure. This internal torsion serves as the basis for politics insofar as it permanently dislodges the structure's mastery from within. The obstacle to lifting repression is in fact the basis for our political activity, but we must recognize it as such. This is the psychoanalytic conception of politics.[30] By identifying with the absent signifier, we do not insist on subverting the system but on adhering to the truth of the signifying system and forcing that truth to manifest itself.

Conclusion

A SOCIETY OF THE DEATH DRIVE

There is no path leading from the death drive to utopia. The death drive undermines every attempt to construct a utopia; it is the enemy of the good society. It is thus not surprising that political thought from Plato onward has largely ignored this psychic force of repetition and negation. But this does not mean that psychoanalytic thought concerning the death drive has only a negative value for political theorizing. It is possible to conceive of a positive politics of the death drive.

The previous chapters have attempted to lay out the political implications of the death drive, and, on this basis, we can sketch what a society founded on a recognition of the death drive might look like. Such a recognition would not involve a radical transformation of society: in one sense, it would leave everything as it is. In contemporary social arrangements, the death drive subverts progress with repetition and leads to the widespread sacrifice of self-interest for the enjoyment of the sacrifice itself. This structure is impervious to change and to all attempts at amelioration. But in another sense, the recognition of the death drive would change everything. Recognizing the centrality of the death drive would not eliminate the proclivity to sacrifice for the sake of enjoyment, but it would change our relationship to this sacrifice. Rather than being done for the sake of an ultimate enjoyment to be achieved in the future, it would be done for its own sake.

The fundamental problem with the effort to escape the death drive and pursue the good is that it leaves us unable to locate where our enjoyment lies. By positing a future where we will attain the ultimate enjoyment (either through the purchase of the perfect commodity or through a transcendent romantic union or through the attainment of some heavenly paradise), we replace the partial enjoyment of the death drive with the image of a complete enjoyment to come. There is no question of fully enjoying our submission to the death drive. We will always remain alienated from our mode of enjoying. As Adrian Johnston rightly points out, "Transgressively 'overcoming' the impediments of the drives doesn't enable one to simply enjoy enjoyment."[1] But we can transform our relationship to the impediments that block the full realization of our drive. We can see the impediments as the internal product of the death drive rather than as an external limit.

The enjoyment that the death drive provides, in contrast to the form of enjoyment proffered by capitalism, religion, and utopian politics, is at once infinite and limited. This oxymoronic form of enjoyment operates in the way that the concept does in Hegel's *Logic*. The concept attains its infinitude not through endless progress toward a point that always remains beyond and out of reach but through including the beyond as a beyond within itself. As Hegel puts it, "The universality of the concept is the *achieved beyond*, whereas that bad infinity remains afflicted with a beyond which is unattainable but remains a mere *progression* to infinity."[2] That is to say, the concept transforms an external limit into an internal one and thereby becomes both infinite and limited. The infinitude of the concept is nothing but the concept's own self-limitation.

The enjoyment that the death drive produces also achieves its infinitude through self-limitation. It revolves around a lost object that exists only insofar as it is lost, and it relates to this object as the vehicle for the infinite unfurling of its movement. The lost object operates as the self-limitation of the death drive through which the drive produces an infinite enjoyment. Rather than acting as a mark of the drive's finitude, the limitation that the lost object introduces provides access to infinity.

A society founded on a recognition of the death drive would be one that viewed its limitations as the source of its infinite enjoyment rather than an obstacle to that enjoyment. To take the clearest and most traumatic example in recent history, the recognition of the death drive in 1930s Germany would have conceived the figure of the Jew not as the barrier to the ultimate enjoyment that must therefore be eliminated but as the internal limit through which German society attained its enjoyment. As numerous theorists have said, the appeal of Nazism lay in its ability to mobilize the enjoyment of the average German through pointing out a threat to that enjoyment. The average German under Nazism could enjoy the figure of the Jew as it appeared in the form of an obstacle, but it is possible to recognize the obstacle not as an external limit but as an internal one. In this way, the figure of the Jew would become merely a figure for the average German rather than a position embodied by actual Jews.

Closer to home, one would recognize the terrorist as a figure representing the internal limit of global capitalist society. Far from serving as an obstacle to the ultimate enjoyment in that society, the terrorist provides a barrier where none otherwise exists and thereby serves as the vehicle through which capitalist society attains its enjoyment. The absence of explicit limitations within contemporary global capitalism necessitates such a figure: if terrorists did not exist, global capitalist society would have to invent them. But recognizing the terrorist as the internal limit of global capitalist society would mean the end of terrorism. This recognition would transform the global landscape and deprive would-be terrorists of the libidinal space within which to act. Though some people may continue to blow up buildings, they would cease to be terrorists in the way that we now understand the term.

A self-limiting society would still have real battles to fight. There would remain a need for this society to defend itself against external threats and against the cruelty of the natural universe. Perhaps it would require nuclear weapons in space to defend against comets or meteors that would threaten to wipe out human life on the planet. But it would cease positing the ultimate enjoyment in vanquishing an external threat or surpassing a natural limit. The external limit would no longer stand in for a repressed internal one. Such a society would instead enjoy its own internal limitations and merely address external limits as they came up.

Psychoanalytic theory never preaches, and it cannot help us to construct a better society. But it can help us to subtract the illusion of the good from our own society. By depriving us of this illusion, it has the ability to transform our thinking about politics. With the assistance of psychoanalytic thought, we might reconceive politics in a direction completely opposed to that articulated by Aristotle, to which I alluded in the introduction. In the *Politics*, Aristotle asserts: "Every state is a community of some kind, and every community is established with a view to some good; for everyone always acts in order to obtain that which they think good. But, if all communities aim at some good, the state or political community, which is the highest of all, and which embraces all the rest, aims at good in a greater degree than any other, and at the highest good."[3] Though later political thinkers have obviously departed from Aristotle concerning the question of the content of the good society, few have thought of politics in terms opposed to the good. This is what psychoanalytic thought introduces.

If we act on the basis of enjoyment rather than the good, this does not mean that we can simply construct a society that privileges enjoyment in an overt way. An open society with no restrictions on sexual activity, drug use, food consumption, or play in general would not be a more enjoyable one than our own. That is the sure path to impoverishing our ability to enjoy, as the aftermath of the 1960s has made painfully clear. One must arrive at enjoyment indirectly. A society centered around the death drive would not be a better society, nor would it entail less suffering. Rather than continually sacrificing for the sake of the good, we would sacrifice the good for the sake of enjoyment. A society centered around the death drive would allow us to recognize that we enjoy the lost object only insofar as it remains lost.

Notes

INTRODUCTION

1. The great Marxist defense of sacrifice for the sake of a future enjoyment comes from Maurice Merleau-Ponty in his wrongfully dismissed *Humanism and Terror*. There Merleau-Ponty defends the violence of Stalinism by pointing out the fundamental difference between Communist violence and oppressive capitalist violence. He claims: "Bourgeois justice adopts the past as its precedent; revolutionary justice adopts the future. It judges in the name of a Truth that the Revolution is about to make true" (Maurice Merleau-Ponty, *Humanism and Terror: An Essay on the Communist Problem*, trans. John O'Neill [Boston: Beacon Press, 1969], 28). The new world that present violent sacrifice makes possible justifies the sacrifice here and now, not simply retroactively after the new world comes about. Because Communist sacrifice aims at the creation of a new world, it has a valence different from capitalist sacrifice.

2. Sigmund Freud, *New Introductory Lectures on Psycho-analysis*, in *The Standard Edition of the Complete Psychological Works of Sigmund Freud*, vol. 22, trans. and ed. James Strachey (London: Hogarth Press, 1964), 181.

3. Sigmund Freud, *Civilization and Its Discontents*, in *The Standard Edition of the Complete Psychological Works of Sigmund Freud*, vol. 21, trans. and ed. James Strachey (London: Hogarth Press, 1961), 115. One of the seemingly damning critiques of Freud from the Left consists in claiming that he directed all of his political statements against Communism and few against Fascism or Nazism. This is a thesis made popular by Michel Onfray in his vitriolic attack on Freud, during which he contends, "One would search in vain in the 6,000 pages of the complete works of Freud for a frank critique of capitalism, but equally of fascism or of National Socialism — while one will find at several points very argumentative attacks against socialism, communism, and Bolshevism. Between 1922, the date of Mussolini's arrival in power, and 1939, the date of his death, Freud published more than 1,000 pages in which

one finds no critical analysis of European fascism" (Michel Onfray, *Le crépuscule d'une idole: L'affabulation freudienne* [Paris: Grasset, 2010], 477–78, my translation). What Onfray's critique misses is that Freud's statements about Communism always reflect a tinge of admiration for the project itself and, more importantly, that the entirety of psychoanalysis functions as a condemnation of Fascism. Freud spells out his criticisms of Communism and not of Fascism precisely because he finds something fundamentally appealing in the former and not in the latter.

4. Juliet Mitchell, *Psychoanalysis and Feminism: Freud, Reich, Laing and Women* (New York: Random House, 1974), xiii, Mitchell's emphasis. Mitchell's contention that psychoanalysis has a political value for what it reveals has widespread echoes within feminism. In her articulation of a feminist film theory, Laura Mulvey makes a claim very similar to that of Mitchell. In the opening of her landmark essay "Visual Pleasure and Narrative Cinema," Mulvey explains: "Psychoanalytic theory is appropriated here as a political weapon, demonstrating the way the unconscious of patriarchal society has structured film form" (Laura Mulvey, "Visual Pleasure and Narrative Cinema," in *Movies and Methods*, vol. 2, ed. Bill Nichols [Berkeley: University of California Press, 1985], 305).

5. Feminist theoretical attacks throughout the twentieth century are numerous, though they have abated significantly in recent years as an increasing number of feminist theorists have come to take up an explicitly psychoanalytic outlook. Some of the most significant critiques include Simone de Beauvoir, *The Second Sex*, trans. Constance Borde and Sheila Malovany-Chevallier (New York: Alfred A. Knopf, 2010); Betty Friedan, *The Feminine Mystique* (New York: Norton, 2001); and Shulamith Firestone, *The Dialectic of Sex: The Case for Feminist Revolution* (New York: Morrow, 1970).

6. One of the predominant contentions among those who appropriate psychoanalysis for political ends is that one must always historicize its insights. This claim, while seeming commonsensical on the surface, attests to the hegemony of a historicism that is fundamentally at odds with psychoanalysis. By historicizing the insights of psychoanalysis, one effectively dilutes these insights of their power.

7. See Aristotle, *Politics*, trans. B. Jowett, in *The Complete Works of Aristotle*, ed. Jonathan Barnes (Princeton NJ: Princeton University Press, 1984), 2:1986–2129.

8. See John Rawls, *A Theory of Justice*, rev. ed. (Cambridge MA: Harvard University Press, 1999).

9. Jacques Lacan, *The Seminar of Jacques Lacan, Book VII: The Ethics of Psychoanalysis, 1959–1960*, trans. Dennis Porter (New York: Norton, 1992), 70.

10. Conservative political theorist Carl Schmitt attacks the progressive attempt to do away with the enemy. He sees the friend/enemy distinction as essential to politics, but sustaining this distinction has for him the status of a good. Even though we don't tend to think of war as part of a good society, Schmitt does. War, which has its basis in the friend/enemy distinction, makes social life worth living.

Without it, life becomes merely "interesting." Due to the extreme conservatism of this position, Schmitt reveals the extent to which the idea of the good seems inextricable from politics. For more on Schmitt's theorization of the friend/enemy distinction, see chapter 6.

11. Julia Kristeva, *The Sense and Non-sense of Revolt: The Powers and Limits of Psychoanalysis*, trans. Jeanine Herman (New York: Columbia University Press, 2000), 29. For a further development of Kristeva's understanding of psychoanalysis as a politics of revolt, see also Julia Kristeva, *Intimate Revolt: The Powers and Limits of Psychoanalysis*, trans. Jeanine Herman (New York: Columbia University Press, 2002).

12. See Claude Lévi-Strauss, *The Elementary Structures of Kinship*, trans. James Harle Bell, John Richard von Sturmer, and Rodney Needham (Boston: Beacon Press, 1969).

13. Karl Marx, *Capital: A Critique of Political Economy, Volume Three*, trans. David Fernbach (New York: Penguin, 1981), 358–59.

14. Sigmund Freud, "'Civilized' Sexual Morality and Modern Nervous Illness," in *The Standard Edition of the Complete Psychological Works of Sigmund Freud*, vol. 9, trans. and ed. James Strachey (London: Hogarth Press, 1959), 204.

15. Sigmund Freud, "The Psycho-analytic View of Psychogenic Disturbance of Vision," in *The Standard Edition of the Complete Psychological Works of Sigmund Freud*, vol. 11, trans. and ed. James Strachey (London: Hogarth Press, 1957), 215.

16. As Reich sees it, the sexuality of the child provides a model for this unrepressed sexuality because it has not yet succumbed to the repressive forces of society. Idealizing the naturalness of unrepressed infantile sexuality, he contends: "Here, in the aliveness of infantile nature lies the guarantee for a society of really free human beings, and only here" (Wilhelm Reich, *The Sexual Revolution: Toward a Self-Governing Character Structure*, rev. ed., trans. Theodore P. Wolfe [New York: Farrar, Straus and Giroux, 1945], 259).

17. There is a version of the death drive in Erich Fromm's thought that he calls "necrophilia," but necrophilia emerges only out of a failure of biophilia. It is not an independent drive, as the death drive is for Freud.

18. Marcuse accepts the idea that we can never overcome repression altogether, but he believes, in keeping with the early Freud, that we can lower or even eliminate what he calls "surplus repression," the repression that is not necessary to keep society functioning but results from the structure of an exploitative society. Marcuse's work thus avoids utopianism—no matter how free our society becomes, it will never overcome the existence of a certain level of necessary repression—but he cannot incorporate Freud's discovery of the death drive into his political vision. It appears here only in its evanescence beneath the power of eros. He writes: "Eros, freed from surplus-repression, would be strengthened, and the strengthened Eros would, as it were, absorb the objective of the death instinct" (Herbert Marcuse, *Eros and Civilization: A Philosophical Inquiry into Freud* [Boston: Beacon Press, 1955], 235).

19. Marcuse's reduction of the death drive to aggression was common throughout much of the history of psychoanalytic thought, and it was Melanie Klein and her followers who provided the main impetus for this reduction. It is primarily Jacques Lacan who breaks from this way of thinking and begins to divorce the death drive from aggression and to conceive of it as the paradigm for all drives. Rather than stressing aggressive destruction, Lacan thinks of the death drive in terms of the repetitive encircling movement.

20. Freud, *Civilization and Its Discontents*, 145.

21. Jacques Lacan, "Kant with Sade," in *Écrits: The First Complete Edition in English*, trans. Bruce Fink (New York: Norton, 2006), 656.

22. Sheila Kunkle interprets the sadistic carving up of the other's body during the mutilations that occur in genocidal violence as the manifestation of the subject's effort to destroy itself, to enact loss on itself: "The carving up of others' bodies marks ... the attempt to deal with the uncanny intimate kernel of one's being, the Thing that is too unbearable to face and that is now found directly in the body of the other" (Sheila Kunkle, "The Ugly Jouissance of Genocide," *Journal for the Psychoanalysis of Culture and Society* 4, no. 1 [1999]: 121).

23. Norman O. Brown, *Life against Death: The Psychoanalytical Meaning of History*, 2nd ed. (Middletown CT: Wesleyan University Press, 1985), 284.

24. Jacques Derrida, *Specters of Marx: The State of Debt, the Work of Mourning, and the New International*, trans. Peggy Kamuf (New York: Routledge, 1994), 59.

25. Derrida insists repeatedly that justice-to-come is the basis of deconstruction and at the same time what is immune to deconstruction. In *Specters of Marx* he explains: "A deconstructive thinking, the one that matters to me here, has always pointed out the irreducibility of affirmation and therefore of the promise, as well as the undeconstructibility of a certain idea of justice (dissociated here from law)" (Derrida, *Specters of Marx*, 90).

26. Even before Derrida's political and ethical turn in the late 1980s and early 1990s, the idea of progress nonetheless animates his thought through deconstruction's critique of metaphysical binarism. At times, the call for a political change within philosophical thought becomes explicit. In the opening essay of *Writing and Difference*, for instance, Derrida contends: "It is necessary to seek new concepts and new models, an *economy* escaping this system of metaphysical oppositions" (Jacques Derrida, "Force and Signification," in *Writing and Difference*, trans. Alan Bass [Chicago: University of Chicago Press, 1978], 19). Here, long before Derrida aligns deconstruction with a certain form of Marxism, he calls for a new economy, and he clearly views this new economy as progress; otherwise, he would simply content himself with metaphysics as it already exists.

27. Immanuel Kant, "An Answer to the Question: 'What Is Enlightenment?,'" in *Practical Philosophy*, trans. Mary J. Gregor (Cambridge: Cambridge University Press, 1996), 18, Kant's emphasis.

28. The Enlightenment conception of the relationship between knowledge and progress informs George Santayana's famous claim that "those who cannot remember the past are condemned to repeat it" (George Santayana, *The Life of Reason or The Phases of Human Progress: Reason in Common Sense* [New York: Scribner's, 1924], 284).

29. Jacques Lacan, "Le séminaire XXI: Les non-dupes errent, 1973–1974," manuscript, session of 23 April 1974, my translation.

30. The unending questions of the child addressed to the parent seem to challenge the psychoanalytic idea that there is no desire for knowledge, no innate curiosity. But these questions are never just random questions about the nature of the world. The child poses them in relation to the desire of the parent. As Lacan puts it, "Everything that [a child] poses as a question, finally, is done to satisfy what he/she supposes that the Other wants him/her to ask" ("Le séminaire XXI," session of 9 May 1974, my translation).

31. Sigmund Freud, "Analysis Terminable and Interminable," in *The Standard Edition of the Complete Psychological Works of Sigmund Freud*, vol. 23, trans. and ed. James Strachey (London: Hogarth Press, 1964), 252.

32. To say that progress is an illusion is not to say that progress never occurs in certain empirical instances (like from the Middles Ages to modernity). It implies rather that progress never occurs ontologically: no amount of progress can ever heal the loss that founds subjectivity, even though this is precisely what the ideology of progress promises. And even instances of empirical progress — say, the civil rights struggle of the 1960s in the United States — are accomplished through a repression whose content inevitably returns (in the form of segregated housing, private schools for affluent whites, and so on). This is not to say that one must accept something like racism as inevitable but only that the investment in the idea of progress always produces its opposite as an obscene supplement — and this is what the embrace of repetition works to counter.

33. A leftist politics based on hope for a different future becomes especially tenuous under capitalism because the latter relies on hope as one of its predominant ideological foundations. Capitalism takes hold of subjects insofar as it offers the commodity as that which will heal an ontological chasm within them. The commodity becomes the elixir for the gap that defines subjectivity, but it acts in this way only in the future tense and thus nourishes hope without ever fulfilling it. It is very easy for hopeful leftists to fall prey to the hopefulness of capitalist ideology. In this sense, the conversion of student radicals from the 1960s into successful dentists should not be surprising.

1. THE FORMATION OF SUBJECTIVITY

1. The difference between Schopenhauer and Nietzsche concerns the attitude that they adopt toward the will. In the vein of Buddhism, Schopenhauer views the will as a curse that the subject must try to escape, whereas Nietzsche embraces the

will as the source of all creative power. Though they both recognize that the will brings suffering, Nietzsche opts to embrace this suffering, while Schopenhauer seeks some respite from it through transcending will. Despite this radical divergence, they share a turn away from the priority of knowledge that was prominent in the tradition of Western philosophy.

2. This is the problem with the assertion that Freud's thought simply elaborates the insights of Nietzsche. This is the position of Michel Onfray, who fails to see that Freud breaks decisively with Nietzsche's biologism. Onfray writes: "I pose the hypothesis that Freud represses a constitutive Nietzscheanism that is the base of his own thought. Because, like Nietzsche, Freud thought the body as the great reason, as the ultimate anchoring point of everything, *including the unconscious*" (Michel Onfray, *Apostille au "Crépuscule": Pour une psychanalyse non freudienne* [Paris: Grasset, 2010], 77, my translation). In order to transform Freud into a Nietzschean, Onfray must ignore a sine qua non of psychoanalysis — that the subject and the unconscious emerge out of the collision between biology and culture. The unconscious is not a remnant of biology that remains after the entrance into culture but rather an excess or deformation that owes its existence directly to culture.

3. It is actually Hegel, rather than Schopenhauer and Nietzsche, who has the most proximity to Freud in the history of Western philosophy. Even though Hegel retains the subject of knowledge, the entirety of his thought aims at showing the fundamental limitation that the project of knowledge cannot escape. Absolute knowledge, for Hegel, names the point at which the subject recognizes an unsurpassable limit, a point of nonknowledge, within its field of knowledge. This point of nonknowledge is, though Hegel wouldn't have put it like this, the unconscious desire of the subject embarked on the project of knowledge.

4. Sigmund Freud, "On Narcissism: An Introduction," in *The Standard Edition of the Complete Psychological Works of Sigmund Freud*, vol. 14, trans. and ed. James Strachey (New York: Norton, 1957), 77.

5. Jacques Lacan, *Le séminaire, livre IV: La relation d'object, 1956–1957*, ed. Jacques-Alain Miller (Paris: Seuil, 1994), 36, my translation.

6. Sigmund Freud, "Negation," in *The Standard Edition of the Complete Psychological Works of Sigmund Freud*, vol. 19, trans. and ed. James Strachey (New York: Norton, 1961), 237–38.

7. Richard Boothby, *Freud as Philosopher: Metapsychology after Lacan* (New York: Routledge, 2001), 188.

8. Boothby, *Freud as Philosopher*, 189. In *Seminar X*, Lacan notes: "We do not live our lives, whoever we are, without ceaselessly offering to some unknown divinity the sacrifice of some little mutilation, valid or not, that we impose on ourselves in the field of our desires" (Jacques Lacan, *Le séminaire, livre X: L'angoisse, 1962–1963*, ed. Jacques-Alain Miller [Paris: Seuil, 2004], 320–21, my translation).

9. Lacan's name for the lost object is the *objet petit a*, a concept that he invented while discussing the agalma that Alcibiades sees in Socrates in Plato's *Symposium*. The agalma in Lacan's eighth seminar on the transference, after transmutations in the two intervening seminars, becomes the famous objet petit a in his eleventh seminar, *The Four Fundamental Concepts of Psychoanalysis*. See Jacques Lacan, *Le séminaire, livre VIII: Le transfert, 1960–1961*, ed. Jacques-Alain Miller (Paris: Seuil, 2001); and Jacques Lacan, *The Four Fundamental Concepts of Psychoanalysis*, trans. Alan Sheridan, ed. Jacques-Alain Miller (New York: Norton, 1978).

10. See Naomi Wolf, *The Beauty Myth: How Images of Beauty Are Used against Women* (New York: Doubleday, 1991).

11. One might hazard the wild psychoanalytic explanation of Naomi Wolf's embrace of the right-wing Tea Party after the election of Barack Obama as the ultimate result of her failure to see anorexia as a political act rather than simply a symptom of female oppression. This reading of anorexia reflects an inability to grasp the nothingness of the object, the precise inability that animates the thinking of the Tea Party and prevents it from being a radical, rather than a reactionary, political movement.

12. Elizabeth Grosz, *Volatile Bodies: Toward a Corporeal Feminism* (Bloomington: Indiana University Press, 1994), 40.

13. The privileged status of the anorexic testifies to the precariousness of the intersection of the psyche and politics. If our society was more egalitarian and had a less oppressive ideal of female beauty, it would have no anorexics. The structure of the drive would manifest itself elsewhere.

14. The initial bond with the maternal figure, either in the womb or in early infancy, does not provide an originary completeness for the child. Even in this apparently perfect bond, absence intrudes, and it is only after the fact that the bond gains the wholeness that we imagine it to have.

15. Karl Marx, *Capital: A Critique of Political Economy, Volume Three*, trans. David Fernbach (New York: Penguin, 1981), 959.

16. Georg Simmel, *The Philosophy of Money*, 2nd ed., trans. Tom Bottomore and David Frisby (New York: Routledge, 1990), 80.

17. Freud's insistence that psychoanalysis would simply not work if it was given away for free or at a discount price stems from his understanding of the constitutive dimension of loss. The analysand's sacrifice of money gives the psychoanalytic session value that it otherwise does not have. In his analysis of Freud, Erich Fromm reduces this insistence on payment to Freud's own obsession with money, and Fromm himself proudly offered psychoanalysis for free to those who were unable to pay. The problem with this critique and this practice is that it completely abandons the theory of value inherent in psychoanalytic theory and posits no alternate theory. For Fromm, there is value simply in life itself.

18. The labor theory of value, which was discovered by Adam Smith and then worked out by Marx, takes the association of loss and value as its basic premise. The loss (of time, of energy, of freedom) that occurs through work produces a valuable object that one can sell. An object that demands no work can produce no profit, and this is true even of objects that one finds in the natural world rather than creates. This is why it is only rare metals that require work to find or to mine, like gold or diamonds, that have value.

19. Though there are of course many ideologies, what all ideologies share is the idea that one can profit on one's loss. For capitalist ideology, the loss involved with hard work results in wealth; for Christian ideology, the sacrifice of immediate pleasures produces an eternal reward; for Marxist ideology, the struggle of workers today makes possible the socialist society of tomorrow; for therapeutic ideology, the pain of the therapy sessions leads to the bliss of a normal life. Despite wide divergences in content, all ideology promises recompense in some form or another, even if that recompense is simply the pleasure of being one of the privileged few in the know, as it is for the ideology of cynicism. As a result, one can speak of ideology as such rather than always discussing it in the particular, and at the same time one can distinguish between ideological ideas and ideas that challenge ideology.

20. The vitalist heresy within psychoanalysis insists on our capacity for avoiding loss altogether. According to this position (first made fashionable by Wilhelm Reich), we can become beings of pure productivity and live without any necessary loss. The justification of loss is, for this position, always ideological.

21. Though the description of Hegel's process of identification with loss in the *Phenomenology* appears similar to the approach of the deconstruction that Derrida practices, they are in fact opposites. Derrida discovers loss through distancing himself from other philosophical positions rather than identifying with them. As a result, he is unable to conceive of the possibility of embracing loss itself. The loss always remains, for Derrida, the loss of the other — loss at a distance. This is why he asks in *Aporias*, "Is my death possible?" (Jacques Derrida, *Aporias*, trans. Thomas Dutoit [Stanford CA: Stanford University Press, 1993], 21).

22. G. W. F. Hegel, *The Phenomenology of Spirit*, trans. A. V. Miller (New York: Oxford University Press, 1977), 492.

23. Though Nietzsche rightly sees that we cannot reduce subjectivity to the desire to survive, he nonetheless does not go far enough in grasping the subject's removal from the processes of life itself. Nietzsche's conception of the fundamental human desire, the will to power, is an organic drive that he often describes in biological terms. At one point, Nietzsche analogizes the will to power to the activity of trees in a jungle.

24. It is Jean-Paul Sartre, in many ways a disciple of Heidegger, who first articulates this critique of Heidegger's assumption of Dasein's worldliness. As he notes, "The ontological co-existence which appears as the structure of 'being-in-the-world' can

in no way serve as a foundation to an ontic being-with, such as, for example, the coexistence which appears in my friendship with Pierre or in the couple which Annie and I make" (Jean-Paul Sartre, *Being and Nothingness: A Phenomenological Essay on Ontology*, trans. Hazel E. Barnes [New York: Washington Square Press, 1956], 334).

25. Sigmund Freud, *Beyond the Pleasure Principle*, in *The Standard Edition of the Complete Psychological Works of Sigmund Freud*, vol. 18, trans. and ed. James Strachey (London: Hogarth Press, 1955), 15–16.

26. Many interpreters of Freud distinguish between repetition compulsion and the death drive because Freud's discussion of the latter through a biological metaphor seems to associate the death drive with actual death rather than repetition. But the structure of *Beyond the Pleasure Principle* provides the clues for how to read the concept of the death drive. After providing instances that imperil the standing of the pleasure principle as a law of the psyche, Freud turns directly to an extended discussion of repetition compulsion before moving to the death drive. What is most striking here is that Freud makes no explicit distinction between repetition compulsion and the death drive even as he shifts from one to the other. In light of this structure, one can see the concept of the death drive as Freud's way of theorizing repetition compulsion rather than as an altogether new concept. If one doesn't read it this way, the death drive seems to emerge out of thin air, since none of the examples with which Freud begins the book involve seeking out death itself.

27. As Juan-David Nasio puts it, "To be reduced to a state of ruin constitutes enjoying" (Juan-David Nasio, *Le fantasme: Le plaisir de lire Lacan* [Paris: Petite Bibliothèque Payot, 2005], 90, my translation).

28. Freud, *Beyond the Pleasure Principle*, 63.

29. This conception of the relationship between the death drive and pleasure also offers us a way of thinking about Freud's dualism—his insistence on the opposition between eros (or sexual drives) and the death drive. In *Civilization and Its Discontents*, Freud conceives of this opposition in terms of unity and dissolution. Eros is a uniting force, and the death drive dissolves the unities that eros creates. Despite Freud's own insistence on the dualism of his thought (as opposed to the monism of Jung), it is clear that, for Freud, one drive—the death drive—has absolute priority in the psyche and that we must see eros as simply part of the way that the death drive functions. This is a pattern in Freud's thinking: earlier in his career, he opposes the sex drives to the ego drives in a dualistic structure, but he constantly shows the power of sexuality to trump the concerns of the ego. Freud's dualism is never really dualism but instead his method of conceiving how drives contradict themselves internally and thus derail all monism. It should be properly called dialectics rather than dualism, despite Freud's own preference for the latter term. The opposing force (the ego drives for the early Freud and eros for the late Freud) is nothing but the indication of a deadlock within the primary drive (the sexual drives and the death drive). Eros works in the service

of repetition. We create unities, enter into symbolic bonds, and make connections that foster identity not because a primordial drive impels us in this direction but because these formations forge the possibility of re-creating and repeating our founding experience of loss.

30. Aristotle, *Poetics*, trans. R. Kassel, in *The Complete Works of Aristotle*, ed. Jonathan Barnes (Princeton NJ: Princeton University Press, 1984), 2:2320.

31. According to Hegel, the difference between the classical hero and the modern subject consists precisely in the former's capacity to accept responsibility for what clearly lies beyond the scope of personal responsibility, like Oedipus's act of killing his father and marrying his mother. In the *Aesthetics*, Hegel says: "A man nowadays does not accept responsibility for the whole range of what he has done; he repudiates that part of his act which, through ignorance or misconstruction of the circumstances, has turned out differently from what he had willed, and he enters to his own account only what he knew, and, on the strength of this knowledge, what he did on purpose and intentionally. But the heroic character does not make this distinction; instead he is answerable for the entirety of his act with his whole personality" (G. W. F. Hegel, *Aesthetics: Lectures on Fine Art*, vol. 1, trans. T. M. Knox [Oxford: Clarendon Press, 1975], 187–88).

32. Lee Edelman, *No Future: Queer Theory and the Death Drive* (Durham NC: Duke University Press, 2004), 11.

33. Of course, no sane person would oppose efforts to reduce or even eliminate childhood abductions, but this is precisely the point. Sanity itself in the contemporary world is identical with the apotheosis of the child and the insistence on sustaining the child's purity.

34. The authority figures that nostalgia tends to rely on are typically positioned outside the mainstream, and this location allows them to fill the gap in the social order in a way that recognized leaders cannot. Figures such as the acupuncturist and the homeopathic doctor and the guru appeal to us because they seem to have access to exactly what mainstream authorities do not. Their authority stems from their connection with what is missing in the chain of signification, not from the signifier itself, in direct contrast to mainstream authority figures.

35. Jacques Lacan's name for social authority is the "big Other," an anonymous force that sets the implicit and necessarily inconsistent rules for social interaction. When he proclaims that the big Other does not exist, Lacan is simply insisting on its inconsistency and on its inability to authorize definitively any statement.

36. Slavoj Žižek, *Enjoy Your Symptom! Jacques Lacan in Hollywood and Out*, 2nd ed. (New York: Routledge, 2001), 216.

37. The ultimately conservative nature of paranoia as a political position — and of Stone as a filmmaker — becomes apparent in his *World Trade Center* (2006), which seamlessly replaces the right-wing conspiracy from *JFK* as the thief of American enjoyment with Islamic terrorists.

38. Peter Knight, *Conspiracy Culture: From Kennedy to the X-Files* (New York: Routledge, 2000), 143.

39. The paranoid tradition in the American novel since the 1960s has had a clear critical edge to it. Writers such as Thomas Pynchon, Toni Morrison, Don DeLillo, and E. L. Doctorow have used paranoia in order to expose the connections that permeate contemporary American capitalism. But what separates these from someone like Oliver Stone is that they maintain a distance from the paranoia that they depict and employ. Paranoia serves as a tool for explication, not as a position in which to invest oneself. As a result, one reads a novel such as Don DeLillo's *Libra* (probably the most paranoid of the paranoid novels) and recognizes how the geopolitics of contemporary capitalism produces paranoia without at the same time succumbing to it. In this sense, one might say that American paranoid fiction is part of the struggle against paranoia as a political form.

40. Fredric Jameson, *The Geopolitical Aesthetic: Cinema and Space in the World System* (Bloomington: Indiana University Press, 1992), 79.

41. Sigmund Freud, *The Complete Letters of Sigmund Freud to Wilhelm Fliess 1887–1904*, trans. and ed. Jeffrey Moussaieff Masson (Cambridge MA: Harvard University Press, 1985), 264.

42. Jean Laplanche, *Essays on Otherness* (New York: Routledge, 1999), 212.

43. Walter Davis, *Deracination: Historicity, Hiroshima, and the Tragic Imperative* (Albany: State University of New York Press, 2001), 144.

44. Sigmund Freud, *New Introductory Lectures on Psycho-analysis*, in *The Standard Edition of the Complete Psychological Works of Sigmund Freud*, vol. 22, trans. and ed. James Strachey (London: Hogarth Press, 1964), 105.

2. THE ECONOMICS OF THE DRIVE

1. See Sigmund Freud, *The Project for a Scientific Psychology*, in *The Standard Edition of the Complete Psychological Works of Sigmund Freud*, vol. 1, trans. and ed. James Strachey (London: Hogarth Press, 1966), 281–397.

2. The *Project* is a key text for Jacques Lacan because he sees the physiological theory of the psyche as the foreshadowing of a structural or linguistic one. According to Lacan, Freud's lack of access to the thought of someone like Ferdinand de Saussure limited his ability to theorize the role that language plays in structuring the psyche, thereby forcing him to fall back on another field—physiology—in order to represent this structure in other terms.

3. The trajectory moving from dissatisfaction to satisfaction is what links so many forms of therapy to the capitalist economic system. When conceived according to this model, therapeutic efficaciousness becomes like any other commodity. It promises to fill the lack that the consumer experiences and provide complete satisfaction. But like all commodities, therapy that aims at curing dissatisfaction inevitably reproduces it in order to sustain its own value as a potential cure.

4. In *Seminar XVI*, Lacan notes that "the drive is undoubtedly mythological, as Freud himself has written. But what is not mythological is the supposition that a subject is satisfied by it" (Jacques Lacan, *Le séminaire, livre XVI: D'un autre à l'autre*, ed. Jacques-Alain Miller [Paris: Seuil, 2006], 211, my translation).

5. The drive's "constancy of thrust," as Lacan says in *Seminar XI*, "forbids any assimilation of the drive to a biological function, which always has a rhythm. The first thing Freud says about the drive is . . . that it has no day or night, no spring or autumn, no rise and fall. It is a constant force" (Jacques Lacan, *The Four Fundamental Concepts of Psycho-analysis*, trans. Alan Sheridan [New York: Norton, 1978], 165).

6. This is, of course, a paradoxical situation. No one would come into analysis if she or he were not, on some level, dissatisfied, but this dissatisfaction occurs on a second level: aspiring analysands are dissatisfied with the way that they obtain their satisfaction.

7. Lacan, *Four Fundamental Concepts*, 166.

8. Joan Copjec provides a masterful explanation of the structure of the drive and its relation to disruption. She notes: "The death drive achieves its satisfaction by *not* achieving its aim. Moreover, the *inhibition* that prevents the drive from achieving its aim is not understood within Freudian theory to be due to an extrinsic or exterior *obstacle*, but rather as part of the very *activity* of the drive itself" (Joan Copjec, *Imagine There's No Woman: Ethics and Sublimation* [Cambridge MA: MIT Press, 2002], 30).

9. Lacan uses the neologism *sinthome* to describe the fundamental symptom that animates each subject.

10. A similar structure exists in *Beloved*, *Jazz*, and *Paradise* as well. In the latter, for instance, the citizens of the town of Ruby view the wild women living at the former convent on the outskirts of town as their symptom. The respectable members of the town heap scorn on these women for their sexual promiscuity and general licentiousness while nonetheless relying on them for clandestine sexual encounters and assistance with terminating unwanted pregnancies. The novel concludes with an armed assault on the convent, an attempt to obliterate the symptom through physical force, but the subsequent reappearance of murdered women reveals that the symptom is indestructible due to its role in the way that subjects organize their enjoyment.

11. Slavoj Žižek, *Tarrying with the Negative: Kant, Hegel, and the Critique of Ideology* (Durham NC: Duke University Press, 1993), 206.

12. Marx's early essay "On the Jewish Question" permits a clear contrast between Marxist politics and a politics with its basis in psychoanalysis. In this essay, Marx argues in favor of the political emancipation of Jews, but he also identifies Judaism as the symptom of capitalism. He aligns Judaism with capitalist excess and argues for the elimination of this excess where psychoanalysis would advocate identification with the symptom. Though this doesn't make Marx a proto-Fascist, it does indicate his belief in a social order without a symptom — a social order perfectly

in balance: "The *social* emancipation of the Jew is the *emancipation of society from Judaism*" (Karl Marx, "On the Jewish Question," in *The Marx-Engels Reader*, 2nd ed., ed. Robert Tucker [New York: Norton, 1978], 52). In contrast, the psychoanalytic political project would involve neither the emancipation of the Jew nor the emancipation of society from Judaism but instead emancipation into the position of the Jew. Rather than curing the symptom, we must identify with it.

13. Lacan, *Four Fundamental Concepts*, 166.

14. The intrinsic link between desire and the death drive makes it possible to transition from desire to drive through fully insisting on one's desire. This is why Alenka Zupančič claims: "In order to arrive at the drive, one must pass through desire and insist on it until the very end" (Alenka Zupančič, *Ethics of the Real: Kant, Lacan* [New York: Verso, 2000], 239).

15. The mantra of capitalist ideology is almost perfectly articulated by Lorelei Lee (Marilyn Monroe) in her admonition directed at her friend Dorothy Shaw (Jane Russell) in Howard Hawks's *Gentlemen Prefer Blondes* (1953): "I want you to find happiness and stop having fun."

16. Adam Smith, *An Inquiry into the Nature and Causes of the Wealth of Nations* (Hamburg: Management Laboratory Press, 2008), 412. In *Capitalism and Freedom*, Milton Friedman argues for capitalism against governmental redistribution of wealth. Governmental action is, for Friedman, an obstacle to the attainment of the ultimate satisfaction that capitalism itself promises. Much more than Smith, Friedman sees the ultimate satisfaction as a genuine possibility impeded only by the state's restrictions on accumulation (Milton Friedman, *Capitalism and Freedom* [Chicago: University of Chicago Press, 2002]).

17. Karl Marx, *Grundrisse*, trans. Martin Nicolaus (New York: Penguin, 1993), 92.

18. The incestuous relation that Cross has had with his own daughter (Faye Dunaway) in the film is the product not of his status as a primal father who can enjoy all women with impunity but rather of his investment in the logic of capitalism. His daughter — and, it is suggested at the end of the film, his granddaughter — becomes a viable love object because she embodies the future. *Chinatown* anticipates the fetishization of the child that has become fully realized today in multiple forms, perhaps most heinously in the child beauty pageant, satirized effectively by the film *Little Miss Sunshine* (Jonathan Dayton and Valerie Faris, 2006) and subjected to a thoroughgoing critique in Walter Davis, *An Evening with JonBenet Ramsey* (Bloomington IN: iUniverse, 2004). One of the great ironies of recent history is that the director who so effectively criticized the fetishization of the child was convicted of having sex with a minor.

19. Karl Marx, *The Economic and Philosophic Manuscripts of 1844*, trans. Martin Milligan (New York: International Publishers, 1964), 150.

20. Karl Marx, *Capital: A Critique of Political Economy, Volume One*, trans. Ben Fowkes (New York: Penguin, 1976), 742.

21. There is a kind of perverse Socratic logic at work in capitalism's demand for accumulation. For Socrates, of course, the more we know, the more we become aware of our ignorance. Within capitalism, the more we accumulate, the more we become aware of how little we actually have, relative to the possibilities. In both cases, the recognition that we really have nothing works to energize the process of acquisition (either of knowledge or of capital).

22. Frank Norris, *McTeague* (New York: Penguin, 1982), 360–61.

23. Theodor W. Adorno, "The Schema of Mass Culture," in *The Culture Industry: Selected Essays on Mass Culture*, ed. J. M. Bernstein (New York: Routledge, 1991), 67.

24. See Max Horkheimer and Theodor W. Adorno, *Dialectic of Enlightenment: Philosophical Fragments*, trans. Edmund Jephcott (Stanford CA: Stanford University Press, 2007).

25. See, for instance, Gilles Deleuze and Félix Guattari, *Anti-Oedipus: Capitalism and Schizophrenia*, trans. Robert Hurley, Mark Seem, and Helen R. Lane (Minneapolis: University of Minnesota Press, 1983); Alain Badiou, *Manifesto for Philosophy*, trans. Norman Madarasz (Albany: State University of New York Press, 1999); and Paolo Virno, *A Grammar of the Multitude: For an Analysis of Contemporary Forms of Life*, trans. Isabella Bertoletti, James Cascaito, and Andrea Casson (Los Angeles: Semiotext[e], 2004).

26. Karl Marx, *Capital: A Critique of Political Economy, Volume Two*, trans. David Fernbach (New York: Penguin, 1978), 199.

27. Sigmund Freud, "Instincts and Their Vicissitudes," in *The Standard Edition of the Complete Psychological Works of Sigmund Freud*, vol. 14, trans. and ed. James Strachey (London: Hogarth Press, 1957), 122.

28. In *Time Driven*, Adrian Johnston attempts to link Freud's description of the structure of the drives in the pre-1920 "Instincts and Their Vicissitudes" to the later discovery of the death drive, a task that Freud himself left unexplored. This allows him to identify the structure of the death drive as divided between two equally exigent and yet contradictory forces that he locates in the four components of the drive named in "Instincts and Their Vicissitudes." According to Johnston, "the metapsychological structure of *Trieb* is split along the lines of two irreconcilable, incompatible axes—an *axis of iteration* (source-pressure) and an *axis of alteration* (aim-object)" (Adrian Johnston, *Time Driven: Metapsychology and the Splitting of the Drive* [Evanston IL: Northwestern University Press, 2005], 149).

29. Quoted in Giorgio Agamben, *The Coming Community*, trans. Michael Hardt (Minneapolis: University of Minnesota Press, 1993), 53.

30. Freud, *Project for a Scientific Psychology*, 324.

31. Jacques Lacan's wholesale opposition to all forms of psychoanalysis focused on the ego stems from his recognition that the ego emerges through rivalry and never transcends it. The development of a strong ego produces rather than prevents

relations of rivalry with other egos. The alter ego is never simply an other but also a competitor for the ego's own strength.

32. Melville's Bartleby the Scrivener provides the perfect antipode to Ahab. It is not that Bartleby has a weak ego in contrast to Ahab's strong one but that he doesn't really develop an ego at all. Bartleby is able to become a wrench within the functioning of capitalism — he is a model for many anticapitalist theorists writing today, including Giorgio Agamben, Slavoj Žižek, Eric Santner, and others — because he has no concern for his own ego and the sense of wholeness that the other might provide for him.

33. The form that profit takes hides its source in the appropriation of surplus value. Because capitalists makes a profit at the moment of the sale of a commodity, they mistakenly view the act of selling as the act that creates value, not seeing that it is production that creates value and selling (or circulation) that realizes it. According to Marx, this deceptive structure of the capitalist mode of production renders both the capitalist and the worker blind to the essence of profit. It requires the theorist — Marx himself — to locate correctly the site where value is created.

34. Sigmund Freud, *Jokes and Their Relation to the Unconscious*, in *The Standard Edition of the Complete Psychological Works of Sigmund Freud*, vol. 8, trans. and ed. James Strachey (London: Hogarth Press, 1960), 120.

35. In her superb discussion of comedy (which she distinguishes from the joke), Alenka Zupančič describes the precise way in which comedy allows us to see connections. Rather than linking everything together in an all-encompassing unity or wholeness, comedy renders visible the absence or loss that connects the apparently disparate elements of our reality: "We could say that the comic short circuit is a manifestation of the missing link which, in the very fact that it is missing, holds a given reality together, whereas Unity functions as a veiling of this missing link" (Alenka Zupančič, *The Odd One In: On Comedy* [Cambridge MA: MIT Press, 2008], 65).

36. When capitalism does employ the joke, it attempts to profit on the economizing that takes place rather than submitting itself to this economizing. For instance, factory owners who share the latest joke with their workers are attempting to use the joke as a way of smoothing over the antagonism between classes that the disparate positions in the factory make evident. In so doing, they use the connections within the joke to obscure the connections that workers might make between their own situation and that of the factory owners.

3. CLASS STATUS AND ENJOYMENT

1. Kojin Karatani, *Transcritique on Kant and Marx*, trans. Sabu Kohso (Cambridge MA: MIT Press, 2003), viii.

2. In a representative sentence from *Capital*, Marx claims: "And the most fundamental right under the law of capital is the equal exploitation of labour-power

by all capitalists" (Karl Marx, *Capital: A Critique of Political Economy, Volume One*, trans. Ben Fowkes [New York: Penguin, 1976], 405).

3. Richard Rorty, *Philosophy and Social Hope* (New York: Penguin, 1999), 205.

4. Isaiah Berlin, "Two Concepts of Liberty," in *The Proper Study of Mankind* (New York: Farrar, Straus and Giroux, 1997), 240. The liberal like Richard Rorty or John Rawls believes that it is possible to reconcile the competing demands of freedom and equality with a social arrangement that limits both while at the same time creating some space for both.

5. The one political philosophy that stresses freedom over equality and yet attacks capitalism from the Left is anarchism. But anarchism in all its forms relies on a romantic conception of subjectivity: it imagines that subjectivity can emerge outside of social restriction altogether, when it is social restriction that provides the subject with all the coordinates of its being. Even if the subject has a purely oppositional relationship to the social order, it nonetheless relies on this order in a negative sense.

6. Of course, the practice of psychoanalysis has not often been guided by the ideal of a classless society. Many psychoanalysts work to accommodate their patients to the demands of class society rather than leading them to a recognition of the incompatibility between class society and an emancipated subjectivity.

7. Immanuel Kant, "What Is Enlightenment?," in *Kant: Political Writings*, trans. H. B. Nisbet, 2nd ed. (Cambridge: Cambridge University Press, 1991), 54.

8. Though class inequality existed well before the birth of capitalism, psychoanalysis could not emerge prior to capitalist modernity because it requires the Enlightenment ideal of freedom as a backdrop. The lack of freedom in previous socioeconomic systems was not at all contradictory. The feudal system, for instance, includes no pretensions of freedom from authority.

9. Sigmund Freud, "On Beginning the Treatment," in *The Standard Edition of the Complete Psychological Works of Sigmund Freud*, vol. 12, trans. and ed. James Strachey (London: Hogarth Press, 1957), 133.

10. Even in the founding text of psychoanalytic treatment, *Studies on Hysteria*, Freud notes that the treatment of the lower-class country girl Katharina goes much easier than the treatment of his typical middle-class and upper-class patients because she experiences less repression. See Sigmund Freud and Joseph Breuer, *Studies on Hysteria*, in *The Standard Edition of the Complete Psychological Works of Sigmund Freud*, vol. 2, trans. and ed. James Strachey (London: Hogarth Press, 1955).

11. For the complete poll results and a detailed analysis, see http://www.policy andtaxationgroup.com/pdf/BNATaxReport.pdf.

12. The fantasy of the upper-class figure who rejects the constraints of the social order for an unfettered existence isolated from the rest of society is just that—a fantasy. Though there are undoubtedly people who live out an isolated existence purchased by wealth (like the eccentric antigovernment billionaire Jubal Harshaw

in Robert Heinlein's science fiction classic *Stranger in a Strange Land* and the equally fictional Howard Hughes), this isolation is fundamentally false. Harshaw and Hughes both live apart from the rest of society, but they do so surrounded by the commodities that this society produces and buttressed by their own sense of individual identity. Their physical isolation is not a psychic one. It depends on a material and psychic investment in social recognition that creates an identity capable of rejecting the outside world. In this sense, there is no parallel between the isolation of a character like Jubal Harshaw and Antigone. Antigone's isolation at the end of Sophocles's play depends on her abandonment of any attachment to her symbolic identity, while Jubal's isolation relies on the symbolic identity he has acquired.

13. Sigmund Freud, *Jokes and Their Relation to the Unconscious*, in *The Standard Edition of the Complete Psychological Works of Sigmund Freud*, vol. 8, trans. and ed. James Strachey (London: Hogarth Press, 1960), 101.

14. The call for more enjoyment, not less, is a tricky proposition because it threatens to devolve into erecting enjoyment as a social duty, which is the fundamental form of contemporary authority. We must also clearly distinguish enjoyment, which one endures and suffers, from pleasure and happiness, both of which promise the overcoming of loss.

15. As Freud conceives it, Bill Gates, whom most of us imagine to be awash in satisfaction, would actually have one of the most difficult paths to it. The intensity of his striving to expand his monopoly certainly and of his contradictory efforts at grand charity projects suggests that this is so, that his unequaled accumulation has done nothing to provide him satisfaction with his satisfaction.

16. *Fight Club* also reveals the great difficulty of emancipation from class status. Though Jack accomplishes it on his own, he can do so only by splitting himself in two — becoming Jack and Tyler Durden. He must experience his emancipation as the result of Tyler's agency rather than his own because it would otherwise remain unthinkable. What Fincher's film indicates through this splitting is the necessarily psychotic dimension of the rupture with social class. Though the subject who abandons an investment in class status does not need to become a psychotic, the break does require a quasi-psychotic moment wherein the subject loses the very ground beneath its feet.

17. Eschewing popularity is not the automatic path to freedom and enjoyment. Most of those who fail to achieve popularity invest themselves in it through yearning, and many others establish alternate networks for finding a sense of class status. There are no guarantees of access to enjoyment that accompany any social position whatsoever.

18. The relative liberty of fashion and behavior that the subject experiences after the teen years is completely illusory. It depends on a fundamental capitulation that occurs during the teen years and silently informs the subsequent existence of the subject. The demands that the Other makes are more overt and extreme during

the teen years because this is the time when the subject has yet to fully invest itself in those demands.

19. One of the great achievements of the television series *The Sopranos* is its ability to show the fundamentally conservative nature of those involved with organized crime. Despite the excessive violence and sexuality of their lives, they are, politically speaking, among the most docile and obedient subjects, as evinced by the fierce patriotism of the characters, their devotion to the ideal of the family, their respect for institutional hierarchies, and so on.

20. Joan Copjec, *Imagine There's No Woman: Ethics and Sublimation* (Cambridge MA: MIT Press, 2002), 167.

21. Slavoj Žižek, *The Parallax View* (Cambridge MA: MIT Press, 2006), 313.

22. Sigmund Freud, *Civilization and Its Discontents*, in *The Standard Edition of the Complete Psychological Works of Sigmund Freud*, vol. 22, trans. and ed. James Strachey (London: Hogarth Press, 1961), 86.

23. Here I accept Fredric Jameson's argument that modernity cannot be separated from capitalism. See Fredric Jameson, *A Singular Modernity: Essay on the Ontology of the Present* (New York: Verso, 2002).

24. G. W. F. Hegel, *Phenomenology of Spirit*, trans. A. V. Miller (New York: Oxford University Press, 1977), 115.

25. Jacques Lacan, *The Seminar of Jacques Lacan, Book XVII: The Other Side of Psychoanalysis*, trans. Russell Grigg (New York: Norton, 2007), 79.

26. Lacan, *Seminar XVII*, 107. In the seminar from a year earlier, Lacan claims that the master emerges as a master only through the act of renouncing enjoyment, which is what renders appropriating the slave's enjoyment impossible. According to Lacan, "The renunciation of enjoyment . . . constitutes the master, which means that the principle of the master's power is formed out of it" (Jacques Lacan, *Le séminaire, livre XVI: D'un autre à l'autre, 1968–1969*, ed. Jacques-Alain Miller [Paris: Seuil, 2006], 17, my translation).

27. In his late writings, Michel Foucault idealizes classical Greek society for its ability to provide mastery without subjection to a universal law. He correctly recognizes that this is possible only through the exclusion of slaves and women, but he contends that this exclusion is actually less oppressive than the modern system of universal inclusion. What his analysis fails to account for is the role of the slave's recognition in the seemingly self-sustaining mastery of the Greek master.

28. The frame story in *Titanic* that depicts Rose as an elderly woman recounting her experience the night that the ship sank has the effect of qualifying Rose's earlier rejection of recognition. When she flies out via helicopter to a salvage ship that is anchored above the shipwreck, we see her come aboard with multiple suitcases, indicating her return to the upper class and her betrayal of the freedom that she had achieved. This image of the elderly Rose reveals the difficulty of sustaining the break that she accomplishes after her rescue from the wreckage. Cameron

includes the frame story in order to emphasize the betrayal and to show the possibility for repeating the act of freedom. When the elder Rose throws the valuable necklace that she and Jack had stolen from her fiancé into the ocean at the end of the film, she repeats the gesture of freedom that she had betrayed through a life of accumulation. Through this depiction of freedom, its betrayal, and its subsequent reassertion, Cameron illustrates both the difficulty of sustaining freedom and the ever-present possibility of asserting it.

29. The infinite enjoyment of precapitalist epochs is an example of Hegel's bad infinite, where infinite is envisioned as a straight line advancing ever farther in the distance. The infinite enjoyment that capitalism makes possible accords with what Hegel sees as the proper idea of infinity: here, the endless movement of the circle provides the model for thinking infinity.

4. SUSTAINING ANXIETY

1. This is not, by the way, a personal example. No such compliment has ever been directed toward me.

2. As Hegel famously puts it, "*Self-consciousness achieves its satisfaction only in another self-consciousness*" (G. W. F. Hegel, *The Phenomenology of Spirit*, trans. A. V. Miller [Oxford: Oxford University Press, 1977], 110, Hegel's emphasis).

3. John Rawls, *Lectures on the History of Moral Philosophy*, ed. Barbara Herman (Cambridge MA: Harvard University Press, 2000), 333.

4. There was a similar Hegelian reading of psychoanalysis in the early thought of Jacques Lacan, who initially saw the analyst as a stand-in for social authority who might provide recognition for the patient, who suffers from detours on the path to this recognition. In his first seminar, Lacan expresses in completely unambiguous terms his investment in recognition. He claims: "Thank God, the subject inhabits the world of the symbol, that is to say a world of others who speak. That is why his desire is susceptible to the mediation of recognition. Without which every human function would simply exhaust itself in the unspecified wish for the destruction of the other as such" (Jacques Lacan, *The Seminar of Jacques Lacan, Book I: Freud's Papers on Technique, 1953–1954*, trans. John Forrester, ed. Jacques-Alain Miller [New York: Norton, 1988], 171). Lacan would subsequently move away from this position as he began to grasp that what he calls here "the unspecified wish for the destruction of the other as such" remains fully operative within the mediation of recognition. Recognition ceases to provide salvation, and Lacan turns to a form of psychoanalysis that no longer seeks to escape destructiveness but to find a way to integrate it into subjectivity.

5. The paradigmatic statement of Hegel as an apostle of recognition occurs in Robert R. Williams, *Hegel's Ethics of Recognition* (Berkeley: University of California Press, 1997).

6. Emmanuel Levinas attempts to bypass the nonexistence of the other as a symbolic entity by rooting his ethical philosophy in the encounter with the other's face,

which is not reducible to the other's symbolic identity. The problem is that Levinas assumes the ethical bearing of the other's face, an assumption that requires a surreptitious reference to a signifying structure that determines this bearing. Without reference to the larger structure of signification, one could never know that "the nakedness of the face is destituteness" and that it calls one to ethical responsibility (Emmanuel Levinas, *Totality and Infinity: An Essay on Exteriority*, trans. Alphonso Lingus [Pittsburgh: Duquesne University Press, 1969], 75).

7. See, most importantly, Slavoj Žižek, Eric L. Santner, and Kenneth Reinhard, *The Neighbor: Three Inquiries in Political Theology* (Chicago: University of Chicago Press, 2005).

8. Kenneth Reinhard, "Toward a Political Theology of the Neighbor," in Žižek, Santner, and Reinhard, *The Neighbor*, 32.

9. Neither the choice of clinging to the other's demand nor that of seeking the other's desire necessarily leaves the subject any better off. In both cases, the subject finds itself dependent on the other, either directly in the one case or indirectly in the other. Psychoanalysis intervenes in order to free the subject from this dependence by bringing the subject to the recognition that the other does not exist. This means that while the other's demand does conceal a secret desire, the secret is not properly that of the other but that of the subject itself.

10. As Renata Salecl notes, "The problem with a society of 'too much choice' is that, on the one hand, there seems to be less and less demand coming from the other and that the subject is much freer than in the past, while, on the other hand, the subject is constantly encouraged to pursue his or her own *jouissance*" (Renata Salecl, *On Anxiety* [New York: Routledge, 2004], 62–63). See also Renata Salecl, *The Tyranny of Choice* (London: Profile Books, 2011).

11. For a fuller discussion of this transformation, see Todd McGowan, *The End of Dissatisfaction? Jacques Lacan and the Emerging Society of Enjoyment* (Albany: State University of New York Press, 2004).

12. Slavoj Žižek, "Afterword: Lenin's Choice," in *Revolution at the Gates: Selected Writings of Lenin from 1917*, ed. Slavoj Žižek (New York: Verso, 2002), 204.

13. Eric L. Santner, *My Own Private Germany: Daniel Paul Schreber's Secret History of Modernity* (Princeton NJ: Princeton University Press, 1996), xii.

14. Perhaps the most striking of these displays of enjoyment is the use of the telephone while one is using a public bathroom. Here, the subject confronts others in the public bathroom with an ostentatious show of enjoyment while simultaneously bombarding the interlocutor on the phone with the sounds of what used to be a completely private activity.

15. The problem with a society structured around the imperative to enjoy like ours is not that it produces anxiety but that it produces anxiety along with the belief that one might enjoy without it. The images of enjoyment with which consumer culture bombards us everywhere universally elide the traumatic dimension of

enjoyment. They present enjoyment in an imaginary form in order to encourage the pursuit of it, but this form is one that can never be realized.

16. One must resort to cognitive mapping, according to Jameson, because the old revolutionary project of class consciousness is no longer possible in the contemporary cultural landscape. The increasing spatialization of time demands above all a political effort that allows subjects to locate themselves spatially within the cultural terrain. At the end of his *Postmodernism,* Jameson explains his choice of the term "cognitive mapping" throughout the book in this way. He claims: "'Cognitive mapping' was in reality nothing but a code word for 'class consciousness' — only it proposed the need for class consciousness of a new and hitherto undreamed of kind, while it also inflected the account in the direction of that new spatiality implicit in the postmodern" (Fredric Jameson, *Postmodernism, or, The Cultural Logic of Late Capitalism* [Durham NC: Duke University Press, 1991], 417–18).

17. Marion's attempt to qualify her brief fling only adds to the idea of her as an enjoying other for both Ralph and the spectator. She initially describes the sexual encounter through the offhand words of her lover, who said to her (as she reports), "Do you want to have a go at it?" After acknowledging the act, Marion then insists that it didn't mean anything and that the man didn't ejaculate inside of her. She details the infidelity in this way in order to lessen the blow to Ralph, but because he posits her as an enjoying other in this scene, everything she says has the opposite effect.

18. The focus on the performativity of identity that marks constructivism as a philosophical position goes awry not in its assessment of symbolic identity, which is wholly a social construction, but in its inability to account for the enjoyment that we continue to posit even after we see that symbolic identity is performed rather than natural. There is no symbolic identity that doesn't appear to hide a real other who possesses some secret means of enjoyment.

19. Even when the specific War on Terror begun by George W. Bush ends, the phenomenon that it represents will continue. It includes all activities motivated by the anxiety that occurs when the West confronts suicide bombers and their open displays of horrific enjoyment.

20. Luis Buñuel's final film, *Cet obscure objet du désir* (*That Obscure Object of Desire,* 1977), presents a conception of terrorism that is wholly different from the one that predominates today. It envisions terrorism as a response not to the miniskirt but to the veil. That is, the film shows terrorist bombings that seem to be occasioned by the impenetrability of women's desire rather than their open display of enjoyment. The terrorist attacks occur in the background of a story recounted by Mathieu (Fernando Rey), who describes the impossibility of attaining the object of his desire, not least because the role of this one woman is played by two different actors (Carole Bouquet and Ángela Molina).

21. Martin Heidegger, "What Is Metaphysics?," trans. David Farrell Krell, in *Basic Writings,* ed. David Farrell Krell (San Francisco: Harper and Row, 1977), 103.

22. Heidegger, "What Is Metaphysics?," 110.
23. Heidegger, "What Is Metaphysics?," 106.
24. Jacques Lacan, *Le séminaire, livre X: L'angoisse, 1962–1963*, ed. Jacques-Alain Miller (Paris: Seuil, 2004), 75, my translation.
25. Lacan, *Séminaire X*, 67, my translation.
26. Thomas Doherty articulates the standard criticism of the film (which he nonetheless appreciates for other reasons). For Doherty, *Rebel without a Cause* blames the castrating mother and the weak father for Jim's experience of anxiety. He notes that "much of the film's pop Freudianism has dated badly" (Thomas Doherty, *Teenagers and Teenpics: The Juvenilization of American Movies in the 1950s* [Philadelphia: Temple University Press, 2002], 84).
27. Žižek, "Afterword: Lenin's Choice," 208. In her unsurpassed study of political subjectivity, Molly Rothenberg clarifies this point in her discussion of the excess attached to every subject that produces anxiety in others. She writes: "As far as I can see, the suspension of the defense against excess — or the neutralization of the more destructive defenses — is the only way that the subject's transformation of its relation to its own *jouissance* can affect others. This suspension means that the subject accepts the relation of nonrelation, giving up its fruitless but often destructive efforts to locate the excess outside itself or to eradicate it. By refusing to defend itself (or by refusing to deploy destructive defenses such as narcissism, aggression, projection, and scapegoating), the subject decreases its contribution to the affective storm in a social field that circulates excess like a hot potato" (Molly Anne Rothenberg, *The Excessive Subject: A New Theory of Social Change* [Malden MA: Polity, 2010], 207).
28. Lacan, *Séminaire X*, 76, my translation.
29. Jacques Lacan, *The Seminar of Jacques Lacan, Book VII: The Ethics of Psychoanalysis, 1959–1960*, trans. Dennis Porter (New York: Norton, 1992), 198.
30. The cultural turn away from loud radios and toward small devices with headphones (such as the iPod) does nothing to eliminate the anxiety produced by the encounter with the enjoying other. The fact that the other's enjoyment is silent or barely audible has the effect of making it seem more foreign and more inaccessible, not less so.
31. Because Fascism enjoys through the figure of the Jew that at the same time it works to eliminate, Fascism will always remain a failed political program. The successful Fascist society would cease to be a Fascist society, having destroyed the figure that serves to organize the society's enjoyment. Success, as Fascism itself defines it, is structurally impossible.

5. CHANGING THE WORLD

1. Max Horkheimer and Theodor W. Adorno, *Dialectic of Enlightenment: Philosophical Fragments*, trans. Edmund Jephcott (Stanford CA: Stanford University Press, 2007), 150.

2. Georg Lukács, *History and Class Consciousness: Studies in Marxist Dialectics*, trans. Rodney Livingstone (Cambridge MA: MIT Press, 1971), 83. Though on the final page of *Being and Time* Heidegger specifically denies that his philosophy targets reification, Lucien Goldmann convincingly shows the shared nature of their philosophical project (at least in its negative dimension): "The fundamental problem common to Lukács and Heidegger is that of man's inseparability from meaning and from the world, that of the subject-object identity: when man understands the world, he understands the meaning of *Dasein*, the meaning of his being and, inversely, it is in understanding his own being that he can understand the world" (Lucien Goldmann, *Lukács and Heidegger: Towards a New Philosophy*, trans. William Q. Boelhower [Boston: Routledge and Kegan Paul, 1977], 40). Goldmann's study makes evident that Heidegger clearly had Lukács in mind when writing *Being and Time*, and the presence of Lukács as a philosophical predecessor produces the disavowal concerning reification at the end of Heidegger's magnum opus.

3. In *Difference and Repetition*, Gilles Deleuze emphasizes the priority of difference relative to the stable sameness of normality. His project consists in emphasizing this priority and thereby undermining the ideological dominance of normality: "We must show not only how individuating difference differs in kind from specific difference, but primarily and above all how individuation properly *precedes* matter and form, species and part, and every other element of the constituted individual" (Gilles Deleuze, *Difference and Repetition*, trans. Paul Patton [New York: Columbia University Press, 1994], 38). Even though at this relatively early point in his thought Deleuze has not yet embraced schizophrenia as a radical anticapitalist position, we can see that the seeds have already been planted for this idea.

4. Alain Badiou, *Being and Event*, trans. Oliver Feltham (New York: Continuum, 2005), 192. Though Badiou attacks the normality of the situation, of all the thinkers that I discuss here he remains the closest to the political project of psychoanalysis as I envision it.

5. Badiou's hostility toward the normal leads him to reject any dealing with the established political system. His *Organisation politique* intervenes through taking up radical positions on various issues and enjoining militant action, but it doesn't involve itself at all in party politics. Electoral politics, for Badiou, is inextricably part of the rule of the normal situation, which is why he proclaims in his book on Nicolas Sarkozy that "the vote in general . . . is a state mechanism that presents disorientation itself as a choice" (Alain Badiou, *The Meaning of Sarkozy*, trans. David Fernbach [New York: Verso, 2008], 17).

6. Jean-Paul Sartre, *Being and Nothingness: A Phenomenological Essay on Ontology*, trans. Hazel E. Barnes (New York: Washington Square Press, 1956), 103, Sartre's emphasis.

7. Robert Pfaller, "Negation and Its Reliabilities: An Empty Subject for Ideology?," in *Cogito and the Unconscious*, ed. Slavoj Žižek (Durham NC: Duke University Press,

1998), 236. Pfaller sees Marxist science as the only possible route out of ideology's trap, but he never lays out precisely how one arrives at the position of the Marxist scientist from an ideology in which negation is illusory.

8. See Michel Foucault, *The History of Sexuality: An Introduction, Volume I*, trans. Robert Hurley (New York: Random House, 1978).

9. Foucault's vision of normality as a completely oppressive force appears throughout his career. As he sees it, a normalizing structure provides the coordinates that play a determining role in every activity undertaken within a culture. As he says in *The Order of Things*, "The fundamental codes of a culture — those governing its language, its schemas of perception, its exchanges, its techniques, its values, the hierarchies of its practices — establish for every man, from the very first, the empirical orders with which he will be dealing and within which he will be at home" (Michel Foucault, *The Order of Things* [New York: Random House, 1994], xx).

10. Sigmund Freud, *Introductory Lectures on Psycho-analysis*, in *The Standard Edition of the Complete Psychological Works of Sigmund Freud*, vol. 16, trans. and ed. James Strachey (London: Hogarth Press, 1963), 338.

11. Sheila Kunkle, "Embracing the Paradox: Žižek's Illogical Logic," *International Journal of Žižek Studies* 2, no. 4 (2008), http://zizekstudies.org/index.php/ijzs/article/view/166/260.

12. Freud practically invites this critique in his general statements about the psychoanalytic project. In his lecture "On Psychotherapy," he describes the analytic process as a correction back to normality for the patient: "The transformation of this unconscious material in the mind of the patient into conscious material must have the result of correcting his deviation from normality and of lifting the compulsion to which his mind has been subject" (Sigmund Freud, "On Psychotherapy," trans. J. Bernays and James Strachey, in *The Standard Edition of the Complete Psychological Works of Sigmund Freud*, vol. 7, trans. and ed. James Strachey [London: Hogarth Press, 1953], 266).

13. Heinz Hartmann, *Ego Psychology and the Problem of Adaptation*, trans. David Rapaport (Madison WI: International Universities Press, 1958), 81.

14. To be fair to Hartmann, the title of his work sounds worse than it is. He defines adaptation as the negotiation between conformity to social norms and the attempt to modify these norms, not as pure capitulation on the part of the subject.

15. See, for instance, Walter Davis, *Inwardness and Existence: Subjectivity in/and Hegel, Heidegger, Marx, and Freud* (Madison: University of Wisconsin Press, 1989), 232–313. *Inwardness and Existence* represents perhaps the only attempt to conceive psychoanalysis and Marxism (along with Hegelian dialectics and existentialism) as part of the same philosophical project. The association with Marxism gives psychoanalysis here a much more explicitly political dimension than we are used to seeing.

16. Joseph Breuer and Sigmund Freud, *Studies on Hysteria*, in *The Standard Edition of the Complete Psychological Works of Sigmund Freud*, vol. 2, trans. and ed. James Strachey (London: Hogarth Press, 1955), 305.

17. In this sense, psychoanalysis seems to function like reform rather than revolution. From the perspective of the revolutionary, all reform is ultimately conservative because it has the effect of dampening revolutionary fervor through the amelioration of the present system. This is why so many revolutionaries have seen fellow-traveling reformists as posing a far greater danger to the revolution than its outright enemies.

18. Not surprisingly, the one disorder that no one celebrates for its potential political power is obsession. With its hypervigilance to the public law as a way of preserving its private enjoyment, obsession bespeaks a fundamental conservatism that is difficult to interpret away.

19. Sigmund Freud, "The Loss of Reality in Neurosis and Psychosis," in *The Standard Edition of the Complete Psychological Works of Sigmund Freud*, vol. 19, trans. and ed. James Strachey (London: Hogarth Press, 1961), 185.

20. Frances Restuccia has made one of the most compelling cases for the revolutionary dimension of hysteria in her discussion of its occurrence in Lars von Trier's film *Breaking the Waves* (1996). About the hysteric, Restuccia notes: "Her fantasy persists and can be in a sense forced to materialize" (Frances Restuccia, "Impossible Love in *Breaking the Waves*," in *Lacan and Contemporary Film*, ed. Todd McGowan and Sheila Kunkle [New York: Other Press, 2004], 206). It is this materialization of the fantasy that I will later associate — and claim that psychoanalysis associates — with normality.

21. Hegel makes a similar point about the project of knowledge. In the *Encyclopedic Logic* he says: "It is not humility that holds back from the knowledge and study of truth, but a conviction that we are already in full possession of it" (G. W. F. Hegel, *Logic*, trans. William Wallace [Oxford: Clarendon Press, 1975], 26).

22. Following Hegel, Carl Schmitt defines the bourgeois as the one occupied entirely with private enjoyment and not at all with public concerns. What Schmitt fails to mention is how this turn away from the public sphere marks the essential contribution of the bourgeois to capitalist society. According to Schmitt, "The bourgeois is an individual who does not want to leave the apolitical riskless private sphere. He rests in the possession of his private property, and under the justification of his possessive individualism he acts as an individual against the totality" (Carl Schmitt, *The Concept of the Political*, trans. George Schwab [Chicago: University of Chicago Press, 1996], 62).

23. Gilles Deleuze and Félix Guattari, *Anti-Oedipus: Capitalism and Schizophrenia*, trans. Robert Hurley, Mark Seem, and Helen R. Lane (Minneapolis: University of Minnesota Press, 1983), 35.

24. Freud, "Loss of Reality," 185.

25. Sigmund Freud, *Five Lectures on Psycho-analysis*, in *The Standard Edition of the Complete Psychological Works of Sigmund Freud*, vol. 11, trans. and ed. James Strachey (London: Hogarth Press, 1957), 50.

26. Slavoj Žižek, *Organs without Bodies: On Deleuze and Consequences* (New York: Routledge, 2003), 98.

27. The trauma associated with the exposure of the fantasmatic core of subjectivity or of the subject's fundamental deception is part of what makes Franz Kafka's *The Trial* so disturbing. Faced with an accusation that has no explicit content, Joseph K. responds in a way that lays bare the fantasmatic structure of his subjectivity — his image of how power operates, his class prejudices, his paranoia, and so on.

28. When fantasy and external reality come together for the film spectator, this creates an experience of the gaze — an encounter with the object-cause of desire in the visual field. There are several directors who privilege this encounter in their films, including Jane Campion, Andrei Tarkovsky, Alain Resnais, Alfred Hitchcock, Wim Wenders, and David Lynch. For a fuller explanation of the cinematic encounter with the gaze, see Todd McGowan, *The Real Gaze: Film Theory after Lacan* (Albany: State University of New York Press, 2007).

29. As Philippe Van Haute nicely explains, "The phantasy stages the manner in which the subject relates itself to the incompleteness of the Other, the cause of desire; it 'imag(e)-ines' the loss of a *jouissance* that continues to fascinate the subject" (Philippe Van Haute, *Against Adaptation: Lacan's "Subversion" of the Subject*, trans. Paul Crowe and Miranda Vankerk [New York: Other Press, 2002], 134).

30. The capacity to lie — and to lie in a singular fashion — is the sole basis for the subject's singularity. Any humanist insistence on a fundamental dignity accorded to every person represents an attempt to evade recognizing the source of uniqueness in deceit.

31. The exception is Michael J. Fox. In *The Secret of My Succe$s* (Herbert Ross, 1987), Brantley Foster (Michael J. Fox) works as a mail clerk at a large company and fantasizes about being an executive there. Through a tenuously worked out deception that relies on the knowledge he gains in the mailroom, Foster manages to pose as newly hired executive Carlton Whitfield while at the same time retaining his job as a mail clerk. The realization of the fantasy in no way traumatizes him, although the one traumatic moment in the film does occur when the fantasmatic nature of Carlton Whitfield as an identity is publicly exposed.

32. When I was in high school, one of my fellow students would regularly brag about his love for masturbation, which had the effect, contrary to what one would expect, of enhancing his reputation in the school rather than impairing it. However, he did this from a position of great popularity.

33. Bruce Fink, *A Clinical Introduction to Lacanian Psychoanalysis: Theory and Technique* (Cambridge MA: Harvard University Press, 1997), 180.

34. The embrace of one's own mode of enjoying is not narcissism. The narcissist takes its own ego as a love object and finds pleasure in this object. In doing so, the narcissist attempts to short-circuit the necessary path through the encounter with the other through which the subject finds satisfaction. Embracing one's own mode of enjoying, in contrast, necessarily involves embracing that of the other as well.

35. William Shakespeare, *Hamlet*, 1.5.189–90.

36. Despite Hamlet's resistance to becoming the fool early in the play, his insistence on questioning does display a form of subjectivity that anticipates the position of the fool. Through the process of questioning, one prepares oneself for discovering the insufficiency of all answers, which is the discovery that produces the subjectivity of the fool. But acceding to this form of subjectivity requires that one abandon the questioning at some point. To insist on questioning as an infinite task is to presuppose that some authority has the ultimate answer.

6. THE APPEAL OF SACRIFICE

1. John Locke, *Two Treatises of Government* (New York: Cambridge University Press, 1988), 283.

2. For almost all of his detractors and most of his enthusiasts, Hegel rather than Marx represents the apogee of the dialectical tradition that stresses the importance of social forces over the insignificance of the individual. The famous statement from the *Philosophy of History* — "The particular is for the most part of too trifling value as compared with the general: individuals are sacrificed and abandoned" — seems to bear out this conclusion (G. W. F. Hegel, *Philosophy of History*, trans. J. Sibree [New York: Dover, 1956], 33). But Hegel minimizes the significance of the individual, on the one hand, only to elevate it, on the other. His philosophy shows that it is those who insist on beginning with individuality (or particularity) who never arrive at authentic singularity, which only emerges once one thinks the universal. The universal that his dialectic conceives is not opposed to the singular but is its homologue.

3. Karl Marx, *Grundrisse*, trans. Martin Nicolaus (New York: Penguin, 1993), 496.

4. The thinker who best exemplifies the effort to sustain the tension between the individual and society is perhaps Simon Critchley, who situates his thought between the singularity of ethics, which concerns the individual subject, and the universality of politics, which concerns the social order. He concludes *Ethics — Politics — Subjectivity* with a statement echoing Kant that recognizes the impossibility of opting for one side or the other. He says: "If ethics without politics is empty, then politics without ethics is blind" (Simon Critchley, *Ethics — Politics — Subjectivity: Essays on Derrida, Levinas, and Contemporary French Thought* [New York: Verso, 1999], 283).

5. Sigmund Freud, *Group Psychology and the Analysis of the Ego*, in *The Standard Edition of the Complete Psychological Works of Sigmund Freud*, vol. 18, trans. and ed. James Strachey (London: Hogarth Press, 1955), 121.

6. In *Absalom, Absalom!* William Faulkner presents the related idea that war exists not because of the inherent antagonism between different societies but in order to provide respite from the antagonisms that proliferate within each society. As Faulkner describes it, the American Civil War allows half-brothers Henry Sutpen and Charles Bon to experience the trauma of battle rather than confront the antagonism that will lead Henry to kill Charles after the war ends.

7. Marcel Mauss, *The Gift: The Form and Reason for Exchange in Archaic Societies*, trans. W. D. Halls (New York: Norton, 1990), 16.

8. Georges Bataille, *The Accursed Share, Volume I*, trans. Robert Hurley (New York: Zone Books, 1991), 33.

9. Bataille's conception of the relationship between the release of energy and enjoyment mirrors that of the early Freud. It is an unacknowledged version of the Freudian pleasure principle, which views pleasure as the result of discharging excess excitation. Freud began to formulate this theory in a rudimentary form as early as the 1895 *Project for a Scientific Psychology*, where he puts it in biological terms, claiming that "neurons tend to divest themselves of Q [or quantity of excitation]" (Sigmund Freud, *The Project for a Scientific Psychology*, in *The Standard Edition of the Complete Psychological Works of Sigmund Freud*, vol. 1, trans. and ed. James Strachey [New York: Hogarth Press, 1966], 296).

10. The further limitation of Bataille's theorization of sacrifice lies in his inability to see how sacrifice functions on the level of the individual subject. He argues that people don't recognize the primacy of sacrifice because they are too caught up in the perspective of what he calls a restrictive economy. They fail to look from a general perspective, from a perspective that envisions that society as a whole, and thus they fail to see how sacrifice operates for the society as such. They miss the exuberance of the sacrifice while focusing on the anguish of the individual being sacrificed. Bataille's call for a general perspective has the effect of unintentionally minimizing the ubiquity of sacrifice. The proclivity of societies to sacrifice has a direct correlate in that of individual subjects, and Bataille's theory leaves this unexplained.

11. The central role of utility in modernity has the effect of rendering utilitarianism the implicit philosophical position. Even when utilitarianism doesn't have numerous proponents, it nonetheless functions as the position that other philosophies seek to define themselves against precisely because it appears as the natural attitude to take up. Beginning with Kant, the great ethical philosophers of modernity all define their ethical systems against a utilitarian ethics, despite the relative paucity of philosophers espousing it.

12. As Bataille points out, "Religion is the satisfaction that a society gives to the use of excess resources, or rather to their destruction (at least insofar as they are useful)" (Bataille, *Accursed Share, Volume I*, 120).

13. Private conversation, 20 May 2007, Burlington VT.

14. Aristotle, *Physics*, trans. R. P. Hardie and R. K. Gaye, in *The Complete Works of Aristotle*, ed. Jonathan Barnes (Princeton NJ: Princeton University Press, 1984), 1:332.

15. The great philosophical critic of thinking in terms of the final cause is Spinoza, and his *Ethics* is an attempt to construct a system without any recourse to final causes.

16. Aristotle's insistence on the final cause is correlative to his conception of the good as the sole possible motivation for our actions, as the opening of the *Nichomachean Ethics* makes evident. There, Aristotle claims: "Every art and every inquiry, and similarly every action and choice, is thought to aim at some good; and for this reason the good has rightly been declared to be that at which all things aim" (Aristotle, *Nichomachean Ethics*, trans. W. D. Ross, in Barnes, *The Complete Works of Aristotle*, 2:1729).

17. Because power analysis remains within the terrain of the final cause, Foucault and Deleuze, despite similarities in their thought, make strange bedfellows. Though Deleuze consecrates a laudatory book to Foucault, and Foucault writes a famous encomium to Deleuze in his preface to *Anti-Oedipus*, Deleuze's proximity to Spinoza and the critique of the final cause should have completely alienated him from the power analysis of Foucault. But in Foucault's celebration of the resistance to power — which is itself motivated not by power but by life itself — Deleuze finds their intellectual kinship. As he puts it in his book on Foucault, "Life becomes resistance to power when power takes life as its object" (Gilles Deleuze, *Foucault*, trans. Seán Hand [Minneapolis: University of Minnesota Press, 1988], 92).

18. Joan Copjec, *Read My Desire: Lacan against the Historicists* (Cambridge MA: MIT Press, 1994), 207.

19. See Thomas Dipiero, *White Men Aren't* (Durham NC: Duke University Press, 2002). The definitive psychoanalytic response to Dipiero's position occurs avant la lettre. In *Desiring Whiteness*, Kalpana Seshadri-Crooks explains that race and sex have a fundamentally different relationship to the signifier and that this accounts for the privileged status of sexual difference. She notes: "Race is entirely captured and produced by language. The racial symbolic is not lacking; it is not missing a signifier that wholly and adequately captures the compass of the raced subject" (Kalpana Seshadri-Crooks, *Desiring Whiteness: A Lacanian Analysis of Race* [New York: Routledge, 2000], 44).

20. It is of course Gilles Deleuze and Félix Guattari who give this critique its most celebrated articulation. In *Anti-Oedipus* they contend that psychoanalysis reduces social antagonisms to familial ones: "The political, cultural, world-historical, and racial content is left behind, crushed in the Oedipal treadmill" (Gilles Deleuze and Félix Guattari, *Anti-Oedipus: Capitalism and Schizophrenia*, trans. Robert Hurley, Mark Seem, and Helen R. Lane [Minneapolis: University of Minnesota Press, 1983], 95).

21. As Alexandre Stevens points out, "The question of sexuation is not solely posed in terms of identification, but also in terms of a position of jouissance, a way of enjoyment, namely, a way of life" (Alexandre Stevens, "Love and Sex beyond

Identifications," in *The Later Lacan: An Introduction*, ed. Véronique Voruz and Bogdan Wolf [Albany: State University of New York Press, 2007], 216).

22. Carl Schmitt, *The Concept of the Political*, trans. George Schwab (Chicago: University of Chicago Press, 1996), 38.

23. Fascism represents the ultimate political extension of the male logic of exception. The Fascist regime promises to reconstitute society as a unified whole, but it does so through the radical exclusion of an enemy—Jews, immigrants, and so on.

24. Jacques-Alain Miller, "On Semblances in the Relation between the Sexes," in *Sexuation*, ed. Renata Salecl (Durham NC: Duke University Press, 2000), 22. It should not be necessary to mention that male and female subjectivity here constitute structural rather than biological or cultural terms, referring neither to the physical sexuality of subjects nor to the gender identity that they adopt.

25. Jacques Lacan, *The Seminar of Jacques Lacan, Book XX: Encore 1972–1973*, trans. Bruce Fink (New York: Norton, 1998), 72–73.

26. Kenneth Reinhard, "Toward a Political Theology of the Neighbor," in Slavoj Žižek, Eric L. Santner, and Kenneth Reinhard, *The Neighbor: Three Inquiries in Political Theology* (Chicago: University of Chicago Press, 2005), 58.

27. For Alain Badiou, the "we" articulated by the French editorial writer was not motivated by an identification with American loss but rather an identification with American civilization in the face of an assault by the barbaric hordes. In this sense, the headline is simply racist. What Badiou rules out with this attack is the appeal of loss as such and its constitutive role for our enjoyment. Even though France would subsequently support the attack on Afghanistan, the headline itself envisions no enemy but instead creates collectivity through the shared experience of loss. For Badiou's fully elaborated critique, see Alain Badiou, "On September 11, 2001: Philosophy and the 'War against Terrorism,'" in *Polemics*, trans. Steve Corcoran (New York: Verso, 2006), 15–35.

28. Of course, one cannot discount the fact that societies also go to war simply to defend themselves and survive. But even the seemingly pure war of defense produces sacrifice that allows subjects to enjoy the social bond, and in this way it goes beyond simple defense.

29. Freud's awareness of the link between enjoyment and cost led him to insist that one should never give away psychoanalysis for free or even at a reduced rate. Doing so out of charity would not benefit the recipients but deprive them of the ability to enjoy the sessions. One only enjoys what one pays for, because it is the act of paying—the act of losing—that functions as the source of enjoyment. This is one of the key points that separated him from apostate Wilhelm Reich, who was exceedingly charitable within his psychoanalytic practice and charged patients based on their ability to pay. For Freud, this largesse detracted not simply from the wallet of Reich but from the effectiveness of the analysis that he offered. A free analysis is a thoroughly unenjoyable analysis.

30. As Slavoj Žižek notes, "Rightist ideology in particular is very adroit at offering people weakness or guilt as an identifying trait: we can find traces of this even with Hitler. In his public appearances, people specifically identified themselves with what were hysterical outbursts of impotent rage — that is, they 'recognized' themselves in this hysterical *acting out*" (Slavoj Žižek, *The Sublime Object of Ideology* [New York: Verso, 1989], 106).

31. The sense of relief and pleasure that accompanied the killing of Osama bin Laden did not last more than a couple of weeks. Soon, other terrorist leaders had to be targeted and other plots uncovered. Most importantly, the public approval of Barack Obama's job performance that spiked after the killing of bin Laden soon plummeted, as if the pleasure that Obama's success gave to the American public actually increased its overall disappointment. This is not to discount the role that the economic crisis has played in Obama's declining popularity. But even in an economic boom, the pleasurable effect of bin Laden's death would necessarily be evanescent.

32. Slavoj Žižek, *Tarrying with the Negative: Kant, Hegel, and the Critique of Ideology* (Durham NC: Duke University Press, 1993), 203.

33. Ludwig Wittgenstein, *Philosophical Investigations*, trans. G. E. M. Anscombe (New York: Macmillan, 1958), 223.

34. Wittgenstein, *Philosophical Investigations*, 222.

35. Joan Copjec, *Imagine There's No Woman: Ethics and Sublimation* (Cambridge MA: MIT Press, 2002), 164.

7. AGAINST KNOWLEDGE

1. Foucault never identifies the diffusion of power with the development of capitalism but rather leaves the driving force behind this shift unexplained. He sees it as an expansion of the control exercised by social authority, and he works to expose and thereby oppose this expansion. But the enemy he opposes is not at all an economic system; it is instead the system of knowledge itself. Thus, he must conceive of forms of knowledge, like the genealogy form (which he takes over from Nietzsche), that do not function in the way that knowledge typically does in order to avoid becoming part of the problem he analyzes.

2. Anthony Giddens, *The Consequences of Modernity* (Stanford CA: Stanford University Press, 1990), 27.

3. Karl Marx and Frederick Engels, *The Communist Manifesto: A Modern Edition*, trans. Samuel Moore (New York: Verso, 1998), 38.

4. Capitalism's universal equivalence marks a decisive break from all prior systems that constitute a social order through a royal exception. Though capitalism employs a general equivalent (money), this general equivalent remains on the same level as the commodities for which it determines their value, while the king exists on a different level from his subjects. This is the problem with Jean-Joseph Goux's otherwise pathbreaking work *Symbolic Economies*. In this book, Goux notices a

homology between the economy's general equivalent and the role of the father in society. According to Goux, "The phallus is the general equivalent of objects, and the father is the general equivalent of subjects, in the same way that gold is the general equivalent of products" (Jean-Joseph Goux, *Symbolic Economies: After Marx and Freud*, trans. Jennifer Curtiss Gage [Ithaca NY: Cornell University Press, 1990], 24). Here, Goux fails to see how the father has an exceptional status that gold lacks. The general equivalent does not rise to the same exterior position relative to the structure as the master signifier does.

5. Karl Marx, *The Economic and Philosophic Manuscripts of 1844*, trans. Martin Milligan (New York: International Publishers, 1964), 141–42. Marx's effort to construct a practically oriented thought has had a decisive — if often unacknowledged — influence on the subsequent history of thought, even among those thinkers who seem most explicitly opposed to the concerns of Marxism. For instance, Martin Heidegger's emphasis on the need to understand Dasein through its productive relation to things rather than as a subject separated from the object world owes a tremendous debt to the step in this direction that Marx takes. Without Marx, one could not imagine Heidegger saying, "There is immediately present in productive comportment toward something the understanding of the being-in-itself of that to which the comportment relates" (Martin Heidegger, *Basic Problems of Phenomenology*, trans. Albert Hofstadter [Bloomington: Indiana University Press, 1982], 115).

6. Georges Bataille constructs an intriguing defense of Stalin — and Stalinist violence — as necessary for the transition of Russia from a feudal society into an industrial one. According to Bataille, Stalin's bureaucratic expertise makes this difficult leap feasible, and this expertise includes the willingness to enforce massive societal changes through violence. For Bataille's full explanation, see Georges Bataille, *The Accursed Share: Volumes II and III*, trans. Robert Hurley (New York: Zone Books, 1993).

7. Bertolt Brecht, *Galileo*, trans. Charles Laughton (New York: Grove Press, 1966), 69.

8. The potential of the Enlightenment to turn against itself and become a force for the expansion of social authority is what Max Horkheimer and Theodor Adorno label the "dialectic of Enlightenment." Within this dialectic, even the experience of liberation and freedom becomes the expression of its opposite. See Max Horkheimer and Theodor W. Adorno, *Dialectic of Enlightenment: Philosophical Fragments*, trans. Edmund Jephcott (Stanford CA: Stanford University Press, 2002).

9. Ulrich Beck, *Risk Society: Towards a New Modernity*, trans. Mark Ritter (Newbury Park CA: Sage Publications, 1992), 58.

10. Eric L. Santner, *My Own Private Germany: Daniel Paul Schreber's Secret History of Modernity* (Princeton NJ: Princeton University Press, 1996), 86.

11. Santner, *My Own Private Germany*, 87. According to Santner, Daniel Paul Schreber is the archetypal victim of expert authority, but he also offers an insight

into a possible ethical or political response to this form of authority. This response includes what Santner calls identifying with the symptom produced by the regime of the expert — that which blocks the full realization of this regime.

12. Georg Lukács, *History and Class Consciousness: Studies in Marxist Dialectics*, trans. Rodney Livingstone (Cambridge MA: MIT Press, 1971), 53.

13. Thomas Frank, *What's the Matter with Kansas? How Conservatives Won the Heart of America* (New York: Henry Holt and Company, 2004), 1.

14. In *Seminar XXIII*, Jacques Lacan points out that our enjoyment is "enjoyment of the real" and that "masochism is the main enjoyment that the real gives" (Jacques Lacan, *Le séminaire, livre XXIII: Le sinthome, 1975–1976* [Paris: Seuil, 2005], 78, my translation).

15. Alenka Zupančič, *Ethics of the Real: Kant, Lacan* (New York: Verso, 2000), 225.

16. A friend recently apologized for smoking while we were walking together outside and confessed that when he smokes he feels as if he is masturbating in public. He meant to indicate the shame associated with the action, but his parallel suggests more importantly the enjoyment now attached to smoking.

17. Of course, not every smoker enjoys smoking. It is possible to smoke or perform a harmful activity without any knowledge of the harm that it does. In this case, one simply obtains pleasure, though simple pleasures are more difficult to find than one might imagine. Once knowledge intrudes on our experience, enjoyment intrudes on our pleasure.

18. Jacques Lacan, *The Seminar of Jacques Lacan, Book VII: The Ethics of Psychoanalysis, 1959–1960*, trans. Dennis Porter (New York: Norton, 1992), 177.

19. See Jonathan Wells, *The Politically Incorrect Guide to Darwinism and Intelligent Design* (Washington DC: Regnery Publishing, 2006); Phillip E. Johnson, *Defeating Darwinism by Opening Minds* (Downer's Grove IL: InterVarsity Press, 1997); and William A. Dembski, ed., *Uncommon Dissent: Intellectuals Who Find Darwinism Unconvincing* (Wilmington DE: ISI Books, 2004).

20. The conservative campaign against the idea that human activity contributes to global warming represents another species of conservative populism, and it relies on the same tropes as scientific creationism. If one doubts the scientific consensus on global warming, one can cast oneself as a rebel against the rule of the expert, whose authority governs contemporary society. The environmentalist who fights against global warming, in contrast, takes the side of knowledge and invokes the authority of the expert as a weapon in the struggle.

21. Slavoj Žižek, *The Ticklish Subject: The Absent Centre of Political Ontology* (New York: Verso, 1999), 391.

22. The combination of obedience and rebellion is evident in the tactics employed by the antiabortion group Operation Rescue in the 1990s. The group would engage in protests that defied the law styled on those of the Left in the 1960s (and its fringe members would even perpetuate violence against abortion providers), while at the

same time everyone involved enjoyed obeying God's law, which manifested itself through the directives of Operation Rescue's leaders.

23. An exemplary case of emancipatory sympathies among the upper class revealing themselves to be nothing but sympathies occurred when left-leaning actor Alec Baldwin visited the Occupy Wall Street movement in October 2011. Expecting to find people with whom he agreed, Baldwin discovered that the movement went too far, that it called into question capitalism itself. Baldwin's recoil from Occupy Wall Street does not reflect his personal insincerity but rather the extreme difficulty for the upper class to align itself with the emancipatory project. Just as Christ made clear the problems that the rich have in attaining heaven, we must recognize as well the barriers that distance the rich from universal emancipation.

24. The agent in hysterical discourse is the divided subject itself, which creates a problem for a social link grounded on this discursive structure. Because the divided subject constantly seeks a master to heal its division, hysterical discourse leads back to the discourse of the master. This is why revolt tends to result in more extreme forms of mastery.

25. Mladen Dolar, "Hegel as the Other Side of Psychoanalysis," in *Jacques Lacan and the Other Side of Psychoanalysis: Reflections on "Seminar XVII,"* ed. Justin Clemens and Russell Grigg (Durham NC: Duke University Press, 2006), 136.

26. Dolar, "Hegel as the Other Side," 136.

27. Alenka Zupančič, "When Surplus Enjoyment Meets Surplus Value," in Clemens and Grigg, *Jacques Lacan and the Other Side*, 168.

28. Sigmund Freud, *The Ego and the Id*, in *The Standard Edition of the Complete Psychological Works of Sigmund Freud*, vol. 19, trans. and ed. James Strachey (London: Hogarth Press, 1961), 48.

29. Jacques Lacan, *Le séminaire, livre XVIII: D'un discourse qui ne serait pas du semblant, 1971*, ed. Jacques-Alain Miller (Paris: Seuil, 2006), 177–78, my translation.

30. Lacan's theory of sexual difference justifies Freud's apparently misogynist claim that female subjects have a less developed superego than male subjects. If the superego employs an ideal of ultimate enjoyment with which to berate the subject, this ideal does not exist in the case of female subjects as it does for males. The male ideal of the ultimate enjoyment — the image of the noncastrated primal father — is the source of energy for the male superego, and no corresponding female ideal exists. Ironically, however, the result is not that male subjects are more ethical than females (as Freud intimates) but the opposite. Despite its link to ethical imperatives, the superego cannot function as a force for ethics because it produces a paranoid subject replete with envy for the other's enjoyment. While not the exclusive province of male subjects, this envy is the necessary product of the male structure, making males more prone to it.

31. The problem with both *Roger and Me* and *The Big One* is that they target individual capitalists who act against the interests of their workers as the problem with

the contemporary economy. By doing so, both films fail to register the structural dimension of corporate downsizing — how this process is an effect of capitalism itself rather than just a few malevolent capitalists. Moore rectifies this error in the later *Capitalism: A Love Story* (2009).

32. Many critics of Moore's filmmaking contend that his presence in the films is their greatest weakness, but this critique is based on the mistaken idea that the most effective documentary is the purest one. Moore's presence in the films is obscene — it pollutes the objectivity of the argument and disturbs the straightforward communication of knowledge — but this is precisely the source of its political effectiveness. Critics want Moore to subtract himself from his films because they want the films to fail, not because they are advising him how to make better films.

33. *Sicko* (2007), the film that follows *Fahrenheit 9/11*, returns to the position of Moore's earlier films. Rather than attacking insurance executives and health care professionals for their excessive enjoyment, *Sicko* illustrates how various systems of universal health care provide more enjoyment than the private system in the United States. One of the strengths of the film is Moore's inclusion of interviews with a doctor in England who lives in a luxurious house and drives an upscale car despite working in the British system of universal health care.

34. Hilary Neroni, "The Nonsensical Smile of the Torturer: Documentary Form and the Logic of Enjoyment," *Studies in Documentary Film* 3, no. 3 (2009): 246.

35. Remarkably, on the basis of this novel, Crichton received an invitation to testify before Congress on the subject of global warming.

36. Michael Crichton, *State of Fear* (New York: HarperCollins, 2004), 182.

37. The films of Michael Moore (outside of *Fahrenheit 9/11*) and other documentaries that adopt an autobiographical form, such as Agnès Varda's *Le glaneur et la glaneuse* (*The Gleaners and I*, 2000), do manage to shift the focus from knowledge to enjoyment and thus escape the seemingly inherent limitation of documentary form. For an analysis of the role of enjoyment in the autobiographical documentary, see Hilary Neroni, "Documenting the Gaze: The Autobiographical Turn in Judith Helfand's *Blue Vinyl* and Agnes Varda's *The Gleaners and I*," *Quarterly Review of Film and Video* 27, no. 3 (2010): 178–92.

38. Jacques Rancière, *Hatred of Democracy*, trans. Steve Corcoran (New York: Verso, 2006), 8.

39. Rancière, *Hatred of Democracy*, 41.

40. In the *Politics*, Aristotle classifies democracy as a perversion, though he sees it as the least objectionable one. The chief problem with it is that democracy lends itself to neglect of the public functions. He says: "For that which is common to the greatest number has the least care bestowed upon it. Everyone thinks chiefly of his own, hardly at all of the common interest; and only when he is himself concerned as an individual. For besides other considerations, everybody is more inclined to neglect something which he expects another to fulfill; as in families many attendants

are often less useful than a few" (Aristotle, *Politics*, trans. B. Jowett, in *The Complete Works of Aristotle*, ed. Jonathan Barnes [Princeton NJ: Princeton University Press, 1984], 2:2002).

41. John Locke, *Two Treatises of Government* (New York: Cambridge University Press, 1988), 350–51.

42. The increasing disjunction between capitalism and democracy is not visible solely in China. It is also apparent in Russia and the United States, where the absence of controls on political spending has led to a near-total economic takeover of electoral politics.

43. Yannis Stavrakakis, *The Lacanian Left: Psychoanalysis, Theory, Politics* (Albany: State University of New York Press, 2007), 278–79.

8. THE POLITICS OF FANTASY

1. Jacques Rancière, *Disagreement: Politics and Philosophy*, trans. Julie Rose (Minneapolis: University of Minnesota Press, 1999), 19. In *Class Ideology and Ancient Political Theory*, Ellen Meiksins Wood and Neal Wood give the classic form of this argument. They contend that "Socrates, Plato, and Aristotle ... thought that the way of life and values of the nobility could be reformed and revitalized so as once more to become the foundation of civic life in order to stem the levelling tide of democracy, the tyranny of the majority, and the vulgar commercialism that they felt were engulfing Athens and the whole of Greece. In a significant way their political thought can be conceived of as the supreme intellectual expression of the increasing class consciousness of the aristocracy during the fourth century, a consciousness that seemed to become more pronounced as the class was progressively threatened with extinction" (Ellen Meiksins Wood and Neal Wood, *Class Ideology and Ancient Political Theory: Socrates, Plato, and Aristotle in Social Context* [New York: Oxford University Press, 1978], 3). The problem with this reduction of Socrates, Plato, and Aristotle to their class origins is that it fails to see how philosophizing itself involves a betrayal of established social coordinates. In the act of conceiving the allegory of the cave, Plato reveals for the first time how ideology functions, and this constitutes a class betrayal, even if Plato himself was consciously trying to justify existing class relations.

2. In the *Philosophy of Right*, Hegel claims: "Taken without its monarch and the articulation of the whole which is the indispensible and direct concomitant of monarchy, the people is a formless mass and no longer a state" (G. W. F. Hegel, *Philosophy of Right*, trans. T. M. Knox [London: Oxford University Press, 1952], 183).

3. Baruch Spinoza, *Theological-Political Treatise*, 2nd ed., trans. Samuel Shirley (Indianapolis: Hackett, 2001), 8.

4. Of course, Western philosophy is not a homogeneous body of thought, and there are significant countercurrents within it. My claim here is not that every philosopher shares a critical view of fantasy (or of experience structured like fantasy)

but simply that this is a prevailing thread that unites the major thinkers, even those belonging to vastly disparate traditions.

5. Ludwig Wittgenstein, *Philosophical Investigations*, trans. G. E. M. Anscombe (New York: Macmillan, 1958), 49.

6. One could viably make the argument that Kant's *Critique of Pure Reason*, written in 1781, provided an essential building block for the 1789 French Revolution by demolishing the fantasmatic role that reason played in thought. The attack on the fantasmatic uses of reason perhaps enabled the toppling of the hierarchical structure of French society, which also had its basis in a similar fantasy structure.

7. Plato, *The Republic*, trans. G. M. A. Grube, in *Plato: Complete Works*, ed. John M. Cooper (Indianapolis: Hackett, 1997), 1133.

8. Plato, *Republic*, 1136.

9. Immanuel Kant, *Critique of Pure Reason*, trans. Paul Guyer and Alan Wood (Cambridge: Cambridge University Press, 1998), 637.

10. Kant, *Critique of Pure Reason*, 621–22.

11. Though the Kant of the first *Critique* takes philosophical fantasizing as the bugaboo that he must dismantle, a radical transformation occurs with the publication of the second *Critique*. Here, Kant positions the moral law as a kind of fantasy through which the subject finds its true freedom. The moral law has no basis in the understanding or the world of theoretical reason, and it applies to the subject only as an agent in the world, not as a thinker. That is to say, one cannot allow it to alter one's theoretical conception of things even though it must fundamentally change one's practical being if one is to be ethical and comply with it. This turn toward fantasy that Kant makes in the second *Critique* becomes foundational for the subsequent figures of German Idealism — Fichte, Schelling, and Hegel. As Fichte makes the second *Critique* the starting point for his theoretical philosophy, German Idealism becomes the one moment in the history of Western philosophy where philosophers treat the fantasmatic disturbance or illusion as the source of theoretical fecundity rather than as a burden to be overthrown. Hegel's method in the *Phenomenology*, for instance, consists in showing how our fantasmatic errors are productive and move thinking forward, and his absolute knowledge is not the final overcoming of fantasy but the recognition that the fantasmatic disturbance is what thought can never overcome. For an analysis of the turn to fantasy in Kant's second *Critique*, see the conclusion of Todd McGowan, *The Impossible David Lynch* (New York: Columbia University Press, 2007).

12. Gottlob Frege, *The Foundations of Arithmetic: A Logico-Mathematical Inquiry into the Concept of Number*, trans. J. L. Austin (Evanston IL: Northwestern University Press, 1980), vi.

13. Ludwig Wittgenstein, *The Blue and Brown Books* (New York: Harper & Row, 1958), 27.

14. Ludwig Wittgenstein, *On Certainty*, trans. Denis Paul and G. E. M. Anscombe, ed. G. E. M. Anscombe and G. H. von Wright (New York: Harper and Row, 1972), 62.

15. Wittgenstein never espouses the idea of freedom as the result of recognizing one's insertion into the language game. And yet, this ideal nevertheless silently informs the entire project.

16. Alfred Jules Ayer, *Language, Truth and Logic* (New York: Dover, 1946), 34.

17. Karl Marx, "Theses on Feuerbach," in *The Marx-Engels Reader*, ed. Robert C. Tucker (New York: Norton, 1978), 145, Marx's emphasis.

18. Étienne Balibar, *The Philosophy of Marx* (New York: Verso, 1995), 17.

19. Karl Marx, *Grundrisse*, trans. Martin Nicolaus (New York: Penguin, 1993), 84.

20. Marx, *Grundrisse*, 286.

21. Karl Marx, *Capital: A Critique of Political Economy, Volume Three*, trans. David Fernbach (New York: Penguin, 1981), 127.

22. Karl Marx, *Capital: A Critique of Political Economy, Volume One*, trans. Ben Fowkes (New York: Penguin, 1976), 165.

23. Laura Mulvey, *Fetishism and Curiosity* (Bloomington: Indiana University Press, 1996), 4.

24. When we see the importance of shattering commodity fetishism for Marxist politics, it becomes clear why Brecht's aesthetic predominates among Marxist artists. Brecht aims at producing a *Verfremdungseffekt* in his audience, an experience of alienation in which the power of fantasy becomes evident — and in which the audience gains critical distance from fantasy. Through this process, the audience begins to see through the structure of commodity fetishism and to see the labor at work behind the commodity (as they see the labor at work in producing the work of art).

25. Yannis Stavrakakis, *Lacan and the Political* (New York: Routledge, 1999), 110. In *Lacan and the Political* Stavrakakis interprets the idea of traversing the fantasy as overcoming fantasy's power over the subject so that the subject can act as a political being. This is not the only possible interpretation. Richard Boothby sees traversing the fantasy in almost the opposite way, as a way of devoting oneself completely to the kernel of the fantasy. He claims: "To traverse the phantasy in the Lacanian sense is to be more profoundly claimed by the phantasy than ever, in the sense of being brought into an ever more intimate relation with that real core of the phantasy that transcends imaging" (Richard Boothby, *Freud as Philosopher: Metapsychology after Lacan* [New York: Routledge, 2001], 275–76).

26. Stavrakakis, *Lacan and the Political*, 107.

27. Even though Stavrakakis attempts to formulate a specifically Lacanian conception of politics, his starting point is actually politics itself, not Lacanian thought. That is to say, he comes to Lacan with a clear basis in Ernesto Laclau and Chantal Mouffe's politics of radical democracy, and he looks to psychoanalysis to buttress this project. As a result, in this work he does not see that psychoanalysis might take up a different attitude toward fantasy. In his later work, *The Lacanian Left*, he

moves away from Laclau and Mouffe and roots his political project more firmly within psychoanalytic thought, and this enables him to see the political possibilities inhering in fantasy and in the enjoyment that fantasy provides.

28. Fabio Vighi grasps perfectly the paradoxical attitude that psychoanalytic politics takes up toward fantasy. He claims that "the two dialectical moments (to dispel and reconfigure the fantasy) are part of the same move" (Fabio Vighi, *On Žižek's Dialectics: Surplus, Subtraction, Sublimation* [New York: Continuum, 2010], 163). Vighi's book focuses its conception of psychoanalytic politics specifically around the formation of an alternative to global capitalism, and, as the book's title suggests, he takes the philosophy of Slavoj Žižek as his point of departure for this political challenge, though the book should not be seen as simply a commentary on Žižek.

29. Sigmund Freud, "Screen Memories," in *The Standard Edition of the Complete Psychological Works of Sigmund Freud*, vol. 3, trans. and ed. James Strachey (London: Hogarth Press, 1962), 317.

30. Sigmund Freud, *Introductory Lectures on Psycho-analysis*, in *The Standard Edition of the Complete Psychological Works of Sigmund Freud*, vol. 16, trans. and ed. James Strachey (London: Hogarth Press, 1963), 372.

31. Fantasies about the end of capitalism are widespread within the world of science fiction. *Star Trek*, for instance, envisions a socialist economy in which money no longer motivates human behavior. But even in more realistic art, such as James Cameron's *Titanic* (1998), the image of the destruction of what seems indestructible hints at a fantasmatic rendering of capitalism's end.

32. Ursula K. Le Guin, *The Left Hand of Darkness* (New York: Ace Books, 1969), 12.

33. Le Guin, *Left Hand of Darkness*, 93.

34. The unraveling of gender identity in *The Left Hand of Darkness* should not be seen as a rejection of all opposition between male and female. Even in Le Guin's fantasmatic world, subjects do take up a sexed identity during the sexual part of their monthly cycle. As a result, the inhabitants of Winter do not elude what Lacan calls the failure of the sexual relationship.

35. Even though there are obviously different ideologies, one can speak of ideology in the singular because every ideology operates in the same way relative to trauma. Constituting a social reality free of the traumatic kernel that creates that reality is what all ideologies share, and it is their fundamental task.

36. We become susceptible to the encounter with trauma in fantasy and the dream because these experiences marginalize consciousness. In our everyday life, consciousness functions as a defense mechanism, preventing us from encountering the traumatic kernel at the same time as it guides our activity.

37. Boothby, *Freud as Philosopher*, 275.

38. Lacan continually draws attention to the pseudoscientific — and thus wholly contingent — origins of psychoanalysis. This is why he refers to Freud and Fliess, as

they are beginning to work out the ideas that would eventually become the basis for psychoanalysis, as a couple of "pipsqueaks."

39. Jacques Lacan, *The Seminar of Jacques Lacan, Book II: The Ego in Freud's Theory and in the Technique of Psychoanalysis, 1954–1955*, trans. Sylvana Tomaselli (New York: Norton, 1988), 154–55, Lacan's emphasis.

40. Lacan, *Seminar II*, 176–77.

41. For the definitive account of the link between fantasy and origins, see Jean Laplanche and Jean-Bertrand Pontalis, *Fantasme originaire; Fantasme des origines; Origines du fantasme* (Paris: Fayard, 2010).

42. Ursula K. Le Guin, *The Lathe of Heaven* (New York: Avon Books, 1971), 167–68.

43. Karl Marx and Frederick Engels, *The German Ideology* (Moscow: Progress Publishers, 1976), 53. Marxism's reliance on the promise of a future complete enjoyment in order to encourage subjects to adopt the proper class consciousness attests to another potential problem with antifantasmatic politics. This image of the future is itself the ultimate fantasy, and it indicates that Marxism itself cannot do without fantasy (albeit in a form different from commodity fetishism). Thus, the example of Marxism suggests that perhaps fantasy is inescapable, even for those most deeply committed to combating it.

9. BEYOND BARE LIFE

1. Osama bin Laden, "Declaration of War against the Americans Occupying the Land of the Two Holy Places," http://www.pbs.org/newshour/terrorism/international/fatwa_1996.html. bin Laden's statement is not an isolated proclamation of the love for death among fundamentalist leaders; many of them have expressed similar sentiments.

2. Erich Fromm, *The Anatomy of Human Destructiveness* (New York: Picador, 1973), Fromm's emphasis.

3. In early 2008, I was part of a panel devoted to a discussion of atheism where two analytic philosophers argued that extreme religious belief simply wasn't rational and thus fell outside the bounds of what we all could agree on. The fact that such belief could lead someone to proclaim a love for death substantiates this claim. But telling someone that her or his belief is not reasonable is unlikely to eliminate it and will most likely have the effect of further entrenching it.

4. Alan Dershowitz makes this point in his article "In Love with Death," though he then blames the culture of death on deranged imams, which, like every claim about ideological manipulation, does nothing to explain why would-be suicide bombers take the imams seriously or why the imams themselves embrace death in the way that they do. His prescription — defeating fundamentalism abroad before it comes to American shores — fails to recognize the similarity between American fundamentalism and the Islamic variety. Furthermore, Dershowitz sees no link between capitalism's insistence on bare life and the emergence of fundamentalism.

See Alan Dershowitz, "In Love with Death," *Guardian*, 4 June 2004, http://www.guardian.co.uk/saudi/story/0,,1231172,00.html; and "Worshippers of Death," *Wall Street Journal*, 3 March 2008, http://online.wsj.com/public/article_print/SB120450617910806563.html.

5. Of course, the stated reason for the love of death is almost always the eternal reward that a glorious death will occasion. But this image of the afterlife functions as a fetish enabling the believer to embrace the value-creating power of death itself.

6. The link between the finitude of death and the infinitude of enjoyment is made apparent in Michel Foucault's stated desire to die at the moment of the most intense enjoyment: "I would like and I hope I'll die of an overdose of pleasure of any kind" (Michel Foucault, *Politics, Philosophy, Culture: Interviews and Other Writings 1977–1984*, ed. Lawrence D. Kritzman, trans. Alan Sheridan et al. [New York: Routledge, 1988], 12).

7. Martin Heidegger, *Being and Time*, trans. John Macquarrie and Edward Robinson (San Francisco: HarperCollins, 1962), 294.

8. The destruction of value that accompanies the embrace of pure life explains the hostility that greets acolytes of life, from Spinoza to the flower child of the 1960s. The exponent of life doesn't simply threaten the destructive values associated with the established system (whether it be Judaism in the case of Spinoza or the military-industrial complex in the case of the flower child). The devotion to life and the turn away from death call all values into question. This position even precludes the capacity for love.

9. The link between capitalism and life is one of the reasons why it appears to be a natural rather than an historical economic form. But this link cannot actually serve as an ethical or political justification for the capitalist mode of production. As subjects, we are by definition alienated from the world of nature, so that even a natural economic form has an unnatural status for us.

10. The fact that modern science leads to the building of bombs capable of destroying all life on the planet seems to suggest that science is on the side of death rather than life, and psychoanalytic theorists such as Jacques Lacan and Slavoj Žižek have aligned science with the death drive. But the drive for the new discovery that animates science, like the capitalist drive for accumulation, is fundamentally life affirming because it refuses all limits. If this refusal leads to total destruction and the end of science, that destruction will necessarily be an external limit that will not touch the scientific project in itself.

11. One of the great renewals of an established commodity in the history of capitalism occurred with the introduction of New Coke by the Coca-Cola Company. Widely panned as one of the greatest marketing disasters in history, this failed product had the effect of renewing traditional Coca-Cola as a commodity. Not long after the public rejection of New Coke, the Coca-Cola Company reissued traditional Coca-Cola under the name "Coca-Cola Classic." With this new moniker,

traditional Coke effectively became a new commodity and began to generate more value than it had previously.

12. Following Heidegger's critique of the modern retreat from an authentic being-toward-death, Hannah Arendt makes the connection between modernity and the philosophy of life in *The Human Condition*. She notes: "Life asserted itself as the ultimate point of reference in the modern age and has remained the highest good of modern society" (Hannah Arendt, *The Human Condition* [Chicago: University of Chicago Press, 1958], 313–14).

13. Heidegger's critique of the inauthentic relationship to death prevalent in our everyday lives is a response to the specific rejection of death that occurs with modernity. Though Heidegger never puts it in quite these terms, his philosophy attempts to recapture what we've lost with the turn to modernity, to reassert the primacy of death amidst the modern repression of it.

14. For the classic account of this shift, see Alexandre Koyré, *From the Closed World to the Infinite Universe* (Baltimore MD: Johns Hopkins University Press, 1957).

15. Jacques Lacan, *The Seminar of Jacques Lacan, Book III: The Psychoses, 1955–1956*, trans. Russell Grigg (New York: Norton, 1993), 13.

16. Marx's conception of the relationship between the forces of production and the relations of production receives its most well known treatment in the preface to *A Contribution to the Critique of Political Economy*. In this preface Marx says: "Just as one does not judge an individual by what he thinks about himself, so one cannot judge a period of transformation by its consciousness, but, on the contrary, this consciousness must be explained from the contradictions of material life, from the conflict existing between the social forces of production and the relations of production. No social order is ever destroyed before all the productive forces for which it is sufficient have been developed, and new superior relations of production never replace older ones before the material conditions for their existence have matured within the framework of the old society" (Karl Marx, *A Contribution to the Critique of Political Economy*, trans. S. W. Ryazanskaya [New York: International Publishers, 1970], 21). Here, Marx sounds like a philosopher of life, though throughout the three volumes of *Capital* he comes closer to being a philosopher of the death drive, as he recognizes the role that sacrifice plays in the creation of value.

17. Gilles Deleuze and Félix Guattari, *Anti-Oedipus: Capitalism and Schizophrenia*, trans. Robert Hurley, Mark Seem, and Helen R. Lane (Minneapolis: University of Minnesota Press, 1983), 231–32.

18. Giorgio Agamben, *Homo Sacer: Sovereign Power and Bare Life*, trans. Daniel Heller-Roazen (Stanford CA: Stanford University Press, 1998), 114. As Agamben's own statement suggests, his analysis doesn't interpret Hitler's actions relative to the Jews. He simply takes Hitler and the Nazis at their word, which assumes that they aren't just lying and, more significantly, that they knew on a psychic level what they

were doing. The task of the theorist of Nazism is interpreting the movement and its statements, not simply accumulating them. Elsewhere, this is what Agamben does, but concerning the crucial point of the Nazi attitude toward the Jews, he fails to see that Hitler's effort to stress the animality of the Jews covers up the Jewish mode of enjoying that is his real target.

19. Of course, Jews were not first reduced to bare life and then sent to death camps. The two sets of camps function as a metaphor for the overall process that the Nazis unleashed on the Jews: the isolation of the Jewish excess and then its elimination. Most often, the Nazis targeted different people for the different operations.

20. For a thorough analysis of the film's sadism, see Walter Davis, *Death's Dream Kingdom: The American Psyche since 9-11* (London: Pluto Press, 2006), 30.

21. In *The Edge of Evolution*, intelligent design advocate Michael Behe accepts many of the premises of evolution (concerning the existence of evolutionary change, for instance), but he insists that evolution provides an insufficient account of mutation or change. Intelligent design exists, for Behe, in the gaps that evolutionary theory cannot explain. In this vision, a theory of evolution that acknowledges its limits becomes an acceptable theory of evolution. See Michael J. Behe, *The Edge of Evolution: The Search for the Limits of Darwinism* (New York: Free Press, 2007).

22. Peggy Noonan, "In Love with Death: The Bizarre Passion of the Pull-the-Plug People," *Wall Street Journal*, 24 March 2005, http://www.opinionjournal.com/columnists/pnoonan/?id=110006460.

23. Jean-Paul Sartre, *Being and Nothingness: A Phenomenological Essay on Ontology*, trans. Hazel E. Barnes (New York: Washington Square Press, 1956), 42. Sartre takes this point from Martin Heidegger.

24. Deleuze and Guattari, *Anti-Oedipus*, 207.

25. Roland Barthes, *Mythologies*, trans. Annette Lavers (New York: Hill and Wang, 1972), 146.

26. One of the most notable attempts to break from mythical language and inaugurate a productive mode of signification was the French feminism of the 1970s and 1980s. By adopting a nonlinear mode of writing (*écriture féminine*) that challenged the exceptions of readers, French feminists such as Hélène Cixous and Luce Irigaray tried to link the production of signifiers in the act of writing to the production of actual history. As Cixous describes it, authentic women's writing is engaged in a way that traditional writing is not: "Her discourse, even when 'theoretical' or political, is never simply linear or 'objectivized,' universalized; she involves her story in history" (Hélène Cixous, "Sorties," in *The Newly Born Woman*, trans. Betsy Wing [Minneapolis: University of Minnesota Press, 1986], 92).

27. G. W. F. Hegel, *Lectures on the History of Philosophy: Medieval and Modern Philosophy*, vol. 3, trans. E. S. Haldane (Lincoln: University of Nebraska Press, 1995), 288.

28. In *Surplus*, Kiarina Kordela offers a compelling—though not ultimately, to my mind, convincing—argument in which she contends that Spinoza does in fact

privilege the negative. See A. Kiarina Kordela, *Surplus: Spinoza, Lacan* (Albany: State University of New York Press, 2007).

29. As Nietzsche puts it, "If a temple is to be erected *a temple must be destroyed:* that is the law" (Friedrich Nietzsche, *The Genealogy of Morals*, trans. Walter Kaufmann and R. J. Hollingdale [New York: Vintage, 1989], 95).

30. It is not merely coincidental that Freud's first book—which was not at all a psychoanalytic work—concerned aphasia. Even while he was working as a neurologist, Freud's attention focused on the point at which signification stops. Though he and Breuer developed the talking cure, the key moment in this analysand's talking is what cannot be said rather than the seemingly endless stream of words that are said.

31. Wittgenstein also implicitly identifies the act of keeping silent with the assertion of subjectivity at the end of the *Tractatus Logico-Philosophicus* when he famously states: "What we cannot speak about we must pass over in silence" (Ludwig Wittgenstein, *Tractatus Logico-Philosophicus*, trans. D. F. Pears and B. F. McGuinness [Atlantic Highlands NJ: Humanities Press International, 1961], 74). In this work Wittgenstein constructs a complete system of logical symbolization, but by ending with the space of silence, he leaves a space for subjectivity as that which the system cannot accommodate.

32. It is not possible for evolutionary theory to simply correct its elision of the gaps and to become more attuned to the role of the death drive in the movement of history. The illusion of perfect continuity is inherent in every scientific investigation because science moves forward without regard for subjectivity. If science were to take the subject into account, it would lose its objective dimension and cease to be science as we know it. But scientific inquiry will necessarily produce an unconscious — and provide an opening for psychoanalysis — because of this elision.

33. Jacques Lacan, *Le séminaire, livre VIII: Le transfert, 1960–1961*, ed. Jacques-Alain Miller (Paris: Seuil, 2001), 120, my translation.

10. THE NECESSITY OF BELIEF

1. While I was speaking on this idea at a conference, someone in the audience pointed out that this bracketing of the ontological question of God's existence bespeaks the limitation of psychoanalytic thought, the moment at which we must supplement it with some other theoretical approach. But this is to give too much credit to the ameliorative power of God's existence. Neither the existence nor the nonexistence of God can alter the trauma of existing—death and eternal life represent equally unattractive alternatives — and this is precisely what psychoanalysis emerges in response to. (Unfortunately, the questioner did not find this line of argument entirely satisfying.)

2. Pierre Daviot, *Jacques Lacan et le sentiment religieux* (Paris: Éditions Érès, 2006), 22, my translation.

3. Sigmund Freud, *Civilization and Its Discontents*, in *The Standard Edition of the Complete Psychological Works of Sigmund Freud*, vol. 21, trans. and ed. James Strachey (London: Hogarth Press, 1961), 32.

4. Alain Badiou, *Metapolitics*, trans. Jason Barker (New York: Verso, 2005), 77. Jacques Rancière, a fellow student of Louis Althusser, also locates the origin of politics in social antagonism. He claims: "There is politics from the moment there exists the sphere of appearance of a subject, the *people*, whose particular attribute is to be different from itself, internally divided" (Jacques Rancière, *Disagreement: Politics and Philosophy*, trans. Julie Rose [Minneapolis: University of Minnesota Press, 1999], 87).

5. In this precise sense, the otherwise misleading (and thoroughly ideological) term applied to Al-Qaeda and other militant Islamic organizations by right-wing commentators, "Islamofascism," is accurate. Like traditional Fascism, twenty-first-century Islamic militancy aims at healing the social antagonism by eliminating modernity and bringing about a society fully reconciled with itself. Of course, it aims to do so without the state apparatus that the term "Fascism" implies.

6. As Lacan notes, "Religion is made to cure men, that is to say, in order that they don't perceive what doesn't work" (Jacques Lacan, *Le triomphe de la religion précédé de discours aux catholiques* [Paris: Seuil, 2005], 87, my translation).

7. See Victor J. Stenger, *God — the Failed Hypothesis: How Science Shows That God Does Not Exist* (New York: Prometheus Books, 2007); Daniel Dennett, *Breaking the Spell: Religion as a Natural Phenomenon* (New York: Penguin, 2006); Sam Harris, *The End of Faith: Religion, Terror, and the Future of Reason* (New York: Norton, 2004); Sam Harris, *Letter to a Christian Nation* (New York: Alfred A. Knopf, 2006); Michel Onfray, *Atheist Manifesto: The Case against Christianity, Judaism, and Islam*, trans. Jeremy Leggatt (New York: Arcade Publishing, 2007); Christopher Hitchens, *God Is Not Great: How Religion Poisons Everything* (New York: Twelve Books, 2007).

8. Richard Dawkins, *The God Delusion* (Boston: Houghton Mifflin, 2006), 5.

9. Harris, *The End of Faith*, 149.

10. Stenger, *God — the Failed Hypothesis*, 248.

11. One might say that it is not that the laws of probability put an end to the question of God's existence but that the question of God's existence challenges the basis for thinking in terms of probability. What calculations of probability necessarily fail to take into account is the power of an event — in this case, a revelation of God — to retroactively change the probabilities. An authentic event is not possible until it happens, and then it appears to have been inevitable because of its power to retroactively change how the past appears. For instance, prior to the collapse of the Soviet Union, those who assessed probabilities considered World War III much more likely than this collapse and counted its probability at almost zero. But after it occurred, the fall of the Soviet Union appeared to have been evident for all to see. By the same token, if God's existence was revealed tomorrow, all the signs

pointing to it today would immediately become visible, even to Richard Dawkins and Victor Stenger. (I am indebted to Sheila Kunkle for pointing this out to me.)

12. Blaise Pascal appears to contend that the wager for belief represents a good investment because the possible reward surpasses to an infinite extent what one wagers. One stakes this life, which has the value of a nothing, for eternal life, which is a life without limit, a life of infinite value. Most critics read Pascal's wager as the ultimate in utility-style thinking (and this is why Dawkins claims that God himself, if such a being existed, would disapprove of the gambit and reward those who wagered for disbelief), but in the act of making his wager, Pascal actually affirms the significance of what cannot be reduced to calculation. He recognizes that there is a point of nonknowledge within the known world that no amount of speculation or scientific discovery can penetrate, and he opts to take the side of this nonknowledge over all the calculable certainties in the world of utility. One cannot, Pascal sees, gain any purchase on this fundamental uncertainty.

13. Karl Marx, *The Grundrisse*, trans. Martin Nicolaus (New York: Penguin, 1993), 409. Though Marx does point out that capitalism involves a tremendous waste of human material, from the perspective of capital itself this waste is not waste but simply proper business practice that follows from the dictates of the mode of production itself. It is only from a moral perspective that Marx himself imports the idea that capitalism becomes guilty of waste. He says: "It squanders human beings, living labour, more readily than any other mode of production, squandering not only flesh and blood, but nerves and brain as well. In fact it is only through the most tremendous waste of individual development that the development of humanity in general is secured and pursued, in that epoch of history that directly precedes the conscious reconstruction of human society. Since the whole of the economizing we are discussing here arises from the social character of labour, it is in fact this precisely social character of labour that produces this waste of the workers' life and health" (Karl Marx, *Capital: A Critique of Political Economy, Volume Three*, trans. David Fernbach [New York: Penguin, 1981], 182).

14. The hold that religious belief has over America—in stark contrast to its power in European countries such as France and Germany—occurs not in spite of the influence of American pragmatism but because of it. The most pragmatic nation will be the most believing in order to compensate for the elimination of pure wastefulness in everyday life.

15. Though not every believing subject embraces the necessity of the leap of faith conceptualized by Kierkegaard, there is nevertheless no believer who does not accept a fundamental distinction between belief and disbelief. Without this distinction, the imperative to believe loses its attractiveness.

16. Jacques Lacan, *The Seminar of Jacques Lacan, Book XX: Encore 1972–1973*, trans. Bruce Fink (New York: Norton, 1998), 45.

17. Lacan, *Seminar XX*, 45.

18. Jacques Lacan, *The Four Fundamental Concepts of Psychoanalysis*, trans. Alan Sheridan (New York: Norton, 1978), 59, Lacan's emphasis.

19. Charles Ramirez Berg, "A Taxonomy of Alternative Plots in Recent Films: Classifying the 'Tarantino Effect,'" *Film Criticism* 31, nos. 1–2 (Fall–Winter 2006): 39.

20. Berg, "Taxonomy of Alternative Plots," 40–41.

21. Jon Kilik, interview with Todd McGowan, University of Vermont, Burlington, 23 April 2007.

22. Daniel Lazare, "Among the Disbelievers," *Nation*, 28 May 2007, 29.

23. Fyodor Dostoyevsky, *The Brothers Karamazov*, trans. Richard Pevear and Larissa Volokhonsky (New York: Alfred A. Knopf, 1990), 69.

24. Because freedom is the ability to act against one's own interest or good, Kant paradoxically sees the existence of law itself as the proof of human freedom. Only free beings could give themselves laws. The law implies that one might act otherwise, whereas beings without laws can only follow their nature, which operates in the direction of the useful. One could not imagine a law for plants not to encroach on the space of other plants.

25. Daniel C. Dennett, *Freedom Evolves* (New York: Penguin, 2003), 13.

26. George W. Bush, "State of the Union," 28 January 2003, http://www.whitehouse.gov/news/releases/2003/01/20030128-19.html.

27. This is the problem with Milton Friedman's conception of freedom in *Capitalism and Freedom*. As Friedman sees it, freedom involves one necessarily in an economy that has ideological and structural dictates, but he fails to see how following these dictates might lead toward unfreedom. Freedom lies simply in the opposition to governmental power. He claims: "The preservation of freedom is the protective reason for limiting and decentralizing governmental power" (Milton Freidman, *Capitalism and Freedom* [Chicago: University of Chicago Press, 2002], 3). Freidman's simple opposition between freedom to make money or do what one wants and governmental control derives from a strictly empirical — and unsustainable even on that level — conception of freedom.

28. Jean-Paul Sartre, *Being and Nothingness: A Phenomenological Essay on Ontology*, trans. Hazel E. Barnes (New York: Washington Square Press, 1956), 620.

29. The attempt to formulate the Kantian ethic as a viable contemporary position requires sidestepping the link between freedom and law. This is apparent in Alenka Zupančič's *Ethics of the Real*, which represents the definitive attempt to preserve the radical disruptiveness of this ethic. Zupančič treats the Kantian ethic as purely formal and thereby empties it of the content that connects it to law — such as the admonition to treat others never merely as a means. As a result, she can claim (which would seem audacious to a devoted Kantian): "Following Kant — but at the same time going against Kant — we thus propose to assert explicitly that *diabolical evil, the highest evil, is indistinguishable from the highest good, and that they are nothing other than the definitions of an accomplished (ethical) act*. In other words, at the level

of the structure of the ethical act, the difference between good and evil does not exist. At this level, evil is formally indistinguishable from good" (Alenka Zupančič, *Ethics of the Real: Kant, Lacan* [New York: Verso, 2000], 92).

30. J. G. Fichte, *The Science of Knowledge*, trans. Peter Heath and John Lachs (New York: Cambridge University Press, 1982), 176.

11. THE CASE OF THE MISSING SIGNIFIER

1. The political stumbling block repeats on the social level the structural obstacle that each subject confronts. As Joan Copjec notes, "The psychoanalytic subject is not infinite, it is *finite*, limited, and it is this limit that causes the infinity, or unsatisfiability, of desire. One thing comes to be substituted for another in an endless chain only because the subject is cut off from that essential thing that would complete it" (Joan Copjec, *Read My Desire: Lacan against the Historicists* [Cambridge MA: MIT Press, 1994], 60–61).

2. Psychoanalytic politics has much in common with the project of Hegel's philosophy. Philosophy has a political edge, for Hegel, because it involves the recognition that a seemingly external limit is actually an internal one. This recognition fundamentally transforms the concept of the political for the subject.

3. In *Psychoanalysis and Feminism*, Juliet Mitchell, responding to the charge that psychoanalysis supports patriarchal sexual relations, rightly identifies psychoanalysis as a descriptive rather than a prescriptive account of patriarchy. As Mitchell sees it, psychoanalytic theory helps us to separate what is necessary within the social structure from what is not necessary. It can thus, according to Mitchell, be the foundation for "a struggle based on the theory of the social non-necessity at this stage of development of the laws instituted by patriarchy" (Juliet Mitchell, *Psychoanalysis and Feminism: Freud, Reich, Laing and Women* [New York: Vintage, 1975], 414).

4. To imagine feminist struggle as the effort to break the link between the feminine and the missing signifier indicates an implicit valorization of the master signifier — the signifier that is *not* missing — and an implicit desire to thrust some other identity into the position of the missing binary signifier.

5. Paul Verhaeghe, *Does the Woman Exist? From Freud's Hysteric to Lacan's Feminine*, trans. Marc du Ry (New York: Other Press, 1997), 247.

6. In his conception of the four discourses that constitute the various social bonds, Lacan defines the binary signifier as knowledge because, strictly speaking, there is no other binary signifier. The missing binary signifier does not exist.

7. Jacques Derrida, *Specters of Marx: The State of Debt, the Work of Mourning, and the New International*, trans. Peggy Kamuf (New York: Routledge, 1994), 29.

8. Dan Brown, *The Da Vinci Code* (New York: Random House, 2003), 238.

9. See, for instance, Slavoj Žižek's claim that "*the Da Vinci Code* effectively reinscribes Christianity into the New Age's paradigm of seeking balance between

masculine and feminine principles" (Slavoj Žižek, "Revenge of the Global Finance," *In These Times*, 21 May 2005, http://www.inthesetimes.com/site/main/article/2122/).

10. Jacques Lacan, *The Seminar of Jacques Lacan, Book XX: Encore, 1972–1973*, trans. Bruce Fink (New York: Norton, 1998), 32.

11. The condemnation of zealotry in *The Da Vinci Code* reveals an investment in the prevailing belief—a belief conditioned by the widespread acceptance of capitalist relations of production as the natural denouement of human civilization—that evil is the product of too much virtue rather than a lack of it. Alain Badiou labels this attitude "Thermidorean" and sees it as a way of vacating politics of its fundamental source of energy. He notes: "For every Thermidorean, whether from 1794 or the present day, the category of virtue is declared to be *devoid of political force*. Virtue is an unsustainable effort that necessarily leads to the worst: Terror" (Alain Badiou, *Metapolitics*, trans. Jason Barker [New York: Verso, 2005], 132).

12. In one sense, Roman Catholic opposition to abortion is different from fundamentalist opposition, since the Catholic Church opposes the death penalty as well. But a fundamentalist undercurrent informs even the Catholic antiabortion position, which is why the opposition to abortion has priority over the opposition to the death penalty. This prioritizing manifests itself in the political activity of certain priests who deny the Eucharist to prochoice politicians while offering it to supporters of the death penalty.

13. Jacques-Alain Miller, "On Semblances in the Relation between the Sexes," in *Sexuation*, ed. Renata Salecl (Durham NC: Duke University Press, 2000), 17.

14. Richard Dawkins, *The God Delusion* (Boston: Houghton Mifflin, 2006), 374.

15. See Stephen Jay Gould, *Rock of Ages: Science and Religion in the Fullness of Life* (New York: Ballantine, 1999).

16. The celebration in *The Da Vinci Code* of the Paris meridian or Rose Line as a repressed alternative reveals clearly the problem with this attitude toward the missing signifier. The Paris meridian is important only insofar as its repression shapes our prevailing system of mapping the world; it does not offer a viable alternative that one might call into existence. If the world replaced the Greenwich meridian with the Paris meridian as its fundamental meridian of reference for determining longitude, nothing would change: the system of mapping would continue to have a center and a site of repression, but the content of each would have reversed. The adoption of the Paris meridian would represent a massive change and no change at the same time.

17. Brown, *Da Vinci Code*, 444.

18. See Ernesto Laclau and Lilian Zac, "Minding the Gap: The Subject of Politics," in *The Making of Political Identities*, ed. Ernesto Laclau (New York: Verso, 1994), 11–39.

19. Chantal Mouffe, *The Return of the Political* (New York: Verso, 1993), 8.

20. Jacques Derrida, *Without Alibi*, trans. Peggy Kamuf (Stanford CA: Stanford University Press, 2002), xxxii.

21. Jacques Lacan, *The Four Fundamental Concepts of Psycho-analysis*, trans. Alan Sheridan, ed. Jacques-Alain Miller (New York: Norton, 1978), 8.

22. Lacan, *Four Fundamental Concepts*, 7.

23. Even though Alain Badiou rejects the position of Derrida and Heidegger that insists on respecting the gap in signification rather than fully identifying with it, he fails to think the relation between signification and the gap (or, to put it in his terms, between situation and void). For Badiou, this is a relation of nonrelation or of subtraction. The mistake of most contemporary theorists consists in failing to save truth (which is located in the structural position of the void) as absolutely distinct from or in opposition to knowledge (which concerns the situation and fails to touch the void). The philosophical and political task, as Badiou conceives it, involves an effort to discover truth through a process of subtracting the void from the situation, thereby grasping the disjunction of these two terms. But by sustaining the nonrelation between the void and the situation, Badiou at once idealizes the void and defames the situation. He works to sustain a situation-free politics and inveighs against the fall from politics back into the situation. Badiou's emphasis on the nonrelation between the void and the situation leaves him in the position of advocating permanent revolution, which occurs through fidelity to event, a rupture within the situation located in the position of the void or missing signifier. Since the subject must avoid falling back into the inauthenticity of the situation, no political gain can ever be enough. The ultimate point of Badiou's thought is not changing the situation through the political act but the very effort to engage in the political act itself. Politics for Badiou is an end in itself, though it only becomes so insofar as he isolates it from the everyday life of the situation.

24. The great filmic representation of conceiving the missing signifier from the perspective of the symbolic system is John Ford's *The Searchers* (1956), which famously concludes with a shot from inside a house with the door closing on Ethan Edwards (John Wayne). Though Edwards returned the kidnapped daughter to her family, he cannot remain within the civilized structure that he helped to constitute. He stands as a necessary absence, and the film's final shot makes this apparent. But the opposite psychoanalytic position relative to the missing signifier takes place during a scene from Nicolas Winding Refn's *Drive* (2011) that clearly quotes the conclusion of *The Searchers*. In a scene in an elevator toward the end of the film, the unnamed driver (Ryan Gosling) must kill a man sent to kill him, and he does so in front of the woman with whom he has fallen in love. Because he has no weapon and the killer is armed, the driver kills the man through extreme physical violence, a violence so brutal that it leaves his lover completely alienated from him. In order to safeguard both himself and the woman he loves, the driver must make sure that the killer is dead, but this requires that he reveal the horror of which he is capable. After this display, Irene (Carey Mulligan) is no longer able to envision herself with the driver. As she steps out of the elevator with a terrified look on her face, the film shows the door closing

from within the elevator, leaving the spectator in the elevator with the driver and the dead man while the door shuts on Irene. Here, the film places the spectator with the missing and excluded signifier, in direct contrast to the final shot from *The Searchers*. This scene from *Drive* reveals the political project of psychoanalysis in an image form.

25. The French feminism of the 1970s and 1980s fell into the trap of believing that the missing signifier concerned a space external to the signifying structure or the space of an alternate signifying structure. French feminists produced the concept of *écriture féminine* as a type of writing foreign to the phallocentric chain of signifiers, emerging from the gap within that chain of signifiers. But *écriture féminine*, despite the efforts of those creating it, necessarily remained internal to this chain insofar as the missing signifier itself was internal to it, which is why texts written in this way did not lead to substantive political change. The limit of French feminism as an effective political project was linked directly to its failure to locate the missing signifier as an internal gap within signification.

26. Simone de Beauvoir, *The Second Sex*, trans. Constance Borde and Sheila Malovany-Chevallier (New York: Alfred A. Knopf, 2010), 148.

27. Beauvoir, *Second Sex*, 80.

28. Juan-David Nasio, *Le fantasme: Le plaisir de lire Lacan* (Paris: Éditions Payot & Rivages, 2005), 79, my translation.

29. Any politicization of male subjects requires an identification with the structural position that female subjects occupy. The female position is that of the missing signifier, and it is only through what is missing that politics as such can be envisioned. This is what Jennifer Friedlander grasps when she notes that "the feminine pole [is] the province of the subversive, of the political, of the cure" (Jennifer Friedlander, "How Should a Woman Look? Scopic Strategies for Sexuated Subjects," *Journal for the Psychoanalysis of Culture and Society* 8, no. 1 [2003]: 107).

30. My position here is proximate to that of Henry Krips, who sees "politics as a matter of working *within* rather than against the system of conventions, but at the same time *pushing the conventions to the point that they become overstretched, and loosen their grip — in Hegelian terms, pushing them to the point that they negate themselves*" (Henry Krips, "A Mass Media Cure for Auschwitz: Adorno, Kafka and Žižek," *International Journal of Žižek Studies* 1, no. 4 [2007], http://www.zizekstudies.org/index.php/ijzs/article/view/67/132, Krips's emphasis).

CONCLUSION

1. Adrian Johnston, *Time Driven: Metapsychology and the Splitting of the Drive* (Evanston IL: Northwestern University Press, 2005), xxii.

2. G. W. F. Hegel, *Science of Logic*, trans. George di Giovanni (Cambridge: Cambridge University Press, 2010), 572.

3. Aristotle, *Politics*, trans. B. Jowett, in *The Complete Works of Aristotle*, ed. Jonathan Barnes (Princeton NJ: Princeton University Press, 1984), 2:1986.

Index

abortion, 42, 177, 232–33, 235, 240–41, 268, 335
Absalom, Absalom! See Faulkner, William
Adler, Alfred, 2
Adorno, Theodor, 2, 64–65, 121–22, 318n8
Afghanistan War, 160–61, 163
agalma, 293n9
Agamben, Giorgio, 71, 230–31, 301n32, 328–29n18
aggression, 12–13, 50–51, 224, 227, 290n19, 308n27
alienation, 63, 75, 199, 324n24, 327n9
All the President's Men. See Pakula, Alan
Al-Qaeda, 331n5
alternative medicine, 42
Althusser, Louis, 2, 3, 331n4
Altman, Robert: *Short Cuts*, 105–12, 307n17
Amber Alert, 41
American Civil War, 152, 314n6
American Indians, 273
American society, 83, 159–61, 163, 177–78, 185–86
Amores Perros. See Iñárritu, Alejandro González
analytic philosophy, 201–203, 326n3

anarchism, 302n
Anderson, Paul Thomas: *Magnolia*, 105
Anger Management. See Segal, Peter
anorexia, 29–31, 293n11, 293n13
antagonism, 4, 7–8, 58, 131, 154–56, 165, 228, 239, 245, 274, 314n6, 315n20, 331n4
antiglobalization, 42
Antigone. See Sophocles
anti-Semitism, 58–59
anxiety, 98–120, 306–7n15, 308n26, 308n30
aphasia, 56, 239, 330n30
Arab Spring, 174, 194
Arendt, Hannah, 328n12
Aristotle, 5, 38–39, 151–52, 191–92, 198, 251, 315n16, 321–22n40, 322n1
Armstrong, Gillian: *Charlotte Gray*, 174
atheism, 243–62
Auschwitz, 234
autoeroticism, 26, 36
Ayer, A. J., 203

Babel. See Iñárritu, Alejandro González
Badiou, Alain, 2, 65, 122–23, 245, 300n25, 309n4, 309n5, 316n27, 335n11, 336n23

339

INDEX

Baldwin, Alec, 320n23
Balibar, Étienne, 2, 203
Barthes, Roland, 237–38
Bataille, Georges, 148–49, 314n9, 314n10, 314n12, 318n6
La Battaglia di Algeri. (The Battle of Algiers). See Pontecorvo, Gillo
Beatty, Warren: *Reds*, 174
Beauvoir, Simone de, 278–79, 288n5
Beck, Ulrich, 170
Behe, Michael, 329n21
belief, 243–62, 326n3, 332n14
Beloved. See Morrison, Toni
Benjamin, Walter, 71
Berg, Charles Ramirez, 254–55
Bergman, Ingrid, 64
Berkeley Free Speech Movement, 228
Berlin, Isaiah, 80
Berlusconi, Silvio, 103
Bible code, 265
bin Laden, Osama, 223–25, 234–35, 317n31, 326n1
Bion, Wilfred, 2
Bloch, Ernst, 71
Bogart, Humphrey, 64
Bolshevism, 287–88n3
Bond, James, 190
Boothby, Richard, 29, 214, 324n25
bourgeoisie, 7–8, 126, 134, 287n1, 311n22
Braveheart. See Gibson, Mel
Bread and Roses. See Loach, Ken
Breaking the Waves. See von Trier, Lars
Brecht, Bertolt, 324n24: *Galileo*, 169
Breuer, Joseph, 126, 239, 330n30
The Brothers Karamazov. See Dostoyevsky, Fyodor
Brown, Dan: *The Da Vinci Code*, 266–74, 278–79, 334–35n9, 335n11, 335n16
Brown, Norman O., 15
Buddhism, 291–92n1

Buñuel, Luis: *Cet obscure objet du désir (That Obscure Object of Desire)*, 307n20
burqa, 268
Bush, George W., 43, 45, 111, 161, 186–88, 224, 260, 307n19
Butler, Judith, 127

Cameron, James: *Titanic*, 86, 97, 304–5n28, 325n31
Campion, Jane, 312n28
capitalism, 4, 7–9, 21, 33, 42–43, 48, 58–85, 89–98, 247, 266, 284, 294n19, 301n32, 317–18n4, 320n23, 325n31; and authority, 167–69, 173, 181–82, 185; and commodity fetishism, 205–7, 291n33, 297n3; and demand, 52, 103, 300n21; and democracy, 191–95, 322n42; and enjoyment, 284, 285, 299n15, 305n29, 311n22; and excess, 298–99n12; and freedom, 260–61, 302n5; and fundamentalism, 223; and individuality, 144, 203–5, 320–21n31; and life, 226–31, 326–27n4, 327n9; and modernity, 302n8, 304n23; and normality, 121–22, 125, 129, 133, 309n3; and possibility, 212; and profit, 301n33, 301n36; and violence, 287n1; and waste, 249–50, 332n13
Capitalism: A Love Story. See Moore, Michael
Capra, Frank: *It Happened One Night*, 132
castration, 4, 113, 155, 157, 183, 216
Cather, Willa: *Death Comes for the Archbishop*, 228
Catholic Church, 335n12
Central Intelligence Agency, 47
Charlotte Gray. See Armstrong, Gillian
Chase, David: *The Sopranos*, 304n19

Chinatown. See Polanski, Roman
Chomsky, Noam, 247
Christ, 232, 266, 272
Christianity, 32–33, 40, 231–35, 267–72, 294n19, 334–35n9
Christmas, 62
Cinderella Man. See Howard, Ron
civil rights struggle, 291n32
Cixous, Hélène, 127, 329n26
class struggle, 7
Clinton, Bill, 114, 163
Coca-Cola, 327–28n11
cognitive mapping, 48, 105–6, 307n16
Cold War, 35, 46
Columbine, 234
commodity, 38, 62, 69–71, 79–80, 85, 122, 205–7, 226–27, 284, 291n33, 297n3, 302–3n12, 317–18n4, 324n24, 327–28n11
Communism. See Marxism
continental philosophy, 203
contingency, 34–35, 106, 215, 217, 254–62
Copjec, Joan, 90, 154, 165, 298n8, 334n1
Crash. See Haggis, Paul
creationism, 177, 191, 234, 241, 319n20
Crichton, Michael, 321n35: *State of Fear*, 189–90
Critchley, Simon, 313n4
CSI: *Crime Scene Investigations*, 172
cynicism, 114–15, 294n19

Dahmer, Jeffrey, 129
Darwinism, 177, 235, 319n19
The Da Vinci Code (film). See Howard, Ron
The Da Vinci Code (novel). See Brown, Dan
Daviot, Pierre, 244
Davis, Walter, 49, 310n15, 329n20: *An Evening with JonBenet Ramsey*, 299n18

Dawkins, Richard, 246–51, 270, 331–32n11, 332n12
Dayton, Jonathan: *Little Miss Sunshine*, 299n18
Death Comes for the Archbishop. See Cather, Willa
Deleuze, Gilles, 65, 127, 129, 229–30, 236–38, 300n25, 309n3, 315n17, 315n20
DeLillo, Don: *Libra*, 297n39
Dembski, William A., 319n19
democracy, 20, 190–95, 197, 198, 273–74, 321–22n40, 322n42
Dennett, Daniel, 246, 260, 331n7
Derrida, Jacques, 16, 121–22, 198, 265, 274, 275, 290n25, 290n26, 294n21
Dershowitz, Alan, 326–27n4
Descartes, René, 169, 218
dialectics, 100, 143, 261, 295–96n29, 310n15, 318n8, 325n28
Diogenes, 114
Dipiero, Thomas, 154, 315n19
The Dispossessed. See Le Guin, Ursula K.
Doctorow, E. L., 297n39
Doherty, Thomas, 308n26
Dolar, Mladen, 181–82
Dostoyevsky, Fyodor: *The Brothers Karamazov*, 259
Drive. See Refn, Nicolas Winding

economics, 52–78, 167–68, 290n26
Edelman, Lee, 41
Ehrenfel, Christian Von, 9
ego, 9–10, 26, 29, 67, 72–74, 126–27, 182, 188, 295–96n29, 300–301n31, 301n32, 313n34
Eiffel Tower, 161–62
empiricism, 47, 157, 260, 274
Engels, Friedrich, 173, 218
Enlightenment, 17, 81, 87, 169–70, 180, 184, 210, 243, 246, 252, 291n28, 302n8, 318n8

341

Enron: The Smartest Guys in the Room. See Gibney, Alex
environmentalism, 42, 189–90, 319n20
Ephron, Nora: *Sleepless in Seattle*, 67–68
Epistemology, 118
equality, 145, 165, 181, 196–97, 220, 279, 293n13, 302n4, 302n5, 302n8
An Evening with JonBenet Ramsey. See Davis, Walter
evolution, 150, 177, 234–35, 241, 247–48, 251, 253, 260, 329n21, 330n32
existentialism, 310n15

fantasy, 21, 125–38, 266, 302–3n12, 311n20, 322–23n4, 323n11; and capitalism, 229, 325n31; and enjoyment, 67, 70, 118–20, 312n29; and origins, 326n41; and politics, 196–222, 245, 323n6, 324n24, 324n25, 324–25n27, 325n28, 326n43; and trauma, 312n27, 312n28, 312n31, 325n36
Farris, Valerie: *Little Miss Sunshine*, 299n18
Fascism, 20, 46, 58–59, 118–19, 156, 178, 192, 230, 246, 287–88n3, 298–99n12, 308n31, 316n23, 331n5
Fast Times at Ridgemont High. See Heckerling, Amy
Faulkner, William: *Absalom, Absalom!*, 314n6
feminism, 29–31, 212–13, 278–81, 288n4, 288n5, 334n3, 334n5
fetishistic disavowal, 175, 207
feudalism, 94
Fichte, J. G., 262, 323n11
Fight Club. See Fincher, David
Fincher, David: *Fight Club*, 85–87, 303n16
Fink, Bruce, 135–36
Firestone, Shulamith, 288n5
Fleischer, Ari, 187

Fliess, Wilhelm, 49, 215
Food and Drug Administration, 47
Ford, Henry, 169
Ford, John: *The Searchers*, 336–37n24
Fort Sumter, 152
Foucault, Michel, 121, 124, 152, 167–68, 304n27, 310n9, 315n17, 317n1, 327n6
Founding Fathers, 40
Fourier, Charles, 17
Frank, Thomas, 173, 178
Frankfurt School, 64–65, 207, 263
freedom, 17, 21–22, 31–32, 43, 48, 86–87, 91, 139, 239, 263, 303n17, 304–5n28; and anxiety, 112, 114; and atheism, 259–62; and bad faith, 123; and capitalism, 79–82, 181, 193, 302n4, 302n5, 302n8, 333n27; and fantasy, 211; and knowledge, 170; and law, 333n24, 333–34n29; and liberalism, 143; and philosophy, 197, 199–202, 324n15
Frege, Gottlob, 201–2
French feminism, 329n26, 337n25
French Revolution, 323n6
French society, 161–62
Freud, Anna, 2
Freud, Sigmund, 114, 308n26, 325–26n38; and antagonism, 4, 7–9; and anxiety, 112–13; and castration, 4; and class, 82–85, 92, 303n15; and Communism, 287–88n3; and cure, 19, 293n17, 316n29, 330n30; and death drive, 1–2, 10–13, 15, 21, 35, 38, 53–55, 236, 289n17, 289n18, 295n26, 295–96n29, 298n4, 298n5, 298n8, 300n28; and desire, 18; and economics, 52–55, 76–77, 302n10; and ego, 72–73; and enjoyment, 67–68; and fantasy, 134, 209–11, 215; and fort/da game, 37–38; and free association, 153; and good, 6; and Hegel, 292n3; and homosexuality,

342

4; and justice, 145; and neurosis, 59–60, 125–31, 239; and Nietzsche, 292n2; and normality, 310n12; and Oedipus complex, 4; and physiology, 297n2; and pleasure principle, 67–68, 314n9; and psychosis, 127; and religion, 244–46, 250–51; and seduction theory, 49–50; and sexual difference, 3, 320n30; and sexual drives, 9–11, 13; and subjectivity, 25–27, 36; and suffering, 1; and superego, 182–84; and violence, 50
—Works: *Beyond the Pleasure Principle*, 9–10, 13, 37–38, 53, 68, 295n26; *Civilization and Its Discontents*, 3, 13, 92, 236, 244, 295–96n29; *The Ego and the Id*, 182; *Five Lectures on Psychoanalysis*, 130–31; *The Future of an Illusion*, 244, 246; "Instincts and Their Vicissitudes," 68, 300n28; *Introductory Lectures on Psycho-analysis*, 125, 211; *Jokes and Their Relation to the Unconscious*, 76–77, 83–84; "Negation," 26; "On Narcissism," 26; "On Psychotherapy," 310n12; *Project for a Scientific Psychology*, 53–55, 72–73, 297n2, 314n9; "Screen Memories," 209; *Studies on Hysteria* (with Joseph Breuer), 126–27, 302n10
Friedan, Betty, 288n5
Friedlander, Jennifer, 337n29
Friedman, Milton, 60, 299n16, 333n27
Fromm, Erich, 2, 10–12, 223–24, 236, 289n17, 293n17
Frost, Mark, 111
fundamentalism, 21, 33, 35, 103, 109–11, 115, 223–24, 227, 229–35, 243, 326n1; and Catholicism, 335n12; and politics, 245; and signification, 266–69, 274

Galileo, 169
Galileo. *See* Brecht, Bertolt
Garcia, Jerry, 76
Garden of Eden, 40, 219
Gates, Bill, 82, 303n15
gay marriage, 42–44, 88
Gentlemen Prefer Blondes. *See* Hawks, Howard
German Idealism, 323n11
Gibney, Alex: *Enron: The Smartest Guys in the Room*, 190
Gibson, Mel: *Braveheart*, 40–41; *Passion of the Christ*, 232, 329n20
Giddens, Anthony, 167–68
Le glaneur et la glaneuse (*The Gleaners and I*). *See* Varda, Agnès
global warming, 189–90, 319n20, 321n35
Goldmann, Lucien, 309n2
good, 2–3, 5–9, 16–22, 26, 31, 117, 136, 152–53, 192–95, 241, 283–86, 288–89n10, 315n16
Gore, Al, 189
Gould, Stephen Jay, 270
Goux, Jean-Joseph, 317–18n4
Grateful Dead, 77
Gross, Otto, 10, 12
Grosz, Elizabeth, 29–30
Guattari, Félix, 65, 127, 129, 229–30, 236–38, 300n25, 315n20
Guggenheim, Davis: *An Inconvenient Truth*, 189

Habermas, Jürgen, 258
Haggis, Paul: *Crash*, 105
Haider, Jörg, 156
Hamlet. *See* Shakespeare, William
Hardt, Michael, 230, 238
Harris, Sam, 246–47, 250, 331n7
Hartmann, Heinz, 126, 310n14
Hawks, Howard: *Gentlemen Prefer Blondes*, 299n15

343

Hayek, Friedrich, 60, 80
Heckerling, Amy: *Fast Times at Ridgemont High*, 132
Hegel, G. W. F., 33–35, 88, 196–97, 238, 292n3, 294n21, 296n31, 305n2, 310n15, 311n22, 322n2, 337n30; and fantasy, 323n11; and infinity, 226–27, 284, 305n29; and knowledge, 311n21; and limit, 334n2; and master/slave dialectic, 93–94; and recognition, 99–100, 305n4, 305n5; and singularity, 313n2
Heidegger, Martin, 36, 80–81, 112–13, 116, 121–22, 156, 198, 294–95n, 329n23; and death, 225, 240, 328n12, 328n13; and Marxism, 309n2, 318n5; and phenomenology, 201–2
Heinlein, Robert: *Stranger in a Strange Land*, 302–3n12
hermeneutics, 266, 270–75
Hill, Anita, 114
Hitchcock, Alfred, 312n28
Hitchens, Christopher, 246, 250, 331n7
Hitler, Adolf, 224, 317n30, 328–29n18
Hobbes, Thomas, 143
Hollywood, 64, 67, 131–32
Holy Grail, 266–73
Horkheimer, Max, 65, 121, 318n8
Horus, 272
House M.D., 172
Howard, Ron: *Cinderella Man*, 40; *The Da Vinci Code*, 266–74, 278–79, 334–35n9, 335n11, 335n16
Hughes, Howard, 302–3n12
Husserl, Edmund, 201
hysteria, 49, 126–27, 179, 181, 239, 311n20, 317n30, 320n24

ideology, 3, 60, 123–24, 133, 154, 189, 198, 208–9, 219–20, 294n19, 309n3, 322n1; and capitalism, 64–72, 205, 247, 291n33, 299n15, 309–10n7; and individuality, 254–55; and life, 225, 231, 294n20; and possibility, 210–13; and progress, 291n32; and religion, 250, 251, 326–27n4, 331n5; and repression, 263, 266; and signification, 237, 259–60, 267, 273; and suffering, 31–35; and trauma, 213–16, 325n35
immigrant, 276–77
imperialism, 161, 224, 227
Iñárritu, Alejandro González: *Amores Perros*, 254; *Babel*, 254–57; *21 Grams*, 254
An Inconvenient Truth. See Guggenheim, Davis
Inquisition, 169
intelligent design, 177, 234, 329n21
Iraq War, 45, 111, 160–62, 188, 260
Irigaray, Luce, 121, 329n26
Islam, 33, 35, 110, 223–25, 231–32, 268–69, 273, 296n37, 326–27n4
It Happened One Night. See Capra, Frank

Jameson, Fredric, 47–48, 105–6, 304n23, 307n16
Jazz. See Morrison, Toni
Jefferson, Thomas, 80
JFK. See Stone, Oliver
Johnson, Phillip E., 319n19
Johnston, Adrian, 284, 300n28
jokes, 76–78, 83–84
Judaism, 40, 248, 298–99n12
Jung, Carl, 2
justice, 79–82, 145, 165, 193, 267, 290n25

Kafka, Franz, 30: *The Trial*, 312n27
Kant, Immanuel, 14, 17, 18, 81, 100, 198, 200–201, 218, 252, 261, 269, 274, 313n4, 314n11, 323n6, 323n11, 333n24, 333–34n29

Karatani, Kojin, 79
Keats, John: "Ode to a Nightingale," 234
Kennedy, John Fitzgerald, 47
Kierkegaard, Søren, 252, 332n15
Kilik, Jon, 257
Klein, Melanie, 2, 290n19
Knight, Peter, 47
Knight, Phil, 185
Koran, 110
Kordela, A. Kiarina, 329–30n28
Krips, Henry, 337n30
Kristeva, Julia, 6–7, 289n11
Kubrick, Stanley: *Paths of Glory*, 150–51
Ku Klux Klan, 272
Kunkle, Sheila, 125, 151, 290n22
Kutcher, Ashton, 64

Lacan, Jacques, 264, 269, 292n8, 300–301n31, 325–26n38, 331n6; and anxiety, 113, 117; and authority, 296n35; and cure, 4, 55; and death drive, 1, 290n19, 298n4, 298n5, 327n10; and evolution, 241; and fantasy, 210, 215, 324n25, 324–25n27; and God, 251–52; and good, 6; and *jouissance* (enjoyment), 91, 93–94, 117, 176, 304n26; and knowledge, 17, 291n30, 334n6; and language, 3, 275–76, 297n2, 305n4; and masochism, 14–15, 319n14; and neurosis, 59; and *objet a*, 26–27, 293n9; and sexual difference, 154, 157, 267, 320n30; and suffering, 127; and superego, 182–84; and symptom, 298n9; and university discourse, 179–82
Laclau, Ernesto, 2, 273, 324–25n27, 335n18
Laplanche, Jean, 49, 326n41
Lasch, Christopher, 106
The Lathe of Heaven. See Le Guin, Ursula K.

Lazare, Daniel, 258
The Left Hand of Darkness. See Le Guin, Ursula K.
Le Guin, Ursula K.: *The Dispossessed*, 210, 220–21; *The Lathe of Heaven*, 210, 216–17; *The Left Hand of Darkness*, 210, 212–13, 325n34
Le Pen, Jean-Marie, 156
Levinas, Emmanuel, 305–6n6
Lévi-Strauss, Claude, 8
Lewinsky, Monica, 114, 163
liberalism, 7–8, 143–44, 156
Libra. See DeLillo, Don
Little Miss Sunshine. See Dayton, Jonathan; Farris, Valerie
Loach, Ken: *Bread and Roses*, 174
Locke, John, 80, 143–44, 192
Lost Highway. See Lynch, David
Love. See Morrison, Toni
Lukács, Georg, 173, 207, 309n2
Lynch, David, 312n28: *Lost Highway*, 111; *Mulholland Drive*, 111; *Twin Peaks* (television series), 111

Magdalene, Mary, 266, 271
Magnolia. See Anderson, Paul Thomas
Marcuse, Herbert, 12–13, 15, 289n18, 290n19
Marx, Karl, 65, 105, 251, 294n18, 301–2n, 313n2; and accumulation, 63; and antagonism, 7–10; and class struggle, 91; and communist society, 218, 298–99n12; and desire, 61; and fantasy, 196–97, 203–7; and freedom, 32, 181; and knowledge, 168–69, 173, 318n5; and life, 229–30, 237–38, 328n16; and morality, 79, 332n13; and satisfaction, 62–63, 66; and society, 144; and surplus value, 75, 94–95, 205–6, 301n33

345

Marxism, 126, 150, 169, 203, 253, 258, 287–88n3, 290n26, 294n19, 309–10n7, 318n5; and commodity fetishism, 207, 324n24; and critique of ideology, 64–65; and emancipation, 1–2, 229; and fantasy, 208–9, 211, 217–21, 326n43; and injustice, 79–80, 82; and praxis, 7; and psychoanalysis, 10–12, 82, 223–24, 298–99n12, 310n15; and revolution, 65; and suffering, 32; and utopia, 20, 242; and violence, 287n1
masochism, 14–15, 28, 175, 219, 319n14
Masson, Jeffrey, 49
The Matrix. See Wachowski, Andy and Larry
Mauss, Marcel, 147–48
McDermott, Jim, 187–88
McDonald's, 188–89
McTeague. See Norris, Frank
Megan's Law, 41
Melville, Herman, 301n32: *Moby Dick,* 74
Merleau-Ponty, Maurice, 287n1
messianism, 16, 71
metaphysics, 201–2, 290n26
Middle Ages, 291n32
Mill, John Stuart, 7, 143
Miller, Jacques-Alain, 157, 269
Milton, John: *Paradise Lost,* 33; *Paradise Regained,* 33
Mitchell, Juliet, 3, 5, 288n4
Moby Dick. See Melville, Herman
Modernity, 121–22, 149–50, 226–27, 230, 232–34, 291n32, 304n23, 328n12, 328n13
Monde, Le, 160
Moore, Michael, 184–90, 321n32, 321n37: *The Big One,* 185–86, 320–21n31; *Bowling for Columbine,* 185–86; *Capitalism: A Love Story,* 320–21n31; *Fahrenheit 9/11,* 186–90, 321n33; *Roger and Me,* 185–86, 320–21n31; *Sicko,* 190, 321n33
Morrison, Toni, 297n39: *Beloved,* 58, 298n10; *Jazz,* 298n10; *Love,* 57–58; *Paradise,* 298n10
Moses, 63
Mouffe, Chantal, 2, 156, 159, 273–74, 324–25n27
Mulholland Drive. See Lynch, David
Mulvey, Laura, 207, 288n4
Mussolini, Benito, 287–88n3

narcissism, 26, 85, 103, 308n27, 313n34
Nasio, Juan-David, 280, 295n27
nationalism, 217
National Liberation Front, 256
natural selection, 253
Nazism, 156, 230–31, 285, 287–88n3, 328–29n18, 329n19
Negri, Antonio, 230, 238
neighbor, 101–2, 185–86
Neroni, Hilary, 189, 321n37
Neurosis, 55–56, 59, 125–30, 135–36, 208
Nietzsche, Friedrich, 25, 80–81, 131, 152, 197–98, 251, 253, 291–92n1, 292n2, 294n23, 317n1, 330n29
Noonan, Peggy, 234
normality, 121–30, 208, 309n3, 309n4, 310n9, 311n20
Norris, Frank: *McTeague,* 63
nostalgia, 39–46, 50, 296n34

Obama, Barack, 194, 293n11, 317n31
Cet obscure objet du désir (That Obscure Object of Desire). See Buñuel, Luis
obsession, 311n18
Occupy Wall Street, 320n23
"Ode to a Nightingale." *See* Keats, John

Oedipus Tyrannus. See Sophocles
Onfray, Michel, 246, 287–88n3, 292n2, 331n7
ontology, 47, 113, 157, 200, 226, 235, 243, 252, 264, 270, 291n32, 291n33, 330n1
Operation Rescue, 179, 319–20n22
Oppenheimer, Robert, 226
Opus Dei, 267, 273

Pakula, Alan: *All the President's Men*, 48
Paradise. See Morrison, Toni
Paradise Lost. See Milton, John
Paradise Regained. See Milton, John
paranoia, 44–50, 164–65, 246, 297n39, 312n27
Pascal, Blaise, 110, 251, 332n12
Pascal's Wager, 332n12
Passion of the Christ. See Gibson, Mel
pathological narcissism, 85, 103
Paths of Glory. See Kubrick, Stanley
patriarchy, 3–5, 29, 213, 264, 266–67, 269, 273, 277, 288n4
perversion, 64, 91, 127–29, 135–38
Pfaller, Robert, 124, 309–10n7
phenomenology, 201
phobia, 113
Picasso, Pablo, 275
Plato, 18, 191–92, 196–99, 201, 204, 218, 283, 293n9, 322n1
pleasure principle, 12
Polanski, Roman: *Chinatown*, 61, 299n18
Pontalis, Jean-Bertrand, 325n41
Pontecorvo, Gillo: *La Battaglia di Algeri (The Battle of Algiers)*, 256
Portman, Natalie, 64
positivism, 266, 270–71, 274
potlatch, 147
Priory of Scion, 271
progress, 15–20, 25

proletariat, 7–8, 11, 94, 204, 206, 207
psychosis, 99, 125–29, 135, 146, 245, 303n16
La Pyramide Inversée, 271

Quine, Willard Van Orman, 198

Rancière, Jacques, 2, 191, 196, 331n4
Rand, Ayn, 143
Rawls, John, 5, 7, 75, 100, 302n4
Ray, Nicolas: *Rebel without a Cause*, 114
Reagan, Ronald, 43
reality principle, 12
Rebel without a Cause. See Ray, Nicolas
Reds. See Beatty, Warren
Refn, Nicolas Winding: *Drive*, 336–37n24
Reich, Wilhelm, 2, 10–12, 289n16, 294n20, 316n29
reification, 122, 309n2
Reinhard, Kenneth, 101, 158, 306n7
religion, 21, 149–50, 243–63, 284, 314n12, 326n3, 332n14
repression, 11, 21, 236–37, 263–81, 289n16, 289n18, 302n10, 335n16
Resnais, Alain, 312n28
Restuccia, Frances, 311n20
revolt, 7, 289n11
revolution, 4, 7–8, 21, 25–26, 65, 127, 173, 181, 207, 307n16, 311n20, 336n23; and loss, 220; and reform, 311n17; and signification, 237–38, 240
Ricardo, David, 60
Rorty, Richard, 79, 302n4
Ross, Herbert: *The Secret of My Success*, 312n31
Rothenberg, Molly, 308n27
Rumsfeld, Donald, 161
Russian Revolution, 3
Ruth, Babe, 77

Sacrifice, 27–31, 81, 232, 236, 293n17, 314n10, 328n16; and communism, 287n1; and difference, 122; and enjoyment, 2, 13–14, 39, 71, 84, 89–94, 175–76, 192–95, 283, 286, 316n28; and neurosis, 135; and recognition, 97–99, 101, 103; and religion, 248–49, 292n8; and society, 143–66
Sade, Marquis de, 14
sadism, 14–15, 290n22, 329n20
Salecl, Renata, 306n10
Santayana, George, 291n28
Santner, Eric, 104, 172, 301n32, 306n7, 318–19n11
Sarkozy, Nicolas, 103, 309n5
Sartre, Jean-Paul, 121–23, 235, 261, 294–95n24, 329n23
Saussure, Ferdinand de, 297n2
Saving Private Ryan. *See* Spielberg, Steven
scarcity, 12, 35, 226
Schelling, F. W. J., 323n11
Schiavo, Terri, 234–35, 241–42
Schindler's List. *See* Spielberg, Steven
schizophrenia, 127, 129, 309n3
Schmitt, Carl, 156, 159, 311n22
school prayer, 42–44, 177
Schopenhauer, Arthur, 17, 25, 291–92n1, 292n3
Schreber, Daniel Paul, 318–19n11
The Searchers. *See* Ford, John
The Secret of My Success. *See* Ross, Herbert
Segal, Peter: *Anger Management*, 171–72
September 11, 2001, 159–61, 187–88, 316n27
Seshadri, Kalpana, 315n19
Shakespeare, William, 265: *Hamlet*, 39, 137–38, 313n36
Sheen, Charlie, 103
Short Cuts. *See* Altman, Robert

Simmel, Georg, 32
Sleepless in Seattle. *See* Ephron, Nora
Smith, Adam, 60, 294n18, 299n16
Smith, Roger, 185
Socrates, 199, 300n21, 322n1
Sophocles: *Antigone*, 39, 302–3n12; *Oedipus Tyrannus*, 39, 296n31
The Sopranos. *See* Chase, David
Soviet Union, 3, 11, 35, 156, 331n11
Spears, Britney, 85
Spielberg Steven: *Saving Private Ryan*, 40, 151; *Schindler's List*, 138
Spinoza, Baruch, 101, 197, 238, 315n15, 315n17, 327n8, 329–30n28
Spurlock, Morgan: *Super Size Me*, 188–89
Stalin, Joseph, 318n6
Stalinism, 3, 169, 287n1, 318n6
Star Trek (television series), 325n31
State of Fear. *See* Crichton, Michael
Stavrakakis, Yannis, 194, 208, 324n25, 324–25n27
Stenger, Victor, 246–47, 331n7, 331–32n11
Stevens, Alexandre, 315–16n21
Stone, Oliver, 297n39: *JFK*, 47, 296n37; *World Trade Center*, 296n37
Stranger in a Strange Land. *See* Heinlein, Robert
suffering, 1, 7, 31–35, 127, 244, 286, 291–92n1
superego, 63, 182–84, 320n30
Super Size Me. *See* Spurlock, Morgan
surplus value, 75, 95–96, 205–6, 229
symptom, 20, 55–60, 239

Talmud, 138
Tarkovsky, Andrei, 312n28
Tea Party, 293n11
terror, 39, 159–61, 187–88, 224, 234, 285, 307n20, 317n31, 335n11

Thomas, Clarence, 114
Titanic. See Cameron, James
tragedy, 38–39
trauma, 22, 36–38, 41, 73, 102, 160–62, 166, 240, 256, 266, 314n6, 325n35, 330n1; and anxiety, 116; and castration, 19, 113, 157; and enjoyment, 14, 172, 221–22, 242, 306–7n15; and fantasy, 131–32, 134, 210, 213–17, 312n27, 312n31, 325n36
The Trial. See Kafka, Franz
Trotsky, Leon, 156
Trump, Donald, 131
21 Grams. See Iñárritu, Alejandro González
Twinkies, 175
Twin Peaks (television series). *See* Lynch, David

uncanny, 101
unconscious, 4, 18–19, 25–26, 30, 51, 81, 206, 250, 288n4, 292n2, 310n12, 330n32; and desire, 87, 153, 164, 211, 292n3; and recognition, 100; and religion, 253–54, 260, 262; and sacrifice, 149
universality, 4, 54, 95, 97, 313n2, 313n4
utilitarianism, 314n11
utopia, 6, 15, 17, 20, 165, 208, 237, 242, 283, 284

Van Haute, Philippe, 312n29
Varda, Angès: *Le glaneur et la glaneuse* (*The Gleaners and I*), 321n37
veil, 110, 307n20

Verhaeghe, Paul, 264
Vietnam War, 47, 150, 228–29
Vighi, Fabio, 325n28
violence, 13, 35, 41–42, 49–51, 108–11, 165, 185–86, 227, 232, 269, 318n6, 336–37n24; and obedience, 304n19; and sadism, 290n22
Virno, Paolo, 65, 300n25
vitalism, 294n20
Voltaire, 241
von Trier, Lars: *Breaking the Waves*, 311n20

Wachowski, Andy and Larry: *The Matrix*, 91
War on Terror, 46, 109–11, 163, 256, 307n19, 316n27
Wells, Jonathan, 319n19
Wenders, Wim, 312n28
Winnicott, Donald, 2
Wittgenstein, Ludwig, 164, 204, 324n15, 330n31
Wolf, Naomi, 29, 293n11
Wood, Ellen Meiksins, 322n1
Wood, Neal, 322n1
World Trade Center. See Stone, Oliver
World War II, 151

Zac, Lilian, 273, 335n18
Žižek, Slavoj, 2, 46, 58, 91, 104, 116, 131, 164–65, 178, 229, 301n32, 307n7, 317n30, 325n28, 327n10, 334–35n9
Zupančič, Alenka, 175, 181–82, 299n14, 301n35, 333–34n29

IN THE SYMPLOKĒ STUDIES IN
CONTEMPORARY THEORY SERIES

Enjoying What We Don't Have:
The Political Project of Psychoanalysis
Todd McGowan

Tragically Speaking: On the
Use and Abuse of Theory for Life
Kalliopi Nikolopoulou

To order or obtain more information on
these or other University of Nebraska Press
titles, visit www.nebraskapress.unl.edu.

www.ingramcontent.com/pod-product-compliance
Lightning Source LLC
Chambersburg PA
CBHW021340300426
44114CB00012B/1016